Death of a Notary

Death of a Notary

Conquest and
Change in Colonial
New York

DONNA MERWICK

Cornell University Press Ithaca & London

First published 1999 by Cornell University Press

Printed in the United States of America

Library of Congress Cataloging-in-Publication Data

Merwick, Donna.
    Death of a notary : conquest and change in colonial New York /
Donna Merwick.
        p.   cm.
    Includes bibliographical references and index.
    ISBN 0-8014-3608-7 (cloth : alk. paper)
    1. Ilpendam, Adriaen Janse van, d. 1686.   2. Notaries—New York
(State)—Biography.   3. Notaries—New York (State)—History.
    I. Title.
    KF363.I44M47   1999
    347.747′016—dc21   99-11943

Cornell University Press strives to use
environmentally responsible suppliers and
materials to the fullest extent possible in the
publishing of its books. Such materials include
vegetable-based, low-VOC inks and acid-free
papers that are recycled, totally chlorine-free,
or partly composed of nonwood fibers. Books
that bear the logo of the FSC (Forest
Stewardship Council) use paper taken from
forests that have been inspected and certified as
meeting the highest standards for
environmental and social responsibility. For
further information. visit our website at
www.(

Cloth

ACC Library Services
Austin, Texas

FSC FSC Trademark © 1996 Forest Stewardship Council A.C.
SW-COC-098

FOR NANCY

and all those we love together

Contents

Illustrations

Acknowledgments

For almost a decade I have lived with the puzzle of Adriaen Janse van Ilpendam's life and death. During that time, the chance to pursue that puzzle and find a way of writing about it was often made possible by others. I was given financial support for travel and research; I was alerted to manuscript collections and archives. Colleagues and students listened to what I was trying to write about; many offered criticisms and (as students are likely to do) suggested new ways of considering the puzzle of his life.

Janse's story has taken me around the world — several times, in fact. My expressions of gratitude are a retracing of that journey. In Holland, archivists and librarians in Leiden, Haarlem, The Hague, and Amsterdam were invariably generous to me. Research undertaken for me by Mr. Pieter Wagenaar initiated me in the holdings of the Gemeentearchief Leiden. His careful work allowed me confident access to the city's public records, especially notarial registers and sentencing books. These were graciously provided to me at all times. Librarians at the University of Leiden gave me privileged access to their collections. In Haarlem, and in a small building where the municipal records are housed, Ms. Mieke Meiboom extended every assistance. Staff in the special collections of the Koninglijke Bibliotheek oversee a remarkable collection of seventeenth-century books and were generous in sharing these treasures with me as well. Notarial papers held at the Gemeentearchief Amsterdam were important to me. The curators of the collection went out of their way, as they have done in the past, to be helpful in making them available. The new reading rooms still look out on the Amstel River and make it easy (despite the busy barges) to think about seventeenth-century Dutch life. The kindness of my friend and fellow New York historian Jos van der Linde made the months of residence in Lisse in 1993 an unforgettable pleasure.

Janse was at home in New York City and Albany, and I was made to feel at home there as well. Staff of the Manuscripts and Rare Book Division of the New York Public Library and the New York City Municipal Archives provided me with important seventeenth-century correspondence, reports, and notarial papers. In the New York State Library in Albany, curators such as Jim Corsaro in the Manuscripts and Special Collections Room were attentive to my needs, as were the scholars who direct the New Netherland Project. To them, but particularly to Peter Christoph and Charles Gehring, I am only one of many historians of early New York greatly indebted. Janse's papers are in the Albany County Hall of Records: I have often wondered what he would think of his papers' being preserved in an Edson vault regulated at a temperature of exactly 68 degrees. To staff in the Hall of Records and in each of the institutions that permitted me to reproduce material as illustrations in this book, I offer sincere thanks and acknowledge their courtesy in captions accompanying the illustrations.

Bernard Bailyn invited me to be an associate at The Charles Warren Center for Studies in American History at Harvard University during the autumn months of 1993. They were valuable months for me, working in the Harvard collections, especially the law library. The staff of the Boston Athenaeum made the notarial papers of William Aspinwall available with a graciousness that is characteristic of their service. Lori Nussdorfer and Karen Kupperman invited me to speak about notaries and notarial papers at Wesleyan University and the University of Connecticut. Lori and her colleagues led me to realize how the dimensions of an already engrossing subject were being enlarged by imaginative scholars.

Here in Melbourne, debts have piled up like the stacks of a notary's papers in the Holland archives. The University of Melbourne funded overseas travel as well as the research assistance of Heide Marfurt, Nicole Provoost, and Pieter Wagenaar. The university and the department of history made study leave available so that I might take up a Scholar-in-Residence grant from the Rockefeller Foundation at the Study Center in Bellagio, Italy. There, in a small garden hideaway, Il Polenta, I read Jonathan Spence's *The Question of Hu*, knew then that I could write a narrative of Janse's life, and wrote the first chapter of this book. As resident directors of the center, Frank Sutton and his wife, Jackie, made every effort to make writing easy, and I thank them and the foundation. Many years after looking out at Lake Como from Il Polenta, I had a finished manuscript and asked Colleen Isaac to read it. The present book owes much to her sensitivities about narrative and style as a creative writer. Stan Katz, Hendrik Hartog, and Tom Green moved the manuscript one step closer to publication and I thank them.

From the first days of working with Peter Agree at Cornell University Press, I realized my good fortune in having a generous and prudent editor. I enjoyed our relationship and know that the final presentation of the book is due in large part to him. My admiration for the press grew as I became a beneficiary of the careful editing of Barbara H. Salazar, Senior Manuscript Editor, and Trudie Calvert. Often they knew what to do with words when I did not. I am greatly in their debt.

"Acknowledgments" is, I think, a rather hard-edged word. In my dictionary it connotes obligation, almost a sense of something legal. Many colonial North Americans had in their vocabulary a better way of saying thanks. They are very apt words for pointing to how a book comes about. The book is the outcome of many remarkable providences. Over the years and to each of us, extraordinary teachers and outstanding writers extend their gifts, offering them to unknown audiences and on behalf of unknown futures, maybe those of writers. In *The Death of a Notary*, these teachers and writers have a strong presence: Svetlana Alpers, Roland Barthes, Michel de Certeau, Inga Clendinnen, Merle Curti, Natalie Zemon Davis, Greg Dening, Michel Foucault, Rhys Isaac, Stan Kutler, Wim Schulte-Nordholt, William R. Taylor, David Voorhees, Hayden White, and Charles Zika.

My husband, Greg Dening, read all of this book, in many versions and many times. Like all the writing I will ever do, I offer it to him.

D. M.

Melbourne

Epitaph

He was the only one. He was the only man to have committed suicide in the town's seventeenth-century history.

I first met him when I was writing another book on Albany, New York. He was the town notary. In a way he stood in the background, bearing witness to the contracts, promises, and pledges of other townspeople. His occupation put him somewhere within the Dutch legal system. I, however, have always thought of him as being someone like myself, a historian. He was surrounded by stories, those he listened to and recorded, the hundreds he archived in a chest or trunk, where they receded into the past.

Adriaen Janse van Ilpendam hanged himself on March 12, 1686. I wish I knew how it happened. My concern arises not from prurience, I think, but from the hope that there was some comfort in the moment of his death, that it was not too terrible. Only one man that I know of, an early twentieth-century archivist, has puzzled over Janse's suicide. He guessed that it was related to the English conquest of Janse's home, New Netherland. Since he earned his living by writing legal papers in Dutch, the demand that they be written in English moved him to his tragic decision.

The archivist was, I believe, correct. And perhaps he was right, too, in leaving the matter at that. I am still puzzled, however, at how it was that an imperial power's designs for territorial acquisition, military invasion and occupation, visions of continental hegemony, how those forces met with and made a casualty of so small a life as Janse's. England's grand designs did not include his death. He was so incidental.

Janse's life, which you will read about, was not a prelude to his suicide. Only later readers of his life would see it that way. It was a sequence of experiences. That, at least, is what we have to think after reading the records. And I have presented them for you in that way. Like his suicide, they are also mysterious happenings in a culture that is not ours, each a meeting place of circumstance and structure, of particularities and generalities. Some were under his control; most were not. We can know only some of them. Puzzling over his experiences, I have come to think that no society, neither New Netherland before the English invasion of 1664 nor New York after it, makes it easy for someone to get along. Getting along in the New World in the seventeenth century was immensely difficult. Perhaps the difficulties were great enough to let us think that some people, some colonists like Adriaen Janse, would have been better off had they never come.

As we begin, I owe Adriaen Janse an apology. He never referred to himself as Adriaen Janse or Adriaen Janse van Ilpendam. He always wrote Adriaen van Ilpendam. You will see why. How he would otherwise tell a different story of himself to the one I tell, I do not know. I do know that, like me, he would pull it together from fragments. He would draw on bits of memory, records, perhaps the oft-repeated anecdotes of others. He would shape it to suit his audience. Some facts or memories he would call upon if he were testifying in court. Others were good for yarning with friends. His selection would satisfy the occasion. I hope that in telling Janse's story, I have judged the occasion of your reading about him correctly.

We are told that in any military adventure, the first casualty is truth. I think it is not. Janse is a reminder that the first casualties are people.

Death of a Notary

CHAPTER I   "New Albanij"

JUNE 10, 1669
Ordinary Session: Court of Albany,
Colonie of Rensselaerswijck and Schenectady

Adriaen Janse appears in the small courtroom on a Thursday in early summer. Two magistrates are present representing Albany. A third man is seated with them. He is the highest official of the surrounding *colonie* of Rensselaerswijck. They are attended by the *schout*, the local law enforcement officer. Tuesdays and Thursdays are days when they usually convene.

He has known the men for years. Jacob de Hinsse is the town's surgeon, well educated, experienced as a trader, trusted by the French in New Canada. Rychart van Rensselaer is the resident director of Rensselaerswijck. He is respected and shares the *colonie's* responsibilities with Jeremias, a younger brother, who is eager but inexperienced. Jan Verbeeck is also well regarded. He has nothing of Rychart's power in the town but is addressed as "Master Jan" because he is a schoolmaster. Townspeople trust him with legal affairs. Gerrit Swart is present as *schout*. He is the legal adviser to the court and, as prosecutor, its presiding officer. Swart is fifty-three years old and has held his office for seventeen years. The *schout* in nearby Schenectady, a much smaller community, says he cannot earn a living from the office and has opened an inn. Ludovicus Cobus is the court's secretary. He writes a beautiful script but is irascible and can be devious. When the magistrates need to have Latin translated, they call on him. Now he is recording the proceedings, sprinkling Latin into his Dutch words, announcing the magistrates as *presentibus.*

Janse presents his papers. He asks to exercise his office as public notary in Albany and the neighboring district. He is old to be seeking such a position. He has just turned fifty-one. Eleven weeks ago was the Feast of the Annunciation, and he counts his age by the legal year that begins on that day, *Maria-Boodschap,* the day of Mary and the Wonderful Message, March 25.

Approval has been delayed for a month, but that is not necessarily a cause for worry. Four weeks ago, he had put a request into proper form and come to the courthouse, appearing before the same men. He thought he needed their permission before seeking the approval of the governor-general of the province. If Petrus Stuyvesant were still governor of New Netherland, he would not have been uncertain. At present, however, an English military commander holds the office. He and his predecessor have done so for almost five years. Care must be taken to follow the proper procedures. Now it has all worked out. He has a commission from the governor-general and awaits the court's final decision. He is in luck. The magistrates direct that the words *fiat . . . in pleno* be written on the margin of his petition and into the minutes. "Let it be done," they direct, "with full agreement."

They also administer what they call an "oath of fidelity." It is a solemn pronouncement, sometimes very lengthy, with seven or eight paragraphs. The notary will serve everyone who comes to him; he will not write acts known to be fraudulent; he will take no gratuities; on and on. Five years from now a candidate down on Manhattan Island will pronounce his oath, swearing "in the presence of almighty God that I will faithfully and justly carry out this office: that I will write and execute all acts and instruments between one man and another, without respect for the rank of persons and keep a proper register of everything that passes before me." He will further promise and swear "that I will faithfully promote the justice of all those cases which may be recommended to me in my role as attorney. And further that I shall comport myself and so discharge my duties, directly and indirectly, as an honest and faithful notary . . . is bound to do. So help me almighty God."

These may not be Janse's exact words. Cobus has not entered them into the minutes. The magistrates, however, accept his oath and hear one more case. Then they discharge themselves for the day.

Janse has begun his life as a notary. He is already a respected burgher of the town and has been for about eighteen years. He lives quietly with his wife. As he grows older, he will find her welfare to be a nagging worry. Then he will write about her several times. Only once will he write her name, Tryntje Jans. For now, neither he nor anyone else mentions her. They have no children. For many years he has been a schoolmaster. Like Jan Verbeeck, he is addressed as master. "Master Adriaen" they call him. Such a man is expected to be meek, *sachtmoedich*: it is the quality expected of him by the admired writer on Dutch schooling of the day, Dirck Adriaensz Valcooch. Over the years, Janse has done nothing to indicate that he is not such a man.

People will not be surprised to find him seeking to be a notary. Schoolmasters in small towns at home in the Netherlands and down on Manhattan Island commonly supplement their income by learning the arts of the *notariaat*. Albany is also a small town, with about 120 households and another 40 or 50 families living on outlying farms. It is on the Hudson River, barely set back from the water and lying along flat land that soon rises steeply up a dominant hill. One might have thought that the town would have grown up farther south, around the old fort built years ago by the West India Company. Instead it takes about twenty minutes to walk north from the fort to the town and its south gate. All along is a strand where oceangoing vessels and rivercraft load and unload. Palisades enclose the town, with gates and blockhouses that oversee thirty or so acres dotted with tiny medieval houses, most with gabled roofs. The merchants in furs have their storerooms and large properties near the river's edge. Their trafficking in pelts has given a name to the street that runs along the river. It is called Handelaarsstraat, but sometimes, later, it is Brouwersstraat, for the brewers who have their works here as well.

Janse lives north on this street. His property faces the river and puts him within easy walking distance of the north gate. About a fourth of the way from the south gate and after crossing a small stream, some way before reaching his house, Handelaarsstraat intersects at a right angle with Jonckerstraat, a busy street that climbs to the better houses on, as everyone calls it, "the hill." The burghers think of Albany as an independent *havenstad*, a port town along the river. As in market towns at home, everyone's prosperity is determined by the attractiveness of the town's wares to outside buyers. It will prosper on the cargoes of fur and grain that are loaded and sent downriver, reaching New York in two or three days or marketed for direct sales overseas.

So there is need for a notary, even more than one. The scores of negotiations that go forward each year must be in correct form before the courts — here and overseas. The deals involve thousands of guilders every year. At the present time, the burghers have only two notaries. It had seemed that Dirck van Schelluyne, the first man to practice among them, a notary trained at The Hague, would be around for a while longer. Only last year he was in court representing one of the town's leading burghers. He had even requested the renewal of his commission. Yet he hadn't stayed. So there are just Ludovicus Cobus, but he is openly greedy and deceitful, and Jan Juriaensz Becker. Becker too is a notary and schoolmaster, but he is not entirely trusted. Some years ago, a company official refused to let him come near his papers "especially to copy letters and other things, for he is only a tell-tale." Four months from now his authorization as notary will be revoked. The magistrates learn of slanderous words written about themselves. They forbid him "for one year and six weeks from executing any writings that are to be submitted to the court." Even when he later earns a reprieve, he will be admonished to behave himself decently.

Janse knows him. For something that happened twenty-four years ago, his presence may be an unwelcome ghost.

JULY 12, 1669
Albany

Janse must know that he can now expect to be regarded with a certain dignity. Yet the first of his clients give his new career a very ordinary beginning. He meets with two farmers, helping them arrange a one-year lease of a house, barn, and land. Possibly the meeting is in his house: once his practice gets under way, he may imagine, it will be the scene of much coming and going. The men could, however, be sitting together in one of many places, one of the farmers' houses, an inn, the rooms of one of the witnesses. He begins to move the meeting forward, carefully getting necessary details and adding those that the men might want to include: that the land is "on the south side" of the farmer's house in Schenectady, that eight hogs "old and young" are left for the tenant. He needs to include words about "similar seed," "risks" to the lease, and final payment of "nine good whole merchantable beaver skins." Two men act as witnesses. All can sign their names except the owner, who makes a mark. It is not their witnessing that will count, however; it is the propriety of the papers and his signature.

The farmers are not particularly important men. The lease of a property twenty miles away in Schenectady — a frontier village of men and women meant to be farmers but always muscling into Albany's fur trade, untrustworthy, lacking control — is not noteworthy either. Yet with this act, Janse has begun the register of his notarial papers. It is the beginning of the capital of his life. One day, if he is fortunate, he can expect to be financially secure. The collection of his papers will be in the hundreds, ten inches high or more; the sand that he uses to blot his pages will fall onto the laps of respected people. The individual documents will accumulate and become an archive. He will leave them loose or maybe thread them into quires — thread is something he will take care to order one day. They will form the *pakken* or bundles of acts that other learned notaries keep in their care. As a schoolmaster he already has the pens and mixtures for ink. But ordering the materials of his new office will be his concern for a lifetime.

He also has a chest for storing his papers. Four years ago he had paid a high price for one offered at public auction. He can make use of it now, beginning to place his papers in its recesses, locking them away. He is sworn to guard his papers, to make them available for clients but otherwise to maintain them in strict confidentiality. In the case of his death or resignation, he or his family will be fined if they are not promptly delivered to a town secretary. He must make copies upon request. Those he retains are sometimes the originals but often the *grossen* or copies. Still, they must be perfect. Someone should be able to say of each of them, "'*T staat als of 't is geprent*" (Why, it looks just like it's printed). There must be no erasures or blotting, no elusive Latinisms or abbreviations. Roman numerals must be avoided because they can be easily doctored. No contract may be notarized to which he, the notary, is a party and beneficiary. There are many rules to obey.

August brings seven more townspeople to him. An elderly woman has died and her second husband and daughter must come to an agreement about her estate. Janse knows each of them. Years ago he would have encountered some of the family in New Amsterdam, now called New York. Soon he will call upon another family member, a notary like himself, for assistance in settling other affairs. He knew the woman's first husband well. Once he had sued him for failure to pay school fees. Perhaps they were for the daughter, who now, along with her husband, reaches agreement with her stepfather and, unlike most of the women he knows, is able to confirm it with her signature.

The settlement has opened a window on the family's private affairs. It is a small one and not left ajar for long. For some moments the three family members and Janse peer into "debts and claims" and an estate "personal and real, present and to come." They take into view the clothing of the girl's dead mother, especially "a colored silk skirt trimmed at the bottom with four rows of gold braid." This her stepfather "keeps for himself." Then the window closes shut and Janse arranges for the signing of the paper. To the right of the page, the older man makes a mark, while his stepdaughter and her husband sign below him. Just below these signatures and to the left, four burghers write their names as witnesses They are prominent men, testimony to the importance of the family. They also have windows onto their affairs, and these too open only a crack when necessary and just as quickly close. Everyone in the room understands the value of discretion.

His first two documents, with their required formalities and their narratives — *verhaelstof*, story matter, they call it — are all in order. Making them accurate and professional presents no problem. Already he has found a comfortable style for covering the page before him. Usually he gets a whole agreement on a single folio sheet, perhaps because clients want their money's worth. He covers the white of the paper with 46 lines and about 450 words set closely together. For signatures, he allows sufficient, but not excessive, space.

He leaves a wide left-hand margin but almost none on the right. This is customary. The wide margin will allow for *achterblijven*, afterthoughts and necessary postscripts. Merchants use them all the time: mostly they bring the story of a transaction up to date. They give a contract its own little history, its story matter. People want to see things brought up to date, and many authors answer this craving by forever adding to the titles of their books "this volume improved" (*verbetert*), "this volume enlarged" (*vermeerdert*). Marginal notes please the eye, too. They act as a kind of design, giving the surface detail that adds interest. It's the same space where the magistrates would have scribbled "Fiat . . . in pleno" on his petition.

Janse has not written any marginalia or threaded slips of paper onto a document. His pen distributes the ink uniformly, in line after line of clear cursive script. Those looking for some division of time in his papers — did he begin to write one day, tire, return, and use a wider pen or thinner ink? — will not find it in the shape of his writing.

The acts are the first of all that are to come. They are the prototypes of at least 260 others and many more that men and women in a series of futures will somehow manage to hand on or somehow fail to hand on. They will have the permanence that their nature requires. How could he guess that his signature would find its way to New York City and Amsterdam and remain in those cities for over three hundred years?

But these first acts of his are marked by some confusion. He is uncertain of the exact source of his authority. Always with his Dutch words, he

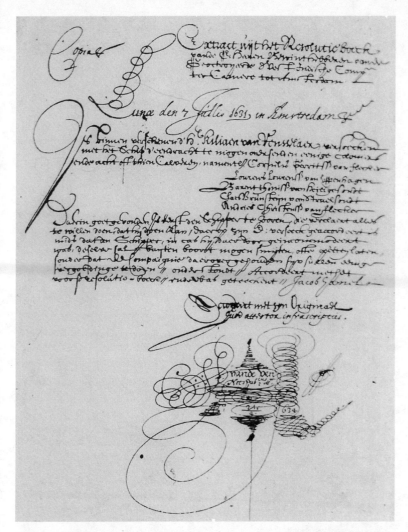

1. Notarial copy of extract from minutes of the Amsterdam Chamber of the West India Company, July 7, 1631. In The Art of Describing, *Svetlana Alpers reminds us that seventeenth-century Dutch men and women did not distinguish as we do between visual representation and verbal sign. They enjoyed the joining of words and images on the same page. Here the notary's text joins a complex visual presentation of his signature. (Collection Nederlands Scheepvaartmuseum Amsterdam)*

identifies himself as appointed by the magistrates "with the approval of the Right Honorable Françoys Lovelace on behalf of his Royal Highness James, Duke of York, governor-general over all his territories in America." He is wrong. His authority does not really flow from the local Dutch officials,

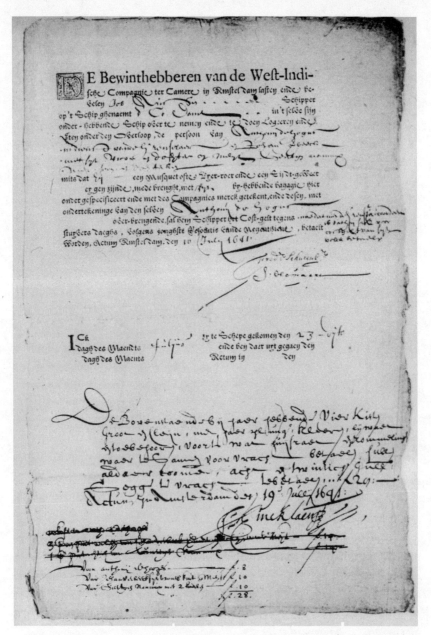

2. *Order of the West India Company, July 10, 1641. Here the eye is entertained by print jostling script and an illuminated letter suggesting a page not yet fully released from medieval pictorial impulses. (Collection Nederlands Scheepvaartmuseum Amsterdam)*

3. Detail from Profile Views of Leiden and Haarlem and Two Trees, *Pieter Saenredam, 1617 and 1625. Here the artist counts on the well-known Dutch enjoyment of mixed images and calligraphy. (Staatliche Museen Preussischer Kulturbesitz, Berlin)*

with the English governor-general simply giving "approval." His appointment is firmly in Lovelace's hands. Other notaries have come to recognize this. On their acts they have been writing, "appointed by the Right Honorable François Lovelace, on behalf of his Royal Highness James, Duke of York."

He cannot know it, but this is only the beginning of confusions that will always be his about authority and how to represent it. Dutch rules, like those that everyone followed under Stuyvesant and the earlier West India Company men, were easy to know. Everything fitted together. But the English laws and ordinances: how do you know the laws and practices when you haven't words about the rules in your head? Soon he will not make any attempt, except in wills, to define the source of his authority. He will just write "notary public residing in Albanij."

The name "Albanij" is confusing too. He at least seems to know that living here he is somewhere in the province of New York. Yet Jan Baptiste van Rensselaer, writing from Holland, thought that his brother Jeremias was now living in New England, and downriver at Harlem a man thought that he and his town were part of New England too. But if he knows that Albany is in New York, Janse seems uncertain of what "Albanij" means. It's not like "Beverwijck," familiar, the same name as the river town settled under the jurisdiction of the old city of Haarlem, having a history in Holland and one in New Netherland as well. So, as often as he locates himself in "Albanij," he writes "residing in New Albanij," as though a relationship existed like that between New Amsterdam and old Amsterdam along the Ij River in Holland. Was there a similar dependency, an old Albany somewhere, whose special history makes this place mean something special too? The town's name was changed from Beverwijck to Albanij by the English officer who led the troopers into town five years ago. Is it, somewhere, an English city?

NOVEMBER 26, 1669
Albany

Janse is being drawn into greater familiarity with the town's "poor community." Everyone knows it exists. "Poor community" is the court's own term. Now, late in the year, he is writing up papers for Arnout Cornelisse Viele and Paulus Martensz van Benthuysen. Viele is selling Martensz the lot next to his own. Immediately the divide between the rich and the poor — they use those words too — shows itself. Viele enjoys a position of some power in the area — and with the English authorities — because he knows the languages of the nearby native tribes and will act as interpreter for people buying natives' lands or, for whatever reason, looking for their friendship. But Martensz is a loser. Last year he tried to earn something from making a wagon — which he failed to deliver — and soon he will be one of the many who default regularly when called to answer charges of indebtedness. And in buying the property, he is placing himself next door to someone much like himself, Huybert Janse. Janse does odd jobs around the town. He is paid a pittance to stand near the gates of the town and turn away any "savages" who arrive to trade in furs. In two years he will still be desperate for stray jobs such as keeping open holes in the river ice during winter in case water is needed to quench fires. Everyone knows how swiftly a man or woman can sink into the swamp of the poor community. Today's Child of Luxury, 't Kind van Weelde — a local man will be called that one day — may be tomorrow's Child of Poverty, 't Kind van Armoede. It happens regularly.

If Janse can match his earnings to the esteem offered by his position as notary, there is no reason why he should be part of the poor community.

The court, after all, has just expressed its anger at confronting documents that are "not in notarial form." It is continually examining itemized accounts, brewery books, and book debt. It deals with papers of all kinds: it wants them to be in "satisfactory" form. And last month, the magistrates made him one of the "good men" of the town. Because they use the bench as a place of arbitration, the magistrates relegate a good deal of time-consuming work — bringing quarrelsome parties together, examining disputed accounts, just maintaining patience — to qualified men. In places like Amsterdam, these are the "good men" invited to search the books of wayward merchants or dispose of other litigious civil actions. It is another way of learning that service to the local court will be almost as much a part of his new life as writing up attestations. All of this should give him work and confidence.

NOVEMBER 1, 1669
Fort James, New York

Francis Lovelace is engaged in routine bureaucratic work. He is completing some papers regarding Jan Juriaensz Becker. He must recommission Becker as notary. He needs to make the appointment because, as he writes, Albany is a place where "there is no person to execute that office." Somehow he has entirely forgotten commissioning a man named Adriaen Janse van Ilpendam.

THE TRADING SEASON, 1670
Albany

In the early months of this new year, Janse has had little opportunity to practice his learned skills. His days, if they are filled, are filled with other things. Only eleven townspeople and farmers have appeared before him during the cold months of winter and spring, ordinary people with their required witnesses, sixteen altogether.

The concerns of their lives are very particular and very material. Elisabeth Drinckvelt hopes to earn something by contracting with a fellow burgher to bake in her house alongside her husband. For the same reason, Robbert Sanders and Meyndert Fredericksz lease farmlands out beyond the palisades. Gertruyt Pietersz Vosburgh sells off some of her house lot because she sees some profit in the eagerness of four neighbors to extend theirs.

Janse gives consideration to small, particular needs in each of the contracts. One carelessly forgotten detail — that the baker must lay in the same quantity of grain as Drinckvelt's husband, that Fredericksz's leaseholder must plant an orchard of two acres but the lessor will furnish the trees — may cost dearly.

Space and time are in small measures. The minutes of a meeting, bounded rectangles of farmland, spaces within a single house, these are small quantities. But this is not all of it. Large rhythms of time and endless reaches of space catch up all their days. The townspeople know that their lives are set by the unpredictable and often hostile movements of the French far to the north, trappers and farmers whom most of them would never even have seen. The Frenchmen and -women have never shown any particular animosity toward Beverwijck: competition for furs and for the friendship of natives willing to provide them, but that's all. Their enmity toward the English, however, is deep. Sometimes this is an embarrassment when distant ambitions temporarily make allies of their kings, but the enmity is always encouraged and rewarded. It stains everyone's days, spreading into the town as surely as the rumors of impending attack. It now runs onto Janse's pages. Writing up both of the farmstead leases, he has to insert that certain arrangements will be altered "in case of general war."

All the dangers of the nearby natives stalk the town as well. Even the Mohawk, for all their promises of special friendship, are fearsome and temperamental, not to be trusted. And all around, there are more of their faces than yours. Your land does not surround theirs — your farmers' tight little acres with their six or seven cows, the soldiers' four-sided fort, the burghers' houses furnished with chests protecting legal papers and dresses "trimmed with gold braid." Their lands and their savage ways encircle you. They are, all of them, another kind of people. Names were invented for them and are still used: sometimes *de luiden*, meaning just "the people," but usually *de wilden*, "the creatures of nature." Even a Jesuit priest writing to Jeremias van Rensselaer endorses the letter from the place where he is in Canada: "*apud barbaros*," among the savages.

Everyone is especially at risk when the natives war among themselves. The hostilities between the Mohawk and the River Indians, the Mahican, have been going on for six years. One merchant seems to remain calm about it and just says it is "very detrimental to this place." But a year from now he will be less reserved and convey to his brother exactly the fear that Janse's farmer-clients feel. One of his tenants will say that he doesn't even care to negotiate a farm now. "And no wonder," the correspondent will add, "for this summer we hardly knew what was to become of us." Rumors from the "Mohawk Country" tell of several thousand French soldiers and their native allies moving south, taking the usual route, down from the great northern river and across the lake. They have already been seen not far to the north.

Yet if their presence is a continual menace, it is still the "savages" who trade in furs and bring wealth. Everyone's life is arranged around the seasonal movements of the beaver, the natives, and the trade. So, deep in winter, Elisabeth Drinckvelt is thinking ahead. She is arranging rent with the baker at the present time. But he will not be welcomed until May. He will move in and begin his work on May 1, the first day of *handelstijd*, the trading season. Then he will begin to bake, as agreed, "for Christians and for Indians." Vosburgh has also made the four buyers who have come together in early February think about "the beginning of the next trading season." That is when she will need cash and expect them to pay. Sanders's and Fredricksz's tenants will move onto their farms on May 1.

For everyone, *handelstijd* is always the expectation of something new. Fortunes will surely take an upward turn. Even the rituals of the court of justice entice people to think this way. On May 1, the longest-serving magistrates make way for newcomers. The incoming officials prepare themselves for what the season will bring: more frequent court sessions and longer lists of plaintiffs and defendants. The men of the town gather outside the palisades for the *papegaaischiet*. They try to prove themselves superior marksmen by aiming for one or another part of an elevated wooden parrot. The contest and the subsequent disorder — "the king of the marksmen" paraded into town with fellows ready for drink, horseplay, and violence — inaugurate the trading contests of *handelstijd*, which will not end until November 1, the close of the season. By midsummer, the natives arrive in dozens. Some bring their families; most carry furs to exchange for brandy, blankets, guns, and strung shells. Traders, as they say, "walk in the woods" outside the town to intercept them: one native here in the dense underbrush, another along a path. Everyone knows how they are cheated and robbed, beaten, made drunk.

The natives who come inside the palisades are lured off the streets and into traders' houses. Now it matters where a man's house is located. Janse and his neighbors are not in an advantaged set of streets. They know that, so they would understand one burgher's request for a lot "on the hill" because he is located "in a street where there is no business." Some natives are found housed in sheds on people's properties. It is all illegal. Last summer, one of the traders protested that yes, some "savages" were in his house, but they had forced their way in and he had dismissed them "without having bartered a single beaver." Later another man insisted that natives were in his yard, but no, he had no knowledge of it and hadn't "a hair of the beavers" they were carrying.

Traders regularly lie in such outrageous ways. They become abusive when called to task by the law enforcement officer. Men, and women too, gamble on making profits: they mortgage properties, sell assets, ignore the risk of fines, get drunk for whatever reason. Many lose out. They have only empty hands to contemplate when the end of *handelstijd* comes, bringing the cold days before the onset of winter.

JUNE 23, 1670
Albany

The violence of *handelstijd* infects Adriaen Janse's papers as well. He too responds to the rhythms of the trading year. On this day he writes up an act in which the parties are not Dutch men or women, not even the town's English soldiers or New England traders. Those who appear before him are three natives, two men of the Katskill people and a woman. They are accompanied by Joris Christoffels, an interpreter. The trader Jan Hendricksz Bruyn will be in court later on this same day. He will have to answer charges of violating the ordinance by entertaining the three natives in his house and — everyone knows what such lodging means — giving them brandy for furs or the promise of furs. He needs them to swear that he is innocent. They must say that they were at his house but he knew nothing of their presence. He needs the deposition this very day.

The natives begin their recitation. Janse takes notes. Last Sunday evening "they came to the house of Jan Hendricksz." The trader told them that they should leave and return in the morning. They did this. They left the town and went down to the shore of the river and slept the night under some boards set up against a fence. At daybreak they reentered the town through the gate and again "came to the old house" of the trader. (Janse continues to write, just what they say, leaving the gaps that are there.) They encountered a black servant and said they were hungry and wanted to cook. Hendricksz was still asleep. One of the natives "laid himself down to sleep." Then a "Maqua Indian and squaw with a child" came into the old house where the natives, the "negro," and Hendricksz were either sleeping or cooking. They too seemed only to want a place to sleep. Eight people now, listless if not drunk or hung over, are drawn in small indifferent groups. That is their story. Janse writes, "All of which has been interpreted as the truth to me, the notary."

Since the incident, the natives have been around the town for four days. Now each of them makes a mark on Janse's page. They have names, of course. The townspeople call them Mamanichtack, Teffenichki, and, the woman, Memechtiemach. It is what they hear of the native tongue, and these are the sounds that Christoffels hears and offers to Janse. Janse does not describe the natives, whether they are shy or looking steadily at the floor, perhaps standing arrogantly aloof. Reluctance to speak, evasiveness, awkwardness at giving words to a closely listening notary — these are moods and feelings: they never reach his pages. Perhaps he thinks for a moment that the old house and the whole feral scene in it deserve the dingy words that would be their counterpart. He, however, draws no discriminations. He brings the episode, brooding squalor and all, under the elaborate language of the honored *ars notariatus*, the art of the notary.

Perhaps he is familiar with the old house. Less than two years ago, Hendricksz owned a place down by the south palisades and very near the river. Its precincts, like the palisades and the town gates, should have been barriers against the wilderness. That's what Huybert Janse's job as sentry is all about. But the wildness seeps in. Like everyone else, Janse also lets it into his life. If the allure of the forest distresses him or causes him to think, he writes nothing. Beneath the natives' strange marks, he writes words that are probably just as exotic to most townspeople, "*Quod attestor*," and signs his name.

JUNE 27, JULY 4, 1670
Albany

Within days he is again drawn into the lives of townspeople caught in their own violence or that of others. But this incident is directly about his own power as a notary: how it can be abused, how it can be sharpened into a weapon against others. Ludovicus Cobus is about to be charged, or so it seems, with behaving abusively on the night of Friday, June 24. He had appeared on the streets shouting taunts at Wijnant Gerritsz and then threatening his wife. At least four households were disturbed and a woman directly menaced.

Gerritsz has asked witnesses to make depositions. Three householders come forward, two of them on the Monday after the incident. Janse puts their stories of the affray into the necessary legal form. Jan Andriesz Kuyper is "aged about 30 years" and speaks first. He cites the date and hour when Cobus reached the street. Then he offers the words of the infuriated, and possibly drunken, notary as clearly as he remembers them. Cobus, as he recalls, shouted toward Gerritsz's house, "I shall have the fool hung." Andriesz cannot offer more because, as Janse writes it, "I . . . went to bed, partly because I was sleepy and because I did not want to listen to another man's abusive language."

Janse then takes the testimony of Catalyntie Barentsz, "about 32 years." Her memories of the violence are sharper. As her story unfolds, Janse elicits the details, especially the words that Cobus will one day have to deny. Barentsz is willing to testify that Cobus ridiculed Gerritsz's wife in her role as midwife, called her a slut, and added other "abusive words." He also threatened, "Do you want any thing written down, I must be present thereat."

The next Monday, Marytie Pietersz comes to him answering Gerritsz's request. He begins again, listening for words remembered, putting descriptions into order. She has her version of Cobus's wild and intimidating language. It is like the others, but she remembers many more of the secretary's lewd words. Janse will not write them into the document.

The testimony of one of the deponents, Barentsz, raises uneasy questions. She draws attention to the fact that Cobus knows he can intimidate the couple because he is a notary. If "you want any thing written down, I must be present thereat." Her account makes Janse record that appointment to the *notarisschap* is no protection against a man's own evil. The temptation that beckons to such a man is using the power to terrorize that resides in his writing. Twelve years ago, after Janse had left New Amsterdam and come to Beverwijck, Petrus Stuyvesant had denounced the notaries of New Amsterdam as extortioners "seized by avarice and greed." And in *patria* for decades, notaries had to live with cries of "vulture" and "Lucifer." There was always some truth in these accusations. That was why Janse had taken his oath, but, then again, why Cobus had taken it too.

JULY 5, 1670
Albany

Reijndert Pietersz summons Janse. Sick and anticipating death, he is putting his affairs in order. Soon he will make a will. For the moment, however, he needs to tie up unfinished business from nine years ago. He was then owner of a river scow and, as it seems, failed in all the intervening years to pay the man who had served him as a ship's hand on a trip down to New Amsterdam. Perhaps this oversight now brings the devil into the company of the two men, or at least into Pietersz's mind. A popular saying quoted by the learned commentators on bookkeeping warns that the "devil gnaws . . . [the] bones" of the man who leaves his accounts "rawly" at death. Whether Pietersz holds such fears, Janse would not necessarily know. But the time has come to erase a disturbing and recurrent memory or to put aside the sight of a name and a sum somewhere on an unattended account.

Pietersz also makes Janse turn his mind to those who owe him money. A biblical scene takes place. Write this down: "there is due to me": 240 guilders from a woman for silk, shoes, and bricks; 147:50 guilders from her husband for passage on the river, money lent, clothing, and tobacco. "Furthermore, found in a book": the same man owing 106 guilders. And write down: "due . . . from July 5, 1670, Sweer Teunisz Debit.": five items, 16:16 guilders. And here: "acknowledgment of an obligation," 30 guilders. Adriaen Janse is made custodian of all these papers and, in its own way, Pietersz's peace of mind.

JULY 15, 1670
Albany

Pietersz prepares to dictate his last will and testament. Janse attends to this matter in the house of Jan Evertsz, where the sick man is perhaps renting rooms. Evertsz is a longtime friend of both men and will act as witness. He has worked the river scows too but is now a master shoemaker. Janse walks to his house at ten o'clock in the morning. It's a short walk because he lives almost directly across from Janse on Handelaarsstraat.

He helps Pietersz complete his final testament. Wills are the bread and butter of notaries. If he has been conscientious, a notary may have served a client over many years, made himself readily available, and offered counsel like a family lawyer. Taking dictation on a will can be the last of his trusted services. But if he is appointed the estate's administrator, it can also be the first of many complex, and financially rewarding, tasks. Pietersz now puts this trust in Janse and an associate, Gerrit Swart. He has already said that he wants "one or more copies" of the will. His mother and wife, both of whom are named as his heirs, live overseas in Bolsward, a small Hanseatic town in Friesland, not far from the shallow waters of the Waddenzee. Janse is expressly asked to contact them and provide them with "a proper inventory, accounting and return" of his estate. Undoubtedly they must have copies of the will as well. Pietersz's is an extensive family, and he conducted a range of business dealings in New Netherland. To clear the estate, notaries in such places as New York and Kingston (the Esopus) as well as Friesland will need to be contacted.

Into October and after Pietersz's death, Janse's and Swart's work is still under way. A copy of the accounts dictated on July 5 has been sent to New York. The court there has been asked to allow a local notary to act with their power of attorney on the estate's behalf. Copies of contracts have been sought. Janse receives a copy of a declaration Pietersz made two years ago before another notary of New York, Willem Bogardus. Careful of his custodial obligations, he puts it, folded, with his copy of the will.

But this is not actually where wills belong any longer. The English have introduced the law that all original copies of wills must be lodged in the Office of Records at New York. They can be removed for the purpose of being proved before what they call the Court of Assizes or the Court of Sessions, but then are to be "returned into the office of Records" and "remain there." Administrators, if they wish, may seek a copy. In none of this is anything said of notaries or their role as caretakers of the community's legal papers.

Laws of this sort haven't yet made their way up to Albany.

SEPTEMBER 23, 1670
Albany

While the town is under the English garrison, public offices somehow seem to alight readily on the shoulders of the soldiers. John Povey, for example, can thank the governor-general for landing him the monopoly on butchering in the town. He and another man will share it. The job doesn't really mean much of an income, but everything counts toward a man's subsistence. There are about twenty-five officers and soldiers in the town. A larger number, about ninety, are not far away at the Esopus, but that's not to anyone's surprise: that place is in continual unrest. For the most part, the soldiers are like Povey: they follow their officers' orders and will take up their weapons against uncooperative townspeople. But mostly they are left to their own devices, trying to get work, clumsy, shunned, likely to enlarge the "poor community." Perhaps, like Jeremias van Rensselaer, they haven't "the least idea" that the country will "remain English." They think they'll be home soon. Still, as much as anything else, the military occupation is going ahead on the strength of each soldier's own desperate effort to survive it. They can be seen beginning to buy houses, rent shanties, lurch into the fur trade. Yet they could be gone any day. Even the governor general will say in two years' time that "the Game . . . [might] shift and wee and Holland shake hands."

Meanwhile, a man or woman must be careful in dealing with the men of the garrison, especially the officers. Any falling out over a business deal and the soldier can claim, even as Captain John Baker did earlier this year, that he is not answerable to the local court. "Being a military person," he will carry his case to the general in New York. Generally a burgher will pay dearly for publicly questioning the honesty of a man like Baker. Gerrit Swart has already been chastised by the general for doing so in the course of his duties as *schout*. He is told not to "molest" Captain Baker further.

NOVEMBER 1, 1670
Fort Albany

The court convenes itself in one of its "extraordinary sessions." Each of the magistrates makes himself present. Captain Thomas Delaval, the mayor of New York City and a member of the governor-general's council, is in attendance representing the general. Jeremias van Rensselaer is also present alongside the magistrates. Somehow they are able to announce that by a majority vote of the burghers, Gerrit Swart has been replaced as *schout* by the commander at the fort, Captain Silvester Salisbury. Exactly when the vote was taken and whether Janse was one of the assenting majority or among an embarrassingly uncooperative — a rebellious? — minority cannot be known. Nothing is ever mentioned about the voting procedures and nothing about nonconformists.

The formalities of the session are impeccable: Swart discharged and "thanked for his good services"; Salisbury reciting his oath of fidelity. Then, however, the fifty-four-year-old man points to the fact that he had held the office for more than eighteen years and asks exemption from one of the sets of taxes. The court refuses to discuss the matter, deferring it to the next session.

NOVEMBER 26, 1670
Albany

Jacobus Fabricius is in need of a notary. Perhaps he will not find one willing to take on his affairs. He means to buy property in the town for his own household and also for a church. Newly arrived, he is the pastor to the town's Lutherans or, as the magistrates coldly address them, "those of the Augsburg Confession." Lovelace is determined that the minister will be made a part of the town, even if he and his congregation are treated with scorn by the majority, those of the Reformed church. He has brought him upriver in his personal entourage. Stuyvesant, as people know, wouldn't have done the same.

Fabricius has found that one of the notaries, Adriaen Janse, will write up the papers. It is a delicate business. Arrangements have been made to secure a house and two properties owned by one of the English soldiers. Not every burgher would let himself be a party to such a transaction, but the trooper is an outsider. He can get away with it. The notary has been exceptionally professional in handling the matter. He has seen to it that the soldier has come with all the pertinent papers needed for the conveyance — "certain accompanying writing(s)" the notary writes down — and has instructed the Englishman to hand them over to the minister during the meeting. Prudently, he has anticipated mischievous litigation. He has arranged for the presence of the usual two witnesses but recognized that this is not an ordinary contract and invited the town secretary, Ludovicus Cobus, to act as witness as well. Like the other two men, he happens to be a Lutheran.

The notary is someone whose clientele includes a surprisingly large number of Lutherans. That's curious, but it's his affair.

DECEMBER 8, 1670
Albany

Adriaen Janse and Gerrit Swart are again called upon by the court to act as arbiters in a dispute. In coming together, the two men, both about the same age, would have reason to discuss Swart's replacement by Salisbury a month ago, to guess at reasons, and consider what Swart will do now. What are his prospects now that he is in his mid-fifties and no longer getting the income of his office?

Janse cannot know that soon the same Captain Salisbury will be "lend[ing] him a helping hand." Janse will be trying to collect fines and, in doing so, coping with experiences his friend has had for eighteen years, since the first years of the town's existence, when Stuyvesant named it Beverwijck.

Albany

The end of the year has come after a disastrous trading season for every-one. Janse too has empty hands. Since the beginning of May he has served only thirteen clients. *Handelstijd* should have brought more employment, but it has been an unusually bad year. As late as the last week of August there hadn't been the slightest amount of trading. The farmers' grain was not in demand in New York City, nor would the English allow them to sell it to places like Boston. Even the town couldn't pay its bills. The chill days of November and December have seen the river and creeks freeze over. Logs slide cooperatively across the ice for the millers. But he has met with clients only every eighteen days on an average, and their needs were not nearly as complicated, or financially promising, as those of Pietersz. He is allowed to ask 1:10 guilders for writing a contract, a lease, or a power of attorney. And he must be paid 1 guilder for a copy. If he takes an inventory, he has a right to 1:5 guilders. He may ask 4 guilders if he has to travel to a client or on a client's behalf. Traveling within Albany with a client is different: he can't ask more than 1 guilder. Usually the things he does earn a single guilder or two — not that they can't add up.

Neither, however, were his clients the leading burghers of the town. Philip Pietersz Schuyler, Goose Gerritsz van Schaick, Barent Pietersz Coey-mans, and Jeremias van Rensselaer are powerful men. They engage in con-tinual business transactions that do honor to the town. Yet neither they nor their families have called on him. None has acted as a patron, returning to him time and again, giving his career a solid start. In two years' time, Schuyler will pledge 8,000 guilders for a farm. Much paperwork might be needed, but none is turned over to him. Nor is he in a partnership of any kind. And neither he nor his wife is of a family that will draw him upward into the ranks of men from whom the magistrates are chosen.

He will need to have, as they say, many strings to his bow. Certainly he will need to put his earnings as a schoolmaster alongside the small income he is getting from the *notariaat* and, when it comes his way, his work for the court. Winter is a time of keeping night schools. Starting now, and not counting other young people, apprentices or their parents will be holding the master carpenters or tailors to contracts promising to send them along to the night lessons. The schoolmaster earns a pittance more for night lessons than for teaching during the day.

But the governor-general has surrounded this employment with uncertainty. Just last May someone, maybe Jan Juriaensz Becker himself, got to the general about schoolteaching in Albany. He was told that schoolmasters other than Becker keep school only when they wish — when they have "no other Imployment" — while he "makes it his businesse" year round. Such men were enticing scholars away from his instructions, encouraging them to move "from one school to another." They were also, so said Becker or his advocate, "more backward in their learning." Lovelace was persuaded. He seemed not to know that the town counted on having many day and night schools, and that they were kept by perhaps as many as six masters. He ordered that no one other than Becker might keep a school or, as he worded it, "interrupt him."

Then, after two months, the general came upriver to Albany. He attended a court session held in the old fort. (He and the soldiers call it Fort Albany — one day he'll say that the burghers should consider it as "their Mother & greatest concern," which is a strange phrase that no one else uses.) Among other things, he announced that he was revoking the commission obtained by an unnamed petitioner "to keep school to the exclusion of others." He now thought it was solicited by someone "without proper qualifications."

JULY 6, 1671
Fort James, New York

Lovelace must respond to intelligence he has received regarding Albany. He sends off a letter to Thomas Delaval, a member of his council, who now happens to be in the town. The news has made him impatient and full of sarcasm. The Dutch men are listening to rumors about a French attack of some kind but show no understanding of how to turn the rumors into proper military support for the garrison. They haven't got a proper standing militia. At best, they improvise defenses or prefer not to contribute to their own defense at all. They're "timorous," nervous Nellies who are full of fright, as though the "very Sword were already at [their] Throats." For his own part, he "can not possibly imagine" where they got the idea that the French were about to invade New York. There is peace between England and France, and he has no intelligence to the contrary. Such lack of courage, he promises, will make them "Altogether Useless" when real danger comes.

Still, he can use the Dutch men's sense of alarm to his "best advantage." There is enough fear about now to make them coordinate their efforts alongside those of the garrison: look to the defenses at Schenectady, contribute to the repairs of the fort at Albany, scout among the natives for information. Let the local "Horse likewise make an appearance" and "a strict list . . . [be] drawn of all persons able to bear Armes." Keep the "Guard" of the burghers active but take care that they are "not too much harrast" because if danger really comes they'll "prove inactive." Above all, "keep up their spirits" and don't "lett them know ye Danger (when it shall happen) till they be in the midst of it."

JULY 15, 1671
Albany

Suddenly there seems to be the need for someone who can make up a list of men eligible to carry arms and then see to it that they discharge their responsibilities. They call the post a provost of the burghers.

Janse puts his name forward. If he gets it, he will be responsible for ensuring that the townsmen cooperate with a proclamation ordering all males between the ages of fifteen and sixty to be ready and armed, presumably in case of attack. He wins the appointment at a meeting of four leading merchants — three of his fellow burghers of Albany and one a merchant of New York City and now council member, Thomas Delaval.

Now, however, these men are not merely sitting posed as merchants. They have become military officers. They address themselves as Major General Captain Delaval and the local men as "*De Hooft Officieren in Commissie van de Burgerye*," the chief commissioned officers of the burghers. Calling himself captain major is Abraham Staats, owner of a river sloop, trader, officer of the local burgher guard, and, ordinarily, indifferent custodian of the town's gunpowder. Philip Pietersz Schuyler, merchant and landowner, is captain; Volkert Janse Douw, another man of Schuyler's power as *peltrij handelaar*, is lieutenant. The order to arm will not be to the burghers' or farmers' liking. But the officers expect them to comply. So steadily have rumors of a French descent upon the town persisted that less than three weeks ago a friend of Janse's and several volunteers had been sent to reconnoiter the Mohawk country. They were to remain there for a week while native scouts went to "spy out" everything possible. Then, just twelve days ago, the burghers and men of the *colonie* were ordered to appear in the town "fully armed, ready to march." Many, or some, had not come along at all. Now they will find themselves on his list.

Janse's appointment immediately mentions the fines that will be imposed for noncooperation. Half will be his. To collect them, he will have to make his way around the town, *colonie,* and outlying settlements threatening fellow residents. Such a job, whether as clerk of a so-called council of war or, as in the past, assistant to the law enforcement officer, is something that one would avoid if at all possible. A man can expect resistance and perhaps physical harm. Townspeople would perhaps remember injuries that had occurred before. So Janse and the burghers are told that Salisbury will give him a "helping hand" should anyone refuse to pay. Already the burghers are struggling to meet the ordinary taxes and those laid for the stockade and new fortifications. Janse's chances of collecting fines are not good.

He can, however, use the additional income. For many years he has been a member of the burgher guard and earned a bit of income as its clerk. Now, as the appointee of the *hooft officieren,* he will also act as clerk, writing up the ordinances regarding militia days and seeing that they are posted. On his first day as provost, he composes such a public notice. Male inhabitants over fifteen and under sixty years of age, he writes, must provide themselves with "a gun and side arms, two pounds of powder and four pounds of lead." This is to be done within fourteen days on penalty of a fine of 100 guilders. He concludes the notice, "By order of said Council of War," and signs his name, adding "Clerk."

Probably he is not optimistic that the men will ready themselves for military duty as some kind of civilian militia. Martial affairs, the burghers feel, are for the burgher guard. They are a civic guard, paid to maintain the town's security. So let them keep their guardhouses and stores of wood and candles, let them carry their arms and keep watch. Moreover, it has never been expected that they, the burghers — or even the civic guard — will ride out against an enemy, not the natives or the French. There is no cavalry: Janse, long-standing member of the guard that he is, seems never to have owned a horse. In any case, since the burgher guard earns a bit of income from standing guard, let *them* see to military security, or let it be handled by the soldiers of the garrison.

Through the month of July, affairs are moving ahead. Within five days of Janse's taking up his post, something of a cavalry has been formed and is now given permission to pasture their horses south of town. Van Rensselaer, presumably because he is the largest landowner in the area, has been persuaded to organize and lead a cavalry troop, supposed to be on the ready to move somewhere. They have been drilling off and on. Late last year they exercised, but in a miserable fashion. Van Rensselaer had to admit that the troop was "not quite complete" and "the horses of some . . . were still in the woods." But then Captain Salisbury, or someone he called "Capt. Salsbergen," had instructed them, and it finally "went very well."

Just two weeks after Janse's appointment, Lovelace arrives in town. Publicly he surrounds himself with military men: three from New York City, three new "captains" among the locals, Salisbury, and, if there are minutes to be taken at any of their meetings, provost Adriaen Janse. Undoubtedly he does not share with the Dutch men his thoughts about their cowardice or that he and Delaval are capitalizing on their sense of alarm to their own "best advantage." Let their scurrying about making lists and collecting fines go on.

Over the next ten months, nothing occurs, no sudden attack, no troopers marching from the St. Lawrence. In spring, when the land allows hostile natives and Christians to move over it once again, Janse is reactivated. The men again have to be warned to arm themselves, and late in May he sees them assemble, or some of them, before the courthouse to hear further orders. He hears his own words read out: the eligible men are to appear with "proper hand and side arms." They are now called infantry and cavalry. The local council of war, now four captains, four lieutenants, one cornet, and two ensigns, orders a day of muster. If it strikes anyone that this will be among the first of such martial happenings, no one reports it. They are to assemble at nine o'clock in the morning "where the ensign shall be flung out." The penalty they must consider for nonattendance is 25 guilders. He signs his name and the word "Provost." Undoubtedly it is he who posts the orders.

If he is fortunate, some of the men will not turn up for inspection. He can begin to prod the absentees for his fines. He does not, however, record having collected anything.

Very likely the whole thing does not amount to much.

NOVEMBER 1671
Albany

He is chatting with friends. In just a few hours one of them will leave for the Netherlands. Eldert Gerbertsz Cruyff is soon to depart and may not return for many months. Such a business trip requires a great deal of planning.

Gerbertsz has to think ahead. So must those friends and family members who will invariably ask him to attend to some of their business affairs. Powers of attorney must be arranged for use overseas. Wholesale merchants and notaries in such places as Amsterdam must be empowered to act in a trader's or artisan's interest. Distant relatives must be constituted as attorneys to collect debts, settle inheritances, or settle old scores. At home, the rental of lands or workshops must be arranged for the coming year. If there are outstanding obligations, then a house may need to be mortgaged, a field of grain disposed of. A will may need to be drawn up. All the papers must be properly notarized.

There is work for notaries. Executing papers for Gerbertsz and his family has given Janse considerable work, little as it is. The call upon his services is not entirely unexpected. Eight years ago, Gerbertsz had described him as one of his good friends.

They would have arrived in Beverwijck at about the same time, in the early 1650s. Janse came upriver from New Amsterdam. His friend arrived directly from Amsterdam as one of van Rensselaer's tenants. Janse would have known what everyone soon knew, that Gerbertsz could be a man of violent temper and unsound business sense. He was often in debt, often in court. The van Rensselaers thought him to be a hopeless tenant and just lately had agreed among themselves that the house and barn on his land were "barely fit for use." At the same time, he had to pay them water privileges to run his sawmill and was never out of their debt.

Janse at least has no disputes with him. Just weeks ago, he helped him arrange for the management of his sawmill south of town until the coming spring, when, all going well, his friend could expect to be home. He included conditions covering the tenant's board and the hiring of a second sawyer when the next spring would come. One man could "saw by day and the other by night." Before the meeting was over, he and Gerbertsz had dealt with all eventualities. What if the boards are "thick or thin," "oak or pine"? How much of the "scantling" should go to the tenant and how much to the assistant sawyer? Let them divide it "every week by lot."

Gerbertsz's departure will be from the foreshore, somewhere along the river between the east gate and the old fort. Once, when New Netherland was under the Dutch, sometimes as many as six men or women would make the trip each year, probably more. Perhaps Cobus or Becker has clients who are making such voyages, but Janse has served only Gerbertsz in two and a half years. The town's early notary — but Janse cannot know this — earned about one-third of his income from acts directly to do with Holland, burghers coming and going, conducting their business and that of family and friends. Less than 2 percent of Janse's income will come from the same source. Maybe he senses this but cannot put his finger on it: something has changed. Perhaps it is just as well that he does not know that down in New York City, even during his first year as notary, obligations were being accepted as authentic without any notary's hand. In any case, the yacht should get Gerbertsz to Manhattan Island in three days' time. He ought to leave there quickly. It is already late in the season for crossing to Holland.

Gerbertsz's leave-taking is known to everyone. Janse is among those who are with him in the last hours before the ship leaves. His friend is talking about business, among other things, how a brewing partnership he once had was set up, who got what profits, what should be the earnings of the man who had one-fourth ownership. The others listen. One is the wife of a man who will, at least in seven years' time, be working as a brewer's assistant. The other is only two weeks away from taking the first steps toward buying his own brewery.

So the men and the woman talk together. Perhaps Janse tells his friend what it's like to make the voyage to *patria*, to be in Amsterdam and to return. He made such a journey once, but the circumstances became frightening and everything seemed at risk. Perhaps he says nothing.

APRIL 18, 1672
Albany

The magistrates have taken an unusual step. They have awarded Janse a special seat in the church. It is "in consideration of his long citizenship" and is clearly a mark of their special respect. The townspeople would know why he has received his honored place. He has not grown rich and watched his riches make him a magistrate or a delegate to the new meetings the governor-general convenes in New York. He is not important in church affairs. He is not a deacon, nor has he ever kept the records of the church. He does not take his place because of an eminent family. His achievement has been to have served well, year after year, in all the small particulars of being a low-level civil servant.

The magistrates honor this contribution because in many ways his work — as notary, schoolmaster, provost, sworn assessor, "good man" — is like their own. At times, and now especially, they are asked to play roles in spacious — in fact, imperial — dramas. When they dress up as a council of war, they are acting in a play that encompasses decisive events that are now, as the general likes to put it, "likely to happen in Europe." Cobus, after all,

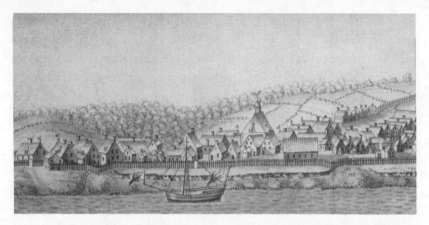

4. Prospect of the City of Albany in the Province of New York in America, *Thomas Davies, 1763. Here the city hall dominates. Such a building was the emblem of a system of government that made the judiciary supreme across the Netherlands. Rather than enshrine a sovereign national law, Dutch men and women devolved sovereignty, entrusting local courts with the interpretation and practice of laws that guaranteed rights and privileges. Holland, Zeeland and Brabant alone had three hundred largely independent courts. Like their counterparts in Albany, magistrates had no legal training, although merchants (who were most likely to make up the court) were often encouraged to study the law. Later historians of New York, looking to find such rights enshrined in popular legislatures and local assemblies in New Netherland, were, of course, disappointed. (Collection of the Albany Institute of History and Art, Gift of Mrs. Richard C. Rockwell; photograph by Joseph Levy)*

now calls the place of the court meetings the "king's house." Even when they assemble on stage to announce, as they will do next month, that all those refusing to pay assessed taxes can expect to quarter soldiers at their own expense and not that of the city, they are, for all that they are bit players, delivering lines in a play that treats of frontiers, defenses, and officials miles away at Fort James and even beyond, in London.

More often, however, their performances are like Janse's. It's true that they have a care for all the affairs of the town — "*het reilen en zeilen*," they call it — everything, lock, stock, and barrel. Yet the cases they hear are not larger than life but on a very human scale. They are figures in scenes of individual dishonesty or cupidity, when often no one more significant than a wagonmaker or innkeeper has to be got out of his or her own violence or misfortune. In a way, they are credible because they never step out of their roles as businessmen. As they would do in their own affairs, and as Janse does, they avoid everything that is showy. They miniaturize: public discord, theirs among themselves, one party against another.

In court, they move things along swiftly. Any one of their ordinary sessions is like a program of the shortest of stage acts, with crisp character entrances and exits, everything concrete and kept to a minimum in time and space. In their relish for accuracy, they choose to perform like Janse. And both his work and theirs is congenial with the ways of the artists so much enjoyed at home, the *fijnschilders* who take time painting the lace of a cuff or feathers of a fowl. They all take pleasure in keeping their part of a record of small day-to-day happenings, a sort of documentary record. Twice this year, the magistrates have called on him to examine accounts, asking him to look patiently at handwriting, check dates, revisit someone's sums. It is work for the nearsighted. That is, it is of little matter that the larger, more distant sights, the big picture, are blurs. So now he works closely over matters of a church foot-stove, a single bushel of buckwheat, and a few allegedly fictitious accounts. He is asked to find — he did it in February — pertinent papers already in his care or, as he sometimes puts it, "resting with me, notary." The interests of the antiquarian are essential, the enjoyment of sorting through old papers, the patience to locate the old stories that the court needs.

Even in his role in the church, the magistrates see in him what Fabricius saw: someone who can deal purposefully with detail, with small things. He is one of the two churchmasters. This really only means that he oversees repairs to the church. He does odd jobs. The fire ladders are in his and Hendrick Rooseboom's care. They hire them out and keep an account. But the sums are trivial, one guilder a day rental, and only part of the income divided between them. He is also in charge of the seats in the church — not that he has a voice in the larger issue of determining the hierarchy of seating arrangements. He is simply to know the order of seating and prevent the mischief that sometimes occurs when someone presumes to sit in another's place.

The magistracy and church leadership are one. So there is nothing out of order in the magistrates' rewarding civic virtue in religious coin. It is also their prerogative to appoint a precentor of the church, a man who will act as gravedigger and inviter to funerals, custodian of the church keys, and *voorlezer*, someone who leads the prayers or singing. Three years ago, they had cast their votes and given the job to Rooseboom. The work earns him a few guilders. Now he is using the church attic for storage space. Rented out, it is another small source of income. He must turn over one-third of his profits to the magistrates. What his overall income is over the year, he would be the last to divulge.

Janse is careful in keeping his own accounts. One day, but only once, he will show us one of them. But what credits and debits he is looking at now is impossible to know. This year he served as notary on nineteen occasions, that is, he met with sixty men and women and filled twenty-one pages with script. That earned him about 30 guilders. If he looks back over the year, he can think that he has worked well on Pietersz's estate (and that work is still going forward), earned something as provost, acted occasionally as attorney for townspeople, completed some work for the court. He hasn't had to hound people into court to collect fees. Cobus had to do this and even then faced angry refusal.

He did not give up on the *notariaat*. A man licensed for Schenectady threw it in just this year.

FEBRUARY 14, 1673
Albany

Ten days ago, Janse helped a fellow member of the civic guard buy a house on the hill. Now his associate is sitting as a judge in court-martial proceedings. It is a trial and execution like none the townspeople have seen before.

A soldier of the garrison, John Stuart, has been found murdered. Apparently he was hacked to death somewhere in the woods. Two natives have been taken up for the murder. Their trial is being conducted before eleven men sitting as something the English call a special court of oyer and terminer. Captain Silvester Salisbury is presiding. Magistrates and officers of the militia are judges as well.

For a full day burghers pass in and out of the fort, one after the other offering testimony and getting their own view of the natives shackled in irons. Townspeople would have known Stuart. He lived in a shanty on the hill and let the forest enchant him into illegal trading. He was a reckless man, whom even the governor-general thought "would dye some violent death." But the two natives have confessed that they met Stuart in the woods and decided to murder him there. The judges find them guilty.

On the next day the sentence of death is pronounced. Townspeople watch as the convicted men, each now desperately accusing the other, are led away. At least in the town's records, it is the first execution of its kind. They are hanged "at the place of execution." The ceremonies — van Rensselaer brought in to parade with his troop, Salisbury wearing the title deputy governor — are as much for the townspeople's intimidation as for that of the natives. Probably they have not thought much about it, but the general has. "Pomp and solemnity," he dictated in organizing the formalities of it all, "commonly strikes as great a terror in Spectators" as in the condemned. Afterward, the bodies are left hanging "in chains," a pleasurably grotesque attraction for onlookers.

In eighteen months' time, Janse will have to think of John Stuart and this incident all over again.

MAY 30, 1673
Albany

Janse has been a notary for about three years. Now he is routinely authorizing a contract binding two parties to the conveyance of a lot "on the slope of the hill near the *plein*." Routinely too he is signing his name as "Adriaen van Ilpendam."

Why doesn't he ever sign "Adriaen Janse van Ilpendam"? Wouldn't it link him more closely with his father? Those who handle his official papers in such places as Amsterdam don't even know that his name is Adriaen Janse van Ilpendam. Why?

AUGUST 9, 1673
Albany

The United Provinces and England are now at war. The fleet under commanders Cornelis Evertsz de Jongste and Jacob Benckes sails into New York Harbor and recaptures New Netherland. Anthonij Colve is commissioned as commanding officer. For months rumors have been abroad that this would happen.

Back in April, Janse was aware of the stories. He was doing his usual thing, writing wills and other legal papers for neighbors and friends. Yet he was especially cautious on their behalf. If New Netherland were retaken, there would certainly be a return to the old formalities demanded by Dutch law. Phrasing used to meet English demands might be rejected. So, in two wills, he wrote that the testaments under his hand would be valid "notwithstanding that certain formalities demanded by law and usage may not be fully observed herein."

Everyone has to take special care in a city or territory that is likely to change hands during wartime. Down on Manhattan Island, Colve has insulted one of wealthiest of the Dutch merchants, a man who was the last mayor to hold office under the English. In an early letter he did not even offer him a courteous form of address. The pointed omission suggested that he had committed treason. Giving service to the enemy as a scribe is equally dangerous. It can mean a man's life. For allegedly translating letters for the enemy, a Dutch man in Brazil was beheaded and his body quartered. First, however, two fingers of his right hand were severed.

It had been the same when the English came nine years ago. In the changeover of authorities, men who seemed learned were especially at risk. One of those, a man who was powerful in Beverwijck when Janse arrived, was Johan de Deckere. He had been a notary and even a "counsellor of state" on Manhattan Island and then administrator upriver for the West India Company, acting as his own secretary and, for that reason, having the powers of a notary. People considered him to be a "proud person." They said he "caused the poor to want." He had been singled out by the English shortly after their arrival and accused of inciting rebellion. Here in Beverwijck and at "other places upon Hudsons River," they charged, he had given speeches alienating the minds of His Majesty's Dutch subjects. He had been forced to flee the town and had not been around for all these years.

The return of the Dutch has served to put Janse's well-being in jeopardy also. His status as a notary is again uncertain. He now has to look to a new set of officials for the renewal of his appointment.

AUGUST 22, 1673
Fort Orange, Colony of Rensselaerswyck and Schanechtade

His appointment as notary has been confirmed. He immediately returns to Dutch ways of presenting documents. He settles into dating acts according to the Gregorian calendar. Everyone used it until nine years ago. The English, however, preferred the "old style" Julian calendar. Now he carefully returns to writing "new style." He also returns to words that revive the familiar notions of local municipal autonomy caught in a phrase that is now once again found in legislation, *stad en jurisdictie*, a city and its jurisdictions. He points to his authority as coming from the local magistrates.

Initially he is unsure of the name of the town, and for a while everyone is as confused as he is. At an early meeting of the Council of War in New York

City (now New Orange), the town's delegates said they were speaking for the "officers and justices of Fort Orange and Beverwijck." He too goes back to early beginnings, when Beverwijck was simply vacant land north of a West India Company *factorij* called Fort Orange. He is, he writes, admitted to office "by the honorable magistrates of Fort Orange." Three months later he is using the town's new name, Willemstadt. At one point, he slips into using "New Albany in America." Except for that lapse, however, he consistently writes "residing in Willemstadt."

For many months there is turmoil and confusion. The magistrates have to ask the new governor where they should convene themselves when holding court. They meet in the fort when they are sitting with military personnel. But on their own? They are curtly directed to meet in the house formerly "used by the English for that purpose." For someone like Cornelis van Ruyven, a man down on Manhattan Island who had served loyally and intelligently under Stuyvesant, only good will come of the restoration. Earlier this year he had carried a letter to Holland full of optimism. The leading merchants had figured it all out and were taking the long view: 25,000 bushels of wheat could go to the Netherlands yearly, and that would come from Esopus alone; closer association with Surinam and Curaçao would ensure increased and easily available supplies here. Increased immigration — another consideration would clinch it: it would secure the "great prospects of the colony."

Others have to think of tomorrow's prospects. For Janse's friend Barent Pietersz Coeymans, the departure of the English means a sudden loss of considerable income. He will not be paid for all the materials he has been furnishing for a house that Lovelace wanted built for himself on the hill overlooking the town. For the Lutherans, it means the revocation of their right to bury their own dead: now Rooseboom will be doing it.

And now a new set of rumors moves like a virus through the province. Any day, the whisper goes, the States General will return New Netherland to Charles II. "Something else will again be seen before Christmas," some are heard saying.

DECEMBER 9/19, 1673
The Hague

Sire,
    In order to manifest to your Majesty [of England] the special esteem which we entertain for your friendship, we hereby also offer the restitution of New

Netherland and of all other places and Colonies which have been won by our arms during the present war.

JUNE 11, 1674
The Hague

Resolution of the States General: "The Amsterdam Board of Admiralty hath prepared a ship to bring away and convoy to this country the State's people who are in New Netherland."

Who "is the person to whom restitution [of New Netherland] shall have to be made . . . and where [is] the person . . . to be met and found"?

MID-OCTOBER 1674
Willemstadt

He attends the funeral of Jeremias van Rensselaer; 151 men and women have been invited to the burial. Van Rensselaer is young to have died, only about forty-five. He leaves a wife in precarious health and a young family. A list of those invited to share the family's sorrow is kept among the family papers. The names of the mourners are in four columns. Janse's name appears in the first column. Except for those of family, magistrates, and the *colonie's* officers, the scores of other names seem to be in no particular order.

During the past fourteen months, much had changed. New magistrates had assumed their places. Swart was again *schout*. A form of municipal government in accord with the "laudable customs" at home had been reestablished. Swart was again ordered to preside over the court, and he and the magistrates could conduct sessions as often as they thought necessary. The burgher guard, or at least the men down at Esopus, once again recalled themselves to being strictly a civic guard: they swore to ensure the "interests of the Burghers entrusted to us." It was now expected that the merchants at home would again be shipping out large quantities of trading goods. Even the natives were told that the days of paying high prices for them were over. Meanwhile, Colve knew what to call Willemstadt: a city.

All the while, Janse aroused as little attention as ever. If he had somehow collaborated with the English by accepting a public appointment earlier from Lovelace, he was not punished for having done so. The services he performed may have seemed inconsequential. Soon his name is once again among those considered by the court as arbiter. Just as soon, however, comes confirmation of the rumors about the return of the English. At least six months ago, the van Rensselaers in Holland suspected this outcome and were taking steps to ensure the *colonie*'s existence under a new English administration. They turned to questioning Jeremias on how he stood with the English. When the garrison left the town, there were serious disturbances. Had he played a part in them? The soldiers were "uncivilly treated by some," he agreed, but he had "showed them nothing but friendship." The family was as much as telling him to prepare for a change.

It set him to worrying. He worried now for prayers he had offered for the English king before Evertsz and Benckes came. He *had* prayed for the king, but mostly on the prescribed days of prayer and "not in secret." But as to the coming again of the English, "we did not count on such a blow, God knows."

OCTOBER 31, 1674
Manhattan Island

General Edmund Andros arrives on Manhattan Island with a company of about a hundred English troopers. He is thirty-eight years old. Some say he can understand Dutch. He will accept Colve's surrender in early November.

During all the months of Dutch rule, Janse executed only fourteen documents. For long periods, no new work came to him. Once, for five and a half months, and again for nine weeks, nothing was heard of him. It was as though he had disappeared altogether.

He wrote nothing of the political changes taking place around him. He did possess something, one thing, that perhaps gave him a sense of steadiness, the hope of a future welcome irrespective of itinerant governors and changing flags. He had a document that he had kept near him now for thirty-four years. It promised that one day he would come into an inheritance.

JANUARY 28, 1675
Albany

Inadvertently he has a bitter confrontation with Robert Livingston. It all began when he was talking in the company of two friends. A third man, Hendrick Rooseboom, came along begging them to speak with the minister, Gideon Schaets, on his behalf. Implore him to go to the lodgings of a man named Robert Livingston and settle a quarrel that arose between him and Livingston at Schaets's house two days earlier. The men agree.

Adriaen Janse does more. He accompanies his friends to the minister's house and assists in persuading him to act as arbitrator. He then makes his way with Schaets to Livingston's rooms in the house of Gabriel Tomasen, just minutes away. The Scotsman is a newcomer to Albany and is not yet a property owner.

It is about ten o'clock at night by the time the men leave the minister's home and arrive as Tomasen's. The figures are of two older men on the street; Schaets is sixty-seven and Janse is now fifty-seven. Janse does the talking. He takes the time to reason with Livingston on Rooseboom's behalf, urging forgiveness in a spirit of Christian love. He pledges his services as adjudicator, offering the time-honored way of avoiding the dishonor and expense of a dispute brought before the court and the public. He isn't successful. He returns to his friends and perhaps Rooseboom. Without hesitation he draws up a brief deposition describing Rooseboom's request and the actions that followed. Janse and the two friends sign it. It will be evidence used, unfortunately, in court.

For some reason Janse cannot let it rest. The next day he takes up the deposition of the previous night and adds another sworn statement. This one is entirely his own. For once he is writing down *his* memories. He details his and Schaets's meeting with the twenty-one-year-old newcomer. He and the old minister, he writes, were making their way along the street "about bell-ringing" time. Arriving at Livingston's, he sought to persuade him to conciliate and forgive. He was able to present "much reasoning" for this line of action. Livingston, or "Lievensteyn," as he consistently spells it, refused.

Livingston will, of course, prevail. He'll have his court case. Schaets is an old man, easily intimidated, someone whom an observer will one day describe as "a poor old ignorant person." Any sworn statement of his regarding the behavior of Livingston will undoubtedly be discarded as unreliable. But it is not so with Janse. His experience as a conciliator is common knowledge. And now he has written a statement that he knows will accompany the deposition of his associates and be honored. Even if Rooseboom loses, it will stand as evidence of the strangely uncompromising attitude of the outsider. People will know of it all. They will soon enough know about the range of arguments he had pressed upon Livingston. The Scotsman's response — that "expenses have been incurred and the matter must be decided before the judges" — will stand as both harsh and unchristian. And

Livingston, or his attorney, will have to deal with his "solemn oath" on all these happenings.

Janse will frequently meet Livingston face to face. He will record the meetings as conducted with civility, as his position requires. Others will encounter Livingston as well, and they too will record the events. Invariably, by something in or about him, they will find themselves as humiliated as Rooseboom. Partly he will intimidate townspeople because he is so obviously useful to the English as a link in the chain of command that stretches from Manhattan Island to Albany. He does not return advancement with unbending loyalty, but he offers ingenuity and fierce energy. He speaks and writes English as well as Dutch. More precisely, he will write a document or minutes in Dutch and then copy it in English, adding "Translated per me Ro: Livingston." This is something Janse will not, and cannot, ever do.

Soon townspeople will realize what Janse is among the first to know, that Livingston, for all his youth, is a man who ruthlessly "takes the meat out of the pot": he spoons up the best for himself. The new English administration has put the ladle in his hand. Within the year, he is secretary and town treasurer; he is also secretary to the commissioners of Indian affairs. Then the private affairs of Rensselaerswijck are his to know because he is made secretary of the *colonie*, keeper of its papers. Next he is tax collector and then sharing the income of the *shout*. His public earnings will not satisfy him, although they are about 800 guilders a year. He is on his way to becoming the wealthiest merchant in the district. The widow of Jeremias van Rensselaer learns to despise him. "He regrets," she will one day offer in summary of his ambitions, "that he has not more in his hands." In coming years, myths about his power and greed will flourish: wasn't Jeremias's brother, the strange mystic Nicolaus van Rensselaer — "Nicolaus the Prophet" he was sometimes called — forced to make a terrifying prophecy about himself and Livingston? Wasn't he on a yacht and waiting for a scribe to take down his last testament when he saw Livingston come aboard and cried out, "Anyone but you, for you will marry my widow"?

Livingston is a threat to each man's survival. He calls himself an attorney and is the voice of the English authorities in cases settled outside the courtroom or, as he prefers, within its precincts. There he is the *kijver*, a wrangler, winning his cases on the fine points of law few others know. He seems made for the new adversarial ways of English law that are coming into the courtroom and in which, as he showed in his dismissal of Rooseboom's pleadings, arbitrators like Janse needn't play a part. People can watch him: how he pursues the suit of the commander of the fort against two insignificant men —

one pasturing a cow and the other a horse on land seized for the use of the soldiers — or computes disadvantageously the tax assessment of a man such as Philip Pietersz Schuyler.

Janse's future is threatened as well. No one sees the larger picture better than Livingston, but he can enjoy being nearsighted too: he does not mind handling receipts, promissory notes, or memorandums. When he was only sixteen, he reminded himself that he must always keep everything in perfect order, even "*op de maniere van Italiaens Boeckhouder,*" the way of men who know double-entry bookkeeping. By the exactitude of his care for them, he will show that his papers — those that are loose and those threaded together, those scribbled and those of fine calligraphy — mean to him what they mean to Janse, although they will be nurtured and tended to deliver so much more power. They are not the ephemera of success but its center.

That is in the future. For the present Livingston at least does not seek to be a notary. He would have been familiar with the *notarisschap* when he was living in Rotterdam as a youth, but he makes no move in that direction. Perhaps he knows that the English have little time for it and, besides, as secretary he already has all the powers of the notary and more.

SUMMER 1675
Albany

The town is full of English-speaking people. Some are strangers and newly arrived soldiers and traders from New England, some are hangers-on from the earlier English occupation. Much in the burghers' lives is being altered. Down on Manhattan Island, the governor-general has already proclaimed that everyone is responsible for reporting on neighbors, friends, or anyone taking mutinous actions against the king. Here the burghers are in their usual pose, guarded.

The general has come to inspect the town. He needs to oversee military affairs. Nearby natives have been aroused to hostility by the war now being carried by New Englanders to natives of other tribes in and around their settlements. This skirmishing and burning must be contained. So the military men are even more than usually present and making decisions about the town's affairs. Over the next four months, from late August to the end of December, townspeople such as Janse will see the magistrates convene the court on seventeen occasions but only five times meet without the presence of the general or his subordinate. A fort is being constructed high on the hill. Later a stranger visiting the town will notice that it "is on the rise of the hill, from which it commands the place." Ordinances and commands for civilians come with frequency and decisiveness.

The general's directives are aimed at remaking the town into one of the province's "English places." He seems intent on change, no looking back. One change leads to the next: the appointment of overseers of "the king's highways"; the vetting of all ordinances passed in Schenectady by the commanding officer of the fort in Albany; the promotion of Nicolaus van Rensselaer, a man ordained in the Anglican church, as minister of the Reformed congregation. Taxes: the usual thing, the eyeing of goods that belong to the vanquished merchants.

AUGUST 24, 1675
Ordinary Court Session Held in Albany on Tuesday

Andros is presiding. On the docket are important, and disturbing, affairs. Nicolaus van Rensselaer has been called a false prophet and temple of the devil. His accuser will be taken as a prisoner to New York City to defend himself there.

Next, the town watch and duties of law enforcement need to be properly regulated. The magistrates will make it their business to choose "constables" from among the town's burghers. Those selected will learn to supervise the watch and carry out duties as "in New York [City] and other English places."

Other matters also fall under the general's direct jurisdiction. The magistrates have thrown some work in the direction of "*Schout* Swart and Mr. Adriaen van Elpendam." They have been undertaking some work clearing up the estate of John Stuart. Now they are ordered to give the magistrates an account of the estate. The general will also inspect the papers and convey further instructions.

The work will take them almost a year to complete. Janse and Swart will dispose of Stuart's property, pay out death duties, convene the creditors, and allocate disbursements — and hope for a reasonable recompense for themselves. At the end and still caught up in their nearsighted work, they will need advice about outstanding debts to the commonest of men: to whom shall they pay the money due to Anthony Glass, who has died, and to Robert Williams and another man who have left the country? Allocate some of it to a local resident. Give the rest to the Englishman who paid for Stuart's burial.

SEPTEMBER 7, 1675
Ordinary Court Session Held in Albany

The right honorable general has left orders that no one other than Ludovicus Cobus and Adriaen van Elpendam are to be notaries public of this place. Somebody has given him their names.

SEPTEMBER 18, 1675
Albany

Janse has his own work to consider. A merchant, Hendrick Cuyler, comes to him with affairs to settle in Holland. Some time ago, he sent about 350 pelts to an agent in Amsterdam. It was a consignment worth about 2,800 guilders. He knows that some pelts have already been sold there, but he has received no payment. Now he seeks a power of attorney authorizing his brother to prosecute his claim in the Dutch courts. Janse sets to work, anticipating the variety of jurisdictions in which the case might be tested in a place such as the Netherlands. Hearings before "Lords, courts, tribunals and judges" should cover it — and allowance for local "custom and procedure." Another merchant, Harmen Bastiaensz, came to him three months ago, also requiring a power of attorney for a resident of Amsterdam. His father had died in Hoorn and he wanted to assign his patrimony to Jan Hendricksz Sijbinck, a merchandise wholesaler in Amsterdam. Janse knows what's planned: the deposited income will fund an account against which Bastiaensz can place yearly orders for trading goods. For many years, the most important traders have been importing goods from Sijbinck's merchant house.

A man with profits from a considerable shipment of furs, another with a patrimony to count on, these are individuals blessed with a good fortune that Janse may not see himself sharing. Winter will come, and he will continue to put on the market the only commodity he has for sale, his work with words, as a teacher and as a scribe. There is no reason to think that anything out of the ordinary will alter the routines of his life. A contract for land, a bond, a six-year lease of a farm: he knows almost on instinct how to put these matters in order for the men who will come to him as the cold months of autumn close in.

Haarlem, in Holland

A man fifty years of age is writing up legal papers. He is not a notary. He is much more than that, exercising as he does one of the most prestigious offices in the city. Dammas Guldewagen is secretary of the city of Haarlem. The papers before him have to do with a cousin in America, Adriaen Janse van Ilpendam. He composes a letter. It is his pleasure to inform Janse that he has been named in two bequests to the sum of 2,000 guilders. An uncle has left him 1,000 guilders. Furthermore, and in a codicil to that bequest, a cousin, Jacobus van Lodesteijn, has named him as beneficiary of a similar amount.

Late in life and suddenly, Adriaen Janse has come into an inheritance.

"In Albany in America"

Janse has been thinking about his inheritance for over a month. Guldewagen's letter arrived just after approval of his request for reappointment as schoolmaster. Yet this news far exceeds the assurance of earning that small and always uncertain income. The yearly interest on 2,000 Holland guilders will buy perhaps four times its value here. He has been busy composing the documents that will be his response. They are two letters and a copy of each for himself. He is now ready to send off his reply.

He is excited and confident, full of a sense of the future. He foresees years when a secure income will mean doing his notarial work with the best paper and good-quality thread. He will seal his clients' documents with the finest sealing wax and have the best black silk for a hood for his wife and blue linen and even heavy white linen from Alkmaar. For himself, he must have neckcloths striped on the ends: even in Albany people are aware of dressing "after the manner of the burghers." Everything that the sudden promise of money means he pours into the prospect of having these needs of his trade and his household.

He addresses a sealed letter to the same overseas merchant with whom Bastiaensz and so many others do business, Jan Hendricksz Sijbinck. His salutation is uncharacteristically flamboyant. He opens, "Mr. Jan Sijbinck:

Salute!" Then he asks grace to place an order. He lists a ream of High Dutch paper with the foolscap and bells and a half pound of fine sealing wax and proper clothing, the things that have so excited his imagination. He offers as security the fact that he has "fallen heir to some money at Haarlem." Sijbinck is to transfer the interest on his inheritance into an account. This time it is not Bastiaensz's account but his own.

He encloses a copy of the letter received from Guldewagen. It is proof that "the money is ready." He becomes exact. Send the goods out of Holland to New York, not Boston. Be prepared to deduct and pay customs charges in Holland and England. And then he becomes the notary, finicky about his watermarked paper: you realize that it "may be loosened and the quires be laid side by side for convenience in packing." And "I send herewith a letter to said Mr. Guldewagen which I have not sealed; when you have read it please close it with a wafer of wax." He concludes the letter exuberantly, commending the merchant's family to the protection of Almighty God.

Writing to Guldewagen, Janse is equally unable to hide his excitement. Although he is Guldewagen's cousin, he cannot fully overcome an awkward sense of dependency on so important a municipal dignitary. He fails to use the proper salutation. He is overly formal. Yet in discussing the details of his inheritance, he overcomes his self-consciousness and writes clearly of his plans for the annuity. As in his letter to Sijbinck, he writes as a notary. He advises Guldewagen that he has executed a power of attorney to Mr. Jan Sijbinck, merchant, residing on the Haarlemmerdijk between the two sluices, in the "Golden Fortune" at Amsterdam. Sijbinck will be presenting it to him, Guldewagen, for the purpose of receiving the interest that may have already accrued and should continue to be generated, year after year.

Other legal paperwork must be attended to as well. It is even more important. A clerk, he realizes, will most likely be attending to the work that Guldewagen must complete on his behalf. Yet all must be done carefully and with an eye to avoiding unnecessary charges. An authentic copy of the codicil to his uncle's will must be transcribed from the original and copied onto a sheet of fine paper like that brought to Amsterdam by postillion from Germany or France. He will pay the scribe "a reasonable compensation for the copying."

He does not need to pay for an authentic copy of the will. He has one. Calling on two scenes that he seems to have revisited again and again in imagination, he describes how it was that on the twentieth of June 1640 his uncle David Janse van Ilpendam dictated a will in Leiden to the notary Jacob Fransz van Merwen. David Janse stipulated that upon his own death and that of his wife, Aefjen Dammas, his nephew Adriaen was to receive a thousand guilders. There was a later scene. He, Adriaen Janse, was about twenty-two years of age and also living in Leiden. He says of the scene only: "It is not necessary to send me a copy of the will of my late uncle, since in my youth I copied the same from an authentic copy, and till this date have it by me."

Janse closes the letter confidently and with consideration. Unavoidably, however, he needs to disclose something of the sharp edge of poverty on which he lives. Perhaps Guldewagen would consider trying to avoid the cost to him of assigning a power of attorney each year when conveying his annual interest to Sijbinck. Wouldn't a yearly letter to Guldewagen be enough? "You ought . . . [to] be able to tell from the writing, style and signature that I had written it, the same as I have written and signed this." He understands that his cousin will not receive these authorizing letters with the regularity one would wish. Maybe, as a result, the interest will not be paid as promptly each year as one would hope. This, however, will not be taken as Guldewagen's fault but rather as something arising from his own decisions. He has, after all, chosen to live far overseas. Letters are sure to go astray. There are "the perils of the sea or other accidents." And, worse, I am here "36 [Dutch] miles inland from New York, where the ships arrive."

A comfortable share in his uncle's and cousin's estates, these are the blessings, the unexpected gifts that have now become his. They are his lien on the future. *Patria* and family have given him the possibility of security. David Janse van Ilpendam, Aefjen Dammas, Jacob Fransz van Merwen, Jacobus van Lodesteijn, Jan Sijbinck, and Dammas Guldewagen, all are names that have taken the landscape of Albany — "36 miles inland from New York" — and thrust it into the wider one of a homeland common to each of them.

For the first time, Adriaen Janse is writing like a man fashioned by something beyond his daily work and the New World settlers and natives, by something beyond the old-timers of Beverwijck and the new English strangers who seem to have become so large a part of his existence. And it is the persistence of that shaping, so inextricably, so predictably made up of family, that now prompts him as an old man to write of himself and his wife. The inheritance from overseas will care for them both.

He turns his hopes to the old country.

CHAPTER 2 *Patria*

1616
Delft, in Holland

In November 1616 Jan Janse van Ilpendam is a young man, about twenty-two years of age. He is living in a city that people regard as one of the most beautiful in Holland. Mapmakers, in their bird's-eye views, try to remind patrons that it is a reincarnation of the mysterious Greek city of gods and oracles. It is the gracious city of Delft.

Jan Janse lives in the center of the city, in the Hypolitusbuurt. From his neighborhood, it takes only a stroll to cross a canal and stand before the Oude Kerk, a building crowned with turrets and begun four centuries ago. Crossing another canal and following Schoolstraat, he or any other tradesman of his neighborhood can quickly arrive at the School Poort. The fortification is like a half-dozen others. It defends a bridge over the river Schie and looks out with distrust across the low open countryside and dunelands. Farther out, at Delftshaven, the city's beauty extends to the magnificent outer harbor. When people want to describe a spacious river, they say it is "as broad as the Mass in Holland at Delftshaven." But Hypolitusbuurt and its artisans really belong to the city's other great church, the Nieuwe Kerk, originally dedicated to St. Ursula. Only the Voldersgracht and a row of fashionable homes separate the small houses of men such as Jan Janse from its massive gothic vaults and magnificent tower and, facing them, the stone walls of the medieval town hall.

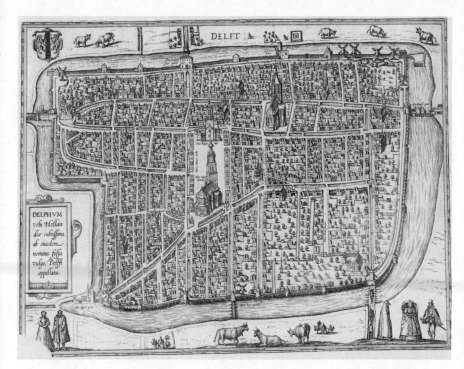

5. Delphum urbs Hollandiae cultissima ab eiusdem nominis fossa, vulgo, Delfft appellata, Braun and Hogenberg, 1547. Hypolitusbuurt was a neighborhood immediately to the right of the marketplace, embraced by the Town Hall and the Nieuwe Kerk. Jan Janse was living here when he was married in 1616. A narrow canal, the Voldengracht, separated his neighborhood from the marketplace. Vermeer lived on a small street along the canal as a child after 1638. Most likely this is "the little street" he depicted some twenty years later. (Harvard University, Map Collection)

On November 4, Jan Janse receives permission to marry Judith Hame Adriaensdr, a young woman who also lives in Delft. If there were an oracle in this Dutch version of Delphi, she could tell them that about half of Jan Janse's days in Holland are over. Judith has only six years to live.

Janse begins to support himself and his wife as a hatmaker. He sells his goods from his home and probably hawks them around the city and countryside as well. The craftsmanship of this work might raise him to the level people call the *brede burgerij*. These are the small, independent artisans, shippers, ministers, and some lower civil servants who exist below the regent classes of the cities. Still, work and wages are uncertain. Just four months ago some women of the city marched to the marketplace raging against the taxes on grain. Being a small entrepreneur is no security either.

As a hatmaker, Janse is protected by his guild, yet he is forced to make his way against other hat merchants in his town, such as his friend Jacob Hugen van Schie.

Some time in 1618 Judith gives birth to their only child. She and Jan Janse name the boy Adriaen for Judith's father. Within two and a half years Judith is dead. Four months later, Adriaen becomes the business of the orphanmasters of Leiden, a city beyond the dunes and flat lands to the north. His mother has left a small trust of 400 guilders and put it in the hands of the city's *weesvaders,* the custodians of orphaned children.

On April 28, 1621, six men meet to draw up a contract in the rooms of the orphanmasters in Leiden. Jacob van der Mij, E. H. van Nieuwehoven, and F. Doijck appear for the *weesvaders.* Jan Janse comes with Jacob Hugen van Schie and Balduwinus Hamens, who is a minister at Woubrugge and one of Adriaen's uncles. Jan Janse agrees to the officials' terms. Until the boy is twenty-five, or married and made the recipient of the bequest, his father may use the interest as he wishes but must guarantee the child's proper upbringing. Because it is not the *weesvaders'* place to do otherwise, they set out the relationship between Adriaen and his father in pragmatic contractual terms. The boy must be given enough to eat and drink. He must have both linen and woolen clothing, and shoes for going to school. He must be given the benefit of godly discipline and an education in a promising trade or craft. He should be cared for in sickness and in good health, even as God cares for us.

Not much is anticipated for the child in the way of achievement or status. Perhaps Judith's small bequest says it all. At least for the *weesvaders* and until 1646, he is on their books simply as "Jan Janse's orphan."

Jan Janse appears to be something of a rolling stone. At the age of thirty-two and when Adriaen is eight, he remarries, taking Cathalina van Straseel as his wife. He has left Delft and is making his living in Leiden, residing in a small house on the Pieterskerkgracht. Again his living quarters and workshop lie in the shadow of a church that is monumental in size and capable of overwhelming the surrounding *buurt* even as it entices small side streets like his to its dark walls and accommodating marketplace.

Choosing to live on the Pieterskerkgracht, he is, for whatever reasons, nesting himself within a family and family-owned properties. They may be dwarfing him as well. Joachim Janse, his eldest brother, owns a large house and a complex of small houses behind the street and in the block between the Pieterskerkgracht and nearby Schoolsteeg. In fourteen years' time, the city will value the properties at the considerable sum of 2,000 guilders. It is likely that Jan Janse is renting one of these *kleine huisjes*. A short block away David Janse, another older brother, owns a large house on one of Leiden's best streets, Breestraat. He is taxed for an assessed value of 3,200 guilders on the house and a further 200 guilders on a *speltuin,* a country house at Zoeterwoude, almost half a mile across the canals and on the outskirts of the city. Everyone knows that its ownership is a sign of arrival, of social status beyond wealth. In the same suburb Geertruijt, Jan Janse's elder sister, lives with her husband, Jacobus van Lodesteijn. Unlike Jan Janse, Geertruijt was established in a good marriage by her parents, and her husband is a minister in Zoeterwoude and a member of two of the most prominent patrician families of the city of Delft. These are family members clearly advantaged over Jan Janse. Perhaps it went back to their years as children. The elder brothers and sisters were old enough to be established in careers or marriage before both parents died of the plague in 1602. Jan Janse was only eight, the same age as his son Adriaen, to whom he now presents Cathalina as stepmother.

Two years after his second marriage, Jan Janse seems to abandon the hope of supporting his family as a hatter. He turns to working the small ships that ply the country's rivers, canals, and inland seas. Why shouldn't he try his hand at it: there is one ship to every hundred Netherlanders, a sign of more than enough business for skippers, supercargoes, and sailors. In January 1628 he is working on *'t Wapen van der Gouda.* Perhaps to accommodate his work on the ships, he has moved his family away from the center of the city and the clustered family and in a line directly opposite to the roads leading to Zoeterwoude. He has taken them beyond the neighborhood called Mare Dorp and out along the Mare, Leiden's most distant encircling canal.

The course of his career is leading him farther and farther from Delft and Leiden. Or, rather, just as Delft and Leiden are determined to reach as far across the globe as possible for wealth, so he is ready to match those desires with ambitions of his own. He is not alone. Half a decade earlier, five Leidenaars had left the city together, sailing to South America for the West India Company and expecting to be gone for at least two years. They had signed on from The Hague. But men who wanted employment with the East India Company — or, as they put it, *als zij op avontuur wilden,* all those who want to search for adventure and profits — would deal with the company's chamber at Delft. Cornelis de Keyser, who lived on the Rapenburg canal and in the neighborhood of the university and the houses of the city's merchant patricians, was married into the family of the registrar of the local count. Yet he too had taken the gamble. Just three years ago he had left everything and sailed. Even one of the city's artists had abandoned his work and gone.

Jan Janse is also ready to throw the dice with fate. Along with scores of other men, he is prepared to cast his fortunes with the newly formed overseas trading venture, the West India Company. Everyone knows that such an enterprise holds high risks. For those who sign up as seamen or clerks, the physical danger is real: many men never return. But even investing in it is a hazardous gamble, just like taking a chance on any one of the other popular lotteries. People call such bets *weddenschappen,* taking a flutter on the market. It can mean quick profits and enormous wealth. Other members of Janse's own family have taken care to try their luck with the company. His cousin will one day sail for Pernambuco, and an uncle will start to collect pay on his behalf from the Delft chamber of the company. Several of the leading families of Leiden are also enthusiastically committed. The de Foreests, the La Montagnes, the de Laets, soon the van Lodesteijns, and later Jan Janse's cousin from Haarlem Dammas Guldewagen, all will be wagering on the profits of the Indies companies.

The West India Company is soundly capitalized. It is thriving. In its first float of shares, Amsterdammers were like people bewitched. They subscribed 3 million guilders. Amsterdam itself is prospering, with merchant palaces along new canals like the Keisersgracht, sometimes hundreds of ships in the harbor, twenty-nine refineries producing sugar imported from Brazil, jewels and furs, spices and rosewood from the Indies. New money.

Yet adventuring in the overseas companies can also mean bankruptcy. It can mean entering something like the Bankruptcy Chamber in the Amsterdam Town Hall on the Dam and relating to oneself its portentous carvings: scenes of empty chests and unpaid bills strewn around a room filled with scuttling and hungry rats.

1635
Pernambuco

Jan Janse is in the service of the West India Company. It has been making decisions about the profitable deployment of its resources and is now gambling thousands of guilders on its capacity to seize the factories established by the Portuguese on the coast of northeastern Brazil. This means capturing and controlling such trading stations as Recife and Olinda and a captaincy such as that of Pernambuco, known to be the richest sugar-producing area in the world. Like the East India Company, the West India Company relies on its war fleet. Superiority is largely, and endlessly, a matter of hit-and-run raids, seizing makeshift forts and sugar factories, and capturing ships laden with sugar or mahogany making for home ports in Portugal and Spain.

Jan Janse is gambling too. He is working the Recife coast as supercargo on a yacht, the *Pernambuco*. Everyone aboard such a vessel is in danger. Yachts are armed cruisers. They menace the coasts, delivering supplies and, when necessary, soldiers. They turn up to support amphibious attacks on enemy installations. Like jackals, they go for strays, a lone caravel with casks of sugar, a single sugar plantation, an isolated fort upriver from the coast. By 1635 the *Pernambuco* is familiar with this sort of hunting. Sometimes it looks for prey with fifteen or sixteen other ships; once it was part of a fleet of forty-seven ships. Often it moves about with the *Windt-hondt.* It has stalked prey around Bahia and as far south as Rio de Janairo. The ship is of middling size for a yacht. While other hunters, such as the *Haringh,* are 280 tons and the *Windt-hondt* is 160, the *Pernambuco* is 200. When it came out for the Amsterdam chamber in May 1633, the ship carried twenty-two cannon and sixty-one sailors. It carried no assault troops, although most other yachts did and the *Pernambuco* did later. Exactly when Jan Janse joined the yacht we do not know.

In March 1635 the company begins the siege of Porto Calvo. The fort is set south of Barra Grande and about five Dutch miles inland from the coast. It controls the Porto de Piedras River and guards the sugar plantations and mills of some 7,000 inhabitants. The fleet sails south from Recife with five companies of men. The *Pernambuco* is in the hunt. Although the enemy holds out at nearby fortifications, Porto Calvo falls. Within days, the *Pernambuco* returns to Recife having snared a victim, a "prize" ship carrying 120 pipes of wine and other trifling sorts of cargo.

In less than two weeks, the *Pernambuco* is again cruising south near Porto Calvo, this time carrying a cargo of supplies, especially bread, to distressed inhabitants and soldiers. Possibly it continues to take its chances, sailing between Barra Grande and Recife. This may explain how Jan Janse, just one of the supercargoes in the *Pernambuco's* fitful history, becomes a prisoner of the Portuguese at Porto Calvo in January of the next year. For the installation reverts to the enemy in that month and somehow Jan Janse is taken captive. With him at Porto Calvo is his nephew, Geertruijt's son Cornelis. There is nothing to suggest that Jan Janse carelessly drew the young man into this dangerous game of chance that he himself has chosen. Historians will write later, and obscurely, only that Cornelis goes into the fighting and is killed.

The Dutch being the Dutch, and the Indies companies attracting artists into their service, a careful engraving made at the time shows the field of battle. Interested parties can see the very tree from which the Spanish commander oversaw his army of some 1,800 men. We do not know how and in what manner Cornelis died or whether his body was among the forty buried in a low trench and covered, for decency's sake, *met veel rijs*, with lots of branches.

Jan Janse is released by the Portuguese and able to reach Holland by the summer of 1636.

1636
Amsterdam

The directors of the West India Company pride themselves on being efficient. Now Jan Janse is petitioning them for 60 guilders he earned before his imprisonment but for which he cannot supply written proof. He would know this place where the directors of the Amsterdam chamber convene, usually on Mondays and Thursdays.

West India House is a proud three-story building along the Haarlemmerdijk near the harbor. Originally its interior was just three large, undivided spaces. The top floor served as an assembly hall for the men of the civic guard — they can still be seen assembling here from time to time. The ground floor was a meat market. The company rented the level in between. So, until about twelve years ago, a man wishing to come into the presence of the directors would find himself mounting an outside flight of stairs to a vestibule and then entering the administrators' large meeting room. Now, however, it is all quite changed. The building has been handsomely enlarged. Two substantial wings have been added, each two stories high. Together with a wall and entrance gate, they join the original building to form a quadrangle and enclose an interior courtyard. So nowadays the directors meet in one wing. Many different offices are in the other.

Altogether, the buildings speak for the solidity behind the company's ambitions: many beautiful windows with stone arches, brick worked with horizontal bands of sandstone, the roof of the Haarlemmerdijk building empowered by its chimneys and a graceful weathervane: two small ships. Of course, the ambitions that the men of the company have worked into their

6. West-India Company House, Haarlemmerstraat, Amsterdam, 1623–1647, *print engraved in 1693. In addition to its main building, the company had warehouses that Jan Janse could see. Directly on Haarlemmerstraat, it was storing grain in a brewery. Much to the directors' dissatisfaction, they did not own this and another warehouse but rented them, one from a burgomaster and the other from a widow. (Gementelijke Archiefdienst Amsterdam)*

buildings are not yet taking on as grand an expression as those of the East India Company and the admiralty, farther away. East India House is the centerpiece of an extensive complex of buildings: warehouses and shipyards with men working away on battle-cargo vessels 600 tons in displacement and 150 feet in length; incomplete hulls are poised on blocks and resemble the rib cages of giant sea monsters. The wharves of the West India Company are modest by comparison: a single large wharf with its house and lands, a ships' carpenters' wharf behind it. But these are early days.

Janse would have known this place but would not have been important enough to appear before the company directors. The chamber's secretary is careful to separate those who may present themselves and those whose business is received in writing or tabled for discussion by a friend who is patrician enough to sit with the directors. Janse's request is simply reported. In fact, it is tabled at least three times before a decision is given in early September. Although his request is for nothing more than the pay of an ordinary employee for one month, it is rejected. The company is known for its niggardliness in paying back wages. This time the excuse is "consistency." Presumably other men held by the Portuguese also came away without written accounts of their wages: all must be denied their livings equally.

Still, the company has plans for him. Or rather, it has a place for him in its own decidedly confused plans for another part of its overseas enterprise, a venture yet to be settled on a firm basis and cursed by discord. For months, the directors and the individual big investors have been at each other's throat over trading privileges in New Netherland in North America. Men holding powerful share portfolios in the company are quick to declare their interest in its corporate well-being. At the same time, they want to exploit the country as private individuals. This situation is not particularly novel. The East India Company has its share of *dolerende participanten*, dissenting shareholders, as they are called. But particularly the dissenting ones in the West India Company want their share of the new settlements' fur trade.

Among them Kiliaen van Rensselaer is particularly mischievous. And his mischief is proving effective because he is a brilliant businessman. He is also determined to enlarge his investments in New Netherland and then reap the profits. To control the trade in furs along *de revier van d'vorst Mauritius* (Hudson River) near the company trading post, Fort Orange, he has begun to settle colonists at his patroonship or *colonie,* called Rensselaerswijck. It isn't much yet, but van Rensselaer is persistently sending over more and more people, equipment, and trading goods. When he wants to, he is able to fit out yachts to facilitate his enterprise — something the lords directors, who have had to concern themselves with, among other things, 806 ships since 1623, cannot always do.

In this September of 1636, Jan Janse is caught up in these power plays. At the same meeting where they feel obliged to deny him his back pay, the directors appoint him as supercargo on the *Rensselaerswijck*. The ship will be fitted out for New Netherland. He will earn 24 guilders a month. Four days later, at its Monday meeting of September 8, however, van Rensselaer is allowed to appear before the assembled directors and even request an extraordinary meeting to consider matters concerning himself and the company — and indirectly Jan Janse.

The discussions are part of a rush of activity that has consumed van Rensselaer's time and attention for some weeks and is driving him all the more decidedly into securing his possessions and trading prospects in New Netherland. Methodical as always, he has convinced Leidenaars such as the de Laets and de Foreests that being equal partners in fitting out a ship for North America will bring them great profits. En route, the vessel can look for prizes on the high seas and then, like the adventurers in Brazil, begin to trade extensively with the Dutch and English settlements when it reaches the continent. It will also — unlike the project in Brazil — convey colonists to Rensselaerswijck. He has already assembled almost thirty people and collected extensive stores and equipment. The *Rensselaerswijck* is his choice.

By the time of its sailing, the *Rensselaerswijck* is clearly not the company's ship but van Rensselaer's. Again and again he calls it "our ship" and will once refer to it as "my little ship." He and Gerrit de Foreest have in fact paid for the construction of the vessel, fitted it out, and purchased its cargo. They have approved if not hired its captain and crew, procured its papers, and met its insurance costs. Someone representing the company has been called in to sign the ship's manifest. But they oversee its departure. They have also contracted for their own supercargo. Not Jan Janse but Dirck Corssen will oversee the 15,000 guilders' worth of cargo. He will board with the last packets of important papers — and report to van Rensselaer. Jan Janse makes the outgoing voyage. Doubtless he boards as the assistant required by the company. What he does to look out for the interests of the directors is unclear. Later van Rensselaer will say of him only, and coldly, "This man is in the service of the Company."

The *Rensselaerswijck* sails from Amsterdam on Thursday, September 25. Only on the next Wednesday, however, does the ship reach Texel, the southernmost of the Friesland Islands, where low-lying stretches of sand are lapped on the east by the waters of an inland sea, the Waddenzee, and other dunes stand along the west and face the fierce storms of the North Sea. Captain Jan Tiepkesz anchors at the east end of the island. Two days later, he attaches the *Rensselaerswijck* to a fleet of twenty-two vessels making their way through the channel between Texel and the northern coast of North Holland and moves out into the open sea.

Kiliaen van Rensselaer writes on October 29 that he expects the voyage to New Netherland to take eight or ten weeks. This is a reasonable estimate. But the voyage takes five and a half months. Even as he writes, the ship is far out to sea but unable to pick up westerlies and so continually drifting east. Week after week it is hit by waves that, as Tiepkesz logs it, rise "to such an awful height that the waves and the sky seem one." In the face of the storms, Tiepkesz can neither take observations to establish latitude nor control the ship. The coast of Spain, the Scilly Islands, the English Channel (twice), the seas south of Cornwall, all are in the log and all are the wrong places to be. Finally, in the middle of November, Tiepkesz brings the *Rensselaerswijck* into the harbor of Ilfracombe on the north coast of Devon and makes repairs before continuing on.

We cannot know what role Jan Janse played in all of this, what fears, perhaps what courage, he may have displayed. He would have been among "the supercargo, the mate and other advisers" whom Tiepkesz assembled on November 6 and who helped him decide "in God's name" to concede to fate and return to the Channel, making for Plymouth or Falmouth. Like the others, he celebrates Christmas and New Year's Day in Ilfracombe. Close to New Year's Day, Tiepkesz takes the opportunity to write to his wife in Amsterdam. Along with other messages of endearment, he commends their children to her care. Particularly he asks that "if you write, have my son Gerrit Jansen write to me too that I may see his writing; tell him that I wish it." Did Jan Janse also wish for letters from his son Adriaen, now nineteen? As a supercargo, he is a man of writing — of inventories and bills of lading and reports and accounts. Does he wish to see Adriaen's writing, to see his progress? Possibly he does. But only Tiepkesz's letter, together with his log, reaches van Rensselaer, who, meticulous man that he is, keeps a copy of it.

The seven-week voyage from the English coast to "the Manhatans" is marked by "beautiful weather," steady winds, clear skies for observations of the sun, and — something Tiepkesz did not have before — time to keep a proper log. Ordinary sailors are often kept in the dark about the exact destination of ships crossing the Atlantic. They speak of voyages to "Virginia or New Netherland and *terra nova.*" But Tiepkesz can now use his charts effectively, those probably kept secret by the company and drawn to provide coastal profiles of the Dutch and English possessions from Virginia north to Newfoundland. Passing Cape Henlopen, reading the islands and coastal profiles, Tiepkesz brings the *Rensselaerswijck* to the headlands on either side of the Narrows. Perhaps he continues to the Manhatans by using the charts authorized by Pieter Minuit seven years earlier: the channels marked, safe anchorages indicated, even the soundings for the bays and harbor, everything made easy. Tiepkesz drops anchor at the Manhatans at four o'clock on a bitterly cold Wednesday afternoon in the first week of March. With a seaman's eye, he sees only an English ship lying before Fort Amsterdam and the entrance to *de reviere van d'vorst Mauritius,* which he must navigate northward to the *colonie.* Just now it is closed because of ice.

1637

At the Manhatans

What Jan Janse sees of Fort Amsterdam and the Manhatans — what he
is looking for — he does not record. Undoubtedly he and others have an
account of it from one of the ship's mates. Hendrick de Foreest is a Leidenaar too and probably a distant cousin. He had sailed to New Netherland
on *de Walvis* in 1632 and stayed until 1633, when he seems to have made the
voyage home. Now arriving with Jan Janse, he may have told of the shel-
tered roadstead, the fort with four bastions, primitive houses, shops for ship
repairs, all of it part of early beginnings. But it *is* beginnings. And perhaps
anyone sailing past Enkhuizen, past den Brielle, or any number of familiar
Dutch trading towns facing the sea and seaborne enemies could recognize
in embryo here the structures so beautifully elaborated at home.

Very likely the Manhatans are what Jan Janse expects. A fort has been
completed, though its walls are more a thing of clay sods than stone. Outside it and along a foreshore are a few large warehouses, two or maybe three
mills, a church, and a city tavern, workplaces for such employees as the sail-
maker, carpenter, and baker. It is already what it should be: a fortified an-
chorage for oceangoing vessels and a *factorij* for trading with native peoples.
Eventually — if it all works out and the profits make it worthwhile to remain — the fort's walls will form part of a larger set of skirts and angles that
will enclose other spaces necessary for the trading station and its personnel.
The usual buildings and open spaces will come alive: a proper church and
hospital, quarters for traders of other "nations" such as the Jews and Scots,
marketplaces, and all the buildings of the customary *ambachtsquartier*:
workers' houses, ship repair shops, a weighhouse. It's all a matter of future
trade. Even Recife and Olinda were just "two heaps of sand and stones"
when Janse was there. Yet to retrieve them and the captaincy of Pernambuco
from the Dutch, the Portuguese had been willing to swap the city of Breda
and pay 200,000 ducats.

Outside the fort will be a moat or set of canals — so there will be *lant-*
and *waterpoortjes* and bridges just as in Delft or Amsterdam. Beyond there
will be vegetable gardens and farms enough to victual the company's personnel and passing ships. About one-third of the personnel will be farmers.
That's enough. The ownership of land is not much to anyone's purpose in
such a place; it's not a primary consideration. The trade in furs, and the explorations made by following the rivers for possible further riches, is. Just

7. Admiral van Tromp's Flagship before Den Briel, *Simon de Vlieger, early 1640. De Vlieger presents Den Briel as part of a beach scene, with ships distributed across the picture, sometimes screening the low-lying land and profile of the city. (Gemeente Musea Delft)*

like the sugar in Brazil. Getting into the trade or "earning a beaver" even as a small-time trader counts. So taking up land alongside the navigable rivers and inlets, well, that is another matter. Land that backs away from water, *that* puts a man along the trade routes and is worth considering. Jan Janse is a minor figure in the company, however, and like any officer in it, he will be forbidden to own much land. It distracts a man's mind from his superiors' business.

Janse knows this. He knows too how his superiors operate, how they run the place from their houses inside the fort. Just the way they come together to make their decisions is a clue. The director acts like the commander of a fleet or convoy at sea. When he wishes to convene a council meeting, he calls together his leading officers and the sea captains who may be in port at the time. He seems to think he is in the great cabin on the officers' deck and has raised a white flag calling officers of the fleet together for consultation.

They are men of two sets of law. They follow the Orders of Governance that the States General has recently imposed on company officers overseas, the usual measure of Roman law and local customs. But as well they are men of South Holland, Zeeland, and Friesland — each an expanse of islands, deltas, and rivers — and of the Noordzee, Waddenzee, and Zuider Zee. They live by the *zee-rechten*, the laws of the sea. A skipper carrying sick

8. Nieuw Amsterdam ofte nue Nieuw Iorx opt 'T Eylant Man *(New Amsterdam now New York on the Island of Man[hattan]): the prototype view, c. 1670 (date depicted, 1650–53). The unknown artist has drawn a beach scene as well, with the foreshore somewhat exaggerated. As in the de Vlieger painting (fig. 7), the composition is one of sea, sky, and low-lying lands and town buildings. (Algemeen Rijksarchief, The Hague, Collection Leupe [4. Velh, inventory no. 619.14])*

seamen must seek the white hospital ship or make for a harbor; a captain must provide wine to his men if he comes to land where there are grapevines; *The Book of Maritime Laws . . . Made in Wisbuy* is available and should be consulted: this is the maritime law they know. It is the *water-recht* that is the other half of the law and the other half of their lives. Even one of the first notaries on Manhattan Island will have his copy of *The Book of Maritime Laws* for easy consultation.

Jan Janse remains at Fort Amsterdam. At least he does not accompany the *Rensselaerswijck*'s crew and passengers as they sail north and anchor at Fort Orange in April, on the Tuesday before Easter. Tiepkesz and Corssen deliver the patroon's consignment of goods to his officer and commissary, Jacob Planck. Van Rensselaer has been obsessive about every detail of administration. Even the natives come into a mind swimming with detail and untroubled by thoughts that they might be different from the Dutch. On the next ship sent out, he will write Planck and remind him that the sawyer can make full use of the mill by building houses for the "chiefs and others of the savages." The houses can be shut "with hinged doors and windows." The smith can provide nails and bolts. For now, Tiepkesz is delivering letters full of Kiliaen's worries about each of the many things that can go wrong and spoil his project. Especially, the colonists must be the artisans and farmers they are meant to be, and nothing more — certainly not independent traders. But what if they begin to trade with the natives for furs? Suppose they trade with them behind his back, making their profits while undercutting his? No, they must not be allowed to do it, even with "products of the soil."

This is exactly what some of the colonists begin to do. And worse: they begin to trade pelts — or promise to trade them — for goods supplied by van Rensselaer's own supercargo, Corssen. The transactions are never meant to reach the patroon's books. All through the summer the inexperienced, and untrustworthy, Corssen is cheated and the illegal trade goes on. Nine men are involved, seven of them here at Fort Orange and the *colonie*. Altogether they owe Corssen about 1,850 guilders in beaver pelts. The furs are undoubtedly payment for merchandise to be used in further bargaining with the natives.

Two men at the Manhatans engage in the illegal trade as well. One of them puts himself in Corssen's debt for 359 guilders two days after the *Rensselaerswijck* arrives back at the Manhatans. He is Jacobus van Curler, a relative of van Rensselaer's. The other man had approached the supercargo the day the ship appeared before the fort. He seems not to have been as well heeled as van Curler and bought goods worth about half that sum, 179:17 guilders. He is Jan Janse van Ilpendam.

Within a year, van Rensselaer knows of the illegal trading and requires justice of each of the deceiving and guilty parties. Planck is to deal with each man individually. Most are warned to turn their payments over to van Rensselaar and "be careful not to do it again." Van Curler, because he is of the family, will not be accused if he pays the sum owed. Jan Janse seems dismissible. "Jan Janse van Ilpendam": "this man is in the service of the Company. If he pays you, I have nothing to say about him."

1641
On the South River

For the next three years, nothing is heard of Jan Janse van Ilpendam. Yet by early 1641 a few people in Amsterdam have contact with him. He is acting as a commissary for the company in New Netherland. His wife,

Cathalina, is with him, but they say nothing of Adriaen. Janse is years behind in the payment of a substantial debt. When the company first includes his name in its records in 1642, it is to signify that he has been serving as *commis* at Fort Nassau along the Suijtrevier (Delaware River). Promotion from supercargo to *commis* is an appointment of considerable responsibility. He will play the role of commissary and commander of a fortified trading station. There, unless other men are appointed to do so, he must be his own secretary and accountant. While he was a supercargo, the company trained him for these responsibilities.

The logic of it all is simple. The same obligations that he had at sea will be his on land: to see to the safe transport and delivery of the company's merchandise and to facilitate its exchange for the goods of the natives, in this case furs. The welfare of commodities ranks ahead of his own. For its defense he must expect to be a soldier, even as in Recife. Or, rather, since the merchandise groans out its bloated presence equally on land and sea, he must be like it: amphibious. To be commander of one of the company forts is much the same as being the highest commissioned officer on any one if its ships. Command at sea entrusts a man with a *handelsschip* carrying a giant anchor. Overseeing a fort puts him in charge of a *handelsschip* anchored to the land.

His post as *commis* at Fort Nassau takes him to a place of violence. It is a place the company considers one of its "distant outlying posts." In fact, it is the destination for violent criminals banished from Manhattan Island — and those driven by the Swedes from their colonies as well. The trading post is reached only by a river located some 105 nautical miles from the Manhatans. A yacht must then maneuver the shallows of Delaware Bay and sail ten leagues upriver. Anyone in command here is well beyond surveillance — or so it seems — and perhaps it is this that lures Jan Janse into waywardness and danger.

The wilderness and the river are a lost and distant meeting place for traders, mercenaries, and river Indians: "Minquase" and "Armewamese," Swedes, English, and Dutch. The natives — or "upper river Indians" or "Minquase" or simply "pagans" — have an abundance of furs to trade. They prefer to trade them for smuggled Dutch cargo, but they will listen to the other Europeans as well. It is like Brazil south of Recife and down to Bahia: hit and run, rob and punish the strays, exploit the natives but stay on-side, look out for yourself, make a little on the side, but don't get caught.

In May 1642 the resident director general, Willem Kieft, and his council send instructions to Jan Janse on how he is to "govern himself." The words are not a warning of potential treachery somehow foreseen. Rather, he is to take a force of men to the Schuylkill River and drive away the Englishmen who have secretly set up trading places. There is to be no loss of life, no bloodshed, nothing that could cause diplomatic embarrassment to the company or the States General. Just as in the days of his twenties in Leiden, Janse is again making his living by adventuring from the deck of a small river craft. He is to take the *Real* and the *St. Merten* — or one or them — and make a landing near the Englishmen, take them captive, and send them to Fort Amsterdam. At the same time, he is to discover the extent of their trade and remove goods stored in their houses, making an inventory of it. Then he is to burn the settlement to the ground. The *St. Merten* is so old that in little over two years' time it will be sold off as unseaworthy. The *Real* has at least one cannon. It will be most useful as a threat.

All through 1643, 1644, and well into 1645, he serves as commissary at Fort Nassau. Some New England merchants try to explore the river, looking for the great lake that they think is the source of the beaver. No further military engagements, however, are asked of him. Now he must be, as each company man is, a "soldier of the pen." The roles are entirely compatible. As much as firepower, writing is the security of the New Netherland enterprise. It is its future. Only accounts and inventories, charts and correspondence give order to the physical world that must be made to give up its treasures to the company and house its merchandise. Only a paper world will give the New World into the company's hands. He must inscribe the signs of empire that make empire possible. To rise through the ranks in a *handelsplaats* — from clerk to bookkeeper to commissary to director — is to rise to higher and higher levels of account keeping. Apparently he is able to fit into this world.

The company makes a fetish of writing. Men can take advantage of this. Not all men write. But all are pulled toward it. Whether they are living in a settlement or out along one of the riverine trade routes — and that is the way they divide themselves up here — they are observers. As much as Janse is paid to put in place the practices of the company, he is there to observe those of the Swedes and English. The company is always in the market for observations. The men of the States General are too. They will reward verbal information: some official will record it and (perhaps) gratefully remember the source. But written information is a commodity it cannot resist. For some of this, it pays a good price. Charting a river is lucrative work. The company might even send a man a writing book, paper, a pen, a ruler, all to ensure his good work. Even in the early years, it grants surveyors 3 guilders a day plus 2 stivers for every two acres laid down and free transportation and expenses. The company needs navigational charts. It expects men to chart from their sloops, giving "every creek, bay and river." It seems to love seeing Dutch words replace those of natives on paper and parchment. It pores over measurements and wants them accurate: the distance from Fort Orange to Wiltwijck (Kingston), the route from one native settlement to the next, the distance from one man's house to his neighbor's.

Constructing coastal profiles, hydrographic maps, and surveys is specialized work. It would not be asked of Jan Janse. Simply reporting to the chamber at Amsterdam or the States General is less demanding. Information about any aspect of the company's venture is welcomed. Even if it is inserted into a story that is little more than tale-bearing, it is still eagerly heard. Especially letters about its officials, their good behavior or treachery, are greeted warmly.

The reports of its own overseas servants — those of men such as Jan Janse — count most heavily. Most men feel this obligation and respond dutifully. They dare not do otherwise. They give *de geheele staet* — the whole situation — of a settlement in detailed correspondence. They try to write three times a year. The more conscientious officials begin with a description and then do a "swing around the circle," describing events at the various settlements. They go off to see birds and fish and natives and then make up descriptions — this is something the directors at Amsterdam like. The company directors — or the States General, or the burgomasters of Amsterdam, or whoever has an interest — expect to pry into everything. They want to *see* things. So employees write reports in the form of tableaux vivants, miniature word pictures no larger than the scene on any familiar wall tile.

Although Jan Janse, at Fort Nassau, is at the far edge of the company's concerns, he is not beyond its scrutiny. About nineteen months after his expedition against the English, Kieft and his council entertain the testimony of two small-time traders about a pack of goods allegedly stolen at the South River. Beyond hearing about the details of thievery and quarreling, they learn that Jan Janse knew of the transaction between the two men and that his wife knew of it as well. They determine to get further information. An informant is sent to the fort to gather "full proof." They want evidence — as much of it as possible — in writing. At the same time, the company's public prosecutor has discovered that Jan Janse is allowing a well-known merchant of the Manhatans to trade guns to the natives for furs. He forbids it, but the man continues his trading and within about five years will have murdered a chief of the "Minquase."

In early September 1645, nineteen months later, the prosecutor lodges a complaint against Jan Janse for possible corruption. In October Janse has to deny that he sold goods to a trader named Jan Juriaensz Becker. Kieft and the council order that he be given a copy of the complaint.

Soon Jan Janse is in court at Fort Amsterdam. He has brought along his accounts, or some of them. He seems to understand what he must strenuously deny: that rather than controlling the trade to the advantage of the company, he has regularly traded goods on behalf of private merchants and for his own personal gain. This could have meant secretly transporting their merchandise to the Delaware River in the company's yachts, trading it, and earning a commission. If so, it meant some form of organized crime at the most and, at the least, forming nothing less than a rival company with other merchants and acting as a factor selling their goods. The prosecutor's evidence is of three such illegal transactions: taking the trading goods of one female trader to the river, receiving two bags of cloth from another, and trading them on behalf of a third man. There is also evidence that he spent months selling the company's goods to the natives at a rate lower than it had set.

Jan Janse's defense of his stewardship is not convincing. The court secretary records him as being indifferently, or evasively, inarticulate. His accounts and the testimony of witnesses are set aside; the accusations of fraud are allowed to stand. The company's fetish for writing falls on him. "Further inquiries" will be made about "the defendant's trade." Lesser company officers at Fort Nassau "and others" will be questioned. The same sort of inventory that Janse made of the Englishmen's goods will now be taken of his personal effects as well as those of the company. The prosecutor will also inventory any goods Janse has at the Manhatans.

He will not find much: in fact, Janse is what he gambled against becoming, a bankrupt. Another man is provisionally put in his place as commissary — and urged to make further reports.

FEBRUARY 1646
At the Manhatans

Jan Janse has been allowed time to answer the charges, but he cannot. Since November 30, he has failed on three occasions to summon proof of his innocence. Again, he seems not to be trying very hard, or he is confused or again dealing carelessly with his life. Neither his words nor those of friendly witnesses are there to be entered in the court minutes. Finally in

February he is condemned for "grossly wronging" the company. With his accounts showing treachery of some kind, Kieft and the others distance themselves from him. As they like to do, they hand the problem over to the directors at home. Jan Janse is to sail by the first ship to Amsterdam, where, with "all his papers and the fiscal's complaint," he can try to defend himself.

Before he can face banishment, further interrogation, and punishment, some time before August 1647, both Jan Janse and his wife die on Manhattan Island. Four years later, a legal document brings him and his son Adriaen together. Or, rather, their names. Two young Amsterdam men will testify that they knew Jan Janse, that he was born in Leiden and was later a *vrijman* (citizen) in New Netherland, that when he died he left behind "more debts than profits." And they know his son Adriaen. He has had to refuse all association with his father's estate in order to protect himself from creditors. The witnesses are correct: through most of his twenties and early thirties, Adriaen will attend to estranging himself from a father who had, for most of his life, estranged him.

The two young men of Amsterdam know something more about Adriaen. Now at the age of thirty, he too is in New Amsterdam. He is a schoolmaster. Little else is to be known about him. He leaves in mystery how and why he has come to the New World. He leaves unanswered why he has chosen, as schoolmaster, a life so different from his father's: the one, exploitative; the other, affirming of structures, even the profession of the guileless. Yet traces of his personality are in the settlement's records as he begins to fashion his life in New Netherland. Clues about himself in statements of 1649 give direction to conjectures.

SUMMER 1649
At the Manhatans and Leiden

During these summer days, Adriaen Janse has his family in Leiden in the forefront of his mind. He must make inquiries about his finances there. Leiden is, as it will continue to be, something of a lodestar. Or, rather, the magnetic point is an uncle, David Janse van Ilpendam, who lived there until five years ago and whose remembrance of Adriaen lives on in his last will and testament. David Janse may have been the boy's "Dutch uncle" in the full meaning of the term. He was married twice, the second time to Aefjen Dammasdr. van der Horn, the daughter of a Haarlem town councilor. His two sons died a week apart in 1635, leaving him childless for the last nine years of his life. Their deaths occurred exactly when Jan Janse decided to enter the service of the West India Company and chose — or found it necessary — to leave Adriaen, then seventeen, fatherless.

David Janse seems to have taken upon himself a special care for the family. In 1640 he provided a home for the illegitimate son of his brother Joachim Janse. The next year he had assumed responsibility for the custody of his sister Geertruijt. Later Geertruijt's son Joost turned to him either to invest money or, more probably, borrow it. He was closely observant of his nieces and nephews. He excluded two of Geertruijt's children from his will because they had not acted well. Toward other nieces and nephews he showed his generous approval. To Adriaen and to three of Geertruijt's children he bequeathed 1,000 guilders each.

In all the moments when Adriaen Janse left a trace on the pages of New Netherland's history, he was bookish. He was teaching, looking for employment as a scribe, getting a world of law and commerce onto paper. In this he was as much like David Janse as anyone who would come into his life. Both embraced professions that had to do with books, both sought employments that even pushed up against — for David Janse literally — the edge of university life and learning.

As much as Leiden prided itself on its cloth industry during David Janse's lifetime, it prized its university even more. Producing fine linen had brought the city riches and status as the second most populous municipality in Holland. In 1632, 8,372 houses, many of them opulent, stood within its encircling canals. Yet it was the university that had ensured its exceptional reputation across Europe. Doctors and professors lectured in the *auditoria* of law, medicine, theology, and philosophy. From across the Low Countries their opinions were sought — often had to be sought — on matters of religious doctrine or maritime law or botanical species. So powerful and well paid were these men that Leidenaars called white bread, one of their luxury items, "professors' bread." Even Kiliaen van Rensselaer knew the authority of the *professoren* of the university and, uncharacteristically, allowed himself to be intimidated by it. Because the professors at Leiden had reservations about the legitimacy of feudal structures in Holland, he rethought the notion of establishing Rensselaerswijck as a feudal holding for himself and his partners.

In 1641, the year after David Janse dictated his last will and testament, the Leidenaar Abraham Commelijn cooperated with another printer in Delft in publishing a comprehensive guidebook to the city. The volume's author, J. J. Orlers, assumed an audience fascinated by the university and eager to see illustrations of its great buildings. One of his own fascinations was the university's library. It was a place of learning open, like the lectures in the *auditoria*, to professors, students, city officials, and "other learned men." To Orlers, the *bibliotheek* was the heart of the university. Its books and maps deserved his unhurried description, those lining the walls or standing in cabinets, those filling the catalogs — and those books too that easily trespassed in and out of the university's walls. They were the volumes trafficked in the bookshops nearby. Not far away, boasted Orlers, stood the honored bookshop of M. Philips. It bore the noble sign Solomon's Temple.

Not far away either was the bookshop of David Janse. His *boekkamer* was across the Rapenburg canal and opened onto Breestraat, no more than 1,200 feet from the university's central building. By 1641 David Janse had been selling books and keeping a hand in the printing and publishing trade for twenty-four years. Matthijs and Isaac Elzevier had opened their shop in the same year. So had the Englishman William Brewster. They were all gone now. Yet Abraham Elzevier was still in business along with some forty-seven men and women who were also selling or printing books — and who were David Janse's competitors.

The book trade was lucrative. More than in other cities, the magistrates and the university protected the merchants' acquisition and movement of large quantities of books. They did not insist that the traders organize themselves into a guild. Instead, they took the protection and expansion of the trade as their own responsibility. They could be counted on to exclude the bothersome peddlers who tried to hawk their hundreds of *boekjes* around the countryside and towns: books filled with astronomical signs, almanacs, those for young and old, those to consult carefully, and those with throwaway pages to pin to the walls of ordinary rooms.

But especially the magistrates and university encouraged regular public auctions of large collections of books. Even better, the regents broke with other cities and allowed booksellers to act as auctioneers and keep the 5 percent fee. In late spring and early autumn, Leiden became the scene of book fairs such as those that merchants like David Janse would have attended in Frankfurt. Leiden's fairs were the most successful in the Low Countries. They enticed buyers by distributing catalogs of all varieties — those listing private scholarly libraries, those that resulted from the inventory of an estate and that mapped, if anyone cared about it, the location of books in the *sterfhuis*, the owner's house at the time of his or her death. There were catalogs that listed prices. Buyers would find that the average cost of a book was a little over one guilder, but many titles could be theirs for half a stiver, less

9. Nederlandse Boekwinkel, *c. 1645, Salomon de Bray. (Rijksmuseum-Stichting, Amster-dam)*

10. The icon "Templum Salomonis" appears on today's letterhead of Burgersdijk & Niermans, booksellers, situated directly across from St. Pieterskerk, where Philips's shop stood in the seventeenth century. I am grateful to them for allowing me to use their logo.

than a dime. If it was law books they wanted, the auctions at The Hague should not be missed. Leiden was for legal treatises but for all the others too: books on geometry, navigation and calligraphy, papers on anatomy, philosophical tracts.

The books were sold singly or in lots. So if a buyer wanted children's schoolbooks in large quantities, Leiden had them — and wholesale, often at less than one-fourth a stiver for a printed sheet. In New Netherland in the mid-1660s, Adriaen Janse needed such books. One man had them, in large quantities. He lived in a settlement along the Hudson River, about four days' sailing from Albany. He had 118 schoolbooks and 100 catechisms. He also had 102 ABC books, 27 "Arts of Letters," 23 "histories of Joseph," 87 copies in various sizes of *Succinct Ideas* by Jacobus Borstius, and 229 other books. He could sell eight small ABC books on parchment. When they were put up for sale at public auction, the books were purchased by a single buyer. He had to pay more for some books that a Leidenaar would. He got Borstius's catechism for about 4 stivers; in Leiden these went for about a stiver (one-twentieth of a guilder). But he got some books for about the same price as the buyers at Leiden, agreeing to 5 stivers for some, 11 for others, and a little over a stiver for the ABC books, sold in a package. Earlier when Janse needed such books in New Amsterdam, it was unlikely that he could even think of owning or using so many books. In any case, there were no bookstores, so he would have had to await the arrival (and probably auction) of a few books from Holland. Perhaps he hoped to be present when, on another occasion, about a hundred books were auctioned in a lottery or, again, when children's books came up in an estate auction.

Orlers did not describe David Janse's bookshop in 1641. Yet since it made him a rich and honored man, it cannot have been unlike the well-stocked and inviting Dutch bookshop that Salomon de Bray pictured four years later. It is a place displaying books but also prints and maps, globes, reams of paper, and writing instruments, all the requirements of merchants, schoolmasters, and notaries. Many books are unbound and layered as folios in cupboards. Others are richly bound in tooled leather and placed on open shelves.

De Bray's viewers walk into a shop that caters to the patrician classes. Men in fine mantles inspect the books, one posing arrogantly with arms akimbo and controlling his hunting dogs. Viewers also encounter the accommodating bookseller. Or rather they meet the merchant and his partner. A woman, who is undoubtedly the bookseller's wife, appears as much in evidence as the male figure. She presents a decidedly patrician bearing and wears personal adornments suggestive of the dignity and prosperity of the publisher's trade. Aefjen may have enacted such a partnership with David Janse. If she did not work alongside him before his death in 1644, certainly she followed tradition and maintained the house's business and reputation until her death in 1647. The publishing house became that of the "Widow of David Janse van Ilpendam."

Even in the first years of its existence, David Janse's bookstore could have been a place where he handled about 20,000 titles, but he left a record of only one volume somehow brought into print with his cooperation and probably distributed by him. In 1637 he was involved in producing an authorized version of the Bible. Such a work would have required the approval of the theologians and magistrates. His skills and reputation would have needed their approval as well.

In 1640 David Janse signed his name to the last of seven folio pages that were *not* displayed for the perusal of bibliophiles or the hope of a quick sale. They were secreted somewhere else in the house on Breestraat, and copies were also in the care of his notary, Jacob Fransz van Merwen. They were the many pages of his last will and testament. Over the years, van Merwen had notarized many documents for David Janse. He was one of at least thirty-one notaries practicing in the city. Soon, in 1641, one of his colleagues, Jacob Verwey, would write one of the most outstanding treatises on the art of the notary, 698 pages long, a beautiful publication and full of enjoyment: models of contracts mischievously spiced with exotic peoples, exempla enlivened with bizarre historical anecdotes. As for van Merwen, five years before writing Janse's will, he was commissioned as notary by an Act of Admission of the Court of Holland. He would have sworn allegiance to the court and fidelity to his profession.

Leiden is rich, so business is good. In just three months of his first year, van Merwen has forty-one clients. He already has papers standing several feet high in his home and representing the confidential wheeling and dealing of his clients — or *handel en wandel,* as they all called it. Some pages hang on the walls, each punctured about three inches from the bottom of the page. They are suspended around him, drying upside down. Somewhere among the loose pages are those registering David Janse's affairs over the years. They are not gathered together under his name, but somehow van Merwen can put his hand on them when necessary.

Most of van Merwen's papers are copies of instruments, so they needn't be completely unblemished. And he is often hurrying, even working on Sundays. Every word of the solemnities is there, to be sure, and all the necessary data. But often a quick line dashed down the left-hand side of the page will do for a margin and even a few crossings-out — sometimes it has to be a full sentence or a full page — will be all right. Inserts and marginal notes are all right too. It will even do to take shortcuts. *Openbaar notaris* is how he should identify himself, but *openbaar nota* or *nota publyx* is quicker. Printed forms for certain documents are becoming available now and would be the best of all. He has a few. They have notary Cornelis van Dosenbusch's name on them so he must repeatedly cross that out and substitute his own. He tries imitating these forms. He switches from cursive script to lettering resembling gothic print but quits — at least he did on one August day when he first began to practice — when it begins to look careless. Still, he has the printed forms in his mind, something like those that his colleague Alewijn Claasse de Man is using regularly. He renews his efforts, trying again to create a few pages with gothic lettering laid down to resemble print: he puts the solemnities in lettering and leaves spaces for the particulars of the transaction. These he inserts in a cursive hand.

From time to time over the years, he gets distracted at his work. He doodles or tests his quills, he writes another notary's name instead of his own and has to cross it out, he adds his sums in the margin of an inventory. Often he gets weary or feels the tediousness of the job. For each instrument, he usually has to create three pages from his notes, and invariably his hand is less controlled as he progresses. But he always embroiders the end of the document with a composed signature of flourishes and curlicues. Like his colleagues he embroiders into its swirling lines the exact date of the instrument: here the day, there the month, there again the year. Van Schelluyne will occasionally do the same. Adriaen Janse will not be so demonstrative.

11. Title page of Notarius Publicus, *Simon van Leeuwen, printed in 1665. The artist depicts a notary and client. Both are prosperous. The notary's clerk is shown at the left, writing. Above his head are bundles of papers to be filed. Others hang while the ink dries. Another scene depicts a sleeping chamber. The notary sits at a table taking notes on a dying man's last will and testament. Three small figures are also present, two women and a child — although women could not act as witnesses to a will. (Stichting tot Bevordering der Notariële Wetenschap, Amsterdam)*

12. The Consultation, Jan Woutersz. dit Stap, *c. 1620–30.* (© *Musée d'art et d'histoire, Geneva*)

Adriaen Janse does not tell us how he was educated. Later the state will go out of its way to require that men like Jan Janse send their children to school. This stricture will apply to those employed to work the canals who either continually move their families on houseboats or employ their sons as helpers on barges. Had a requirement such as this affected Adriaen as a child? The University of Leiden had set up an academy for young boys. Did he attend the school, perhaps owing his enrollment to his uncle? Later did he meet young men his age who were getting their degrees at the university and whom he would encounter in New Netherland: Johannes La Montagne, studying medicine and probably lecturing in the subject until 1636, Adriaen vander Donck and Dirck van Schelluyne studying law?

How often did he enter David Janse's bookstore? Did he aspire to be what van Merwen was so successfully, a notary? Everyone knew that for someone like, say, Adriaen vander Donck, who had given himself great honor by earning his doctorate in law, being a notary was a step down. Yet university professors and doctors aside, for everyone else it was a step up. Having to know something of the laws and regulations of the provinces, something of the *ars dictaminis*, something of Latin — and perhaps other languages — made a young man a *half-intellectueel* and carried respect. Yet everyone knew too that being a notary was almost a family affair. A father or uncle passed his registers on to his son or nephew from one generation to the next.

This was coming to be the practice in Leiden. It will not affect Adriaen Janse. And in New Netherland there will be no time for such things, not with the English coming.

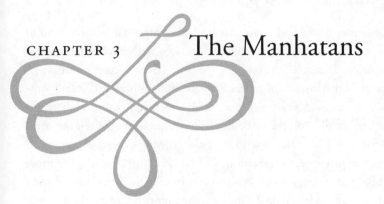

CHAPTER 3 The Manhatans

In the 1640s both Adriaen Janse and his cousin Joost left Leiden for places opened by the West India Company. Joost made the choice of his dead brother Cornelis and his unfortunate uncle, Jan Janse. He sailed for Pernambuco. Adriaen made his way to New Netherland.

Perhaps this was not a wise decision. Perhaps it would have been better if he had never left the city. As a schoolmaster, or perhaps a notary, he might have had a good career and a reasonable income. He will always be scholarly and reliable, he will wear the words "Master Adriaen" well. These virtues might have been signally rewarded in Leiden. Look at one of the notaries in Leiden, someone other than his uncle's friend van Merwen. He is a registered notary and also secretary of the court in the small nearby town of Noordwijck. Another man, one who sold a house to David Janse just before his death, enjoyed similar offices. One day Adriaen will think himself learned enough to be a town secretary. Depending on the size of the town, a secretary at home might draw a salary of 500 guilders or, at the end of the century, 2,000 guilders and additional compensation for official robes. And he has status from other employments that call upon his skills in the law and as a scribe. Everything seems predictable for such men: the dress and obliging demeanor of clients, the solid civilities of their own prosperous lives. Nothing — no strange landscape, no bands of enemies or pagan *wilden* — asks them to refashion their lives, to rethink their world, to be continually uncertain.

At the Manhatans

On Manhattan Island, Adriaen Janse is putting his life into some kind of order. It is midsummer of 1649, and he has been in New Netherland for about two years. Petrus Stuyvesant arrived only twenty-seven months ago and is now at Fort Amsterdam as resident director of the West India Company. He is thirty-seven years old, not much older than Janse. He has not imposed much stability on the settlements. Disputes rage between the company and the many merchants who are now growing powerful enough to demand greater privileges and freedoms. Quarrels continue and grow more raucous. Many think Stuyvesant wishes only to take the bread out of their mouths. They take sides against him and the company, fearing their lives will be ruined and their property swallowed up.

It is all threatening. Janse needs to avoid poverty too. He needs employment. He does not take sides, however. He remains silent, although silence is not a sure hedge against danger. The company, and men like Kiliaen van Rensselaer, distrust silence. Shouldn't the company have him on its books somewhere? Why doesn't he make an appearance? Is his wordlessness a sign that he is off somewhere along the rivers trading privately with the natives — and finding greater success than the company's own officers? Van Rensselaer was one to think this way. The colonists at Rensselaerswijck were always trading furs on their own. The sign that they were doing so was their silence, their failure to report, their failure to write. Even his secretary and bookkeeper would not communicate. "I . . . have received neither goods nor letter from you," he wrote. "You spend too much time in the woods." Where else but deep in the forest trading?

Yet Janse writes nothing. Fate, as he may well have thought, had brought him to New Netherland when others *are* writing — and are feverish to do so. Stuyvesant has inherited many of the enemies of his predecessor Willem Kieft, and, even as it was in his time, writing has become a kind of sorcery widely practiced. Evil men are being undone — Stuyvesant and his allies or burghers like Cornelis Melijn and his — by representations made of them. To see the end of a wicked man, it seems necessary only to construct a representation of him and in it run him through with deadly pins. If the word-doll is well made and the pins driven in expertly, sooner or later the company or the States General will do the rest. He cannot survive.

These are violent times. Many natives have been killed, men imprisoned, and lives threatened. The burghers are divided in their loyalties. Some support the company's director, but most plot strenuously against him and hope that New Amsterdam — free of the director general and the fort — will receive rights and privileges like those of a city at home. They will be free to manage their own trade. But the sorcery spreads. Earlier on, one man had thought to destroy Kieft by making a representation of him as murderous. Another planned his destruction by writing of him as a homosexual. Others, the most learned men on the island, ran him through quoting Linius, Propertius, and Xenephon. Kieft had planned to save himself by his "Little Blue Book" and even had it embellished with pictures in watercolor. He thought he would return to *patria* and survive — not on what he was but on what the book would show him to be.

All package their eyewitness reports as commodities. Some package their words in Latin, one complainant's pages have eighty-nine footnotes, another's is forty-nine pages in length and haughtily called a Remonstrance. They are put on the market for the company at home and the States General to finger, weigh up, and buy. Meanwhile, the voodoo is known to be powerful. Men are still ransacking each other's houses to steal and destroy the images. A trader Janse will know later, a man almost his own age, suffers the deliberate destruction of all his papers and books and imprisonment at the hands of Stuyvesant. Stuyvesant confiscates the papers of Cornelis Melijn and the men who have sent the Remonstrance to the States General. They, in reply, will soon be told they can call themselves the "burgomasters of New Amsterdam." Yet Stuyvesant will not acknowledge them. He seems to trust only his own "highly embellished writings" and the words written by his secretary, the despised Cornelis van Tienhoven.

Still, people can see that the trade is expanding. The city of Amsterdam now controls about half the trade of the Low Countries — and New Netherland as good as belongs to Amsterdam. Whatever side one is on at the Manhatans, everything turns on the success of the merchants, those at home and those on the island. And now there are signs that the earlier uncertain probing of the wilderness is giving way to the customary and solid structures of trade: long-term credit, joint partnerships, and the appearance of wholesale merchants with overseas investments and regular commercial exchanges. Trade is slowly making the Manhatans what it should be: among other things, a place of many "nations": Portuguese Jews, Englishmen, Swedes, those who speak only French.

In every way, the Manhatans is made for the merchants. The States General means to make New Netherland just like any one of the other provincial governments at home. The West India Company will have its rights,

13. Marriage of Giovanni[?] Arnolfini and Giovanna Cenami[?], *Jan van Eyck, 1434. The couple were members of the "nation" of Italian merchants from Lucca living in Bruges. Their presence denoted a flourishing city. As a court merchant, Giovanni would have expected to use the bench of Bruges; that is, a court that recognized the international nature of mercantile law or, as they said, knew that merchants carried their law with them.*

In painting the couple, van Eyck seems to take the role of the notary. He makes himself merely a supportive participant in a scene in which two parties have entered into a contract, in this case a marriage agreement. His painting is something of a permanent and valuable document executed for the couple and authenticated by his grandiose notarial signature. (The National Gallery, London) but it must be obedient to Dutch-Roman law, the imperial statutes of Charles V, and all the pertinent edicts, resolutions, and customs of the United Netherlands. Men like Stuyvesant will know this from their lawbooks — Joost de Damhouder and Bernhard van Zutphen on criminal and civil law, Jacques Thuys on the art of constructing notarized acts, Nicolai Duysentdaelders and Gerard Rooseboom on the ordinances and customary law of Amsterdam, Hugo de Groot on Dutch jurisprudence, the collections of maritime laws. They will find in them that what the merchants are saying is true: that the United Provinces is a union of cities represented in the States General for the commercial well-being of people like us. Yes, they make laws protecting the interests of each class of people. They are everyone's commercial agent. But they protect no class more carefully than the merchants.

This is what Stuyvesant knows but is mismanaging. He wants only to hear "Yes, Lord," as though patronage had any place in men's affairs. It is free trade that is wanted. He should recognize the commonwealth of merchants here, exercise *his* legal rights but recognize that they can govern themselves. He should be facilitating the traffic of sea captains in and out of the harbor. But given his arrogance and high-handedness, what merchant stranger would have the courage to come to buy or bring his wares and merchandise here? How could he or anyone know what was just if there was no court of merchants who dispensed justice to residents and strangers alike and who moved with the changing realities of the trade? Even the company's own judge advocate has called the place an "infant republic." Others are already calling New Amsterdam the "Capital of New Netherland." An independent court and the rights and privileges of a city: that's what's needed. Soon they'll have it.

The hopeful future that some men are envisioning will be to Janse's advantage. He makes no comment and signs no complaint, but he is beginning to establish himself. For a full year now, he has been the servant of a local trader, Jan Laurensz Appel. He would have done whatever Laurensz required, but undoubtedly his skills at writing and bookkeeping would have been used as well. Laurensz is not a prominent trader, but he is clever and has connections. His association with the prominent wholesaler Arnoldus van Hardenberch, for example, goes back to at least 1646. He knows the dangerous world of trading on the Delaware River and has a partner who sells his and Hardenberch's merchandise for furs — possibly illegally — upriver at Fort Orange. Perhaps he chose Janse as servant because some community of Leidenaars existed at the Manhatans. Laurensz, Adriaen Janse

Appel, Adriaen vander Donck, the de Foreests and La Montagnes, all are from Leiden or have married into Leiden families. Most of the learned men are also from Leiden. In a year's time, Dirck van Schelluyne will arrive, having completed a degree in law at the university there, and in five years' time the daughter of Joannes de Laet will arrive along with many other Leiden colonists.

For the moment, Adriaen Janse is simply a servant and gives little indication that he is supported by a family, business associates, or friends. It seems that he has a wife, but there is no record of a marriage. In the coming months, he will be asked to witness the baptism of two children. Others in the church are also from Leiden. Yet because he is not known to be of a solid burgher family — perhaps because the opposite is thought — he will have to think that real eminence in the community will be denied him. In one sense, he has to worry that he will always be someone else's servant, a *doodeter*, someone going nowhere.

Janse is a merchant's servant but also a schoolmaster. He has begun to live by the skills that he seems to trust most, those of writing. The company's insatiable craving to get things in writing is clear now. Merchants and many artisans have the same need; even farmers do. Janse's father was disgraced because of his deeds, but that was to say that his copybooks and accounts could not defend him. The same was true of Kieft. There is a place for someone who can prevent such misfortune from befalling others and their children. There is a good market for the ABC's and legible writing and numeracy.

Over the past months, Stuyvesant and the clergymen have been trying repeatedly, but without success, to procure a schoolmaster for the lower school. It had got under way twelve years ago, and children had been continually instructed since then. Last year, however, the man who had served for almost seven years, Jan Stevensz, took his leave. Now they want to engage someone like him, a teacher willing to offer instruction from his own home and ready to assist the minister by giving consolation to the sick, assisting during church services, and perhaps serving as sexton. The company had paid Stevensz a reasonable salary of 432 guilders and granted him tuition money. Still, the Amsterdam *classis*, or consistory of ministers, likes to have its way in appointing schoolmasters, and it is to them that the director general is now writing.

The Amsterdam ministers say they will choose a man in Holland and send him out. But there is much annoying delay, and the leading merchants are angry. They want a public school with at least two good masters to train the youth in reading, writing, and knowledge and fear of the Lord. Stuyvesant is also uneasy about the irregularly conducted classes. There are now perhaps two hundred children on Manhattan Island. He is insistent with the *classis*: "We need a pious and diligent schoolmaster."

Meanwhile, there are private schools for the children in New Amsterdam. Janse conducts one of them. Stuyvesant knows of the schools and apparently is pleased with them. Yet perhaps because the *classis* must have its way and perhaps because he wants a man prepared to give extensive time to tasks connected with the church and finds no willing candidate among Janse and the others, he does not put a nomination forward but waits another year for the arrival of the ministers' choice.

In the same month, Janse has his mind on the homeland. He has business to settle and prepares to send a friend to contact his family there. It means making his way to the imposing house of Stuyvesant's secretary, van Tienhoven. His need to call on van Tienhoven's services is more evidence of Stuyvesant's failure to see that he must share power more judiciously. People say openly that he is blinded to the power his secretary holds and abuses. Van Tienhoven seems to know everything, and certainly he knows Janse. In eleven months' time, when he is finally called to Amsterdam and made to give an account of his and Stuyvesant's administration, he will take credit for a range of achievements, among them the good work of men and women like Janse. The youth at the Manhatans, he will boast, are not in want of schools. Although the public school has only a temporary master at the moment, "other schoolmasters keep school in hired houses."

Like Janse, van Tienhoven is a man of paper and ink and books. He has managed to keep his job as the company's secretary for eleven years, inscribing Stuyvesant's letters and accounts, recording council meetings, and acting as the province's treasurer. He is also something of a *raadspensionaris*, offering advice on all important matters. One day his books too will be called in and audited. Stuyvesant will come to admit that he should be removed from office "lest some mishap happen to him." He will almost immediately, mysteriously disappear. People will say he committed suicide, but none can ever prove it. Meanwhile, it is common knowledge that any man's name can be trapped in the spidery curlicues of his exquisite handwriting and fear for himself.

Van Tienhoven has also won the right to act as New Netherland's only notary. In a fury at his enemies, Stuyvesant has decreed that no documents will be valid "except those written by the secretary." But in interfering with the authentication of commercial papers, he has gone too far. He and van

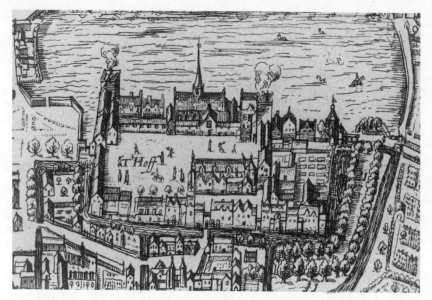

14. *Detail from a map of the Binnenhof, Braun-Hogenberg, 1618. The court buildings of the United Provinces were in the Binnenhof in The Hague. Booksellers and notaries had stalls in the Great Hall (center foreground) and set up shops in the outside galleries of other official buildings. Offices for secretaries were in the building immediately to the right of the Great Hall. Places nearby were allotted to notaries. (Gemeentearchief, The Hague)*

Tienhoven have tried to put a stranglehold on a set of practices to which a trading community has to have free and public access. Small wonder that one of the merchants has complained that "everyone has to do business with him," and that such complaints are being listened to at home.

During these same months, the States General has employed one of the many notaries in The Hague to judge the veracity of the long and detailed Remonstrance. They have selected Dirck van Schelluyne, whose credentials are the reputation of an uncle, once a notary at The Hague, and his own degree in law from the university at Leiden. Many ambitious notaries are among the civil servants, lawyers, and traders who swarm around the court of Holland in the Binnenhof. There a man can practice the notary's art at one of many small desks, some set between the stalls of booksellers and other tradespeople. Within six months, the members of the States General are convinced that Stuyvesant, with van Tienhoven, is throttling the commercial expansion of New Netherland. Van Schelluyne is appointed to act as notary on Manhattan Island and in all of New Netherland. He will arrive in ten months' time.

Janse's business with van Tienhoven is urgent. There are two matters to settle. It is August 20, and some of the summer ships are leaving for Holland. Arnoldus van Hardenberch is departing immediately on the *Valckenier* and now arranging for the management of his business affairs in his absence. He meets with Janse and Laurensz at the secretary's house to put his affairs in their hands, renewing a power of attorney given to them a year ago. Hardenberch is an important merchant. He is one of three burghers chosen to represent the merchants in the city government of New Amsterdam, the Board of Nine Men. The trust he has placed in Janse means something, perhaps the beginning of a special reputation for competence and discretion. As it happens, van Tienhoven is absent from the meeting. His clerk takes his place in drawing up the papers. Van Tienhoven's son is there to act as witness — and get a small remuneration. It's part of the meaning of family.

Janse also has his own affairs to consider. The state of his inheritance has taken some twist or turn in Leiden. His friend Sybout Claesz, a carpenter, is sailing on the same ship as Hardenberch, and now Janse authorizes him to make inquiries and, if necessary, take legal action on his behalf. The language of the agreement is full of the prescribed solemnities found in any power of attorney. His friend is to "collect, demand and receive . . . such sums of money, effects and property as may be coming to him," and so on. The contract's words also suggest, however, an unsettling distance from relatives and their intentions, a loss of touch with the motivations that move family money and estates in and out of a cousinry less and less knowable, less and less tangible. Claesz's must be a secondhand voice in towns and cities where other cousins, other family members can present themselves, reason, make gestures, arouse family kindliness.

Concerning other finances, Janse is taking steps to relieve himself of all liability for his father's debts. Perhaps he sees that doing this in van Tienhoven's house is especially apt, or ironic. About two years ago, his stepmother entered the same house. She too paid van Tienhoven to write up a power of attorney. The company had, she claimed, failed to pay Jan Janse his wages, and she was giving Joannes de Laet authority to collect them. Three days later, on August 19, she signed bonds encumbering her joint estate with Jan with debts amounting to 2,169 guilders. This amount included 1,220 guilders for rent and board in New Amsterdam, presumably since October 1645. Now Janse has called upon Adriaen Keyser, one of the men who acted as witnesses to the debts two years ago, to certify that he has received no part of his father's estate. "On the contrary," he has — as they said — "kicked the same away with his foot."

It is a humiliating admission to be a bankrupt's son. The cruel popular saying catches the anger of such sons toward their fathers. Janse signs the document "Adriaen van Ilpendam," without his patronymic.

But nothing is without its politics on the Manhatans. As the *Valckenier* is about to get under way, there are distressing moments for Claesz and a friend who is sailing with him, Joost Teunisse. Each man is carrying a formal complaint against Stuyvesant and means to present it to the States General. Claesz has had property seized by Kieft and a request for a house lot arbitrarily denied by Stuyvesant. Teunisse had been imprisoned for providing guns to the natives around Fort Orange, then cleared of the charges. Despite sureties later put up by Claesz and Isaac de Foreest, he is still being denied the right to trade. He now petitions for the near-impossible: to transact his business "unwatched."

Stuyvesant interferes with their departure, but the captain connives to bring them along. On Monday, December 13, about sixteen weeks later, their petitions are read before the States General. Another document of far greater weight, also from New Netherland, is read as well. It is the petition signed by eleven of the most powerful burghers on Manhattan Island. They register their plea that the port city on the island have what it would enjoy anywhere in the United Provinces: suitable municipal government like that at home. They seek the right to trade "every way and every where your High Mightinesses have granted to the Netherlanders the privilege of trade and resort." Hardenberch has endorsed the plea. Why wouldn't he, since Kieft had once threatened to jail him, and only a month ago Stuyvesant had given authorization to enter his house, search for, and, if necessary, remove illegal goods.

Claesz, de Foreest, Hardenberch: these are some of Adriaen Janse's friends. Undoubtedly associating with them does not mean drawing Stuyvesant's attention to himself. More likely, his situation is like that of other ordinary men. As the leading burghers say, the common people live in fear and anguish, not knowing "with whom to associate."

Nothing comes of Janse's inquiries in Holland. He continues to earn his living as a schoolmaster. He has no salary and must make his way on the fees he charges to parents. Van Tienhoven was right: he has rented a house for his teaching. Although many of the most ordinary residents have managed to become property owners on the island, he has not. Nor does he seem to have attached a *monster kaart* outside his house with enticing specimens of his handwriting or a picture of the rod used for disciplining children. If he draws attention to his calling by wearing an inkhorn, no one records it. People do write "Master" or "the Worthy" before his name. They are honorable titles, although considerably more humble that those bestowed on merchants. He does not render his name into Latin — that is for the ministers and masters of Latin schools to do.

He seems to be a good schoolmaster. He comes under no public criticism — doesn't keep an inn, collect the excise on wine and beer, or write legal papers in a taphouse. Stuyvesant leaves no record of having given him permission to begin his school. Still, the director has already gone out of his way to make known his concern for the children's well-being and soon will make his authority over schoolteaching clear in the case of a burgher who has been conducting a school for some time without first seeking his approval. The right to keep a school, he decrees, derives absolutely from the *jus patronalis* invested in himself and his council. The master who is now denied his living is Jacobus van Curler, the same fellow who, like Jan Janse, cheated Kiliaen van Rensselaer twelve years ago.

No one, of course, thinks to describe Adriaen Janse's school or schoolday. Undoubtedly he is teaching some lower school children during the day and others in the evenings. His pupils are boys and girls who sit separately on benches — or perhaps on the floor. They work on boards placed on their knees. Or perhaps they rest them on planks or benches, sitting to write and standing to read. Probably they sit, or squirm, before him from eight to eleven o'clock in the morning and from one to four in the afternoon. Those who come in the evening stay from five to seven o'clock and, at least in winter, learn by the light of a candle and perhaps a lantern. But because children have delicate bodies, the most valuable study time for them is in the morning. Those learning writing and ciphering sit nearest to him. Those just beginning the ABCs are at the back, along with children too young to receive lessons in arithmetic.

There is little variation in the lessons offered. Everything should turn around ciphering. Some of the skills of mathematics are essential to children whose parents expect them to be merchants or traders. In a trading city, everyone needs to be numerate in one way or another. Many people have to figure exact measurements every day. People work just fractions of days and have to calculate their pay. Everyone is buying or selling something. Quantities have to be reckoned and remembered: yards of cloth, bushels of grain, the miles of a coastline. Yet everyone knows that things stick faster in memory, as they say, if they are written down. For many, it is foolish and dangerous not to keep records. At any time a man or woman may be diddled or falsely accused of cheating, and the company expects people to keep accounts. Twice in the past two years the burghers have been warned that everyone planning to "sell, barter, trade, ship or export" any "wares or merchandise, of whatever nature" within the lands governed by the company has to be ready to have "his books or accounts examined" whenever it pleases the officials.

Janse is a writing master as well. His pupils will have to make their way in a world of script and become part of it, even the poor children to whom he is obliged to give free lessons. In a way the company officials and leading merchants are responsible for this state of affairs. But they are putting things in place the way they would at home. There too ships would be anchored in harbors and alongside riverbanks with ordinances or placards nailed to their masts, burghers would go about with receipts of one kind or another in their possession, skippers, traders, and tapsters would be ready with receipts to prove they had paid the excise, boatmen would carry signed orders allowing them to land, the court would reject the excuse that someone acted as he did because he failed to read a placard. It goes on and on. Here at the Manhatans, many of the important papers are in van Tienhoven's script. As handwriting goes, it could not be more beautiful. It is the sort of calligraphy that a writing master might present to young people for their imitation alongside his own. Everyone knows that among all languages Dutch is especially charming and sonorous. Here the beauty is not to be heard but to be seen.

If Janse is earning approval, he is nonetheless not earning a substantial income. This is not surprising. There are only about 120 households on Manhattan Island, so perhaps there are no more than two hundred children, and only a small percentage of those would be of lower school age. Janse has at least two competitors for pupils: Jan Cornelisse is teaching in the public school, and David Provoost has a school in the broad street that leads north up the island from the fort. Some burghers have hired private tutors for their children, and probably there are women who instruct small groups of children in their homes: this has never been forbidden. Even in ten years' time and when the population has almost tripled, a master will think himself fortunate to have twenty-five students. Janse probably has closer to fifteen. But the charges to the parents of each pupil for the four quarters of the year are somewhere between 8 and 16 guilders. Altogether, fees would pay for the average cost of house rent and little more than the necessities of bread and beer. His income would be close to, in fact slightly less than, that of an unskilled servant.

Soon, but too late for him, fellow townspeople will think of ways to supplement the schoolmaster's income. For teaching a child the alphabet, spelling, and reading they will give him, above a salary, 30 stivers a quarter; for teaching reading, and writing, 50 stivers; for reading, writing, and ciphering, 60 stivers; and "a fair sum" for those who come in the evenings. But nothing like that exists for him. He is allowed to pursue other ways of using his skills, but only before schooltime and during those evenings when he has no pupils. Many of these livings are either frivolous or out of the question, given the circumstances offered by the Manhatans. He may, for example, help compute the city taxes, cut hair, or cure wounds. He may bind books or compose love letters.

Other jobs on the side would be a possibility. He could be a notary or a court secretary. Valcooch recommended that a schoolmaster consider becoming a notary. He himself had done just that after eight years of teaching. Especially in small towns at home, many men filled both jobs. There were recognized ways of becoming a notary's apprentice. One could contract to be a notary's student and clerk, learning the art of the notary — and perhaps a language like French — and earning 6 guilders and room and board. The same young man might expect to earn — like van Tienhoven's son and stepson — a fee for appearing as a witness. If he were fortunate, a young man's father might pay a notary 200 guilders for the two-year education of his son. The youth would have the theory and practice of the *notarisambt* and a smattering of law as well. Such decisions, however, were ordinarily being made by or for a young man with the support of a family and when he was in his teens or early twenties. Janse is alone and already thirty-one, well beyond the time when young men who will make their mark have begun a career.

Far more important, Stuyvesant continues to see no need for notaries at the Manhatans. He will in fact molest van Schelluyne so continually when he arrives that the newcomer will remain uncertain whether to build on his new farm or leave. Merchants will be afraid to turn their papers over to him, and he will become convinced that those he has are not safe from Stuyvesant's, or van Tienhoven's, invasion of his house. One day there will be eighteen notaries in New Netherland and twelve on Manhattan Island alone. Their records will be more complete than those of any other West India Company settlement. The States General, the merchants here who have made themselves into the Board of Nine Men, and even the directors of the company at home foresee this development. For now, however, it is a chimera.

The position of secretary is, however, another employment that Valcooch recommended and that Janse will soon ambition. Being a secretary somewhere inside the structure of the company or in a town is a considerable step upward. It is a very demanding occupation, especially on Tuesdays: secretaries are always busy on Tuesdays. On that day Janse would have to give up his time to attend meetings of the court and then write up the minutes, ordinances, and necessary correspondence. A fair copy of a morning or afternoon session could mean from two to seven or eight pages of script, hours of work.

The company needs more clerks than ever. It is enlarging its activities around Manhattan Island. It is also expanding its hold along the Delaware River and upriver at Fort Orange. Here in New Amsterdam an Englishman has been hired to write letters in English for the director. Two years ago he was earning 42 guilders a month for this service plus 200 guilders for himself and his boy. The company's secretary is paid about 720 guilders a year and earns additional fees for attending meetings and writing up the minutes. It is a modest enough income but certainly an improvement on a schoolmaster's fees. And the position offers other rewards as well. It means much more than taking dictation. Janse would have to keep secret all that he was instructed to write and all that he heard during deliberations of the company officials. He would become an insider. He could come to know everything about the trade and use his knowledge to his own benefit. This is an important consideration, and any man would take advantage of it.

As secretary, he could also use his skills in a more versatile way. People expect a man's skills to take him in many directions. The ordinary town clerk may be expected to gather the old records and memories of the town and write its history. One of Janse's fellow burghers (and a secretary) will soon be writing a "Description of the Founding or Beginning" of his town. It will serve, he thinks, "for the information of us and our successors" and "for the encouragement and information of their posterity." He knows enough Latin to insert masterly sayings and to make his "book," as he calls it, respectable. Such ambitious projects are only reasonable. A clerk lives continually with books: those made by himself, those required by his work — a sentence book listing lawbreakers, a wages book accounting for soldiers and their pay, a journal and daybook, registers and minutes — and those he must consult, such as de Damhouder's guide to civil and criminal law and Thuys's manual for writing up legal papers.

Janse seems to think himself ready for such a position. The company takes only honorable men as its officers — at least, that's what it says — yet at the moment men are gossiping openly about the company's treacherous secretary. But, for now, the company's need to maintain its own honor will serve to make him look honorable too. Van Tienhoven will continue on for about three years. And if Janse has thoughts about a lesser position, such as that of the secretary's clerk, he is not offered one.

In thirty months' time, he will put his name forward as secretary of another court, this one upriver, almost forty Dutch miles away.

SEPTEMBER 9, 1650
Rensselaerswijck

In September, the colonists of Rensselaerswijck decide their children need a proper school. Many of them are from the eastern province of Gelderland, rather than the urbanized western provinces of the Netherlands. There taking the initiative in such matters is customary.

Gelderland is the van Rensselaer family's home province. It is a place of good farmlands and prosperous cities such as Nijkerk. Farther to the east, however, the sandy soil of the Veluwe dominates, making the land almost unworkable and beneficial to only a limited number of large landholders. Of course, good land is available for every Gelderlander in Rensselaerswijck, or so Kiliaen thought. With its broad river and fast-flowing streams all creating hectares of arable land, every man could be like the wealthy landowners of the high Veluwe. And so, for good or for ill, colonists have come, and the patroonship is now what a later historian will call *de Geldersche Vallei*. The people speak an odd sort of Dutch, as they do in the high Veluwe. Brant Aertsz van Slichtenhorst, the present director and one of the van Rensselaer cousinry, sprinkles the *colonie's* court minutes with quaint sayings. At least for their speech, Amsterdammers find them all *plattelanders*, country bumpkins.

Now, following ancient custom, the people have declared themselves ready to meet the costs of establishing and supporting a school. They present their petition to the *colonie's* officers, who meet on September 9 and agree that the appointment of a suitable schoolmaster is not only a salutary initiative but a necessary one. They remind themselves that they live in a "republic" and that such a form of association needs the presence of a schoolmaster. Two officers volunteer to supervise a collection of funds and oversee the administration of the school. That same day Adriaen Janse is appointed to take the position. He will receive a gift of 50 guilders when he takes up his duties.

The colonists do not record why they invited Janse to come upriver to the *colonie*. Nor has he explained his decision. It's true that the patroonship looks promising. As director, van Slichtenhorst is increasingly asserting the patroon's ownership of an area that reaches for miles along both the east and west banks of the river. In a high-stakes game of chess already begun with the company, he is putting his pieces in all the right places. He means to wipe the board of nothing less than the company's trading post, Fort Orange. Or, rather, he means to break its dominance over the fur trade. He is moving his colonists, his pawns, in two directions. Some are already on farms at a distance far from the fort. Their presence there seems innocent enough. But they are meant to forestall the carrying of furs to the company's men at the fort by natives making their way especially from the northwest and south. Other pawns — as the houses of the colonists surely are — have been moved to spaces pressing on the fort itself. The patroon's trading house is a building directly under van Slichtenhorst's supervision and is standing on the bank of the ditch that immediately surrounds the fort. Two years ago, there were only about eight houses near it. Now there are more and, as van Slichtenhorst moves his pieces in, in two years' time there will be close to a hundred.

Important people are choosing to come to the *colonie* and play van Slichtenhorst's game. At least twenty-eight men have arrived in the past twenty-four months. Jan van Twiller and Gerrit van Wenckum, both distant relatives of the patroon, have arrived. Carpenters have moved in. A master builder has removed from the Manhatans with his wife and child. Philip Pietersz Schuyler has come directly from Amsterdam. There are houses and mills to be built. Ordinary people also take their chances. A boy of seventeen comes as a farmhand. Like everyone else, he will get into the fur trade, even though the patroon reserves it to the family and the company licenses only its own men and about twenty-five free traders.

So the growing *colonie* might seem a promising place. Yet even van Rensselaer, at the same time that he vigorously promoted the *colonie*, had deep reservations about the sort of people who were trying to make a living in Rensselaerswijck. The fact was, he thought, "that the best people seldom go so far across the sea." And just a month before Janse's appointment, one colonist had received permission to leave the *colonie*. He couldn't make a living. Everyday needs were more expensive here than downriver.

Moreover, *de Geldersche Vallei* is a dangerous place. The natives too play on the chessboard. Usually they are just the traders' abused prey, an unpaid workforce that hauls hundreds of pelts to the Dutch, gets cheated, and moves off to await the time of more pelts. They can also be a nuisance and a cause of unease. Many live nearby, farming and grazing cattle. Let a colonist abandon his farmhouse and they will squat in it. From time to time, their leaders threaten raids and the burning of houses.

NOVEMBER 28, 1650
Rennselaerswijck

Janse comes face to face with a native who has a name that looks on paper like "Stichtigeri." Everyone calls him "the Owl." Janse is acting as witness to the sale of the Owl's small house near the fort. The commander, Jan Labatie, wants to purchase it and has the papers drawn up. Stichtigeri and three Dutch men sign the conveyance. If Janse finds this first chance to witness a legal document in Rensselaerswijck strange or disconcerting, if it leads him to momentary reconsiderations about this dangerous new country, he keeps his thoughts to himself.

Besides, there are recurring cycles of living in Rensselaerswijck that leach some of the strangeness from the days' happenings. He is beginning to be a part of these regularities. Labatie, though he is the senior officer at the fort and a more important man than most, is not the only one buying or selling a house lot in November. This is a time for house sales. The *colonie* likes to sell or assign house lots in November, getting ready to collect its rents the next Easter. And *handelstijd* is over, so people are leaving, some permanently; others, such as the bakers, temporarily: they will go to the Manhatans and probably return in May. The Owl, being around in November, is a hanger-on. He, and everyone else, saw most other natives finish their trading and move off one or two months ago. It happens every year.

November brings a sort of stasis to the otherwise frequent demands on the court. It continues to sit on Tuesdays and Thursdays but then less frequently as a quiet descends after the fever of *handelstijd*. Yet something is left over from the trading season that disturbs the quiet. All during the summer months, the native traders were treated cruelly, physically brutalized in the woods, cheated, and left drunk. No one needs to be told these things. Now rumors of the expected retaliation are rife. The sachems are once again threatening to attack the settlements, exercising a sort of desperate blackmail, seeking clothing and guns to see them through the winter. But this time the threats have disturbed van Slichtenhorst's studied game of chess. By mid-September, he realizes that he needs to send emissaries to the Mohawk, men who can make the usual offer of broken guns and blankets in return for continued friendship. Only Labatie, however, speaks the Mohawk language. On September 23, the director humbles himself, asking him to make the journey. Instead, Labatie made his move on the board: we in the fort don't care how it goes, whether it is "war or peace."

The November 28 meeting with the Owl is the admission of stalemate at this moment in the contest between the *colonie* and the company. The parties to the drama know this. Labatie wins the right to buy the house so he can tear it down — and make the point that the company men at the fort will act independent of the *colonie* in controlling the land on its defensive perimeter. He wins this concession, however, in van Slichtenhorst's court and after acknowledging his opponent's authority and the patroon's ownership of the land. The Owl looks on and makes a mark on the agreement. Adriaen Janse watches as van Slichtenhorst adds his signature. Then Anthonij de Hooges signs as secretary of the *colonie*. De Hooges would have seen to the careful wording of the contract, and now his signature gives it the status of a notarized document. Finally, Janse adds his name as witness.

Van Slichtenhorst, de Hooges, and Janse: these men have their employment because they have skills beyond those of the farmers and artisans. Van Slichtenhorst and de Hooges keep the paperwork of the *colonie* in order. Janse is, as so often in other circumstances, a supportive participant. As schoolmaster, he is expected to give colonists advice when it is requested, to help them make up accounts or write letters.

In van Slichtenhorst, Janse can observe someone who never neglects his books. Perhaps because of his age or sense of self-importance, he keeps to his house and the nearby warehouse. He does not go around the settlement much. He is determined to bring the *colonie* into perfect order but is being driven to distraction by the recalcitrant colonists. They rebuff him as a "gray thief and rascal." Everyone knows his ways. When a disgruntled colonist wants to confront him — and ends up stabbing him with a knife the old man uses for sharpening pens — he is in his house "busy writing." At one point, he asks 700 guilders, almost a year's salary, for doing the paperwork on three legal cases for the family. He employs his nephew Gerrit van Wenckum to write as well: the usual family thing, training the young man and putting such sums as 60 guilders in his hands for copying "writings." Small wonder that along the way he charged the patroon for over a thousand sheets of paper. He has farmers and artisans attending to their ledgers as well. Each must itemize his yearly account. Income must be shown "not in gross but in detail" and "with the vouchers." He wants an account of income from the fur trade too, but he will never get that.

Anthonij de Hooges is a man of writing too. If Janse looks for exemplary young men who have the wit to make something of their careers as scribes, he is one. Like Janse's, his is something of a West India Company family but — and perhaps Janse will think of this — without the stain of corruption. When he sailed to Rensselaerswijck from Amsterdam, an older family member was a bookkeeper in the company's Amsterdam chamber, and the directors there went out of their way to ensure that his young relative was assigned a cabin on the ship. During the four-month voyage, he busied himself writing a thousand-word journal that he would hand to van Rensselaer.

In the *colonie*, de Hooges initially assisted Kiliaen's grandnephew Arent van Curler in keeping the accounts and writing letters. The men were friends. Van Curler was twenty-two and de Hooges even younger. Not long out of Latin school, they were boyish, even amateurish, in doing their work. Van Curler adorned the cover of one account book with "Est nomen meum Cato & inquit Rem Tuam" ("My name is Cato and I inquire into your affairs"). He used the Greek alphabet in constructing the index of names. He was still following the schoolmasters in composing letters. Kiliaen wanted this foolishness stopped and admonished him that putting the date at the top and bottom of a page was superfluous. He emphasized that Arent erred by adopting the general style followed in the schools, for example, "If it were otherwise, I should be heartily sorry." Such scribblings filled pages but gave no advice. Eleven years later, Arent was one of the two men who volunteered to get Janse's school under way and to supervise its administration.

De Hooges was more diligent. He too needed to be taught how to construct a proper inventory, but soon he was keeping the wages books of the *colonie*. Then he was unofficially director of the patroonship for four years, until the arrival of van Slichtenhorst.

In meeting de Hooges, Janse is encountering a man who has helped keep the *colonie* afloat by mastering the details of civil and criminal law. There are books to help him. In eighteen months' time, he and van Curler will make a note of all the books in the director's house. Among them will be his copy of Grotius's *Introduction to Dutch Jurisprudence*. As well, the *colonie*'s minister is a university man and has his library, or some of it, with him. Like other ministers, he has supplied himself with treatises on theology and philosophy but also on moral economy, law, and mathematics.

The standard treatises on civil and criminal law have also been available in the *colonie* since the mid-1630s. Kiliaen wanted his court of justice to be conducted like that of Amsterdam. He made a point of sending his untutored law enforcement officers and court members a copy of Joost de Damhouder's treatise on criminal law because the court there, he emphasized, "generally follows this author." He also sent de Damhouder's companion volume on civil law as well as the *Ars Notariatus* of Jacques Thuys. These were three books, he said, to "keep carefully and study diligently." And so they were. De Damhouder's two volumes were useful because they set out to do nothing more than guide law enforcement officers through the practical techniques of applying the law. He wanted to produce something that was "clear and accurate," something like the law itself, mostly a matter of getting the facts straight. So he offered an illustrated handbook. It was shamefully plagiarized but greatly admired.

Ars Notariatus was in the officials' hands to complement de Damhouder's work. It was another instruction manual. The title was meant to entice a wide audience: *The Art of the Notary, That is: The Art and Style of the Office of Notary: Made Clear in Theory and Practice. With Explanations of many obscure Latin and French Words and Terms, which are commonly used in Practice. Very Profitable, Proper and Serviceable for All Legal Practitioners, Businessmen, Merchants and others.* Van Curler and de Hooges would have found themselves led along in this work by a simple question-and-answer format not unlike the articles set out in the catechism. Page 1: What is a notary? A notary is a public office by which the trade and negotiations of a people are recorded in solemn and authentic form and also brought to memory, just as any kind of writing has always been able to do. Who may be a notary? A slave may not be a notary. A farmer is a man well down the social ladder and may not be a notary. And so on, about fifty pages of "De Theorike." Then came models for easy imitation and use in everyday practice: a contract of sale, a petition, how to nominate a substitute notary in another country, how to take an inventory of a deceased person's estate: first, itemize the papers and accounts, then list gold and silver, then the contents of the room with the main fireplace, then . . . All simplified.

These were the sorts of books needed to fit oneself to be administrator or secretary of a town or landholding such as Rensselaerswijck. They were simple manuals. In the case of de Hooges, they helped change an assistant bookkeeper into a court secretary earning 455 guilders a year and someone who, in the absence of a notary, would soon be expected to act in court as its *defensoris loco*, an advocate for defendants needing legal representation.

Janse's chance will come too, but he must wait nineteen years. Then, however, "what is a notary" will have many different meanings.

Rensselaerswijck

Adriaen Janse stays in Rensselaerswijck. It is again November, one year later. The court meets on this day, a Tuesday, and attends to a petition he has written and now presents as schoolmaster. He has taken November as a time to consider his future: perhaps his contract needs renewal and the quarter of the school year that begins on All Saints' Day has arrived. He expects to have difficulty meeting payments for house rent and requests assistance. The court allows him 50 guilders to cover the rent — but just this once. It is a gruff reply but one he may have anticipated. A rent of 50 guilders indicates he intends to reside near the center of the settlement — near the new cluster of houses and warehouses close by the foreshore. He has no interest in living at the margins of the community, say, at places out around Norman's Kill, where the rent is only 20 guilders but, as everyone knows, few go to trade. Perhaps he is involved in the fur trade. Perhaps he does have, as they say, "friends in the game."

In any case, the game changes early in 1652. Stuyvesant takes the company's chess pieces into his own hands. There will be an independent fort and a town around it. Those who wish may be burghers of the town and free to trade, subject to a new court's regulations. Let the new *peltrij handelaars* make of the town what they will.

In four months' time, Adriaen Janse puts his name forward to be secretary of the new court. Within the year, he owns land. Perhaps he is getting lucky.

CHAPTER 4 Beverwijck

1652

Beverwijck

Stuyvesant calls Adriaen Janse's new town Beverwijck. That makes sense. Look at an old map and you will see that the name has to do with Holland's world of sea-lanes and trading cities, with setting sails and moving cargo around the Zuider Zee, or even making for faraway destinations. If you sail into the Zuider Zee through the narrow passage between Den Helder and Texel, you come to Enkhuizen. You must take care here. The shoals lying near the city are especially treacherous. Next, still to starboard, is Hoorn. It is a further one-and-a-half day's sailing: everything is still dangerous channels, shifting sandbars, and sudden storms. After skirting the island of Marken and entering the wide estuary of the Ij River, Amsterdam rises on the port side and stretches for two miles along the shore. There are houses, canals, towers, anchored vessels of all descriptions. Then, still to port and a sail of four or five Dutch nautical miles upriver, you come to the next trading town. The river is petering out, making a last generous offer of easy and cheap transport to merchants willing to settle alongside and trade their goods. Especially it is ready to carry people and goods to and from Amsterdam. The town is Beverwijck.

In New Netherland it is quite the same. After leaving the open seas, you also face the dangers of piloting through narrows and channels before skirting Staten Island and approaching New Amsterdam. You must then navi-

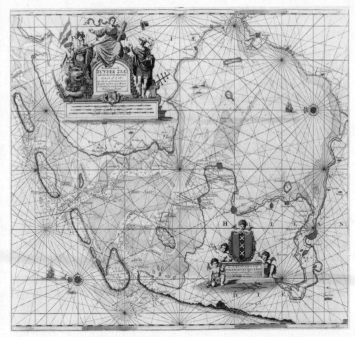

15. Paskaart van de Zuyder Zee, *Jean van Keulen, 1682. This navigational map of the Zuider Zee shows the entrance from the English Channel to the mouth of the Ij River and Amsterdam. The map shows the island of Texel with six towns and villages as well as a fort guarding the entrance to the inland seas. The Ij links Amsterdam and Beverwijck (lower right corner). Haarlem lies to the south of Beverwijck.* (Le Grand Nouvel Atlas de la mer, Amsterdam, Chez Jean van Keulen, 1682. Harvard University, Map Collection)

gate the *raks* or reaches of *de rivier van d'vorst Mauritius* (Hudson River), sailing upstream, at times threading low-lying islands, river flats, and dangerous sandbars. About forty Dutch miles along, a small trading place will appear: a fort and a dispersed settlement of perhaps a hundred houses and farms. It too appears to port and marks the end of waters deep enough for a seagoing vessel. And it too is now Beverwijck.

Beverwijck in 1652 is not much to see. Approaching it from the south, a skipper first observes a broad stream called Norman's Kill emptying into the river on his left and then, about five miles along, Fort Orange appears, with administrators' and traders' houses pinned to its internal walls and a ditch separating it to the north from lands suitable for farming and gardens. Next a low foreshore comes into view and, inland, a cluster of houses, mostly wooden but several of brick. Then comes another kill farther on and finally the sight of a steep and dominating hill casting waters downward into a ravine and thrusting its own bulk forward, almost to the river's edge. Not an orderly settlement. Then the return of dense forest.

Yet parcels of land, houses, farms, none of these are the meaning of Beverwijck. Adriaen Janse would know what its meaning is: the activity of a river town, the trade in furs. Downriver, New Amsterdam is realizing another kind of meaning, drawing itself purposefully into order. In a year's time, the burghers will be city men and women. They will have it all: a market, a wall, and a charter. They will be jurisdictionally independent of the company and have a future — as wholesalers, creditors, transatlantic shippers of goods from an expanding hinterland. Beverwijck's future depends on *not* duplicating New Amsterdam, at least not for the time being. It rests on making use of New Amsterdam in the same way the old river town of Beverwijck at home makes use of Amsterdam. It must learn to manipulate the port town for what it is: a giant wharf.

One day Janse will try, but only once, to describe Beverwijck. He will call on this relationship. He will say that it is a dependent place, that it lies "inland" from New Amsterdam. That's what it must be. Already more than 10,000 pelts are being loaded each year along the strand north of Fort Orange for shipment south. Four years from now, the count will be 36,000 and then, in six years' time — although it will happen only once — 60,000. New Amsterdam is a place that belongs to Beverwijck. In a sense Janse has never really left it.

The new beginning that Stuyvesant now offers requires some consideration. Even Janse and other men and women of little consequence are forced to make decisions. They can remain van Rensselaer's tenants and artisans or choose to become free traders and cast their lot with the company. People worry about loyalties. The call of the *colonie* on people's steadfastness is real. Rensselaerswijck has a history now, a past to remember. It is something that arranges people's memories, whether they like it or not. De Hooges likes to think that two years ago, 1650, was the fifth year of the directorship of Johannes van Rensselaer. One man had hesitated and declared, "I cannot give allegiance to another lord before I am released from the first."

But most go Janse's way. They pin their hopes on becoming townspeople. Stuyvesant has given them a court. They will be under the jurisdiction of the court of Fort Orange and Beverwijck. Johannes Dyckman is its presiding officer. He is the company's chief customs officer at the fort and, if reliable, may be retained in his position for life. Local burghers also occupy the bench. They are "commissaries" or magistrates representing the people and appointed annually from a list of men chosen by the inhabitants and —

half of them — approved by the company. Everyone knows that it is the court that will give shape to their lives and their rights.

Janse shares with everyone a close and uneasy scrutiny of Dyckman. The man is sometimes strange and given to irrational rages. In three years' time, he will be recognized as out of his senses and dismissed. Meanwhile, he is trying to manage the company's business at the fort. He works steadily enough, but his handwriting is careless, almost indecipherable. Still, he must carry on without an assistant bookkeeper or secretary. He must also settle the new town. In these first months, he has already administered the usual burgher oaths and begun to act as law enforcement officer. He has appointed surveyors and a court messenger, approved a marriage, and organized the church and minister. His day-to-day conduct of the court is efficient and fair enough, but it is unusual. He is presiding over the court and — except for the services of a part-time clerk — also keeping its minutes, acting as his own secretary. This is an opening for Janse.

He offers himself as secretary during the first week of August. He has directed a petition to the court and now awaits a judgment: it is the first step toward securing the position. He presents himself as someone who is already serving the community in a special capacity as schoolmaster and begs that the magistrates recommend to Stuyvesant that he be not just appointed but "promoted to the post of secretary." If he were to get the job, he would be writing about a hundred pages of minutes every year, at 30 stivers a page, earning about 150 guilders. And he would be called upon to read legal papers "word by word" to those not able to do so. That would provide a few guilders more. The magistrates consider his petition after hearing five other cases. Dyckman minutes their decision and later writes: "His request is granted." Stuyvesant, however, denies the application and requires Dyckman to continue as his own secretary. At the end of the year, the court will be discussing a place that a clerk, at some time "in the future," might use for writing and for his papers. But it will be four years before Stuyvesant approves a secretary's salary. Then it will be for Johannes Provoost, a man unlike Janse: he has family connections in New Amsterdam, a brother who is a schoolteacher there but also one of Stuyvesant's trusted councilors and a successful merchant. The appointment will give him what Janse will never attain: tenure in the honorable position of secretary, and for eight years.

Janse leaves the matter at that. He does not put himself forward for another public appointment, such as that of court messenger. It brings a small *beneficium*, probably 50 guilders a year and various fees on the side. It is small change: 4 stivers for a burgher's petition to the court, 6 for informing a burgher that he or she has been cited and must appear in court. Or perhaps Janse remembers his first year in Rensselaerswijck when the court messenger was laid up for two months after his face was smashed in while he was trying to serve a summons. Five years ago at the Manhatans a schoolmaster had taken on a similar task. As the *schout*'s servant, he was employed to round up lawbreakers for 26 guilders a year and 100 guilders for board. Perhaps he was supposed to think it was a step up from his previous side jobs of taking in washing and assisting illegal traders.

Such jobs — junior clerk, court messenger (which sometimes includes being jailer), *schout*'s provost — are for lackeys or for men prepared to act aggressively. They are not roles that Janse, judging from the rest of his life, would choose. The secretary's position would have brought a reliable income and perhaps accommodation. The place set aside for the man who is presently serving as court messenger and sometimes clerk is inside the fort, in the company's "little house." Soon a man named Maximillian de Winter comes looking to share this place. He says his need is urgent. The court grants his appeal, "for the present."

1653
Beverwijck

De Winter does not remain in Beverwijck for long. Janse does, staying on as schoolmaster and somehow involving himself in the fur trade. The principal *handelaars* are moving thousands of pelts downriver to New Amsterdam. It's not difficult. Skippers are ready to vie with one another for the work of carrying cargo and passengers. Two years ago, between four and seven of them were offering their services regularly. In four years' time, the traffic will multiply during *handelstijd* and practically be beyond Dyckman's control. Townspeople will be on the river in "canoes, rowboats, and other vessels" while, about every three days, one or other of eighteen captains will be looking for clearance from the strand. Following ancient tradition, some traders will want to accompany their goods to the Manhatans and see to their consignment to a local wholesale merchant or get them directly onto one of the "summer ships" leaving for Holland. The pelts have to be dispatched quickly to their various destinations: the Amsterdam storehouses of people such as Sijbinck, the stalls of the hawkers of furs at Amsterdam kermis, the company's warehouses. But all the sales have to serve as credit on the coming year's supply of trading goods. Some traders have partners who can stay behind in Beverwijck. Others have partners, even wives, in New Amsterdam.

Janse does not have a partner and is not even clear of his father's debts. Just two years ago, the directors of the company in Holland wrote about them to Director General Stuyvesant. Jan Janse had supposedly closed his accounts in 1645, they reported, but there were still outstanding debts, and creditors were angry. Still, even if Adriaen Janse had a partner, such arrangements end as often in quarrels as in profits. They require the court's adjudication. Papers must be examined either by the court or by learned and disinterested men acting for it. In March, the same officials who could not get Janse the position of secretary turn to him as mediator in such a case. He seems to be trusted and is paid a small amount.

Now he is also a property owner. The director general wants the traders who have been living inside the fort to build their own houses outside its walls. Other burghers are also to be given house lots and gardens. The properties have been surveyed and are ready for distribution. A lottery is held. Numbers 7, 19, 11, 22, and 24 are among the lots drawn. Janse draws number 5. It entitles him to a house lot that is 9 rods and 10 feet by 4 rods and a garden. He can keep it intact or subdivide it for sale, or sell it all. It is a lien on the future. One man's property will be worth 2,325 guilders in two years' time. Janse's lot is also near those of important burghers: Jan Baptiste van Rensselaer, the surgeon Abraham Staats, the prominent trader Rem Janse. Like the others, he is expected to build on the property and fence it within the next month, but he cannot meet the costs. He joins with another townsman in petitioning for further time to complete the fencing and is given until October. That will give him all the weeks of *handelstijd* to "earn a beaver" in the trade and take in something additional keeping school.

He seems to do his best in the frenzied trading of *handelstijd*. Like everyone else, he has bought merchandise from one of the New Amsterdam wholesalers and means to exchange it — or arrange to have another trader exchange it — for furs. He is still associating with Sybout Claesz and owes him about thirteen beaver pelts for money advanced to him. By mid-August the natives arrive with furs. That means it's also time for the arrival of New Amsterdam creditors or their debt collectors. Most men and women of Beverwijck are in debt to a number of creditors. So the trick for the men of New Amsterdam is to convince the court that they are the first in line to collect. Then the newly acquired pelts are theirs — and not the property of a hatter in Amsterdam or someone holding a mortgage in Beverwijck.

At the height of this trading season, Jan La Montagne comes upriver to Beverwijck. He is in the market town to sue Janse on behalf of two creditors at the Manhatans: one a merchant, the other his father, a physician. Janse appears in the *stadhuis* to defend himself. The merchant Adriaen Keyser has provided La Montagne with letters proving that Janse purchased merchandise worth 64 guilders on his father's estate. He must now make payment. Always careful, Janse presents a note as evidence that his obligation was only 55:5 guilders and that he has paid it or is prepared to pay. Receiving an adverse decision means handing over almost seven beaver pelts. That's a considerable payment: it would provide a supply of bread for almost a year. The court, although it usually pays close attention to cases brought by the burghers of New Amsterdam, decides in Janse's favor. Keyser is advised to present further evidence. He doesn't.

Janse is also sued by the doctor who cared for his wife during a long illness at the Manhatans many months ago. He has been trying to pay off his account in installments and now declares that he has paid 51:5 of the 88 guilders that La Montagne is claiming on his father's behalf. He does not have a receipt — perhaps because the doctor is a fellow Leidenaar and known to him — and therefore must offer his testimony relying on "the best of his knowledge." The bench orders him to pay only 36:5 guilders but leaves the door open for a further suit. Judging from his dealings with Keyser, he seems to surmount indebtedness by meeting just part of the obligations held by many creditors.

Amounts of 36:5, 88, and 55 guilders are not negligible even to the principal traders or farmers. Jeremias van Rensselaer was careful to pay a debt of 2 or 3 guilders; Gerrit Bancker pursued a debt of 302:18 guilders for seventeen years. Nothing earned is insignificant. And just having a hand in the trade, perhaps earning very little, puts a man in the game: it's a way of coming to know the countryside, of making the same mathematical calculations as everyone else, of learning the river channels and natives' castles, of securing friendships and even marriages. But trading with 88 or 55 guilders puts a man among those whom even they call the "least burghers." There are many least burghers. The rewards from trading in furs or grain are always unequal. Everyone knows that, just as they know where each man stands in the hierarchy of the rich and the poor by observing the cargoes that come and go on the foreshore.

So in these months after *handelstijd* has schooled people to their ranking in the town, there are still those who are impoverished. Others, who are not, wish to say they are. Look at the pastureland just north of the fort, the fine land where house lots and gardens were distributed to townsmen. Few houses and fences have been erected. The place is barren, surely evidence of impoverishment for all to see. But that's not so. The lands on the *plein* are unattended — houses and fences still not in place — because another concern, trading with the natives, engages attention so completely. The authorities, the highest authorities, know this.

OCTOBER 15, 1653
Fort Orange

Stuyvesant comes to Beverwijck and remains for about a week. He has credits and debits on his mind, as well as the lands around the fort. Under his direction, Cornelis van Tienhoven has been busy in Fort Amsterdam writing up conveyances confirming land to the lottery winners of the early spring. Now, in the director general's presence, Janse's *grondbrief* is authorized and dated, October 25. But, giving with one hand and taking with the other, Stuyvesant announces that the company is carrying extraordinary expenses in repairing the fort and improving the village's bridges. It is also building a guardhouse and "executing other works." The answer is a tax on properties. A trader owning a house with interior finishings will pay 15 guilders; if he or she has a vacant lot or garden, 7:5 guilders.

In November, Dyckman loses patience with the property holders on the *plein*. He summons fifteen of them and hears evidence why he should not impose a 25-guilder fine on each. Each man appears in court to offer his excuses and avoid the penalty. Janse is among them. Dyckman gets it all into the minutes. He can not have been pleased with the session, for some men use the occasion to ridicule him. Janse's young friend from Leiden, another Adriaen Janse, offers an explanation "so farfetched" that he is made to pay immediately. Another man does the same and uses abusive language. Dyckman, so often the butt of abuse, adds 3 guilders to the fine. Janse makes his appearance. Of all the offenders, he alone pleases the court by not dishonoring it and offers "sufficient" reasons for his negligence. Dyckman registers "Master Adriaen van Ilpendam, schoolmaster" in his minutes but does not record his excuse.

Janse's careful comportment, the restraint that shows itself in his unwillingness to engage in mocking Dyckman — it is, after all, so easy to do — has seemingly not escaped the notice of the townspeople. One man sees it as being servile, behaving "like the dog of all the burghers."

It happened this way. Earlier, in summertime, the men of the burgher guard had gathered in the fort to keep watch. With them was Janse, who was earning something for himself as clerk of the guard, and Jan Janse Stoll, a man of considerable income but given to drink and extreme physical violence. Janse was his chosen victim on a particularly violent night at the guardhouse. Stoll singled him out as a coward, happy only when he was acting as someone's servant. By implication, he lacked the independence that family or a tough personality would bring. Stoll approached him brandishing a sword and offering a handkerchief with which to fight. Only other members of the guard prevented the attack. Witnesses later said that Stoll saved his vile language for Janse alone, calling him "a burgher's dog and boy, yes, the dog of all the burghers." He then struck him, but no one could say why and Janse did not retaliate.

In the coming winter, in February 1654, the court will investigate the case and prepare to bring judgment. February is a time when the magistrates are frequently required to settle — or at least announce their anger about — cases of outright violence and malicious mischief. Shrove Tuesday is near. The mischievous will think it clever to dress as women, fire off guns, perform sexually disgusting acts in public, and generally flout the rules of good behavior. Is it that people have too little to occupy them? Is it that, more than in other seasons, they have time to gather at the inns and one another's houses to tell their stories, compose and distribute lampoons and verses dishonoring the magistrates, concoct wicked nicknames for the magistrates and prominent traders? Do their huddling together against the snow and their drinking incite memories — like the casual yarning about vicious behavior months ago in the guardhouse that, coming now to the ears of magistrates, becomes court testimony:

"Yes, . . . [Stoll] gave Adriaen, the schoolmaster, a handkerchief to fight against him with his sword and threatened to cut him and hack at him."

"Whether in the guardhouse, after the watch was set . . . [Stoll] used much useless and abusive language to one person and another?"

"Yes, but especially to Mr. Adriaen, calling him a burgher's dog and boy, yes, the dog of all the burghers."

The memories of last summer. Story time. Interrogations. The February court pursues its case against Stoll for three successive weeks. Janse is not summoned, nor does he ask to appear. Months ago, he did not take up Stoll's taunt to fight in the guardhouse, nor did he bring a suit against him.

Others would have done so. Between summertime and now, he has not passed along his interpretation of the event. None of his fellow burgher guards have anything to tell of his side of the story.

Among the storytellers and versifiers, the conjurers of nicknames, and the interrogators of the midwinter quiet, he remains silent.

NOVEMBER 7, 1657
Beverwijck

He has got into the property market. The past year has been an exceptionally profitable one for the traders. Even the new director of the *colonie*, young Jeremias van Rensselaer, is euphoric about the 36,000 beaver pelts sent to Holland. Now a brick kiln is being auctioned and draws a considerable number of bidders. It is a good investment. Only one other burgher is operating an oven nearby, and bricks are in demand. Just eighteen months ago, the poorhouse was coming to completion, and the deacons of the church were paying the owner of the oven 116 guilders for 5,800 bricks. Six months later, just a year ago, they paid for 800 more. The magistrates are also building a church. Any prospective buyer has to think too that the terms of sale of the brickyard are fair: three yearly installments, with the first not due until July.

Against many others, Janse remains the last bidder, pledging 1,100 guilders. Perhaps the crowd thinks his bid is accepted because he is from Leiden. The seller is, after all, Joannes de Laet's daughter Johanna. She is already employing two brickmakers from the Leiden area and — another sign of favoritism? — will soon sell her tile kiln to another Leidenaar, a man who sailed with the de Laet family from Holland four years ago. Another Leidenaar, Janse's associate Adriaen Janse Appel, is witness to the sale of Johanna's house on the next day. The present company commissary, Dyckman's replacement, has no regard for either Adriaen Appel or Johanna. To him Appel is cunning and operates outside the law. So does Johanna. To put it shortly: they're Rensselaerswijck. Appel thumbs his nose at the jurisdiction of Beverwijck. Johanna flouts its authority by holding auctions of things such as wood without his permission and — not like everyone else, those who arrange auctions at inns — in the church or van Rensselaer's house. Nevertheless, Janse buys his brickyard.

He can purchase the business because late last year he sold part of his house lot and garden near the fort for a good price. It brought 1,800 Carolus guilders. Properties anywhere near the angles of the fort and on the *plein* are especially attractive. Perhaps sentimentality about the old fort and its surrounds is already growing up. In the late 1660s and even though it will be passing to a third owner, Janse's property will still be "allotment 5." Townspeople might also be aware of the auction of two houses and a garden — *not even fenced in* — for which Dyckman paid 1,627 Carolus guilders. Still, merchants and artisans are now beginning to build houses along two streets well to the north of the fort. One climbs up the high hill and is called Jonckerstraat. The other extends north of the strand and edges along the river. It is Handelaarstraat: the street of the *degelijken handelsmannen,* the solid and trustworthy dealers in furs.

Janse's sale of some of lot 5 also allowed him to purchase, almost immediately, another lot with a house and garden. He was fastidious about the terms. A bedstead had to be made and delivered by the seller; shingles and some posts for the house had to be provided and in good order. Otherwise, it was the usual thing: he bought it in February of last year but would continue to live in half of his house on the *plein* until its delivery to him three months later — when he seems to have had the choice of taking possession of it or renting it to someone trying his luck in the months of *handelstijd.* During June of this year, he had to pay 1,300 guilders in beaver and seawant, the strings of shells valued by the natives. He was able to meet his obligation and did so with a graciousness that the seller thought had to be noted. "I am paid in full," he had Provoost record on the deed, "and I thank him for prompt payment." Seven months later, Janse invested in his brickyard.

To be owner of a brick kiln, schoolmaster, and small-time trader: this seems a strange combination of interests. It is not particularly so. They are the cards Janse is playing in the game of risk-taking that everyone in Beverwijck has pulled up a chair to join. Others play with different cards — an inn, a pair of house lots, a yacht, a sawmill, and a yearly cargo of trading goods. One cannot know when, or why, a player's hand will change, with a yacht discarded for part ownership of a brewery — or a brickyard. Nothing in Janse's background seems to suggest that he would want to take ownership of a brickyard. He will not keep it for more than ten years. And one day, still a decade away, he will invest money in a joint venture, making himself part owner of the cargo of a transatlantic ship. Winning, or just staying in the game, depends on playing each hand as it comes: cutting the cards with people of your own sort and, above all, not showing your hand.

In this respect, perhaps Janse's appearances in the public records of his town — appearances so few and dispersed that they cast little more than shadows — are not infrequent because of the nature of the records. Perhaps his temperament is such that the scenes he allows Dyckman and Provoost to inscribe about his life are enough for him. They are the times when he cannot avoid (as he would prefer) showing his hand.

Consider these still-life scenes, because — as they will say 340 years from Janse's time — it is the only way he is putting himself in the picture.

Only six sketches drawn about daily life in Beverwijck over the past three years include the figure of Adriaen Janse. The first painting is of an auction in an inn. There are the tiny figures of an auctioneer and twenty-eight men. September light reaches the rim of a pewter plate and the edge of a book, a pail and a pillow, a heap of household goods seen in the yard through a half-open door, things on wooden pegs. The figure of Janse is one of a thirty-six-year-old man. Cornelis Steenwyck's is that of a wealthy merchant of New Amsterdam. The miniature face of Herman Janse Scheel, the mason, shows him to be squint-eyed. The figure of Jan Coster van Aecken is holding seven pictures. Surgeon Jacob de Hinsse clutches a book on health, and five other men hold books as well. Janse stands with two platters and six plates worth 4:05 guilders.

He appears again — almost — in a winter scene in 1655. Six figures are in a second-story courtroom. It has no chimney or ceiling. A trapdoor allows entry to the room. Floorboards slant because the wooden building itself is sagging. A man stands with his hand uplifted in an oath. The others are magistrates, listening. On the desk can be seen a petition yet to be considered. The standing figure is accused of inventing lewd nicknames for the houses of fourteen prominent townsmen and -women. He is in the middle of swearing that the episode occurred while he was drinking after the funeral of a friend's child. He knows only that he heard others saying he contrived the names. The petition on the desk is not a matter of such mischief. It bears the signature of Adriaen van Ilpendam and prays for the exclusive right to keep day and night school. To it is added a marginal note: the honorable court cannot find sufficient reason for doing so.

In a third scene, he is one of four figures. It is three days before Christmas. In a small room somewhere, a quartet of businessmen are posed together. They sit before two copies of a document bearing their signatures. The men know each other. One, Adriaen Gerritsz Papendorp, has the look of a magistrate. He has signed the paper agreeing to pay 1,800 Carolus guilders to a second figure in the scene, Adriaen Janse, for his lot and garden. The figure of Rem Janse is painted into the group portrait as well. He fits in because he will, separately, buy a corner of Janse's property. Andries Herpertsz looks out from the picture as witness.

Two months go by. Adriaen Janse sits for another group portrait. Four of the town's leading men pose together in the fort. It is now the residence of the new commissary, Johannes La Montagne. He is an older man, the physician who cared for Janse's wife in New Amsterdam. Close by are two fellow magistrates and wealthy traders. Their business is obviously a paper lying on the table. Like other such portraits, this one invites us to read some of the writing. It is a confirmation of Gerritsz's ownership of allotment 5. We see that Janse is addressed as "honorable" and "burgher and citizen of this village."

About the end of January 1657: a winter scene. Small houses of darkened wood are shown strewn across the surface of the picture. Tiny bunched figures are braced against the cold. Caspar Jacobsz Halenbeeck's house, and a garden with cherry trees, is a miniature scene within unconnected scenes all around. In it, a vendue master is at work offering the property for sale. Someone else records the bids. Jacobsz stands by, waiting. Harmen Jacobsz Bembos, collector of the excise on beer and spirits, makes the last and successful bid. Adriaen Janse and a carpenter are off to the side and ready to sign their names as Jacobsz's sureties.

In November, the townspeople tumble once again onto canvas. He is with them. Johanna de Laet is auctioning her brickyard. Again, energetic figures are painted in. Janse wins the bid.

But one among the miniaturized faces is missing. Johannes Dyckman has had to let deputies do his work for two years now. For all that time, he has been confined to his house and unable to act as his own secretary. He blames it on a community greatly multiplying in numbers. Others, those waiting to have his job, think differently and want to see the end of him. Whether he is insane or senile or suffering from a stroke — "it is doubtful," writes one, "which is most impeded his understanding or speech" — he should leave. His wife has been spoken to: take him to the Manhatans and then by warship to Holland. She can't, however, make up her mind and will speak directly to the director general. He needs to have an explanation of her husband's behavior because he has already been called to task for some illegible, and illogical, papers of Dyckman's that somehow reached the company directors at home. He has been forced to explain that they are the work of "the drunkard, Johannes Dyckman."

The greatly multiplied community does the usual thing. It makes Dyckman the butt of its humor: the "sayings of Dyckman" are still good for a
laugh. At the same time it is compassionate. Maria and Johannes Dyckman
stay in Beverwijck. In ten years' time, Janse and the congregation of which
he is a part will be providing alms to Dyckman — they will encourage another recipient, but not him, to work off some of the costs by cleaning the
church. Three years later, the deacons will record that "the old set of pau-
pers" has nearly disappeared. But not Johannes Dyckman. It will be another
two years before they will pay 40 guilders to Mother Dyckman toward the
expenses of his funeral.

In 1657 and 1658 the town builds a new *stadhuis*. Its construction seems a
brickmaker's delight. It is a "brick building, with two cellars, each 21 feet
square, separated by a two-brick wall." The stone foundation rises from
ground level in "a brick wall, two feet high and three bricks thick" and carrying the cellar beams. The first story is divided into three parts: at the
north and south ends are rooms with brick chimneys, and in the middle is
a hallway separated from the large north room by a one-brick-thick wall.
The upper story is divided by a half-brick wall. Altogether, it is a strong
building, "the walls below and above . . . being one and a half bricks thick,
provided at each end with a double chimney, braced by 42 anchors and
built of clinker brick."

One guilder for every fifty bricks! Yet if Adriaen Janse is in Beverwijck to
direct any of the work of baking and carting — and taking his earnings —
or if, by some chance, he is not the *steenbakker* the magistrates use, he does
nothing to reveal it.

JULY 22, 1658
Beverwijck

Another auction is held. As usual, payment is due in eight days in beaver
valued at 8 guilders the pelt. About thirty men and one woman come together. There are ordinary household goods for sale. Four or five men stand
around selling their wares. Jan de Groot offers household stuff, a straw mat-
tress and pillow, a bearskin and two books, a shovel and two jugs, an old
suit of clothes. Barent van Marle, waiting for bids, watches over his eight or
nine rolls of tobacco as a clutch of four men look interested. Another man
displays six knives and a pistol. The hatmaker is selling stockings and a ring.

The glassmaker stands with a gun for sale. He interests Janse, who buys it for 20 guilders.

Janse's name is again in the records. Yet if he is anxious about his privacy, he needn't worry. It will be over 260 years before the record of this scene will be translated out of what will then be thought an odd language and written down in English. English is the language of those under whose rule he will live for the last twenty-two years of his life.

For now and at least from the pages of the town's public records, he disappears for the next two years.

CHAPTER 5　Beverwijck:
　　　　　　　The Final Years

SEPTEMBER 1, 1660
Beverwijck

Janse has now been keeping school in Beverwijck for almost ten years.
The years — the regularities of the school quarters, the collection of tuitions — seem to have gone smoothly enough. But this year is different: it
has been so since May, and it has been so for everyone. The trade has not
been good for two years. Competition intensifies, and with it danger. The
woods around the town explode into violence. Like hectares in a bushfire,
the gullies and paths where native traders can be waylaid ignite into beat-
ings and theft. The competition of one burgher against another incinerates
the ground for weeks, sparks of treachery and name-calling fall into the
town itself, men seem not to care if another man's household is ruined.

Survival is uppermost. The burghers do uncharacteristic things. Twenty-
five principal *handelaars* publicly declare themselves. Let no one go into the
woods except those who can employ Indian brokers. Eighty small traders
sign a counterpetition: no, let everyone "be allowed to do the best he can."
The court vacillates, letting grassfires of disobedience and mayhem grow
but knowing that nothing is surer than that Stuyvesant will come upriver
soon, recognize that the company's regulations are a pile of cinders, and
allow the town's magistrates and merchants to regulate the trade. It is the
Manhatans from 1649 to 1653 all over again.

Everyone suffers. Adriaen Janse does not declare himself a trader or put himself alongside any of the public petitioners. He does, however, bring some of the parents of his schoolchildren to court for failure to pay school fees. It is the first time he has had to do so, and he has waited until this day in early September when *handelstijd* is nearly at its end and they may have something coming to them from the trade. He knows all the men and women, three of them well. Only one among them is not a commoner. Cornelis Teunisse Bos was nominated as magistrate four years ago and has frequently been able to act as a guarantor of considerable debts undertaken by his associates. He acted as one of Janse's sureties when he purchased the brickyard. It was only three months after pledging 3,225 guilders to buy his own large house, together with a cow stable, hog sty, bleaching field, and bake oven. Now, at the age of forty-six, he is someone to be reckoned with. Janse and the whole town have watched him become increasingly defiant of the trading laws. He blames the chaos of the trade on self-serving magistrates, each of whom is a prominent *handelaar*. Just recently he announced that he would "wipe his . . . [ass] on the ordinance" until the principal traders were prosecuted for ignoring it, like everyone else. He was fined 1,200 guilders and banished.

Neither Janse nor any of his other creditors expected him to comply, and he did not. Rather, he openly sent his servants into the woods, organized the petition of small traders, and took on a leading trader for calling him and other small traders "a rabble." Now he is in Janse's own situation: debts have piled up, but people will not extend credit. Friends undercut one another and everyone is disadvantaged. Townspeople even betray one another by sending messages to natives, little notes to tell them where they live and can be found. Soon the magistrates will be summoning Teunisse to explain his failure to meet payments on a property. He won't appear. Nor does he come to court now to face Janse.

Janse must also bring suits against Lambert van Valckenburgh and Pieter Lookermans. For several years he and van Valckenburgh have been together as members of the burgher guard. Lambert and his wife, Annatie, arrived in Beverwijck six years ago, with children aged eight and two. The older boy, Jochem, would have required schooling: in the future, certainly by the age of seventeen, he is able to write, perhaps thanks to Janse. It is something his father cannot do. Probably Lambert and Annatie's younger child, now eight, is presently Janse's pupil. They have failed to pay 6 guilders in beaver for about half a year's tuition. It is hardly an exorbitant fee. The local surgeon is charging people the same price, two beavers a year, for his own form of medical insurance. Annatie appears in court, taking the voice that women have in matters of schooling. She admits the debt and agrees to pay.

When Pieter Lookermans enters the courtroom, Janse is facing a friend known for about five years. The young man owned a property next to Janse's lot 5. When Janse needed guarantors to secure his bid for the brickyard, Lookermans joined Teunisse in offering security. He also acted as a witness when Janse purchased his house in town. Lookermans is a builder, so he is no stranger to suits about incomplete work or debt. He is also a fur trader, and he too has put his name to Teunisse's petition. Last month, in August, he sold off some property in the town: a sure sign of being squeezed by a creditor. Now he has let the school fees go unpaid for a full year. He agrees to pay Janse two beavers in six weeks' time.

Janse tries to get justice from three other burghers. Among them, Gillis Pietersz has a large family, which he supports as a carpenter. Hendrick and Maria, ten and eight, are of lower school age and likely to be Janse's pupils. Probably Tryntie, aged twelve, is a pupil of his as well. Pietersz's debt is, like his family, a large one, about 84 guilders, or five years of schooling. Still, he agrees to pay. Willem Brouwer is also a carpenter and a trader. He has never made a secret of flouting the trading regulations. But now he has signed Teunisse's petition and gone further, daring the court to charge him. He is saying in all directions that he has sent his servant into the woods. "You can do as you like." Like Teunisse, he seems dismissive of Janse's suit and fails to appear in court.

Schooling fees: these are a small part of the community's agony. To Janse they are not inconsequential, but there is something petty about them. A schoolmaster's fees are as often reckoned in stivers as guilders, rather like pennies to dollars. His everyday needs are also small and cheap. For about 15 guilders he can get 38 items: 16 books of paper, 8 bunches of quills, 3 pounds of material for ink, 3 penknives, 2 whetstones, 2 almanacs, 2 rulers, 1 small writing book, and a half pound of sealing wax. He is always doing close work, repetitious, relatively trifling. People might know that the rich merchants, even as they do in *patria*, pay more for their summer clothes than for school fees. In church they sit in the front benches. The schoolmaster leads his pupils into the church and sits with them, or he should. It is quite a difference. Back home, in Overijssel, the burgomasters are saying that the schoolmaster should have a special attachment to the church. But they have godly women in mind: he should be, they say, just like the devout housewife. And here a man will ask to be a teacher because he has only one hand. What does that say? Do the happenings in court serve to accentuate in his own mind the pettiness of his interests and occupation and his own unimportance?

Think of Tuesday, September 28. For a second time, he is before the bench awaiting the appearance of Cornelis Teunisse, who again fails to come. Yet within the hour, it could not have been longer, Teunisse does appear. He is responding to the summons of one of the wealthy *handelaars* and faces the man squarely because they have made themselves bitter contestants in the trade. They are powerful men. They have partners who underwrite and enlarge their ventures. Others have partners as well: many have a partner so they can trade with the English "to the north." Some are dealing regularly with the French. A few have joined together to settle two new villages. Janse has none. His "partners" are the parents of his schoolchildren. Their support of him is transient. Nor does he have a patron. Jeremias van Rensselaer, Philip Pietersz Schuyler, Goose Gerritsz van Schaick, people like Rut Jacobsz and Teunisse, they are not men who have any need for him. Yet without a stable partnership with a prominent merchant — everyone calls it "friendship" and waits for it to bring new adventures and profits — he would be among those about whom Kiliaen van Rensselaer once spoke. "One cannot get as far," he warned, "by "well-doing as by having friends in the game."

He also lacks family. He has not, as they put it, been brothered or sistered by his parents. He cannot be to a niece or nephew what David Janse was to him. Nor can they be a safety net for him. Last year his cousin Sophije van Lodesteijn and her husband, Carel de Beauvois, came to New Netherland to live. Janse might have envied Carel for the career that soon opened before him. Within two years he was schoolmaster for the growing congregation at Breukelen on Long Island. He was given public responsibilities and then, in another two years, voted a salary of 75 guilders "to give him more encouragement." There is no one concerned to give Janse encouragement. For twenty-three years more, he will live with his wife, but he will not be able to acknowledge that her family has, even once, been of assistance to him.

Still, the community is growing. Men and women want the protection that written documents provide. Even the magistrates have been counting on writing to give the market town its future. They want page after page of court minutes in which Stuyvesant will read that only the greater independence of the town from the company will prevent a breakdown of authority and, ominously, hostilities with the Mohawk. The whole summer has been a dangerous gamble that before violence tore the trading town apart, the narrative of it would bring its cessation.

But if the power of the magistrates is played out as much in their books as in their day-to-day activities, it is the same for ordinary townspeople. Ledgers accounting for produce and rentals and river trips, bills and receipts, all catch them up and alter their lives almost as much as climate and geography.

Now at the *colonie*, too, old records are at the heart of the year's activities as never before. The van Rensselaer family is questioning van Slichtenhorst's books and his demands for back payment of salary amounting to 13,799 guilders. For months Jeremias has been gathering evidence, making copies of old minutes, and searching for contracts in ledgers like "a thin white book . . . about a finger thick" and "a blue book of the same size, but somewhat thicker." Once found, the original papers and accounts are to be packed up and sent to Holland. Copies will go by another ship. "Everything" written down is wanted. Even if it is not exactly like a skilled bookkeeper's audit, an account, the family tells him, "can be worked out later." Jeremias is instructed to write "by every ship," and "all those [other colonists] who wish to write" may enclose their letters with his. Jeremias can call upon a secretary and accountants to protect him and the family from such exorbitant claims and his own misjudgments. His *schout* is there to offer interpretations of the civil and criminal law. Even the *schout's* provost, as a schoolmaster, is someone from whom ordinary colonists can seek advice about the law or anything else that confuses them.

Now, for the first time, the townspeople are to have such an ally too. They are to have a notary.

JANUARY 1661
Beverwijck

Dirck van Schelluyne has been in Rensselaerswijck for five months now. He has taken up a position as secretary of the *colonie* but is also serving as notary in Beverwijck. Janse would know him from the Manhatans and from early times in the *colonie* when he was schoolmaster and van Schelluyne secretary for a while. He is someone for Janse to study. He seems a model of the honorable and learned notary.

Van Schelluyne's skills have been in demand. Already he has drawn up twenty-three *attestaties*, and over the next four and one-half years he will draw up more than three hundred. If he makes two copies of each, he is writing up about 1,430 pages. People will come to him, or he will go to them, at all hours: eight o'clock in the morning, four o'clock in the after-noon, and nine o'clock in the evening. They will find him every day of the week, but mostly on Tuesdays and Saturdays, less on Fridays and Wednes-days, seldom on Sunday. Sometimes he is away — or ill? or on private busi-ness? — for weeks. His busiest months are July to October. During those months of this year, he will meet with 172 parties to contracts and 162 wit-nesses. Next year, he will meet with 196 clients and 101 witnesses. Among them, about 8 in 10 men and 4 in 10 women are literate: they can sign their names.

Even though he has been a notary elsewhere for about ten years — at home in Gornichem, in New Amsterdam, on Long Island — he has a great deal to learn. He would see in his own papers that he is catching on to ways of simplifying the formalities of documents. He learns, for example, that he need not include the occupations of witnesses, and he picks up tidier phrases, those that reduce detail to a few comprehensive words. He is also learning the town's history as it is being lived out. He knows many of the burghers' secrets. But by bringing them to him, they can begin to settle a di-vorce, recount a crime and at least move the matter toward resolution, have a last testament drawn up. It's a problem solved, at least legally.

In eight years' time, Janse will qualify as a notary. Nowhere does he say how he acquired this learning. Yet later this year he will serve as witness to one of van Schelluyne's acts and will, for the first time, reach for a legal word to put alongside his signature. Self-consciously he writes, "Adriaen van Ilpendam, *testis*." And van Schelluyne's double role as *colonie* secretary and sole notary in Beverwijck — and in the hamlets of Schenectady and Bethle-hem — is a demanding one. A clerk or apprentice might well be needed. Often he is working in the *colonie* and Beverwijck on the same day and for several clients. Frequently his responsibilities would be overwhelming.

From late May to early November, for example, he must meet with about 260 people and complete work on 82 legal papers. He has to lay down about 2,200 lines. August 16 is a typically crowded day. Jeremias's cousin is depart-ing for Holland and has given one of the local farmers power of attorney to collect his debts. He and his witnesses meet with the notary. Like all these things, the matter is complicated, and van Schelluyne must be in the *colonie* for a considerable time. Another meeting takes place in Beverwijck on the same day. He has called six men together. He and three others among them have been arbitrating a dispute between the other two burghers. The note-taking begins. He must work out the wording of the agreement between the two parties and get their signatures. He must then write up the terms reached by the adjudicators, obtain their signatures, and add their statement as a sort of appendix to the agreement. Further time is given to concluding the occasion ceremoniously: the disputants shake hands in the presence of the arbiters and thank them.

Still on the same day, and again in Rensselaerswijck, van Schelluyne assembles witnesses to two parties agreeing to the lease of a house and garden. Again the terms are not straightforward — the walls of the back room of the house have to be faced with brick before sale, the roof must be repaired. He will have to write up two pages. He also has paperwork arising from duties that were his before he came to Beverwijck. And all through August, the departure of Jeremias's cousin keeps him busy with work. The young man has been careful in settling his accounts. He has made dozens of his debtors sign bonds promising future payment. He has also agreed with colonists to act as their legal representative in *patria*. There is no set of uninterrupted days for van Schelluyne until after September 3. Then he begins again on September 7, though the work is not as steady. Meanwhile, he has his obligations as secretary to the *colonie*.

There is a place for a man like Janse. Perhaps it is humiliating to be a notary's clerk, any kind of clerk, at his age. He is now forty-two. Yet if van Schelluyne takes him on, he has access to the notary's books, and if he watches van Schelluyne's work closely and copies his ways, he is learning from a master. For in his instruments, van Schelluyne stays within the limitations that the legal requirements and tradition impose on his use of language. Yet he also finds room for the elaboration of an original style, for the occasional fanciful touch and modulations of expression. In a will made jointly for a man and his wife, for example, he writes, "both being sound in body, walking and standing, and using and being in full possession of their faculties, reason, memory and understanding." Sometimes he adds "as far as one could outwardly judge," sometimes he doesn't. He likes to use an occasional Latin or French term. He enjoys being baroque, writing "the last day of March anno XVIc and sixty-one" rather than "thus done and executed in Beverwijck." Sometimes he spins his signature into curlicues like van Merwen's. To give a sense of urgency, he uses phrases that are repetitious. He enjoys "fully paid and satisfied, the last penny with the first" and "pregnant and with child."

One day Janse will use these modulations himself. He will formulate documents that balance the requirements of the law with the idiosyncrasies of his clients' wishes. He will include statements that disclose the emotions of the parties involved, like van Schelluyne writing, "The parties . . .thank each other for the respect and friendship shown and [intend] to be and

16. *Autograph attestation before Adriaen van Ilpendam, 1676/77. Janse's script is generally more carefully formed than that of van Schelluyne, possibly because he sharpened his pen to a finer point. Neither writes as beautiful a hand as van Tienhoven, Provoost, or the merchant Jan Baptiste van Rensselaer. (Albertsen [Uythoff], Wooter, Manuscripts and Archives Division, The New York Public Library, Astor, Lenox and Tilden Foundations)*

remain good friends." Or he will write, "This is a matter very grievous to both sides."

Even if he is not van Schelluyne's apprentice, Janse must have joined other burghers in noticing the standards the notary sets for himself. To the hundreds of men and women who read his words on one or two of his papers there is evidence of meticulousness, initiative, and familiarity with a complex commercial world. Sensitive to his clients' needs and their expectation of confidentiality, he is what one writer called the *secret professionel.*

And he is that, the professional man of secrets, to others who share his skills. Next year, he will receive a business letter from Salomon Lachaire, notary of New Amsterdam. He will be addressed as *confrater.* Expectations will be expressed about acting with "civility" on Lachaire's behalf. For this courtesy, he may count on "similar service" on future occasions.

Van Schelluyne is a man set apart. In Amsterdam and The Hague, there are special spaces for notaries. This is not the case in Beverwijck, perhaps not even in New Amsterdam. Yet one day, not far off but in places far away, Janse will see just how special they are.

17. De Dam met Stadhuis, *G. Berckheijde, 1673. The Amsterdam Town Hall was completed in the 1660s. The playwright Joost van Vondel praised it as the achievement of civic republicanism. It symbolized Dutch federalism at a time when the economies of other European states were centralized under absolute monarchs. New Netherland shared in this exceptionalism until the English came. The* stadhuis *was also a place of notaries. They served as clerks of the law enforcement officer and city council. They were assigned rooms near the Chamber of the Magistrates. Two councillors examined the credentials of intending notaries and registered their oath of office. By the early eighteenth century, seventy notaries — ten too many, thought the council — were practicing in the city. (Amsterdams Historisch Museum)*

SATURDAY, MAY 26, 1663
Beverwijck

Janse is acting as a witness to the will of Harmen Thomassen and his wife, Catalina Bercx. It is five o'clock in the evening. He and two other neighbors of the couple are watching van Schelluyne at work. Catalina and her husband are in good health. She is in fact pregnant. The writing takes place in their home.

Van Schelluyne is either taking notes or writing the hundreds of words that will complete the testament. The couple are trying to think ahead, imagining all the assets that might one day make up their estate, "claims and credits," even "gold and silver, coined and uncoined," and jewels. So the notary takes notes that either there or later will fill two full pages. On the third page, he writes Janse's name or, more carefully, "Mr. Adriaen van Ilpendam." Janse has agreed to act as a guardian of the couple's children, should that become necessary. A fourth page of writing follows and then the signatures.

Janse knows why Thomassen and Bercx are being so cautious. The improvident ways of Dirck Bensingh are the cause. Bensingh was Catalina's first husband and left her with many debts: he couldn't settle peacefully on a lot he received about the same time Janse got his; he thought the surveyor was robbing him of a few feet; he blamed members of the court, calling them a pack of rascals, villains, and dogs. For years he ran up unpaid bills and, at the same time, tried to collect money in all directions, from the company, from Groningen at home, from distant family.

About nine months ago, Thomassen was in New Amsterdam. Something had to be done about his and Catalina's finances. Already it was the last Saturday in August, and the summer ships would soon sail for Holland. A friend from Beverwijck was preparing to make the voyage and could assist him in calling in debts in Holland. He made his way to the house of Salomon Lachaire and employed the notary to entrust his friend with his power of attorney.

Lachaire would have taken good care of Thomassen — and he would also have been sure to exact his fees. He has provided himself with the most useful books and learned how to use them judiciously. De Damhouder and van Zutphen on criminal and civil law, Rooseboom's introduction to the laws and ordinances of Amsterdam, Gerard van Wassenaar's work on law and the art of the notary are all references in his possession. He has books on Roman-Dutch law. He can locate citations from the works of Grotius: chapter 35 on personal injury, chapter 15 on the execution of a contract of sale. He has a Dutch translation of Justinian's *Institutes*. He consults the printed volumes of *zee-rechten*, using a volume in which the customs of Amsterdam are bound together with those of other cities and towns that also look out on the Zuider Zee: Hoorn, Enkhuizen, Edam, Monnikendam, Weesp, Muiden, and Naarden. These are followed by the maritime regulations of Wisbuy and the Hanse cities. So he will remind the court, for example, that any captain who, without reasonable and lawful cause, discharges his seamen at the place where bulk is first broken must pay their full wages. In these ways, Lachaire serves the community of resident merchants as well as the strangers who continually enter the port of New Amsterdam and expect to find courts and notaries who understand their business. For the resident traders of the small English "nation," he has

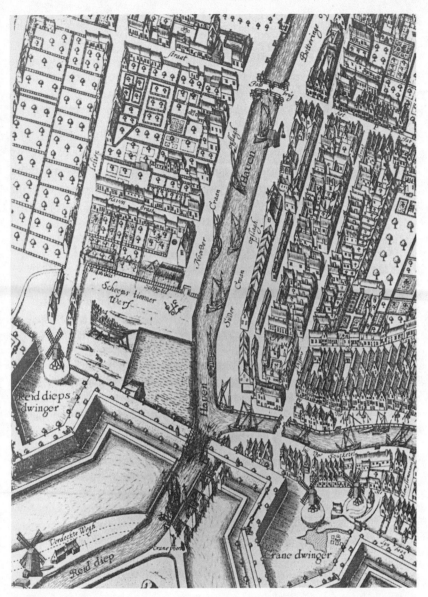

18. *Map of Groningen, Egbert Haubois, c. 1635. In 1656, Dirck Bensingh gave power of attorney to Roelof Gerritsz, cranemaster at Groningen, to collect his wages from the Groningen chamber of the West India Company. The map shows the company's docks, where Gerritzs would have worked amid its cranes, wharves, ropewalk, and warehouses. Negotiations with men and women in the Netherlands were many and important to the colonists. They gave Janse's predecessor close to one-third of his income from 1660 to 1664. For Janse, practicing after the imposition of English rule, they provided less than 3 percent. (Gemeentearchief Groningen)*

learned a bit of English. He helps them and other New Amsterdammers do business in Maryland, New England, Virginia, and Rhode Island.

Thomassen would have found in Lachaire a slightly idiosyncratic man. He has a sharp tongue in court, likely to caricature a client's opponent as "an inexperienced comedian forgetting whose character he represented." He is also a busy man. At all hours, he is found at his writing: at the ferry, in the jail, on shipboard. He is in court, then off to Breukelen, then hastening away for a "verbal consultation" — and his fee. He will work for three hours writing up a single lease. Such busyness — presumably it is such busyness — makes his register an untidy parcel of papers. And at the time of Thomassen's visit, the papers would be even more careless because the ships are leaving for Holland and he will be in great haste. He likes these departures, of course, just as he relishes the arrival of ships, sometimes bothering to scribble the names of incoming vessels riding at anchor. No one would appreciate better the message that the author of a *notarisboek* would one day write about such a man: "The Sea, the Land, the City and the Church all give him brisk employment."

Thomassen will have been well served, however. He will have his papers within three days. Perhaps Lachaire will also remind him, either for his information or for his sense of security when he arrives in Amsterdam, that the magistrates of the city keep a Register Book of Powers of Attorney. Lachaire knows such things.

That was last year. Now, having helped Thomassen and Bercx arrange an estate for themselves and their children, Janse and the two witnesses carry on as their neighbors. Catalina's children are aged from four to thirteen. No one can know that in little over a year's time, they will continue to live in their town but under English rule. In twelve years' time — when the eldest boy is twenty-five and a brother twenty — the two young men will need a contract to buy farmland and will come to Janse. He will write it up in Dutch, a language that will still be theirs. He will, however, identify himself as living in the place with the strange name, and he will have only recently encountered the curiously hostile outsider calling himself Robert Livingston.

FEBRUARY 2, 1664
New Amsterdam

A concourse of citizens gathers to celebrate before the town hall on Wall Street. The ago-old rituals of municipal elections have been set in motion. Four days ago, the city's *schout* called for nominations. The presiding burgomasters and *schepenen* assembled and offered the names of men "peace-loving and . . . fit for that office." Now it is Saturday and they are meeting again in the presence of Stuyvesant's secretary. They are merchants holding the power of the city seated alongside merchants holding the power of the province. The voting is completed, and the crowd plays its part as an enthusiastic audience to the news of the new city officials — or, if not enthusiastic, at least loyal. What is it they say: Either arrange your life and affairs in accordance with the duly appointed authorities or, if there is a problem of conscience, move away.

Yet on this occasion, there is rumor of bloodshed from an impending English invasion and news of other terrible costs that allegiance will require. In six days' time Stuyvesant is using the same fearful word, bluntly warning of "bloodshed" before an assembly of his councilors and municipal officials. The desperate defensive precautions that such independent trading cities as Naarden, Den Brielle, and Leiden had been forced to adopt against enemies at home are now New Amsterdam's and Fort Amsterdam's to make: the long series of decisions that will have to be made over many months, then men quarreling among themselves, then seeing themselves lapse into passivity, finally trying to negotiate while preparing for siege warfare. Unless the enemy can somehow be reasoned with or bought off, armed hostilities must come.

So in late August and early September, Stuyvesant will be writing his enemy with "the utmost respect and civility." He will cite Grotius on the Dutch right of possession to New Netherland based on "first discovery, uninterrupted possession and Purchase of the land." There will be reasoned suggestions that the matter be settled by the two governments in Europe. But for now Stuyvesant is saying to his councilors and the burgomasters that the walls, bastions, and *waterpoortjes* — all notoriously inadequate — must be reinforced. Like it or not, outlivers will flee the countryside and come inside. The military will station itself at whatever outer defenses can be thrown up, but every burgher must defend his place within the city walls. The English will mount their attack directly at New Amsterdam. They have long had "the desire to plunder [it] or obtain booty."

And why not? In two weeks' time, the burgomasters themselves are pointing this out to one another. By their own exertions, the residents have made it a place of "so many fine houses" that "it surpasses nearly every other place in these parts of North America." It is the capital of a veritable granary of cereals, a favored land of "many villages, hundreds of farms, with houses, grain, cattle and nearly ten thousand souls, mostly Dutchmen and

19. Insert from The Island of Manhados, The Towne of New-York. *c. 1664–68 (cartographer unknown). As in the Netherlands, a besieged city such as New Amsterdam counted on water and walls for defense. Here the fortified wall from the Hudson River to the East River is indicated, with one of the bastions, a "half moon," set up before the town hall. The map was probably made for Governor Richard Nicolls soon after the arrival of the English in 1664. (By permission of the British Library)*

some Frenchmen, who in the course of years and with God's blessing" will "grow into a great people." Now, for its safety, the city needs to be encircled. The inner line of defense is obvious. From a bastion erected at the water gate near Pearl and Wall streets, a line of palisades must be driven into the water south and then around to the bulwark in front of the town hall. Palisades must then be in place to the southernmost points of the strand. Then a battery is needed and more palisades to prevent a landing along *'t Noordt Rivier* (Hudson River). Then another bastion will be needed and more palisades running down to the river's edge, and finally a stone wall across the island.

As usual, the merchants and richest burghers must carry the costs of these fortifications. They must lend the city money and await repayment in not less than a year and, more realistically, closer to five. Stuyvesant and his secretary set the example — each offering at least 1,000 guilders — while the municipal officers do the same. By the end of February, more than a hundred loans are arranged. It gives the city a treasury of about 28,000 guilders.

So it goes on. By early March, contracts are let for the building of the fortifications. No one knows that on March 18 the English king, Charles II, has already given New Netherland to his brother James, Duke of York. Yet everyone knows by mid-March that, give or take some accuracy, "the English . . . [will try to] take and possess this place, Fort Orange and the Manhattans within 6 or 8 weeks." War preparations continue to be put in place. By June, it is known that there will be an amphibious landing of English troops. Ship captains are put on alert. By late August, the inhabitants are required to labor at throwing up earthworks, one-third of the available men rostered each day. Now it is known that the invasion will come in the form of four frigates. On August 29 one and then three men-of-war show themselves at Sandy Hook and then anchor up the bay, closer in. Stuyvesant sends a delegation, trying the usual conciliation. "Why does the English hostile fleet . . . [lie] in the bay before New Netherland?" In respect to the government of this place, they are out of order in arriving without announcing themselves. What is "the intent and meaning of their approach and continuing in the harbor?"

Conciliation fails. A letter is delivered to Stuyvesant on the following day. The king of England considers them "fforraigners" and usurpers who have "seated themselves" in his dominions. Their choices are the centuries-old ones. They must surrender all possessions into the enemy commander's "protection" or expect death (the "effusion of Christian blood") and "all the miseryes of a Warr." Stuyvesant and the merchants take the measure of their situation. They summon the ten bakers of the city to discover the number of days that the stocks of grain would allow them to hold out against the siege. Meanwhile, someone does the calculations on manpower: there are enough burghers to post all along the inner defensive line, but even if every man were used, they would be fifty feet apart and useless. Officials in neighboring non-Dutch settlements write saying they cannot assist but, on the contrary, feel obliged to support the invaders. The frigates, they hint, carry about two thousand men: with themselves added, that makes thousands more. On September 4, the warships excite terror by coming to the island under full sail. They train their cannon on the city and position themselves for an immediate assault.

Two days later, Stuyvesant and the magistrates begin the process of surrender, he for the West India Company and the merchants for the trading city of New Amsterdam. They must do what countless other Dutch city regents have done before them: exonerate themselves of responsibility — it is, isn't it, a matter of overwhelming circumstances? — and get it all in writing.

They must also sue for the best possible terms — and immediately look for ways of ransoming the city or otherwise getting it back into their own hands.

WEDNESDAY, JULY 16, 1664
New Amsterdam

Getting things right is occupying Stuyvesant and the city officials in another way. Some time just before this Wednesday of midsummer, Hendrick Janse Smitt left his house near van Tienhoven's in Bridge Street — or perhaps he took his leave from an inn or friend's house. He made his way to the Fresh Pond outside the city walls. There he hanged himself on the branch of a tree. They called such an act self-murder. To churchmen and believers, it meant everlasting punishment among the damned. To the state, it was a capital offense. He had robbed himself of his own life.

Now Pieter Tonneman, the same man who had assembled the burgomasters and *schepenen* for municipal elections five months earlier, must enforce the law. Just as there are protocols surrounding the defense and surrender of a city, there are rules concerning the punishment of a *zelfmoordenaar*. They are codified and clear. Tonneman knows them. He takes custody of the corpse at the small pond and calls for the enactment of the law.

He demands that the magistrates declare Smitt's goods forfeit to the city. His corpse must be "drawn on a hurdle . . . [through the streets] as an example and terror to others." It must then be dragged to the place where the body was found hanging and there "be shoved under the earth." A "stake, pole or post" must be erected there "in token of an accursed deed."

It would have been no different in a city such as Leiden. There from 1600 until the year of Smitt's death, the bench heard only twenty-six cases of suicide. It too expected its *schout* to go to the place of the crime, gather evidence, and then advise on proper sentencing. It heard cases of women — who often murdered themselves by taking poison or slashing themselves with knives — and men who, like Smitt, generally took their lives by hanging. Except that corpses were sometimes given over to the university for medical examination, it was all the same. In about 1660, Leiden's magistrates began to take account of special circumstances: family members said that a man was disturbed, loved ones pleaded that a woman was not herself.

And the burgomasters and *schepenen* of New Amsterdam do the same. They hear Tonneman's case but give judgment against him. Smitt was, after all, "an old Burgher" of the city. Though he was once reprimanded for selling drink at his house on a Sunday and later summoned for keeping late hours and allowing "noisy singing and chanting" to go on into the night, he was a man of reasonably good behavior. Also, eight of his neighbors have put together a petition praying that he be accorded a decent burial. The magistrates yield. They decide that Smitt's body is to be interred in a corner of the churchyard but "in the evening after the ringing of the nine o'clock bell." In Leiden, the magistrates thought it just to do the same thing. The body might be buried in the Vrouwenkerkhof but after ten o'clock and usually at midnight. The family was not permitted to celebrate the familiar rituals of grieving. They could not engage an *aanspreker* to invite relatives and friends to a funeral. All had to be done "in the quiet of the night."

Yet if Smitt's body is put to a peaceful rest, the matter of the city's authority in handling the case is not. When Stuyvesant is told of the proceedings, he approves the sentence against Smitt but not the "form" of its presentation. Judgment in cases of capital crimes, he insists, is in the jurisdiction of the States General and the company. It is not a case for the city court to decide. As he has done for the past eighteen years, he continues to make the municipality fight for every inch of its independence. Even now, the matter remains undecided.

Meanwhile it's clear that, though Smitt has been granted the court's and the provincial council's mercy, the law is unrelenting and the criminal nature of self-murder unequivocal: the *schout*'s act of taking a corpse into custody by removing it from the Fresh Pond is equivalent to apprehending a capital offender off the streets.

Harshly, it is a question of what to do with a murderer.

WEDNESDAY, SEPTEMBER 24, 1664
Beverwijck

An English garrison enters Beverwijck. Johannes La Montagne surrenders. Nine years of military occupation begin.

Adrian Janse says and writes nothing.

CHAPTER 6 · Albany

1665, 1666
Albany

Colonel George Cartwright has retired from Beverwijck. He leaves behind about 60 of the 450 soldiers now occupying New Netherland. Captain John Baker is in command. Cartwright has named the town Albany. The men take over the old fort, hoisting the flag of the New England colonies. They commandeer some of the surrounding land for their horses and stables. Most men need to be billeted. They are unwanted by the burghers, who start to quarrel among themselves about distributing the outsiders to various households. The soldiers intimidate the burghers but are sullenly excluded in return. Just as the townspeople do, they begin to experience the sort of culture of coercion that occupation brings. They're both victors and victims. Like it or not, everyone is involved in days, and then months, of fashioning one another. Like the land around the old fort, all the spaces of life are shifting, the social and moral ones too.

How Adriaen Janse would tell the story of the English conquest and the beginnings of occupation — how the town would tell the story — we do not know. There is a great deal of silence. The English have stories to tell. They are new stories for them, the first ones told of places like Beverwijck — and now from the inside out: administrative reports, a few letters, some accounts of military recognizance, tales told to New Englanders, how it is all going. The people have settled into collaborating, but many are surly and ignorant. Still, they cannot be expected to "love us," a governor-general will one day comment to the local commanding officer.

Janse is part of daily happenings, nothing political, nothing to which exception can be taken. He plays his usual unremarkable role, neither looking for favors nor "dangling a line," as Kiliaen used to say. He acts as trustee of a fellow townsman's estate, he stands surety for a friend.

He goes to the auctions. They are always a way of picking up useful things, perhaps a bargain. In spring, just before the English troopers came, the magistrates took an inventory of Jan Gerritsz van Marcken's estate. He had goods of interest to a teacher of young children: 20 girls' and boys' caps, 10 wooden flutes, 3 rubbing brushes, "16 books great and little," 2 books with maps, a perpetual almanac, 3 little pictures and "2 little square pictures," "4 tin spyglasses," a Shrovetide play toy, "three pieces of false parchment." Perhaps the goods will find their way onto the public market.

Less than three months after the English soldiers march into Beverwijck, he attends an auction of a dead man's things, a fellow from the Katskills. As usual, he and other buyers must make payment for goods in twenty-four hours. Now, however, a guilder paid or pledged is worth only a third of its previous value. Once a cow that sold for 32 guilders was worth four beaver. Now you can get only one and a third. While he stands by, fourteen men make successful offers. Paulus Martensz bids for an old cow, and he guarantees the bid. Then he offers to stand behind a neighbor's bid on a young heifer. Three months later, he attends another auction. People are there whom he knows: Rychart van Rensselaer, Ludovicus Cobus, Hendrick Rooseboom, Adriaen Gerritsz Papendorp, and Paulus Martensz. Domine Schaets and others usually come along as well. He decides to offer 10 guilders for three tin plates and a liquor measure. He hears Rychart bid on goods eleven times the value of his purchases.

In August, eight months into the first full year of the garrison's presence, he attends an auction of another estate. This time there are farm animals and household goods. Provoost has organized the sale and is recording bids. About forty-five townspeople come to bid or look on. Janse is looking for a chest and gets one for 25 guilders. Cornelis Teunisse Bos is there and offers 64:07 for a variety of trifles. Others pay their 7 and 26 and 29 guilders for an old box, a coverlet, and a grindstone. Nothing about Janse's ways are changing. If it were not for the auctions and Provoost's "Doctor Adriaen" written in a book beside his bid, he would, again, almost disappear.

Four months later and now into winter, items from the estate of Rut Jacobsz are auctioned. This time Janse and the other burghers will not enter the bidding. The items are costly, and only the prominent men and women bid against one another. In four separate auctions, most of everything Jacobsz possessed has been exposed for sale and exposed for everyone to see — houses and lots, a yacht, furnishings from his house, valuable luxury items. Two books fetch 30 guilders, a writing slate with a frame brings 10, a "parcel of old books" goes for 17. Six pictures bring the highest price of all: Philip Pietersz Schuyler is able to offer 100 guilders for one picture and 35 for another. Arent van Curler pledges 85 for a third picture and Robbert Sandersz gets one for 36. Provoost pays 17:10 for two small pictures.

A second session of bidding turns to silverware and gold jewels. The number of competitors is reduced even further. Only nine men can stay in the game. Jeremias van Rensselaer remains the highest bidder for a diamond ring and a double ring, a gold bodkin, and a gold chain. He also wins a silver dish and six silver spoons engraved with male and female figures. People watch as he pledges 227 guilders in all. The eight other men win their bids, each acquiring an expensive gold or silver piece. They hand over 285 guilders.

The occasion is nothing more than the sale of luxury goods, the disposal of valuables accumulated by a leading merchant. Yet perhaps there is politics here. Perhaps this auction — although Provoost, writing it all down, offers not so much as a sideward glance — is not like all the others that took place before the English came. Onlookers would know what the rich are doing here. They are the lucky ones, buying their gold and silver, giving themselves security in troubled times, offering their cautious rebuke to the way things are. Like so much else, their rebuke is a guarded flick of critique: like the comment offered by one of the furnishings of Jacobsz's yacht and now brought to everyone's attention — the flag of the Prince of Orange. And at one of the other auctions, an English soldier is among the forty bidders. He takes away leather and cloth breeches for 36:10 guilders. Janse pays 7 for a couple of earthen bowls.

They are terrible times. Jeremias van Rensselaer might well have recorded them if an earlier idea of his had come to fruition. Just before the English came, he thought about producing a sort of news sheet, a New Netherland equivalent of the *couranten* so serviceable to merchants and men of affairs in Europe. He would snatch some of the title from a Haarlem publication, the *Hollandtze Mercurius,* and call it the *Neu Nederlanse Marcurius.* The notion was not an extravagant one. In Rotterdam at almost the same time a baker had taught himself poetry and the law and started a journal. Soon he came to share Jeremias's feeling that people were interested in America, so he produced a sort of travel guide, an *Amerikaansche Wegwijzer.*

20. The Election, *Plate 1: "An Election Entertainment" (February 1755), William Hogarth. Englishmen protested about the adoption of the Gregorian calendar. Here the placard on the floor reads, "Give us our Eleven Days," and suggests something of the resistance to it in 1752. Farmers especially had a sense of dislocation. "Eleven days," wrote one historian, "are quite a long time in the agricultural year" (Poole 1995: 119).*

After the English conquest, a similar change of the calendar year occurred in New York. New Netherlanders were forced to abandon the Gregorian calendar ("new style") and somehow accept the gain of ten days imposed by the Julian calendar ("old style"). Tjerk Claesz was publicly punished for contesting the new calendar year. On another occasion, a plaintiff before the Albany court alleged that he had lost nine days' work from a hired man who insisted that he had completed his work according to the Dutch calendar and not "according to the old style" calendar. Exactly how disturbing it was to farmers as they lived out a traditional agricultural cycle that defied the proper days for sowing and harvesting we cannot know. (British Museum)

Nothing came of Jeremias's plan. If he had somehow gone ahead, however — perhaps reporting routinely to his brother in Holland and expecting him to forward Neu Nederlandse news to a Dutch *courant*—he would have been describing two years crowded with newsworthiness. His journal, if true to form, would tell of events around Albany month by month. There would be no interpretation, no search for causal explanations, just descriptions, especially those that would be useful to merchants looking to make, or withdraw, investments in such a place. Thus he might have written:

New Year's Day, 1665. Albany. A comet has appeared at nine o'clock in the evening. Its tail extends toward the east and is visible for a long time. Another comet was also seen five weeks ago, toward the end of November. Coming up in the south, it showed itself with a tail toward the west that was at least twelve feet long, later twenty-four feet long, but very pale.

May 1665. Kingston, south of Albany. Disturbances have broken out between local burghers and the English garrison. The burgher guards have been deliberately provoked by soldiers. The common people complain repeatedly about quartering soldiers and many are found carrying guns. One householder has been arrested for attacking a soldier quartered with his family. He is to be sent for sentencing to the Manhatans. Another uprising has occurred at the burghers' guardhouse. Sixteen men have presented themselves in armed defiance of English authority.

August 1665. Albany. Governor-General Richard Nicolls has inspected the garrison of about sixty men. He is faced with insubordination from townspeople regarding quartering.

October 1665. Albany. The town expects Mr. John Schutte to be licensed as schoolmaster by the governor-general. Captain John Baker has received orders to inform local magistrates that "the teaching of the English tongue is necessary in this Government." The burghers have been told that they are free to limit Schutte's wages to those given to local Dutch schoolmasters. They are assured that Schutte is to be the "only English Schoolmaster in Albany."

January 1666. Albany. An expeditionary force of 600 French troopers from New Canada, mostly of the Carignan-Salières Regiment lately in combat in Turkey, has been ambushed by Mohawk Indians. The ambush occurred after an unsuccessful raid just outside a nearby Dutch village called Schenectady. Heavy losses have been reported and many wounded Frenchmen taken to Albany. Meanwhile the Indians are in pursuit of a main force retreating to New Canada under Daniel de Remy, Sieur de Courcelles. Sixty soldiers are thought to have been killed before reaching the Richelieu River. Local English authorities are condemning the raid as an armed invasion of His Majesty of England's dominions.

April 1666. Albany. Forty houses and barns have been swept away by surging waters of the Hudson River. Stores of food have been destroyed. A comet appeared in the east at four o'clock in the morning of April 3, its tail threatening toward the south. General fright and alarm prevail: "God Almighty has 3 several times shown us comets." What they will bring townspeople do not know. They say they always see them "with the tail threatening us." They are praying "that He for His Son's sake . . . Jesus Christ, will be merciful."

July 1666. Albany. Several wounded French soldiers have reached Quebec from Albany. Surgeon de Hinsse has received personal letters that offer thanks and tell of harrowing voyages from Albany to Manhattan Island, thence to Boston — "full one hundred leagues by canoe" — finally to Port Royal and Quebec. About twenty soldiers still remain in Albany.

December 1666. Kingston. Captain Daniel Broadhead is reported as having abused a burgher, Tjerk Claesz, for keeping Christmas on the day customary with the Dutch and not the day followed by the English. The village is now on the edge of mutiny.

APRIL 20, 1667
Albany

Adriaen Janse meets with two of the magistrates of Albany, Rychart van Rensselaer and Philip Pietersz Schuyler. They come together in van Schelluyne's presence and that of Jan Janse van Aecken. Janse is present with Albert Gerritsz's power of attorney to convey a house and lot to Jan Janse.

Gerritsz is a brother of Adriaen Gerritsz Papendorp, who now owns part of lot 5. Albert Gerritsz lives in Wiltwijck, now Kingston. Just ten weeks ago, the village was the scene of a violent uprising against the English. Sixty men, the English said, had risen in mutiny against the garrison. Perhaps there were as many as eighty. In the tumult, Hendrick Cornelisse Lyndraer was killed by a soldier, William Fisher.

In five days' time, officials will come up to Kingston from New York City and sit to examine this "rising in armes." A file of soldiers will attend them. They will have the governor's private instructions for proceeding. Let Fisher be the first man tried: "If no other notorious circumstances appear . . . conclude him guilty of . . . [not murder but] manslaughter." Find that the commanding officer did not attack but only threatened the Dutch sergeant of the burgher guard. Find that, instead, the man threatened and abused him. Now call the leading most violent "Actors . . . of the Ryott." Tell them that rising in arms against an established garrison of His Majesty is no less than treason. Accuse no more than six offenders and "conclude them . . . in writing to be guilty of a treasonable and malicious Ryott." Remit the final sentence of punishment to me — and send them to me as prisoners, with an armed guard. Don't berate the soldiers in public "least the Boors insult over them." Admit "very few into the room where you shall sitt."

Albert Gerritsz took no part in the violence. People in Albany would know that. Last month he did attend the auction held to dispose of Lyndraer's possessions. But that says nothing. Now he is selling property granted to him fifteen years ago by the director general and council of New Netherland on April 23, 1652. Last year the general court in New York lost patience with people like him all across the province. It caught up with all those villagers and landowners who had refused to acknowledge that their lands were now held from the Duke of York and *still* would not reconfirm their titles or "even come to fetch or request new ones." Well, now they would learn that no one would continue to "have possession of their land and houses . . . [as] subjects of the States General of the United Provinces."

There is no alternative for men like Gerritsz but to sell their properties or get them registered and risk raising all the issues of taking an oath to the English crown. And what if the property is lost because the English somehow say the original deed is defective? At the least, all of this involves expenses, perhaps even paying the local surveyor to plot the land all over again.

Others seem to be facing the same decision. Among them is a burgher whose present uncertainty or fear will come back to haunt him in twelve years' time. Then he will ask for legal possession of his land but have to admit that he "neglected to secure a patent" from the governor. Among them too is Janse. A month from now he will make sure to renew his grant to his first allotment of land near the old fort. For many like him, these last two weeks of April are a busy time of trafficking in properties, with dummy buyers doing their tricks, quick sales, buying and selling for undisclosed reasons.

It is also a time of past histories. The genealogies of parcels of land recorded long ago are now revisited. Particularly the earliest years of the town's past are recalled. Perhaps Janse remembers those years when he sees the words describing Albert Gerritsz's land as conveyed to him on "the 23rd of April, 1652." It was a time like the week eighteen months later when Stuyvesant came up to Beverwijck, settled the land allotments around the fort, and, on October 25 confirmed his right to a large lot and garden. He was then only thirty-five — not almost fifty, as he is now. Of the other men in the room, Schuyler was a young man, married only three years. Rychart was scarcely in his teens and still in Holland; van Schelluyne was married and just beginning his family. Now, again and again as the lands change hands, words that recall Stuyvesant and the council of New Netherland as well as the years 1652 and 1653 spill from the notary's pen and put the past on paper.

The past is also remembered when the land is registered and the deed finally passed by the English governor and recorded by his secretary. Five days after Janse concludes Gerritsz's business, Abraham Staats receives such a patent to his land near the fort. To describe the property and those abutting on it, the English scribe must commemorate the early association of seven near neighbors: he must write such names as "Mr. Renslaer," "Adriaen Gerrits," and "Adriaen Ilpendam." For the secretary, it is a fleeting revival of a past that belongs neither to him nor to his superiors. But he is also required to record a new kind of past. It is a past that the landowners might not even be able to identify but must now fit into, like it or not. He summons it carefully. He reaches the concluding solemnities of the patent and dates it according to an event in an England of 1648: "25 April, 1667 (19th year of H. Maties Reign)."

JULY, AUGUST 1668
Albany

There is excitement in the town. Skipper Jan Bestevaer is about to take a ship to Holland. Anyone planning to pack her with cargo, make the voyage, or send packets of letters must be ready to do so by the second weekend of July.

Jeremias van Rensselaer has finished three letters to his family and business associates. He has also packed some beaver for the family to sell. But his mind is uneasy about a number of things. The English generals, as he calls them, are due next week. Nicolls and his newly appointed successor, Francis Lovelace, will be in Albany shortly. In his dealings with Nicolls he knows he has been walking a tightrope. Now this anxiety leaks into the letters that Bestevaer will carry. He feels that he has accepted a considerable share of the quartered soldiers and a humiliating reorganization of the *colonie*'s court. He has paid extortion money to the English to save some of the few remaining rights of the *colonie*. "It seems to me," he writes codedly, "that he who draws the hundred beavers, which I had to pay them, has by far the best of the bargain." He is also living in fear that Nicolls will somehow learn that he failed to report two properties still registered in Holland

and therefore subject to confiscation. He dares not sell them and is worried that they will somehow "get . . . [him] into trouble." On top of that, and the family must understand this, selling duffels belonging to the partnership of his brother, a fellow townsman Pieter Hartgers, and Jan Martensz van Wolphen of Amsterdam is fraught with almost impossible difficulties. Hartgers has already had his properties in Albany and New York City seized.

Van Schelluyne is also busy writing. Some townspeople are leaving and need to be assisted in settling their business affairs. Some must also sign papers allowing them to conduct overseas business for relatives and friends. On Friday, July 3, Gerrit van Slichtenhorst meets with him, having agreed to see to the affairs of his sister and her husband. On the same day, Jacob Schermerhoorn attests that he has accepted obligations on behalf of two friends. On Sunday, Lysbet Dircksz van Eps comes along and contracts to act as attorney for her mother and father-in-law.

The next day, van Slichtenhorst appears again together with two others, Stoffel Janse Abeel and Harme Vedder. Each is contracting to act as attorney on a friend's behalf. About three weeks later, van Schelluyne is attending to Vedder's business again. Then Jan Coster van Aecken arrives. He too is departing for Holland.

The travelers will go to many places: Nijkerk in Geldlerland, Gornichem in South Holland, Utrecht, Wieringer in North Holland, and of course Amsterdam. Van Eps must make her way to the house of Jan Hendricksz Sijbinck in Amsterdam. She wants to place orders for trading goods and recover a valuable sealed packet left by her mother six years ago. She may also find her way to the residence of Abel de Wolff. In the past, his merchant house had major interests in New Netherland. For over fifteen years and until just recently, they had employed her husband, Gerrit Bancker, as one of their agents. Harme Vedder must get to West India House in Amsterdam. Van Slichtenhorst means to convene a meeting with Jan Baptiste van Rensselaer somewhere in the same city. Schermerhoorn was in Holland about thirteen years ago. Then his affairs took him to Dordrecht. This time he may travel to Naarden, following up his friend's affairs there.

The six men and women are among the most powerful wholesale traders in the town. They know each other well. They have served as magistrates together, taken risks in business dealings with one another, sued each other in court, intermarried. They are tied to any number of New York City and Amsterdam merchants and to factors in Boston. Few burghers juggle portfolios of investments and shifting partnerships more profitably, or more secretively, than they: now van Aecken exercising power of attorney for Nicolaes de Meyer of New York City, now Vedder in court with van Eps's husband for illegal trading during *handelstijd*.

The court watches Bancker and Vedder closely. The two men interest themselves in Schenectady's illegal trade with the natives. Everyone else watches them because they interest themselves with the de Wolffs. The overseas connection has been much to the traders' advantage — that is, until the English came. Bancker and his wife profited greatly. They got a share of the company's profits for fifteen years and earned an annual salary of 500 guilders. Bancker made a profit of 4,300 guilders on an investment four years ago and shared the use of a farm and house owned by de Wolff on Manhattan Island. And now, how the mighty have fallen. Last year the de Wolffs had to watch while 25,000 guilders in cargo was charged customs duties by the English just for the privilege of trading with New York. The house and farm on Manhattan Island are gone, sold to cover increasing debts. Vedder is now their factor. One of the purposes of his trip is to bring them an account of profits and losses over the past four years. It won't be especially welcome. There are nothing but losses. The company's furs and tobacco are now valued at only 800 guilders. Vedder himself will never see an investment of 4,400 guilders again.

Nothing, of course, betrays the purpose of each trader in preparing to depart for Holland. Over the past months, however, it would have been obvious to any onlooker that some have been selling properties in order to release funds for other kinds of investments. Early last year van Aecken sold two properties, and now this month, on July 6, he is selling another and has been fully paid for it. On July 2, just the day before van Slichtenhorst took on power of attorney for his sister, he disposed of three properties.

A seventh townsman is also leaving for Holland: Adriaen Janse. He too has arranged his affairs before departing. On July 10, he gave his wife power of attorney. She was empowered to sell the houses and lots they jointly owned and to pursue any matters that might arise from such sales. She could collect all payments that were due to him from his debtors. He trusted her. Whatever she thought best to do, he would hold as valid. The next day was one when the generals were expected in town, but he attended to his own business. He sold his brickyard after keeping it for eleven years.

He knows the others leaving Albany. But he is not a man of their importance, and his connections with them are tenuous. In any case, each traveler is concerned for his or her own affairs.

Yet this is not so. They do not travel as individuals. In about five months' time, Janse's name and theirs will appear on a petition to the king of England. He and sixteen other "subjects of the Dutch Nation, Inhabitants of New York in America," will be explaining how they transported themselves "into Holland this last summer" with the intention of settling their business affairs and "propagating the Trade of those Your Mats dominions." They had not anticipated trouble. Of course, it was common knowledge that trading between New York and Holland within the English system as *Dutch* owners of a ship and cargo meant facing charges that made profits almost impossible. The king's council for trade, however, had publicly stated that three ships a year would be allowed to make the voyage. That was just nine months ago. They had obtained the proper permits. Theirs would be one of the three. But something had gone wrong.

Now in November and in Amsterdam, they have managed to freight their ship. It is ready with cargo for New York. The sailors have been paid and all are "ready to set sail." Suddenly an Order in Council has come stating that only one vessel will be allowed to sail from Holland to New York — and it is not theirs. Their proposed voyage has been prevented and now, as they petition, they are in a "ruinous condition." On the king depends their "welfare or Destruction": will he not reinstate the "Privilege formerly Granted" or at least grant a pass to these his "Loyall subjects?"

Back in early July, however, selling his brickyard and readying himself for months of absence, Janse was taking his chances on the profitable outcome of this venture. They called it a *rederij*, a one-off joint-stock venture. Trade in furs had been good. There were beaver pelts to package and sell. The governor-general had promised favorable things for the *colonie* and Albany. Besides, people had mostly accommodated to what one man called this new "jurisdiction." Making his own efforts to find a way within it, Janse had made himself a *reder* in a high-risk and costly venture. Others counting on good fortune were some of the wealthiest merchants of New York City: Oloff Stevensz van Cortlandt, Jacques Cousseau, Nicolaes de Meyer, Jeronymous Ebbingh, and Margaretta Hardenbroeck. Van Slichtenhorst, Vedder, van Aeken, van Eps, and Schermerhoorn had their hopes too. A few overseas adventurers in Amsterdam were also in on the charter party. Jan Martensz van Wolphen had been Jan Baptiste's and Hartgers's partner for at least the past five years. Now he too had elected to make himself a part owner of the ship and its cargo. His judgment should count for something. Usually about 250 tons of goods are hauled aboard such a ship. The profits should be considerable.

July passes. The partners have not set sail. It is only in August that Janse and the others take their leave for Amsterdam. Probably they leave the

Manhatans just after August 21, when Margaretta Hardenbroeck assumes power of attorney for her husband, Frederick Philipse. Their ship is the *King Charles* — van Rensselaer spells it *de Konigh Carel* or sometimes gets closer to the English words with *Cingh Carels*. It arrived in New York sometime in mid-July. Bestevaer will sail it to Holland. It is one of many he has taken across the Atlantic over the past thirteen years: the *Vergulde Beer, Blauwe Duyff, Vergulde Otter, Draetvat,* and *Trouw* were others. Now he takes it through the Narrows and out to sea. The ship carries the partners, their freight, a letter from van Rensselaer for his brother, and possibly Governor Nicolls, now returning to England.

How does it happen that Adriaen Janse is in the company of such eminent people? Even if he is not a full partner and ready to bear the costs and profits of one-seventeenth of the venture, still he is one of them. Is he cut into it because he can act as the partners' notary? Perhaps he was examined by van Schelluyne and given the chance to qualify: the notary did the same for Salomon Lachaire earlier in New Amsterdam. Yet he does not seem to have been licensed for the *notarisschap*. Perhaps, on the high seas, he is meant to act as his companions' secretary.

We know only what neither he nor the others know in this July and August: however smoothly Bestevaer takes the *King Charles's* passengers to Texel, past Enkhuizen, and finally to the harbor of Amsterdam, they will not return to Albany until the early winter months of 1669, and two of them, van Cortlandt and Cousseau, will still be in Amsterdam well into the summer.

1668–1669
Holland

There is a proper way of being a traveler here in Holland. Cosimo de' Medici knows what it is all about. In his two visits during these months, he means to discover why Holland is the wave of the future and the vision of what tomorrow will be like. He is here to observe *het nieuwe leven,* the new way of things that is coming in Europe.

So he seeks out the buildings and ideas that are the most recent. He listens and learns. He follows the customary itinerary: large cities first, Amsterdam, Haarlem, Leiden, and The Hague, then smaller centers such as Deventer and Hoorn. Perhaps he will take a yacht from Rotterdam to Zeeland, then Germany and home.

21. Warehouses of the Dutch East India Company, Amsterdam, *Ludolph Backhuyzen, 1696. The company's four-story* zeemagazijn *serves here as a backdrop to the harbor and ship-yards. Two recently completed hulls are already afloat. Beyond the picture, ropewalks of the company and the Admiralty lay alongside each other. (Fitzwilliam Museum, Cambridge)*

Amsterdam is the place to get to the Schouwberg to see the new *Medea* of Jan Vos. Let churchmen cry out that the theater is the sign of evil days. Others find it exciting. There is the new and magnificent Town Hall, elsewhere something called *architectura moderna,* and the opportunity to get out to Hellevoetsluit to inspect forty drydocked warships of the Dutch admiralty. There is the interior of East India House to examine and company warehouses thought to be the most "remarkable to see in all of Europe." A side trip to Zaandam will give one a firsthand inspection of the most advanced shipworks in Europe. Then off to Haarlem and study of the linen industry, Leiden and viewing of the Hortius Botanicus and the Theatrum Anatomicum, then to The Hague, a place, the young prince thinks, of "youth and vigor," somewhere to be away from a life stunted by ceremonials.

Holland is a land that answers Cosimo's curiosities. Pieter Blaeu, the son of the printer Johannes Blaeu, guides him around Amsterdam. He goes to the workshops of many artists, to that of Mijnheer Rembrandt van Rijn — who had nothing finished for him to see. He examines the self-confident houses of the merchant-patricians, he buys maps, and he uses the busy barges moving on intercity canals and waterways. Most of all, he enjoys listening to men returned from the Indies with stories of traders and sea rovers. He fingers "curiosities" brought to his house and buys a few.

22. Interior of the Church of St. Bavo in Haarlem, *Pieter Saenredam, 1636. Saenredam presents a figure lost in wonder at the great organ of the church. In 1685, a picture identified simply as a church painting by Saenredam was inventoried among the effects of Judith Loreijn, the widow of Dammas Guldewagen. Sixteen years earlier, the year Adriaen Janse returned to New York, the papierkunst belonging to Saenredam's own estate was auctioned in the Prinsenhof in Amsterdam. It included many drawings by two Haarlem painters, Martin van Heemskerck and J. J. Guldewagen. Guldewagen was an artist of some accomplishment and in a lateral line of Dammas's family. (Rijksmuseum, Amsterdam)*

Some of Cosimo de' Medici's days in Holland coincide with those of Janse. The prince thinks life as it is lived in Holland, and especially in The Hague, is *volledigheid*, life in its fullness. He feels he is *er uit*, really in the swing of things. Does Janse think the same? Cosimo pries into every facet of life in Amsterdam — the harbor, fish markets, churches. Does Janse? Does he wander around the wharves of the West India Company? Does he make his way to the bookshops: to 't Groot-Boeck op de Dam, where, among other things, the owner prints and sells manifests to ships' captains; does he look through the collections of the booksellers like Johannes van Ravensteijn, Michiel de Groot, and Cornelis Jacobsz Naenaart, one or another of whose books will eventually find their way to Curaçao and New Netherland? Is he aware of Amsterdam as a city full of music, much of it enjoyed in taverns and inns: the *kunst herbergen*, the musical arts of the wine and beer houses? Is he too overawed by the East Indiamen, the great Return Ships: 50 men unloading each vessel, 300 men aboard, 1,200 men building and fitting them out? Has he ever seen anything like the cargo of the nine ships that came into port from Batavia just a year ago: 2,781 packets of raw diamonds, 100,575 pounds of fine Moluccan tin, 22,831 pounds of Ceylonese ebony, 20,489 pounds of Japanese camphor, and pepper and indigo and more pearls and diamonds?

Does he have curiosity, as Cosimo does, about the Catholics in the city, perhaps as many as 15,000 of them hearing mass in more than twenty-five places named for the house or warehouse where they meet: the Parrot, the Dove, the Three Spotted Crows? Does he share in the dangers and delights of Amsterdam kermis, the great fair days of late September, when, all day and into the night, strangers gawk at freakish sideshows, have their pockets picked, and watch country bumpkins get drunk and give over their coins to jugglers and thieves? Kermis is the high season of the surgeons. As they say, "a hundred Netherlanders, a hundred knives."

Cosimo allows Holland to unfold itself to him by moving from city to city. Does Janse do this? Does he use some of his months in Holland to make his way to his home in Leiden? Does he think of plans to be a notary? Would he have been overwhelmed to find that there are thirty notaries in Leiden alone and that one man, Adriaen den Oosterlingh, is serving 473 clients in this year, that he has so many papers from just three years of his work that they make a stack twelve or fourteen inches high, that he writes in French when necessary and, as Jacob van Merwen did years ago, experiments in writing gothic script?

Was his traveling in fact unlike Cosimo's: was he seeking and finding the past more than the future? Did he go to replenish memories of Leiden? Did he go to Haarlem, to the house of his cousins the Guldewagens to inquire about his inheritance? Did he make comparisons: Albany's few hundred residents and Amsterdam's 200,000; his town's small courthouse and here on the Dam, as they boast, "the palace of the townspeople"; the small-scale work of van Schelluyne in Albany and the scale — the status — of the notary's work here, with three rooms set aside on the second floor of the great Town Hall just for them and their minutes? Does he compare the rule of burgomaster Gellis Valckenier here in Amsterdam with that of the English authorities in New York? People say Valckenier is the monarch of Amsterdam. No Turkish potentate has a "more absolute say" about the lives of his people than Valckenier, says one observer: "Whatever he says is always done without contradiction." Is that how it is in Albany, where the highest-ranking officer should be the *schout* but is — when the final word is said — an English soldier, and where contradiction is carefully disguised?

The Hollanders respect Cosimo's father and, for that reason, they warmly embrace him. Yet he knows he is an outsider to Holland's way of life. Does this trip make Janse feel a stranger? The people of Rotterdam think that American colonies are *vreemde*, strange and exotic. The great overseas merchants of Amsterdam divide the trade into two sorts: *ordinaire negotie* are imports and exports within Europe, the rest is commerce with the *barbaren*. Do they think that the Netherlanders who go overseas are barbarians, just like the natives? When they read the word "Americans" do they differentiate between them and *de wilden*?

Or, perhaps more disturbing, is he different because he is now a "Loyall" subject of the king of England? Better a barbarian or an American than an English king's subject? And does the wording of the partners' petition to Charles II remind him that he is a stranger even in New York? He has to say that he is one of "the Dutch nation" there — like the men of the Portuguese-Jewish nation that Cosimo met here in Amsterdam or those of the English nation in New Amsterdam years ago. Where does he *belong*? The partners themselves do not say that they are living in "New York." To various notaries, they say they reside in "Albany in the colony New Netherland," or in "New Netherland." One says, "living in New-er Amsterdam in New Netherland." Another lives "in New Netherland on Manhattan." Why is this so?

The plans for Cosimo's travels are carefully made. In The Hague, he must be received by the young Prince of Orange. Inspecting the admiralty ship *Dolfijn*, he must be in the company of naval officers. During the evening when he looks over the East India Company warehouses, it is arranged that Dutch merchants who trade with such places as Livorno are in attendance.

What are Adriaen Janse's plans? Does he have business in Amsterdam? Could it be that eight years from now, when he selects Jan Hendricksz Sijbinck to receive the interest on his inheritance, he has already met him? At that time he will ask Sijbinck to accept his power of attorney because they share a bond "from old acquaintance." Could he know then that Sijbinck lives on the Haarlemmerdijk because he is now visiting his home — or perhaps meeting him at an earlier residence on the Nieuwendijk?

In fact, Jan Sijbinck is a common denominator in the business affairs of the distressed owners of the *King Charles*. In one way or another he has been, or will be, a business associate of nine of them. This is understandable. Seventeen years ago, he formed a partnership. A friend would go to New Netherland, take up a house at Fort Orange, and put them into the fur trade. Sijbinck would remain in Amsterdam, forwarding merchandise and disposing of the furs.

The partnership endured. Another, taken up about four years later with another trader, lasted as well. Both gave Sijbinck an entry into the trade of the upper river valley and Manhattan Island that he still enjoys. Very quickly his contacts multiplied. In Amsterdam, he made himself a major supplier to Abel de Wolff and other wholesalers dealing with New Netherland. In New Netherland he was supplying merchandise, especially textiles, to fur *handelaars* like Goose Gerritsz van Schaick in Beverwijck and merchants like Nicolaes de Meyer in New Amsterdam. When they could, his New Netherland partners and clients came across the seas to his house, where together they might examine a *partij* or lot of beaver pelts.

A year before the English came, he set up another partnership, this one with Pieter Hartgers and Stoffel Janse Abeel. By now he knew the names of notaries who could serve him and his clients on Manhattan Island. He acted as one of the Amsterdam agents for Cornelis Steenwyck, one of the wealthiest merchants in New York, and used Cousseau to sell goods there. Hardenbroeck, van Eps, and van Slichtenhorst, each of whom comes to him now extending power of attorney to facilitate their affairs, are not strangers. And later the call on his services made by men like Schermerhoorn, van Cortlandt, and Adriaen Janse will not be unexpected.

Now, on December 28, Lysbet van Eps appears before a notary. She states that she is in Amsterdam only temporarily and gives power of attorney for the management of her affairs to both Sijbinck and Abel de Wolff. All is not going smoothly, however. Although the petition was answered positively and the *King Charles* given a pass for New York on December 11, the ship's departure is still delayed.

The partners, or some of them, are quarreling. On the day before van Eps's appearance before the notary, Steenwyck's legal representative in Amsterdam is insisting that Cousseau and Hardenbroeck place his client's cargo on the *King Charles* and ship it to New York. He knows that the ship is already under Pieter Reyersz's command and that within four days the last lighter will go with goods from Amsterdam to the ship as it lies at Texel. Steenwyck's merchandise must be stored aboard and the ship must sail promptly if it is not to get frozen in. Hardenbroeck will have no part of it and, on her own behalf and that of the other partners, insists that the demand be ignored.

1669
Holland

The dispute between Steenwyck's representative, Cousseau, and Hardenbroeck goes on. Cousseau has been in Amsterdam for months. More than the *King Charles*, another vessel, *'t Fort Albanie*, is at the center of Steenwyck's grievances. He and Cousseau acquired the ship four years ago. It was then the *Hopewell*, a New England vessel of about 400 hogshead burden. Oloff van Cortlandt knew about the ship and about the troubles the two merchants had in interesting others in freighting it and getting it here to Holland. Somehow Frederick Philipse had taken up part ownership. Now Cousseau is delayed either by this affair or by other untidy business. In March, he and Sijbinck agree to fit the vessel out and arrange suitable finances. Late in May and into June, Cousseau is still signing notarized papers about *'t Fort Albanie* and still carrying debts of at least 2,283:80 guilders owed to Philipse.

When, then, does the *King Charles* sail? Even back in mid-November, when the partners were drawing up their petition, the delayed departure was becoming, as they said, "a great hazard (the season of ye year considered)." And who would sail on it? Hardenbroeck is still meeting with a notary on January 5. Van Slichtenhorst is dealing with Sijbinck on February 14. Cousseau is in the city in mid-June. Van Cortlandt is trying to make final arrangements for a power of attorney regarding his estate on July 17 because he is "going to New Netherland."

Where is Adriaen Janse? On a winter's day, not in the year 1668 but sometime in the early months of 1669, he arrives at Texel. The cost of getting there from Amsterdam is about 3 guilders. In three years' time, it will be here that Admiral Michiel de Ruyter will order the removal of all channel markers and their replacement with fishing boats so as to hinder a possible English attack.

Presumably the markers are now set as they should be for a safe passage into the dangerous channel.

Pieter Reyersz takes the ship out to sea. Of Adriaen Janse's four or five months in Holland, this leave-taking and his endorsement of a petition recognizing himself as a subject of the king of England are all that we know.

MAY 12, 1669
Rensselaerswijck

Reyersz has brought the *King Charles* to New York. He is now preparing it for the voyage back to Holland. Perhaps he is embarking after completing an uneventful crossing that took the vessel from Texel in early March and caught all the favorable winds. Perhaps he was able to leave there even earlier. Harme Vedder, for one, seems to be have been home in New York by early April. We cannot know.

Jeremias van Rensselaer sends a dispirited letter to Jan Baptiste along with Reyersz. It is impossible to obtain beavers. He is supporting himself by brewing, but there is little demand for beer because "no money circulates among the common people." He has learned that Nicolls is "no friend" of the *colonie*. It's "strange." The war between the Mohawk and the river Indians goes on: it "has lasted now for six years."

He hopes it will please God that Rychart may make a visit to Holland and bring along some of the *colonie*'s accounts. A year ago he also referred affairs to the pleasure of God. The Lord has ordained, he wrote his mother, "that we must learn English. The worst of it all is that we have already for nearly four years been under this jurisdiction and that I have learned so little. The reason is that one has no liking for it."

In six months' time, he will write of Albany as "this distant and strange country."

MAY 13, 1669
Albany

Adriaen Janse has sailed up the Hudson River and disembarked along the familiar foreshore.

In eleven years' time, a Dutch stranger will make the same voyage. He will describe it as a wild and distasteful experience. His company aboard the yacht is "about twenty passengers of all classes, young and old, who made a great noise and bluster in a boat not so large as a common ferry boat in Holland." Ahead lies the dark interior of the country and Dutch people whom it has made uncivilized. They live "nearer the Indians." So they are "more wild and untamed, reckless, unrestrained, haughty, and more addicted to misusing the blessed name of God."

Adriaen Janse has arrived and begins his life as notary. He is home, isn't he?

CHAPTER 7 "Nieuw Albanij in America"

SEPTEMBER 19, 1678
Albany

Eight years have gone by. Janse's venture with the *King Charles* seems to have come to very little. Nor has his inheritance amounted to much. His income has not increased appreciably after eight years as a notary, and now the matter of the street paving has made this public.

A year ago he and other property owners were ordered to lay stone paths in front of their houses. It was not a burdensome ordinance, actually one of the least irksome imposed by magistrates trying to comply with the directions of the governor-general. But he found it an embarrassment.

For the last four years the English have been afraid that what they call the "daily sad spectacles" occurring "among our neighbors" will be repeated here. It is their way of speaking about the wars between the New Englanders and the distant natives. So orders now come with predictable regularity: nail tight any gate the local commander thinks necessary; expect to be fined if you are found exporting grain; clear the street in front of your house or turn over a fine to one of the soldiers; get a pass from the officer at the fort if you want to travel to Schenectady.

Commands against illegal trading practices are now more rigidly enforced. The English don't want the natives inside the town. Two years ago, the general himself ordered that if a native were found drunk in any street and no one came forward to confess that he or she had furnished the liquor, the whole street would be fined. The sheriff is now empowered to keep close watch on everyone and to punish offenders "without mercy, favor or" — what does he mean? — "connivance."

People seem to know what is expected of them. Ordinances are now proclaimed in Dutch and English from the courthouse steps. Yet misunderstandings occur. One man says that the fence in front of his house was torn down during the night and thrown in the water by the local commander himself. A soldier told him so.

So this ordinance about the streets is of little importance and quite straightforward. The walks are to be made eight feet wide and completed within two months. A month goes by, and only 3 of about 120 householders are unwilling or unable to comply. Janse is among them. Like the others, he is summoned to court for negligence. People have made complaints and a fine of 25 guilders must be paid. He tells the court that he "has done his best" to meet the requirements. Already he has "spent much money but . . . he can not pave so far." The court accepts his word and treats him with leniency: he may use cheaper materials, planks or slates. But he must put the path in order, to prevent further complaints.

He is using every opportunity to secure the income he needs for himself and his wife. Now, among other things, he is waiting for the magistrates' final appraisal of the estate of Arent van Curler's widow, Anthonia. When she died last year there was a chance to declare himself a preferred creditor of the estate and make a claim. The estate is expected to be large.

He had approached the bench along with Jan Verbeeck and asked to be considered a preferred creditor. Each protested that he had given her long years of service, acting as agent and settling other affairs for her. Janse remembered the number of years. He had served her ever since he became a notary, seven and a half years ago. It was a sign of his trustworthiness that Anthonia had chosen him as her notary. She had denied Jan Juriaensz Becker access to her accounts and papers, letting it be known publicly that she would not let him come near her books.

Janse and Verbeeck would remember the court's decision: two old men waiting, he now sixty and Verbeeck with grandchildren already married. They were granted preference as creditors but only for the last year of service to the old woman. Otherwise they were to be treated like other creditors. It meant settling for just a percentage of their claims or, worse, getting nothing at all. Now another year has come around, and still the administrators of the estate are nowhere near an appraisal.

Still today he has ink and paper. He is writing to Dammas Guldewagen. He received two letters from Guldewagen a full year ago saying that his interest had been duly advanced to Sijbinck months before that. Yet apparently no consignment of goods had been put together in Amsterdam. Certainly it had not arrived. Only in spring of this year did it finally reach him. As Guldewagen would expect, he has tried to imagine what could have happened.

Now, he tells him, he understands. "The ship had some accidents." It was entirely predictable but, still, Guldewagen would appreciate the form some of his desperate worries were taking. For months, people had been talking about vessels seized by the Turks on the high seas. Just recently, a collection has been taken up in church for New Yorkers seized off a Dutch vessel and taken into slavery in Algiers. Domine Schaets is still going around collecting. His fear was — as he can now say with equanimity — that his goods could easily have been on that ship.

Rambling a bit, he is careful to draw his cousin back to the routine that should be simplifying the annual transfer of his interest to Sijbinck and his own placing of orders. The whole business, he now sees, is full of risks. Hoping out loud, however, he presents himself as not just a worrier. All is well now: he has "no doubt" that things will go smoothly.

He encloses his letter to Guldewagen in one composed for Sijbinck. He thanks the merchant for his correspondence and for freighting his merchandise, which arrived in good condition. He conveys none of his past worries but does dwell on the long-delayed delivery of his goods to Albany. They had been off-loaded at New York and remained there with a friend consigned to receive the shipment, Pieter Jacobsz Marius. That was in autumn of last year. Marius had taken proper care of things, but the winter weather had prevented him from sending it — and news of its safe arrival — upriver. Sijbinck would know why things went wrong: the Hudson freezing over, goods delayed over winter, sloops first making their way upriver with the breaking up of the ice in spring, not Marius's fault, all well known to him.

"Courteously and earnestly" he then places his order. It is a modest one. He needs a fine penknife with a long white handle and "a turned horn pocket inkstand to hold 3 or 4 pens." He must have some clothing already made up and a variety of materials that his wife, or perhaps a friend, will make into clothes and household furnishings. He and his wife are careful in their ordering. They allow themselves only what is needed. They measure exactly, like 1 and 9/16ths yards of heavy corded silk for a woman's apron.

For just a moment, Janse betrays an awareness of his advancing age. He asks to receive spectacles with large lenses and silver rims. These are for the use of "people who are over sixty years old." He also requests two copies of a Bible that can be read by people with failing eyesight. He would like an edition that provides notes to the text, octavo in size, and bound in black Spanish leather. The Bibles need to have "coarse and clear print" and "black silk ribbons . . . [and] one with a black silk ribbon to carry it by over the arm." Please send the consignment, he concludes, "by the first ship that shall sail directly from Holland or England to New York."

He will wait, as he has done in the past, for the order to arrive. If all goes well, he will see his goods sometime in the coming year. Meanwhile, he sends his letters off to Sijbinck's residence. Copies for himself he places with his notarized papers, secreting them away with the business papers of the community. Yet these he folds in fourths like his others to Guldewagen and Sijbinck, and they become worn. Perhaps he looks at them often, takes out one or another, enjoys the sight of them as a reassurance on paper of another distant and less and less reassuring reality.

What he does not know is that Sijbinck, although he received 204:08 guilders last year, got nothing from Haarlem this year. And during the coming year, he will be notified that only 77:18 guilders can go on Janse's account. For some reason, the interest has dropped by about two-thirds. Nor does he know that Anthonia's estate will not be settled until three years from now and that creditors will receive only 36 percent of the money owed.

It is becoming more difficult to maintain his earnings as a notary. All householders, of course, are pressed very hard these days. They still pay excise taxes and those for the public and military expenses of Albany, but now there are provincial taxes, even those laid according to the street where a burgher lives. Farmers face hardships because often they can't plant much grain. The deacons of the Reformed congregation are no longer able to support the minister out of weekly contributions. Voluntary gifts are encouraged.

Janse's position as notary is especially vulnerable. He must earn an income from his writing. Yet the needs of the townspeople for his services are diminishing. There seem to be new expectations and uncertainties about the legality of documents: just a change here and another there, no pattern but enough to be unsettling. People are turning in new directions for advice. What is to be done in this case, one leading trader inquired last year: a friend bought a house at public auction but found it to be on "an unsure footing" because the seller did not have a deed. For some reason, the trader felt he had to seek advice from the governor's English secretary in New York City.

And perhaps a burgher could now be in trouble if he or she makes a deposition before a notary. Just last year, the governor-general was here and issued a series of new regulations. The first among them was that in future no depositions were to be taken down except in court. Something must have happened. Before this, nobody needed to think twice about making depositions before the notary — in the deponent's house, in the notary's house, in any number of public places. Now, for some reason, everyone has to face up to Livingston, the court's secretary, and watch the notary's business go to him. Isn't a deposition made before a notary legal?

Perhaps there are other negotiations that are no longer within the notary's power to handle. Of course, there were always transactions that were outside his competence, such as the formal negotiations concerning land. Mostly these involved the final transfer of property, the writing up of a deed. When the previous governor-general recommissioned Jan Juriaensz Becker nine years ago, he seemed to think that notaries had the power to endorse deeds. Everyone knows, however, that informal agreements to sell are in the hands of notaries, but the transfer of deeds is not. Town secretaries see to these and record them in their registers.

Now that is changing. The court seems to be adopting new ways of looking at contracts regarding land, at least mortgages, and new ways of making use of a notary. In midsummer last year, a case was brought by the strange domine, Nicolaus van Rensselaer. For the six magistrates and the sheriff, the suit came on a morning long with bothersome disputes. They had dealt with fourteen cases. Then the domine — eccentric and now intensely nervous, entering the courtroom, then leaving, then entering again — presented his case. He produced a bond payable by the English officer John Baker. It was "written by a notary public in the form of a mortgage," with Baker's house and lot offered as security. He expected payment. But the magistrates denied his request, arguing that the mortgage was invalid. It was not written by a secretary and in the presence of magistrates. And they went further. Because it was written only by a notary, "much mischief may be concealed." They had never declared anything like that before.

Janse writes nothing about these curious and unaccountable changes. Yet if he is not alert to the curtailment of his practice, Ludovicus Cobus is. He is wilier than Janse and eager to cooperate with officials, to move with the times. But even for him things are unpredictable. Last year he made a list of claims on the court for his services. Three of them were rejected, including compensation asked for taking a deposition or, as they say now — as though the validity of the act rested on the deponent's word rather than the notary's signature — "swearing any person." Nevertheless, he has found an expanded role for himself as an "attorney." He seems to be operating out of two descriptions of a notary. One is as the man who authenticates the private attestations of clients and the other is as "attorney admitted to practice before this court." And he now uses the court as a place of argumentation. Give me a copy of the papers of my client's opponent, he now says, and I will "reply to it on the next court day." As attorney, he can also take over cases once prosecuted by the *schout*. This would never have happened in the old days.

Janse is seldom before the court. For some reason, he hasn't the energy or interest to adapt as Cobus is trying to do. If he had appeared, he would see that the courtroom is still a place of his own language, but it is also a room filled with the new words and meanings. But what are plaintiffs and defendants hearing? Are they hearing the magistrates use Dutch words for the new terms, for "defective" evidence and "subpeonaed" witnesses? Do the magistrates know what they mean when they state that they consent to a defendant's receiving a copy of a plaintiff's rejoinder "per superabundance"? Or are the magistrates confused and bumbling, with only Livingston as secretary putting the words clearly on paper, writing English words out of his own vocabulary? And do they feel insulted when one plaintiff who knows English takes it upon himself to teach them another new phrase: "yesterday," he instructs them, my "suit remained *in mora*, or otherwise, in English, nonsuited." Does it disturb them — don't they think the townspeople will find it contradictory — that in April two years ago they were reading out the Duke of York's laws to one plaintiff and four months later entertaining the case of another plaintiff supporting his position by citing de Damhouder's *Practycke*, chapter 50?

The courtroom is also busy with new ways of arguing cases. The magistrates seem to assume that their courtroom will now be a venue for adversaries and not parties expecting arbitration. Evidence begins to be marshaled in a military tone. One man, an English soldier, asks that the court arrange the parties standing before them as if they were two battalions facing off in combat. "The plaintiff requests that his witnesses may be heard," he directs, and then, "Now follows the testimony for the defense."

Perhaps the courtroom, with its new ways and new words, is becoming an uneasy place for townspeople, even a place of humiliation. Yes, most evidence is still offered in the traditional storytelling way, and most parties still spin out their accounts to get the best advantage when reconciliation comes. Townspeople can still expect the court to make its decisions in the usual way, not interesting itself in earlier behavior but just looking at the concrete evidence of the present case. But even the most prominent burghers are being told that they are ignorant. Philip Pietersz Schuyler, of all people, will be told by his opponent's attorney that he can expect his case to fail because he is proceeding "according to the old custom and . . . [is] ignorant of any other form."

No one speaks about the cause of these changes. Certainly not Janse, and not the magistrates, who make every effort to muffle complaints. Yet one man utters what they dare not say. Two peoples live here now, Dutch and English. Everyone knows there is a divide. The English are resented. For him, a court decision brought in against him is sound enough proof. He has been mistreated for "being an Englishman." So he'll wash his hands of the court and carry his case to the governor in New York City. No one comments publicly.

Janse served on a jury two years ago. It was the first time he had been called upon. When the English first occupied Manhattan Island, men and women there said they didn't know what a jury was. They were reluctant to serve and distrustful. Now here in Albany, juries are common. Supposedly they replace the traditional arbitrators, the "good men" to whom the court once turned for advice. Janse was called to hear a case of some importance. A magistrate of Schenectady had been publicly accused of rendering false judgments and was trying to clear his name by prosecuting the slanderers. Janse listened to testimony that was exceptionally tangled and badly presented. The wording of his verdict and that of his fellow jurymen, however, was even more snarled and amateurish. It was at times incomprehensible, like the final statement: "If he [the plaintiff] meant that, he could not swear that he had heard it; and on the contrary, if he heard it, he could not swear that he meant that; *ergo*, it is false."

For everyone, it is a time of mangled words and attempted translations. Many are coming up with the new English-language sounds and signs that are now so often required or serve as a safety net. Even important men and women are trying to use English words — and mixing them up with Dutch. One wealthy merchant makes a try at it, describing land he means to sell as "Seventigh Acres of five en Dartigh Morgen," seventy acres or thirty-five morgen. The magistrates try "scandalous" and come up with "schandilas." They are not exceptional. Everyone is groping along the walls of the new language. Livingston means to make money out of it. He alone in the town can put on the market the English words that the authorities and an increasing number of local burghers and farmers have to have. He wants his salary increased for keeping the town's account books because, as he says, he has "more trouble in making translations, etc. than any secretary has ever had heretofore."

For Janse also, language is central to his profession. He is expected to be at home in the native language of his clients; the learned writers have repeatedly said so. But what is the native language? Not that long ago, tapsters were paying for their licenses and calling it the *spinhuiyssedeel*, a tax for the upkeep of the poorhouse. *Spinhuiyssedeel* was part of a ready-made language passed down from generation to generation. Now there is Dutch and there is English.

So Janse is not alone in feeling clumsily along the dark wall. His papers are pointing up his difficulties. Generally, it is English proper nouns that he hears, tries to write correctly, but misspells. A name like Frazier is hopelessly distorted, and for some reason he adds "*ij*" to Jan Connell's name, making it a diminutive. Once he tried to get "Mr. Samuel Willson" right. He was notarizing a property conveyance between the Boston merchant and a local family. He first wrote "Mr. Samuel Wilsen," then possibly saw the signature as "Wollson" but wrote "Wolson." Later he tried to find the English spelling for a yacht, the *Royal Oak*. On the bill of sale he wrote "de Royael Lock" — and repeated the mistake on another contract in the middle of the year. When the sloop underwent two changes of ownership five years later, he tried again, this time writing "De Royael Ock" on both documents.

His clients in these last transactions seem to have been unperturbed by his spelling mistakes. Orthographic variations happen all the time, the burghers may have thought, and, although they were clever enough to sign their names, who were they to improve on the notary's accuracy? Besides, he is trying to be careful. But with the court for some reason beginning to split hairs, was the yacht *Royael Lock* really in law the *Royal Oak*? Would the buyers of Samuel Willson's land have any difficulty claiming the property of "Mr. Samuel Wolson" as contracted years earlier?

Janse did not write up many documents this year. Through January, February, and March he had no clients at all. Then from early April to this day in September, he had fifteen. He will have only eighteen more before the year's end. He had many hours of paperwork but only seventeen meetings altogether — and the last two years were worse. This year, among his thirty-three clients, he served a Schenectady magistrate, an English soldier, and the wife of a New England merchant. Mostly, however, he continued to be called upon by ordinary townspeople.

In these final months of the year, he writes up five wills. The solemnities of each should be the same. But they aren't. Solemnizing the joint testament of one couple, he begins as van Schelluyne had always done and as the manuals had taught it should be done. "In the name of the Lord, Amen. Know

23. Double Portrait of a Married Couple *[Burgemeester Egbert Gerbrantsz and his wife]*, *Dirck Jacobsz, 1541. Adriaen Janse was accustomed to taking dictation on wills made jointly by married couples. Probably he had made a joint will with his wife, just as they jointly owned property in Albany. Female ownership of property was contrary to English practice and soon disappeared in New York. Grotius held that even country folk in the Low Countries were not exempt from dictating wills according to Roman form because "all across the countryside" there were courts and notaries. (Amsterdams Historisch Museum)*

all men that on the fourth day of June, about four o'clock in the evening, in the year after the birth of our Lord and Savior Jesus Christ, one thousand six hundred and seventy-eight, before me appeared. . . ." The others begin in a new way, with words and phrases that he began to use about two years ago. Now he employs them regularly, except when he becomes forgetful or loses concentration. They seem awkward and wooden. "In the name of God, Amen," he begins. "Know all men by the contents of this present public instrument," and he goes on.

He doesn't say why he feels the need to emphasize the public nature of a will or that he is the maker of *public* documents. If he is worrying about the privacy that has always surrounded wills and that the traditional solemnities imply, he has the best Dutch authorities on his side. What is disturbing him? When he drew up the agreement for Samuel Willson, the merchant had demanded that, when it came through, he wanted the deed to his new property written in English. Are these things getting to him?

DECEMBER 10, 1678
Albany

He meets with Jan van Loon, who is buying a large tract of land south of Albany. In eight years' time and despite his often refractory attitude toward the magistracy, van Loon will be appointed coroner. He will be called in when someone dies alone or in uncertain circumstances. Or has committed self-murder. Then he and Adriaen Janse will meet again.

MARCH 5, 1679
Albany

His name appears on a list. For some reason, he is number 47. The townspeople, 146 of them, have been assigned to repair the posts set up around the town's palisades. There are still hostilities between the natives and neighboring Christians, so the town's inhabitants are now given detailed orders about maintaining defenses around the settlement. Someone has already measured the distance as 347.5 rods, "beginning at the gate opposite the new fort, northwards and so back to the said gate."

There had been grumbling about this earlier in the year. People were noticeably uncooperative, especially calling on their ignorance of what was to be done. In response, Livingston as court secretary had posted an order, one version in English, another in Dutch. It was meant to catch all those "who Pretend not to know" where their stretch of the stockade is. If they are so ignorant, let them come to the constables within three days and be instructed.

The list is completed. It's like each of the auctions: another dramatization of who is rich and who is poor. Philip Pietersz Schuyler is the only burgher assigned 6 rods, that's 72 posts. Gerrit Bancker and the widow of Goose Gerritsz van Schaick must each look out for 5.5 rods, while fourteen men are responsible for 5, 4.5, and 4. Among all householders, 80 percent are deemed able to contribute at least 2 rods. Only thirty men fall below that figure and are asked to contribute posts for 1 or 1.5 rods. Janse is among them.

FRIDAY, MAY 2, 1679
Extraordinary Session Held in Albany

A petition of the magistrates and leading *handelaars* is sent to the governor-general. It asks that he rescind an order prohibiting them from carrying on overseas trade. The right to free trade, they argue, has never before been questioned. Shipping flour, grain, and furs across the sea brings more trade and prosperity than just selling it (as he wishes) to New York City. What else is it but an "ancient privilege" that port towns have always had? It makes no sense to suggest that "none of the inhabitants of Albany may be overseas merchants or traders." One of the results will be that others, the many "who can neither trade nor do any manual labor," will have to move away. Artisans too. "Really, no right minded persons" could fail to see that the city's privileges should in fact be extended.

Two men immediately leave for New York City to deliver the petition.

TUESDAY, MAY 6, 1679
Council Meeting, New York

The matter is "for the Present to remaine as settled." The petitioners, furthermore, must know that they were badly advised in carrying, as they were, so "mistaken a Peticon."

MONDAY, MAY 19, 1679
Extraordinary Session Held in Albany

It is reported that the petition was resented by the governor and the matter must remain unchanged. The burghers have been offered an impossible choice: Do business overseas *or* retain the monopoly over the Indian trade.

JUNE 5, 1679
Albany

The magistrates still call on Janse to assess the records of deceased burghers or those whose books are in dispute. But they will do so only three times this year, and then, as often as not, they will call him "Mr Ary van

Ilpendam" — in indulgent recognition of his age? He still shows himself to be meticulous in his nearsighted work. Now he is asked to offer his opinion on an irregularity in the behavior of Cobus. Cobus has acted as legal representative for opposing parties in a case before the court. He assisted the sheriff by taking a number of depositions. Then he served the sheriff's opponent in court by drawing up his answer to them. Janse is summoned to identify the original of the defendant's response because he had later made a copy. He is careful: the defendant's statement is in Cobus's handwriting, he testifies, but he did not actually see him write it. It was simply handed to him by the defendant, for whom he made a copy and returned it. In the end, the case is of little importance.

The court calls him again in October, and again it is to verify claims about accounts and ledgers. After that, for over two years, he makes no appearance at all.

In about two years' time, the town will auction the cattle herder's job. For some reason, Janse will be allowed to earn a bit by conducting the sale, writing down the bids, keeping account of things. Recording it all, he will put himself down as *scrijver*, clerk. It will be the last time he will write the word.

NOVEMBER 4, 1681
"Albanij in America"

From "Albanij in America" he writes Guldewagen a letter that is barely controlled. Little of it has the tone of a proper business letter. He is still able to see a pattern in the transfers going on between Haarlem and Amsterdam, and he takes comfort in thoughts of the old man who thinks of him each spring, sending his interest to Sijbinck, facilitating the usual early summer consignment of goods. And this year's shipment has arrived, though only 69:8 guilders' worth. Was it, he asks, meant to be that little? It has worried him. So he reconstructs his account with Sijbinck. But there are only four entries to list. It tells the story of all he has received: goods worth only 431:8 guilders altogether, in four consignments over five years. Little as it is, he acknowledges that Sijbinck says it is correct. The fault, he guesses, must have been somewhere in the early years, between 1677 and 1679. Still, he refrains from being critical or carping. He is satisfied.

Yet his mind is not on the past but on the future. He writes reflectively. He now knows no one in Holland, and he must shake off worries about his cousin's ill health. Recalling Guldewagen's illness, he is now moved to expressions of joy that his cousin has recovered some of his former health. But these thoughts give way to sentiments of fear that can't be kept down and that rush into the same sentence. He would be certainly lost should it please God not to give his cousin further years: "I hope and pray God that it shall have pleased Him to restore your honor to your honor's good health unto Salvation, Amen. And whereas I neither know nor am acquainted with any one in Holland who could collect what is due to me, therefore I humbly and kindly pray your honor, that it may please your honor, to continue to do so as long as it may please God; for I and my wife are both over 63 years of age and can not earn much here and have need of the [money], but I do not know where it is, nor who has possession of it, nor how I can obtain it."

He stores away his copy of the letter. Only one more will be added to it.

MARCH 7, 1682
Albany

He has made a mistake. It is something that should not have happened. On January 16, Teunis Pietersz sold a house, lot, and some timber to a cooper, Jan Janse Ouderkerk. The parties summoned Janse, and he wrote up the contract of sale. He kept a copy among his papers. Now, two months later, Ouderkerk is declaring that the contract is invalid because he was drunk, "so drunk that the next morning he did not know who had been the witnesses."

Janse is called before the court to testify. He says that he could not tell that Ouderkerk was drunk and that the man insisted that he was sober. Yet the testimony of others goes against him. Gerrit Bancker and Pieter Schuyler swear that Ouderkerk was "not capable of making any bargain." One of the witnesses to the contract, moreover, was "reeling" around, "even more drunk" than the cooper. Dirck Wessels, one of the magistrates, supports this testimony. He adds that he "forbid Mr. Ary, the notary public, to write any contract that day." The court annuls the purchase but chooses not to chasten him for a serious breach of practice.

Four years ago, this would not have happened. Then, too, he had been drawn into a "drunken man's business." He was summoned to write a contract but found one of the parties "so drunk that he did not dare write for him." Is he now becoming careless? Is the court's compassion a worrying sign? Other old men are the subjects of the court's concern. Arrangements have been made just this year for the care of an old farmer during his remaining days. He is in a pitiable state, behaving improperly in front of young people, carelessly throwing a knife, pulling up corn on another farmer's property. His imminent death is discussed. But until that time, his farm will be rented and the lessee will provide him 150 bushels of apples each year for five years.

Old Claes Janse Timmerman is a similar case. His comportment is just as troublesome, and he will soon become a charge on the deaconry. He walks along the streets intoxicated, then promises to behave himself but continues his worrying ways and needs a guardian. By December, he is deemed incompetent. The court requires him to choose two men who will keep him under supervision and be custodians of any earnings. They must keep a correct account and be prepared to have it inspected.

The civil law books have their descriptions of old people who have, as they say, one leg in the grave. They are the most "miserable" of people, *decrepiti senes*. In Amsterdam, the church deacons, of course, have an old people's home. It is along the Amstel River, near the Zwanenbrugwal. Last year, to be eligible as an inmate, a man had to be a widower without children and sixty years old. He needed to have been a resident of the city for twenty years and a member of the church for fifteen. He had to have been receiving alms for one year.

By some of these requirements, Adriaen Janse would qualify, except that he has not been receiving alms and still has his wife with him. At least for this year.

MAY 29, 1682
Albany

Today burghers are meant to celebrate the birthday and restoration of King Charles II. Ministers must call their congregations together for prayers of thanksgiving. All must abstain from employment.

Janse meets with five men. He writes a contract for the sale of a sawmill south of town.

SOMETIME IN NOVEMBER 1682
Albany

He finishes a letter to Guldewagen. He is frightened and melancholy. Jan Sijbinck has died and left his affairs in the hands of his widow. He seems unable to think about his interest and his home country with the same vigor as before. This year 79:14 guilders reached Amsterdam from Haarlem. But the transaction only reminds him of Guldewagen's frail health. So dependent is he on his cousin, he writes, that it would be better if God would be pleased to let him remain in good health more than he himself. For, he despairs, "I should not know how or in what manner I could receive my interest."

Moved by nothing in particular, he cuts to his age and a sense of aloneness that he and his wife feel. "We have no children and it is now more than 31 years ago that I married my wife and she was a widow and has a son, who now more than ten years has been married and has three sons and gets along reasonably well." He recovers a business sense and asks that Sijbinck's widow be sent money next March. But abruptly he returns to his and his wife's tenuous circumstances. "We have two small houses here. Upon one, in which we dwell, we have spent more than the interest of two years amounts to, from the other we receive now not more rent than . . . [torn]."

He sends off the original copy of the letter. His own copy he keeps and seems to place with one of his previous letters. He folds both in fourths. They get worn and stained, unlike his other papers. He undoubtedly also has letters from Holland, but they have long disappeared — and, in any case, he will have few more from Guldewagen. In a little over two years, at the age of fifty-nine, his cousin will be dead.

This letter is a fragment. It is written on the kind of paper he had wanted years ago: good paper watermarked with a foolscap and bells.

Meanwhile, all around Janse the town is living out the seasons of the year: the dull persistence of war with the natives and the French, the sober acceptance of change toward things English, the watchful awareness of difference. Language — finding the words to say things, being tangled up in Dutch — persists as a problem.

Being in a place with two languages makes troublesome things even worse. Notice is taken of it. Some months ago, two Hollanders from overseas met with the commander at the fort. One of the men mentioned in his diary a curiosity in the encounter: they needed an interpreter because the commander spoke no Dutch. Not long after that, an English official, John Lewin, was poking around, trying to establish the number of land patents Andros had passed and the rents that should therefore be reaching the coffers of the king's brother. Constables went out to gather information, getting him his figures and documents. Yet it had all become hopeless. Only one return came in, he reported, "and that from Schenectede which is in Dutch."

Lewin was a novice to strange written words that would neither go away nor give away their meaning. The common townspeople are accustomed to them. In March, two years ago, Wynant Gerritsz asked Thomas Rodgerson, a soldier or English trader, to read a patent for him. Rodgerson complied, and they talked together. For some — but how many? — it is now the way of things.

There is the English-Dutch language of the strange preacher Nicolaus van Rensselaer and his mysterious English-Dutch ways. Words to the English king got him where he was. Years ago he thought himself to be a prophet of God — not the only Hollander to speak with God and send prophecies to churchmen, magistrates, and foreign monarchs. You will one day, he promised Charles II, be returned to your throne. Then he came to Albany, was already ordained in Anglican orders, but appointed by the governor to the Reformed congregation. He preached in Dutch words but twisted meanings and carried out the rituals of the English churches. Janse met him but remained silent. Others said he was unorthodox, perhaps mad. Finally questioned by some in the consistory, he appeared in court to defend himself. He spoke in Dutch. But he read English — and his strange foreign languages — and seemed enamored of the king. Now he is two years dead. He left his widow about two hundred books in "foreign languages" and "13 pictures with the royal arms."

Those for whose fortunes it can make a difference search for the new language of the English lawyers. Secretary Livingston knows this. He has come quickly and remarkably into control of the *colonie*: the distracted domine van Rensselaer was his point of entry. Now he wants more of the *colonie*'s lands, those of Jeremias's widow, Maria, and clear title. One day he will place an order on London for five law books, but for now he means to learn from English lawyers how to carry his case through the courts. Maria will soon learn of this and have to realize just as quickly that London is now the place to learn the law. Yes, writes a New York friend to her, Livingston sought control of the *colonie* by representing himself to the council in England as the only director. An associate of theirs, however, has also promised to consult a jurist in London to see what can be done.

And well might Livingston consult London. For English law has already come to his doorstep and mocked him. Last year a wealthy New York merchant, John de Laval, answered charges brought by Livingston here in the courthouse and taught him a lesson. In the course of the procedings, the words that the six magistrates heard in his defense were entirely new and the notions behind them altogether different. Twelve jurymen, who were also town leaders, listened to the extraordinary string of words as well.

The secretary had been performing his role as excise collector. In that capacity, he accused the merchant of failing to pay 1,020 guilders on 510 gallons of rum brought upriver. In court de Laval offered a devastating response, putting forth a legal case that the local burghers could never have constructed, probably never even imagined. It was written in English but translated into Dutch, the argument coursing forward on a tide of points never before heard in the courtroom. De Laval could prove that the secretary was collecting monies — "this *pacht* or excise, as he calls it" — that were the financial base of any Dutch city or town and in the collection of which a man, particularly a ruthless man, might grow prosperous. These odd taxes, however, had no place in English law. That was his first point. And then he went on to ask "whether we are not to be considered free born subjects of the king? If not, during which king's reign and by which act passed during such king's reign we were made otherwise than free?" Next: "When did the king, lords and commons empower a governor of New York to levy taxes on his Majesty's subjects, since such right belongs to all three of them jointly, and not to one of them alone?"

And again, why didn't Livingston demand the excise as soon as the rum landed? If it is a lawful demand, show me under what law, "on what page or in which book the same may be found?" Finally, should not "a person who demands a tax or excise which is not warrented by law . . . be deemed to be a disturber of his Majesty's peace and, consequently, should he not be proceeded against for attempting to arouse the minds of his beloved subjects and for making him out to be most severe who by all nations is regarded as the most benevolent king in the whole world?"

The jury brought in a unanimous verdict against de Laval. Yet the burghers could use words too, and their decision was carefully ambiguous. Perhaps they were as wise as de Laval at least in one way: perhaps they too knew that the laws of England were one thing and those made for New York another. So they said they could find no provision for an excise tax in "the laws which prevail here" and "*if* the order of the governor must be considered as being law, then the defendant is guilty."

The magistrates also found words to weasel out of resolving the case. They did not, they insisted, have the power to interpret the verdict on the legality or illegality of the order. Send the case to New York City.

Janse writes nothing about these words, things "warranted by law," legal empowerment by the king, lords, and commons. Yet if he had to worry about being examined again as a notary, how much law would he really know? At home, stealing from a church, mill, bridge, or sluice was a special kind of crime. Were there such categories of misdemeanor in England? under English law? And if so, how could he, not knowing them, counsel townspeople? He is sworn not to write an act that violates the laws of the land. Yet even if he could, what law books would he consult? No use learning the laws of England when, even as English-born New Yorkers know, the laws here are those of the Duke of York. Actions are legal if they accord with the methods and practices of England *or* the laws now established: that's how the provincial assembly puts it.

The burghers know that the law is there. But something is coming apart. One man, a baker, puts it down to the changeover from producing written evidence in court to — what the English seem to want — swearing oaths. He can identify the shift only as something happening "nowadays" and something that unscrupulous people are taking advantage of. "It nowadays makes little difference to the people," he says. To gain 20 or 30 guilders "they readily take an oath." Kiliaen van Rensselaer was one of many merchants who thought that oral promises were either useless or the work of papists. Precisely "because words are forgotten or can be twisted," he wrote, "written instruments are made." Another man, a writer, made the same point but directed it to the importance of the notary. "The words, and trade, of a community unsettled in just a few hours or flowing past memory itself will," insisted the author, "by My Writer, endure for ages." Back in 1665, a witness in New York City, when called to court and asked to take an oath, said he needed an explanation of "what an oath means." Things are different now.

JULY 23, 1683
Albany

Janse pays the deacons 10 guilders for the use of a pall to cover the coffin of his wife. It is of black cloth with tassels at the corners. His name and the payment are recorded by Pieter Schuyler, who is serving as deacon and keeping the church accounts. Schuyler writes "Laus Deo" at the top of each page. Making his entries for July, moving down the page, he writes "Abraham van Ilpendam" instead of "Adriaen." He is still young, only twenty-six. Perhaps for that reason he does not know the older townspeople well. He does not write down the name of Janse's wife: it is not meant to be part of the record.

The customary contribution for the pall is 10 guilders. In May, Margaret Schuyler had paid the same amount for the cloth that would cover the coffin of her husband, Philip Pietersz. Johannes Provoost will pay it in November and add a guilder for the small pall for a child.

The pall is the town's lowest common denominator of death. Otherwise families have their own ceremonies and rituals of death, their own words. "What consoles us in our sadness," wrote a member of Philip Pietersz's family earlier in May, "is that he died with sincere repentance for his sins and with a foretaste of eternal joy. We shall go to him, but he will not come back to us."

What Janse's gestures toward death are, we do not know. Since the distribution of invitations to a funeral is customary — in years to come, the *aanspreker* expects to deliver them up and down both sides of the river — it is likely that he calls friends and associates to grieve with him, filling in the hours after the burial with skeins of stories and eating and drinking. He would pay the expenses, and he would pay 30 guilders for a coffin. To the *aanspreker* who is perhaps also the gravedigger, he should make an offering of something like 40 guilders. But we cannot be sure that he did.

Death becomes a matter for the magistrates when a man or woman dies alone or in unknown circumstances. Dying alone is a fearsome thing. Such a death will call up emphatic words, such as he died "all by himself, without anyone being present." Late last year, the sudden death of a child moved the court to undertake the rituals of a formal inquiry. A French couple, recently arrived from Canada and renting a house next to Jan van Loon, had failed to report the child's death. The lapse was seen as "reason for suspicion." A jury of six men and the doctor who had occasionally cared for the child viewed the body and made their report. They were of the opinion that the child had died a natural death. Still, the parents were questioned closely. Why had they sewed up the child's body in a cloth? It was "the custom among the French." Why had they not notified someone? They were "unacquainted with the language," and they did not notify Jan van Loon because "they had troubled him about so many things that they were ashamed." They admitted that they made a mistake in not informing someone that the little child had suffocated by a discharge of phlegm. The court was satisfied.

Last year too the commander at the fort — the man who could not understand Dutch — died suddenly. The formalities of inquest began, but the procedures were different. Thomas Ashton was an important person. Everything had to go smoothly. The magistrates themselves investigated the large room in the fort, the scene of his death. They took an inventory of his effects, sealed a chest, trunk, and desk, and entrusted the keys to the secretary. They summoned an extraordinary session of the bench, selected a jury of twelve men, and questioned soldiers. A corporal swore that, just before he died, Ashton was perfectly healthy. He reported that after dinner he said, "God be thanked, what a good Dinner I have eat," went out to smoke a pipe at the fort gate, and then "lay doun upon ye Bench in ye great Ro[o]m." Other soldiers confirmed that indeed he died suddenly there.

The magistrates and the jury assembled and made their determination. It was a reasonable one: the cause was the sudden intervention of "God's Providence." At the same time, they entertained another time-honored ritual. They suffered the appearance of those burghers who now proposed themselves as preferred creditors against Ashton's estate. This would happen again, early in the coming year and in other circumstances. The estate of a man killed while felling a tree alone in the woods was pounced on by would-be preferred creditors before the day was out. Like contributing to the church for the pall, it was a part of death.

Janse writes nothing about the death of his wife. At such times people would be expected to seek the comfort of the *ziekentrooster,* the man engaged by the church as comforter of the sick. Anthonij de Hooges had comforted a man in great distress just after Janse and his wife arrived in Beverwijck, now thirty-one years ago. The man was "dejected in spirit" and given to crying. He asked de Hooges "to come sometime to console him, as at times he had a hard struggle and suffered great temptation." He knew he needed help and admitted this to a female friend. Perhaps Janse needed help too; perhaps he did not.

DECEMBER 3, 1684
Albany

The fort is on the rise of the steep hill that overlooks the town. From it the English commander has a prospect that an artist like Bruegel worked hard to get, not exactly a bird's-eye view but a focus taken from a dominating elevation. Small houses and sheds are strewn in silence across the surface before him. Jonckerstraat is broad directly in front of him but narrows as it descends into the middle distance and then diminishes even more as the corner of a house falls out of step and almost excludes the view of its sliding down to Handelaarsstraat. The church, set at the foot of the hill, is directly in his view. Off to his distant right, the banks of the river can be seen despite upward-thrusting palisades, the courthouse, and more irregular roofs. Still to his right but closer now, gaining in size, is the Lutheran burying ground. Largest of all, because the yards of road and brick have now come back toward him, are the houses on the hilltop, some of them owned by soldiers or agents of English traders. It is easy to see the stoops and windows of the inns where the men of the garrison drink and the house of a tapster who serves the soldiers and also bakes their bread.

Off to the officer's left the hill soon falls away sharply, again to places miniaturized by distance, to clearances more than a mile away, where tanneries and pasturelands make owners of men like the town secretary. Then the dark shades of the forest dwarf the cleared lands, suffering the existence of only a few farms and a road going north that everyone calls "the road to the patroon's mills." Beyond his seeing, in all directions, is the newly created and unknown "county of Albany."

Spread before him are about 120 houses, perhaps more. Once, to sort them out geographically, they were said to stand on the hill, or lie on the third kill. Now that has changed. They are places set within one of four wards. Today four men have been chosen as aldermen. Four others have been elected assessors. Janse is one of them, assessor for the fourth ward.

The fourth ward is at the far distance from the commander's vantage point. Houses here stand mostly on the flat land that runs along the river. They border both sides of Handelaarsstraat, where it heads north from the intersection with Jonckerstraat and makes its way to the town's northern gate and the road to the patroon's mills. From the intersection to the gate is only a fraction of a mile. The gate is sometimes called Cow Gate and the street Cow Street.

The magistrates have tried to help people locate themselves in the geography of the new wards. Their pronouncements have been useful maps, with the houses of prominent burghers offered as aids to memory and understanding. They map Janse's ward clearly enough: from the Cow Gate near David Schuyler's, along both sides of Handelaarsstraat southward, to the corner of Carsten Fredericksen's, and so on.

His house is not mentioned. If we did not know that his fellow aldermen and assessors lived in their respective wards, we could not be certain that he lives here. We do know that five years ago, he planned to sell fifteen feet of his lot to a wealthy man and that the merchant lived on Handelaarsstraat, near the north palisades. And one day a man will own a house and lot known to have been Janse's and be said to have — as they liked to say in old books — "settled in Albany and for many years occupied the west corner of Maiden Lane and Broadway" (earlier Handelaarsstraat.) About two hundred years from now a scholar will do as the magistrates have done and draw another map. He will make his calculations about land transfers over time and properties divided and sold off. He will draw streets and lots and think he can write Adriaen Janse's name across a rectangle drawn to represent land almost at the corner of Jonckerstraat and Handelaarsstraat, near where the church sits — oddly, some will say — in the middle of the intersection. The scholar's map, however, is not thought to be trustworthy, but no one will be able to say exactly where he lived.

Janse takes his oath sometime after one o'clock this Tuesday afternoon. Six magistrates are present, now empowered to call themselves justices of the peace. The ringing of the bell brings them together. Livingston administers the oath: "Whereas you are chosen by the commonalty to be assessors of the town and county of Albany, you swear by the everlasting God that . . . you will to the best of your knowledge justly and honorably tax or assess the inhabitants of the town and county of Albany for defraying the public expenses. . . . So help you God."

After the ceremony, if he does not join with friends to go to one of their homes or an inn, he can walk the short distance to his own house. There is no reason why it should not be like most of the others. People are aware of which streets are old streets. They have an eye too for acceptable houses, substantial dwelling houses, as they say. Two square rooms in a house of not less than 18 feet in width, a front wall *not* of dark timbers like the rest of the house but of stone or brick and faced with tiles, that's what they expect. There are many to be seen: solid houses, one and a half stories, gable ends to the street. Janse owns a wide lot, or so he indicated six years ago when he had to have the frontage paved.

On this December afternoon, it will get dark early. The winter outside will bring its quiet into the house. A fire and candles will be needed. Their limited light will reduce the size of the room. It will reach to the things, however, that even medieval Netherlanders owned: a table, a chair, and some pieces of furniture for storage. Cabinets and chests are of all kinds, those specially made for prayer books, others designed for weapons, *tafelkastjes* or tabletop boxes for family papers, some boxes in a man's house so small and so many that after his death they are not even inventoried.

If Janse does not have so diverse a collection of hideaway places, he at least has a chest. The old saying among notaries about due vigilance for their papers, "take notes and guard them," may not have come to his attention, but he is not forgetful that, as he once wrote, papers are in his "custody." Perhaps the light of his fire now casts its shadows onto the chest or perhaps it picks up the wood of two chests, one that keeps hidden his own

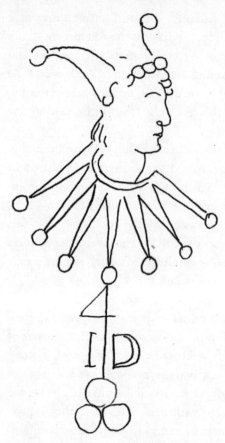

24. *The jester with cap and bells was a common seventeenth-century watermark. There may have been more than 150 versions of the jester watermark. Janse ordered such watermarked paper from Jan Sijbinck, as well as post paper, which was watermarked paper brought by postilion from Bordeaux and Germany. Even in the eighteenth century, most good paper used in England was manufactured in Holland. (Author's line drawing after Churchill,* Watermarks in Paper *[1935], cclxx, Fig. 354)*

papers and another that holds those of van Schelluyne. The moving light may also be illuminating folio pages he would have around the room, sheets pierced at the bottom and hung on the wall to dry, others that he must have to hand at any moment. The pages are, at least some of them, those ordered from Amsterdam and watermarked with the foolscap and bells. The jesters he would see against the light are figures four inches high, some five inches. He would also see pages marked with the coat of arms of Amsterdam.

About two hundred years from this winter day when Janse pronounced his oath, a French writer will reflect on the *curiosités esthétiques* of wintertime and houses. He will write of winter as the sad season and of the winter house taking "reserves and refinements of intimacy" from it. No one, of course, wrote about Janse in his winter house, keeping a fire alive while working at his papers. A scholar in Friesland did earn such a description about this time, one with a reflective tone to match the writer's soundless hours. He was a professor at Franeker University and also a local minister. The scholar's writing took place mostly during daylight, so in winter he could work at only half his capacity. His workplace was like a scriptorium where he sat at his books but was often distracted and needed to gather wood for the fire. The room was, offers the description, "above all very still." The cold made him wrap himself in an *extra-jas*, a sort of overcoat. He wrote with a goose feather and had to sharpen it carefully and often. If his ink was too solidly frozen, he had to postpone his writing. To ward off the cold, he stretched his legs and walked around the room, thinking about his writings. He then went into another room where the *Statenbijbel* rested on a high table. He turned the pages, stirring memories.

We can think that the stillness of the Frieslander's winter hours is part of Janse's experience too. Just as the scholar moves from his writing to recollections stirred by the turned pages of the Bible, perhaps Janse too moves away from his writing and is stirred by the memories that other papers and other objects in the room incite. For winter is a time when the cold confers age on memories. The house and the memories will seem old together. Janse lives with the chests and locked-away places that are the very models of stored memory and intimacy. Day after day he has come home to live with papers that are the secrets of scores of burghers and farmers. In his chest are their behaviors, long gone and stored in a language that is also moving into memory, into the past. For fifteen years, he has lived a life of secrets and old stories, hiding away what he knows.

The painter Rembrandt van Rijn reached old age around this time in Amsterdam. "Zelfs een man als Rembrandt zakte in zijn latere jaren terug," a later admirer wrote: "Even a man like Rembrandt withdrew into himself in later years." If Janse has not become withdrawn, certainly work is not filling his days. Only fifty-one men and two women have come to him over the past year, most seeking him on Saturdays, Sundays, and Tuesdays. Only twice has he undertaken to do some writing outside his own house. One day an old man wanted a will made. But Janse was still unsure about the laws regarding wills. He inserted in it that it was to have full force "notwithstanding that certain formalities required by law and usage may not have been fully observed herein." Notaries often used this clause, but perhaps it now has special meaning. For just last year, the assembly decreed that not wills but all mortgages now had to be drawn up in the English form. Those written before that date were invalid. Soon here in Albany, mortgages that Janse was writing in the early years of his practice will be referred to as "old" and "Dutch."

Directly down the street at the courthouse, another man, in another chill room, is also occupied as a scribe. Janse is not as busy as this man, Robert Livingston. For each act that Janse has written this year, the secretary has drawn up at least five. Much of the work is in writing up deeds as clerk of the town and county.

Janse is earning a small fraction of Livingston's income. Yet the papers of the two men are much the same. Almost all have to do with land. It was not so in van Schelluyne's day. If Janse has his predecessor's papers in his care and if he chooses to compare them to his own, he will discover that about a third of the more than three hundred documents that van Schelluyne notarized were not concerned with land. They were papers legalizing the commercial negotiations of the townspeople with the Netherlands and places like New Amsterdam and Long Island.

His own papers are different. Less than a quarter of them concern affairs outside the district, and only about 3 percent concern the Netherlands. In the past eight years, only two men have asked to arrange papers respecting business with Holland. The trade with *patria* is as good as gone. Even the number of traders in the town has diminished, at least among the women. Before the English came, their number was about forty-six — someone will count them one day — and now there are only six. Beverwijck as the farthest stop on a trade route reaching back to Manhattan Island, then across the sea to Texel, the Zuider Zee, and Amsterdam — perhaps even up to the other Beverwijck — is no longer a reality.

So landownership has become important. Yet the properties that are coming Janse's way to sell or lease are generally townspeople's modest investments: a single house lot, from mother to son; a farm leased because of debt; a house sold but already needing a new shingle roof. There is nothing in all of it that would tell a man that he is important. Nothing offers him a key to important matters around the town.

The properties that are coming Livingston's way are doing just that for him. The frequent entry of natives into the town, two, three, four at a time, has become a clue. Just two months ago five Mahicans appeared in the courthouse, three men and two women. They signed away rivers and lands off to the east of Kinderhoek. It is fertile land on both sides of rivers, with eight hundred acres of woodland and six stretches of rich bottomland. There is land too along the path that goes to New England and, added on, two thousand paces across the path to the south. Three Mohawk sachems had arrived before that, back in August. A high-ranking English officer and a man called John Spragge had arrived from New York City as well. Spragge and the officer were present to accept lands on the governor's behalf. They lay beyond Schenectady on both side of the great river. It was "wood lands, Pastures, Meadows, Marches creeks Rivers Rivulets Creeks Kills, trees timber." An Esopus native came a week before that and conveyed land at the Katskills. So did three natives two weeks earlier, old-timers named Schermerhoorn, Jan de Backer, and Papagay (the Parrot).

These things weren't happening before. And this appearance and reappearance of natives was preceded by occasions when about forty others, in eight different groups, had arrived in the town and stood before Livingston, putting their marks on his papers. A further twenty-one natives will be in his presence at some time in the coming year. But they are just the vendors. It is the buyers who matter: Governor Thomas Dongan, Pieter Schuyler, John Spragge, Sybrant van Schaick, Silvester Salisbury, Livingston himself. In most such arrangements — everyone knows this — men or women are able to buy priceless river lands and creeks because of their exceptional wealth. This is different. Who couldn't gather — it's all the governor had to pay — six fathoms of duffels, three guns, three kettles, three bags of powder, 60 guilders of wampum, twenty-four bars of lead, and six shirts? Becoming a large landowner is all a matter of patronage, dancing attendance on the governor.

Others realize this and feel diminished. Just last February, one of Janse's clients went around the streets shouting that sycophants in the provincial assembly were buying up all the land. But he had "money too," he raved; he could "pay for it too, even for the choicest land." The governor, he burbled on, has more power than the assembly, "and the devil take them all." Some said he was drunk. He said no, he was not as drunk as he "made out to be." Everyone, even if they did not feel as he did, would have known what he meant, but nothing could be done.

Janse was with Livingston at the courthouse earlier on this afternoon of December 3. They were playing their parts in something now called a court of common pleas rather than the old court of *schout* and magistrates. The magistrates also call themselves something novel, justices of the peace. They use the title, although they can't always spell the words and they mix Dutch and English together. Twice over the past four weeks, Pieter Schuyler identified himself as "Justes of de Pees." Others have learned to spell the words properly but don't seem to know what they mean, writing, "Justice of Peace." Still, they were the men who bestowed on him his job as assessor. Helping to compute a city's taxes was always an extra source of income for notaries. Perhaps he would arbitrate disputes in the ward. That too is a tradition and provides income.

He must have known that being a ward assessor was not without its difficulties. Six months ago, another group of aldermen was specifically instructed by the governor to act as their own assessors. Within a week, they'd begun their task, taxing things like Indian goods. But they'd made a mistake. The governor disapproved. He wrote to Livingston, not the magistrates. For some reason, a tax on the trading goods was unlawful.

The cold of the winter night falls over the town. Curfew is at nine o'clock. These are nights when the men of the burgher guard feel the cold in the guardhouse. Each householder is ordered to contribute a load of wood by the first of January. Janse will get to see each of them. As clerk of the guard, he must be notified when they fulfill their obligation. He will make another list.

JANUARY 20, 1685
Albany

The winter still chills the town. There is the need to maintain firewood and to worry about unattended fires. Two burghers think that an old man will have to be removed from their neighborhood because he throws scorching wood around his house. He is endangering his son and will possibly cause a "serious accident." He is a character around the town, one of the earliest inhabitants. Now his children are told to keep him under close supervision. They must either confine him, so he can do no harm "by fire or otherwise," or remove him from the town. The winter also sends the burgher guards out for loads of wood for the guardhouse. They look for good firewood, oak, ash, and elm.

Janse finishes a document. If he knew of the mistake made in it, he would be embarrassed. How unprofessional he has become! He has been meeting with four men, two of whom are engaged in the sale of land, and the others are witnesses. The vendor is selling land north of the town, beyond one of the farms of the Schuyler family. Unlike the others, he makes a mark on the completed paper rather than writing his signature. Janse authenticates it, writing "Quod attestor," signing his name, and identifying himself as notary.

But he tries to write English. He signs himself, "Note Republic." Perhaps there are reasons why he can't get it right. Often enough in an act a notary separated the Dutch words for "notary" and "public" or even reversed them. Decades ago, a notary in Nieuweveen in Holland had inscribed the usual "on this day appeared before me" and then identified himself as "openbaar ende bij den Hove van Hollandt geadmitteerde notaris, ter presentie van de nabescreven getuijgen," that is, public and, by the Court of Holland, licensed notary, in the presence of the undersigned witnesses.

Janse must be aware that he has experimented with English. Yet he apparently remains unaware that he cannot even spell what he is. He continues at his work. Over the coming months, his handwriting is as firm as it has been over the years. His pages are unblotted, filled with writing laid down in his customary straight lines and set within even margins.

There is nothing in them to say there will not be many more.

OCTOBER 2, 1685
"Nieuw Albanij in America"

During the year he has written only four acts. Two are leases of farmlands, one of them drawn up for Jan van Loon. It is full of detail. Another is an agreement to sell a house and lot near the courthouse. The fourth is a tradesman's contract to build a sawmill in Canada. In April, a young man, Andries Teller, was asked to examine some van Rensselaer family accounts and, for some reason, signed himself as a notary. Janse probably would not know of this. In the same month, however, the widow of Joachim Wesselsz was creating problems for the magistrates. The old woman had become, as they said, "not *compos mentis*," and her affairs were in disorder. Soon it was again said that she was "completely out of her mind." Adriaen Janse would know her. It was her husband who had bought his house and lot thirty years ago and had made a point of thanking him for prompt payment.

Now he is writing a letter to Madame Sijbinck in Amsterdam. Both men who were his contacts in Holland have now died. He had written to Guldewagen's widow but had heard nothing from her, not "a line in reply." Jan Sijbinck's wife has at least answered his appeals for information about his income. His letter to her points again and again to his sense of helplessness.

He is grieved about the death of his cousin and feeling betrayed that she has been unable to obtain his interest. He fears he is sounding like a "complainer" and knows that such people "have no friends." But he is forced to it. "I do not seek another's goods, but only what is justly due to me. I am now past 67 years of age," he adds, "so that I can not earn much more and said interest is my chief means of support." He does not know where the son-in-law who is supposed to be managing his affairs is living or even his name. Someone has the 2,000 guilders in his possession, but he has no idea who it is. Still, he takes care to place his plight within a Christian view of reward and punishment. Whoever is at fault, he recalls, "will not easily answer for it hereafter, for the present is but a short portion of life and we ought always to think of eternity."

He also looks to the future. He extends power of attorney to Madame Sijbinck, still half hoping that his interest may yet be handed to her "in a friendly way." He places an order for a ream of paper with the foolscap and bells and a pocket inkhorn. He requests an almanac "which will be good for the next few years." He makes a suggestion for the careful packing of his paper. The ream of paper may be loosened and the quires laid side by side. He commends Madame Sijbinck to God's protection and looks forward to receiving the goods, with God's help, "this summer."

He signs the letter as her friend and servant and adds, "Done in New Albany in America." He saves his copy of the letter. It is on cheap paper.

Three months before the summer comes, he hangs himself.

MARCH 12, 1686
Albany

Janse takes his own life about seventeen days after meeting with his last clients, a young man and a near neighbor who agree that within a year the older man will teach his new apprentice how to make a good cart.

He does not leave a letter. We know nothing of his reasons or feelings from what we have come to call a suicide note. We do not know whether he considered the consequences of his act, that he was condemning his soul to the everlasting torments of hell, that to keep his evil spirit from wandering the earth luring others to sin, his body could be buried at a crossroads with a stake through his heart. If he remembered that he was a notary, a man whose office had made him think often of death, a man paid to help others commit their souls to God and their bodies to the earth, the memory seems

25. *Detail of* Charitas, *Pieter Bruegel the Elder, 1559. In the larger engraving of which this is a part, Bruegel stresses the works of mercy practiced by the laity of a parish. The Christian act of burying the dead was foremost among them. Here two parishioners are placing a coffin in the sacred ground just outside a church.*

Scholars have looked for seasonal patterns to explain the incidence of suicide. In early modern Kent in England, it rose during spring. Perhaps despair deepened when others were experiencing the joys of the season. Perhaps men hanged themselves from roof beams when they could be alone while others were out-of-doors. As in Janse's case, such suicides remain a mystery. (Museum Boijmans–van Beuningen, Rotterdam)

not to have helped him. If the words of the catechism that he had taught to children came into mind — Question 101: How shall the raising up of the dead come about? — or if he gave thought to Judas Iscariot as the symbol of self-murder, these recollections seem not to have helped either.

We know nothing of the circumstances of his dying. Whether he hanged himself in his house or walked out beyond the palisades — unseen? noticed by someone? — we do not know. In eighty-six years' time, almost to the day, an Albany man will write in the family Bible, "Beautiful Weather, plenty of snow. Adieu winter." In another seventy-six years, the temperature on this day will fall to ten degrees below zero and heavy snow will cover the ground. Whether on this day there was early spring weather or snow, we do not know.

If the court followed earlier precedent, it arranged to have his body examined immediately. Nine years ago, a woman's death by drowning incited the magistrates to conduct an autopsy and open an investigation. She was pregnant and alone when she died. Had she deliberately murdered her unborn child? A jury conferred and offered its verdict: nine men voted "Not guilty"; three said "Guilty." Probably only the sheriff and the coroner Jan van Loon viewed Janse's body. His hanging was the first case of self-murder ever to reach the court records. Somehow van Loon took possession of his papers.

No one recorded where the body of Janse was buried or by whom. Only seven families paid for the pall that year. No one paid for him. We have to think that, according to custom, no one tolled the bell, no one invited friends and acquaintances to a funeral. Back in the summer of 1664 in New Amsterdam, as we remember, one of the resident burghers hanged himself. His near neighbors successfully petitioned the burgomasters to allow them to give his body a proper burial. Whether anyone spoke for Janse, we do not know.

We do know that on July 29 the English governor and his council agreed that a cousin from out of town might dispose of any property of "Adriaen Johnson van Elpendam," a suicide. And in mid-August, the local magistrates gave the same man a certificate of his death. He could now claim Adriaen Janse's inheritance or, as they put it, "a certain annuity recorded in Holland."

CHAPTER 8 The Costs
of Conquest

JUNE 24, 1701
City Hall of Albany

For fifteen years now, Adriaen Janse's notarial papers have had a mysterious history. At the time of his death, they should have come into the hands of the town secretary. Had they been the register of a notary at home in the Low Countries and had circumstances been otherwise, they would have passed from Janse to his son or a nephew or to a fellow notary. They would have remained in a town secretary's or notary's rooms, where they would have been consulted, copied, and compared. Hugo Grotius argued in the early 1620s that they gave the notary his public character and thus a kind of perpetuity. Their longevity was his living memory. With Janse it was otherwise.

In this June meeting of 1701, Jan van Loon is called upon to surrender the papers of "Adriaen van Elpendam." For some reason, he has held custody of them for these past fifteen years — but not without opposition. In November 1688, he was summoned to appear before the magistrates and told to release the papers at once. He failed to do so. Now, various people are complaining because the documents cannot be consulted, and he is again summoned by the court. He has twenty-eight days to give them up. Again he refuses. Another warrant is issued, this time calling on him to appear in early September. Only in January of the next year, 1702, does van Loon surrender the papers. He offers no explanation for having retained them for sixteen years.

Exactly where Janse's papers were during all those years or how carefully van Loon had secreted them away we do not know. In 1681 van Loon took ownership of a tract of land far to the south of Albany and soon called Loonenburg (later Athens, New York). Always a marginal man, he had arrived in Albany in the late 1670s. He refused to pay taxes and questioned the authorities' right to collect them. In the census of 1697, he was listed as one of two papists among the 379 householders of the city and county of Albany. Such people, it was thought, were inclined to have sympathies with French officials and traders to the north in Canada. They were distrusted.

Now he seems to have carried Janse's register into his marginal world. Once, in November 1696, he disturbed the papers. He and Cornelis Michaelsz had composed an agreement regarding Michaelsz's claims to land at Loonenburg. Somehow the agreement fell into Janse's papers. Other than that moment of interference with the old notary's papers, we have no evidence of how van Loon carried out his role as their self-appointed overseer.

Clearly he remembered Janse in a way that no one else did. The notary's papers had a significance to him that they had to no one else. But what those memories and meanings were he kept to himself. He lived to be an old man who reared his children as Lutherans. During his lifetime, they remained in Loonenburg, providing land for the Lutheran church and parsonage. Apparently he said nothing to them about his relationship with the stack of over two hundred pages that had belonged to Adriaen Janse.

In 1688, 1701, and 1702 there were moments when van Loon's inexplicable behavior required Janse to be remembered publicly in Albany. Other circumstances also incited council members to recall the old notary who died two, then fifteen, then sixteen years ago. In 1701, for example, his name was carried before Robert Livingston Jr. on a contract of sale referring back to the early 1680s. It could not have been the only occasion.

But memory was short. Undoubtedly there was talk about Janse's suicide in the community in the months of 1686. Interpretations must have been quietly made about such an act. Today we also search for reasons and offer explanations. We speak of the atrophying of the creative imagination, of the difference between gemeinschaft and gesellschaft, or incomplete mourning. It is a phenomenon "underreported" in the statistics, a Protestant rather than a Catholic option, or a "vast and final metaphoric." Then, the community would have pondered and spoken of its shock. Perhaps Janse's suicide brought to memory the supposed suicide of Cornelis van Tienhoven. But that was thirty years earlier; only the old would have remembered. Perhaps the townspeople thought Janse was given to melancholy. If that was the

26. East Side of Market Street from Maiden Lane, South, Albany, 1805, *James Eights. The Reformed Church stands on the right margin of Eights's drawing, at the intersection of Jonckerstraat and Handelaarsstraat, renamed State Street and Market Street. The covered market dominates the center of the picture. To its right, a male figure stands not far from the place where Adriaen Janse's house may have stood. (Collection of the Albany Institute of History and Art, Bequest of Ledyard Cogswell, Jr.)*

cause, then his self-murder was excusable. Melancholia was simply another disease. There is no reason to think they reacted to his self-murder with anything other than pity. It was an incident they could allow to fade away.

Janse's presence faded too because he had no extended family or children in Albany. His wife, her name written just once, leads us to the story of a companionable old age but little more. Tryntje's son by her first marriage remained unnamed and never, from what we can tell, entered Janse's life. There was no genealogy to carry his history forward, neither in the account of child nor in the lifetime of a family house or other property.

Janse's property was sold to strangers. Within eighteen weeks of his death, his estate was the subject of a petition made to the governor's council in New York City by his cousin's son, Jacobus de Beauvois of Long Island. Two weeks later, still in August 1686, the appeal was approved. The two houses and lots about which Janse had written to Guldewagen in 1682 were now de Beauvois's. The young cousin, however, had no reason to retain property in Albany and was soon looking to dispose of it. Within the same month, he managed to sell the house on Handelaarsstraat to one of the city's merchants. After six years, the owner bequeathed it to his son. By now, it was said to stand on the corner of Maiden Lane and Broadway. The new owner occupied it for many years and seems to have placed his own character on the house. By the early nineteenth century, some Albany houses like the old van Rensselaer manor had histories of their own. The credulous asked about resident ghosts. The property at the corner of Maiden Lane and Broadway does not seem to have provoked such questions.

Memory of Janse also waned as that of the Dutch notary generally moved into the past. Jan Juriaensz Becker died shortly before November 1698. Four years earlier, he had made a will and described himself as living at his garden "lying behind the old fort." City officials made an inventory of his notarial papers. Fifty-one documents were found. They bore some of the same family names as Janse's acts, those of people now grown old and those of their children. The sheriff took possession of the papers and delivered them to Robert Livingston. Ludovicus Cobus disappeared from the records in the 1680s. Across the years, his records disappeared as well.

Meanwhile, in New York City, it was becoming necessary to invent procedures to cover what notaries did, such as calling three witnesses to authenticate something like a power of attorney. One Dutch resident explained to an Amsterdam notary in 1693 that the precaution was needed because "there were no Dutch notaries there any longer."

Genealogies and tales of haunted houses are among the many ways the present makes use of the past. It is not really the case that memory is short or long or kept alive or dead. The act of remembering, like the act of forgetting, is a maneuver. A family, community, or nation answers a present need by endowing some event or person of the past with significance. For Janse to be remembered with some positive significance over the many decades that became the history of New York, his existence, configured variously during his lifetime out of his roles as schoolmaster, counselor to the court, and notary, needed to be thought useful enough to be reconfigured in all the narrative forms, or celebratory forms, where remembering might find an entry. His memory needed to have a niche in some of the cultural systems that called upon the past to refurbish the present. It needed to have a place in the representational repertoire of the law and of education, literature, religion, and academic history.

Janse's memory had a place. But because of the English conquest, it became an emblem of something negative. He was something grotesque, a figure of fun. The legal transformations in the New Netherland that became New York and the wider transformations of jurisprudence in England since the last quarter of the sixteenth century were too far-reaching to allow respect for older and different traditions. Through those years and well into the eighteenth century, advocates of English common law were successfully arguing that a sovereign national law should replace the traditional multijurisdictional court system of England. The power of tribunals such as admiralty courts and courts of request should be dismantled in the face of a centralized jurisprudence. This same jurisprudence was to be interpreted by constables, justices of the peace, lawyers, and judges trained at the Inns of Court, all practicing common law.

Courts merchant should be dismantled as well. They were dependent on *lex mercatoria* and operated with an eye to the concerns of merchants engaged in international commerce. They were focused on the practice of business rather than on the symbols of state power. William Blackstone was to deride such courts as functioning according to the "changeable practices of merchants." To him, and to other champions of common law, they were "foreign law," acknowledging the propriety of other ways of doing things. But this foreign law — mercantile custom, maritime law, courts merchant — was the raison d'être of notaries such as Janse. A space had also been opened within the discourse for identifying notaries as foreign and dangerous. The hatred of William Prynne for "Imperial notaries . . . who [had entered the Realm of England] and set up public Offices" that usurped the power "belonging only to our Kings and their Offices" was perhaps excessive and, on that account, unique. Nonetheless, the wider discourse that was identifying and dismantling England's multijurisdictional legal system allowed Prynne to conflate chancery and secular notaries and to present his thoughts to Charles II in 1669, the year Janse assumed his duties as notary in Albany. Notaries, then, personified something distinctly alien.

The Albany setting for this transformation of a legal system was, predictably, primitive. The generation after Janse saw just three men, two of them English, replace attorneys like Cobus. They divided the city's local law business among themselves. For most residents, they made the mayor's court a stage for "bewildering English procedures." An officer of the garrison had introduced these procedures. In his spare time, he was a lawyer.

In New York's memory, Janse could not simply be replaced. Had that been the case, a note of equivalence might have been struck. The new men now finding the law in English treatises and English cultural ways could be seen as merely standing in the place of those who had found it in Dutch commentaries and Dutch cultural ways. The new system, however, could not simply be seeded. The old had to be uprooted.

The conquest of New Netherland was not a gentleman's agreement about replacement. We can recall the declaration carried to Stuyvesant by the captains of the English warships menacing New Amsterdam in late August 1664. The Dutch were "fforraigners" who had "seated themselves" in the dominions of His Majesty of England. Already redefined by the victors as trespassers, the Dutch were living a lie. A legitimate conquest had to make Stuyvesant's earlier appeal to the English that New Netherland was settled upon "first discovery, uninterrupted possession, and Purchase of the land" forgettable. The conquest needed to be remembered from the start — from the first accounts given and those constructed thereafter — not as the replacement for but the first introduction of legitimate government. What had gone before was (where it existed at all) delinquent, primitive, and underdeveloped. It was a grotesque version of civilized — that is, English — lawgiving.

As part of a subordinated population, Dutch men who wished to pursue careers in the law or politics had no choice but to participate in the newly introduced legal practices. Ordinary Dutch residents were similarly constrained, appearing before justices of the peace, submitting papers to courts of assizes, serving as jurors. Invariably their efforts were, and were perceived to be, clumsy or absurd. They were ignorant of the simplest practices, laughable in courtroom situations they could not understand. Those most concerned to imitate the English, even a bicultural man such as Robert Livingston, drew the sharpest ridicule. Others were reported as "very ignorant" because they "could neither speak not write proper English."

Anecdotes proliferated about "the ignorance and peculiarities of what are designated Dutch justices." More generally, the Dutch were a people reluctant with pen and paper. They were even content to let the story of their uprising against the Spanish be told "by the more expert tongues and more eloquent pens of Englishmen." The memory of effective Dutch courtrooms became easy to erase. It was even easier to erase the memory of all that gave context to those Dutch courtrooms a discourse given direction by citing de Damhouder or Grotius, the appearance before the court of nonlawyers such as notaries, the daily drama of a notary and a client, the sight of a woman bent effortfully over an account book that might be required by the court. None of the unspoken rules that integrated a coherent legal system and gave the ordinary citizen a sense of living in a just society were ever brought to memory. As a later reading public peered into the past by looking at the illustrations accompanying Washington Irving's text about Father Knickerbocker, they encountered ludicrous characters from Dutch New York. There they were — slothful, roguish, and lecherous-looking men. Who could entertain the notion of them as having been serious administrators of the law? Who among these grotesques could have cared about notarized papers or acted as "good men" to a court of magistrates?

The representations of men such as Janse were certainly found to be useful, even a cause of popular entertainment. But they were used as a foil to early Anglo-American probity and virtue. For the historian Thomas Janvier, erasing the work of such men as Janse and Lachaire and Stuyvesant was a strategy for arguing that only governors like Richard Nicolls or Richard Coote helped New York achieve "that civic rectitude which was an unknown virtue in the Dutch times."

There is much hegemony in laughter. I encountered Adriaen Janse for the first time in 1976. He had signed a conveyance of land that I was reading at the New-York Historical Society. He identified himself in bowdlerized English as "Note Republic." I don't remember thinking, as Janvier did, of his lack of civic rectitude. But I do remember laughing.

In 1856, Herman Melville gave to New York its most remarkable and enigmatic scrivener, Bartelby. Melville introduced Bartelby through the narrator-employer into whose orderly, and then disrupted, life the legal scribe walked one day. Over the years since I began my research on Adriaen Janse, I have come to feel a special affinity with the narrator. He introduces himself in the opening sentences of the story:

I am a rather elderly man. The nature of my avocation, for the last thirty years, has brought me into more than ordinary contact with what would seem an interesting and somewhat singular set of men, of whom, as yet, nothing, that I know of, has ever been written — I mean, the law-copyists, or scriveners. I have known very many of them, professionally and privately, and, if I pleased, could relate divers histories, at which good-natured gentlemen might smile, and sentimental souls might weep. But I waive the biographies of all other scriveners, for a few passages in the life of Bartelby, who was a scrivener, the strangest I ever saw, or heard of. While, of other law-copyists, I might write the complete life, of Bartelby, nothing of that sort can be done. I believe that no materials exist, for a full and satisfactory biography of this man. It is an irreparable loss to literature. Bartelby was one of those beings of whom nothing is ascertainable, except from the original sources, and, in his case, those are very small. What my own astonished eyes saw of Bartelby, that is all I know of him, except, indeed, one vague report, which will appear in the sequel.

The scrivener and notary Adriaen Janse was "the strangest I ever saw." The strangeness was not, I believe, because of something in him. Although he was like Bartelby — "nothing is ascertainable, except from the original sources, and, in his case, those are very small" — there is no evidence of his being strange, let alone, like Bartelby, obscurely threatening. He was made strange by all the social and cultural systems that postdated Dutch New Netherland and that classified the significant and the insignificant, the strange and the familiar in colonial New York. He was made strange as the victors, the English and then the Yankee Americans, exercised their power to retain or discard archives, to be victors over knowledge and the story of the past.

Many others have recognized this. In 1879 a speaker addressing the Oneida Historical Society warned New Yorkers that they had already given away the power to narrate their own past. "Various historical circumstances," he said, had thrown "the writing of colonial history into the hands of New Englanders." He accompanied this warning with his own re-classification. For example, the settlements in New York after 1664 had become the "private property" of the Duke of York and "never obtained the simplest right save as the spoils of victory."

Earlier in Albany, the printer and publisher Joel Munsell had made himself into a one-man historical society. He too sought to reclassify the stores in the memory bank of New York's colonial years. Along with others, he succeeded in pushing memory backward into the Dutch period. He discovered and published early documents; he had records translated out of Dutch — and apologized for those "not so well done as could be wished." Unavoidably, he rearranged the significant and the insignificant, began to make the strange familiar. He did not pretend to say what the full significance of recovering the early Dutch records might be. He would await the historian who would use work like his "to take great countries in hand, and tell the story of their growth truly and philosophically."

Nor did he especially look to recover the life and significance of Adriaen Janse. But Janse was in the "historical facts" that he published in their tens of thousands, as early records, council minutes, ancient names and places, his "gleanings." Here was Janse as schoolmaster, Janse burying his wife, Janse's papers held by van Loon. Happenings in the court of Beverwijck and early Albany, where Janse had so often appeared, were not yet significant enough to be brought to publication. Committees set up by the city government in the 1830s and 1840s thought they bore no resemblance to the present court system and were therefore irrelevant. The city published some synopses of the records from 1675 to 1685. Munsell said they were of "no use to any body."

Just as Janse was the beneficiary of Munsell's excavations in the relics of New York's early colonial history, so he also benefited from the social impulses of the early twentieth century. Like the philosopher John Dewey or the writer Richard Wright, Arnold J. F. van Laer, New York State's archivist, was fascinated by the relationship between the community and the individual. The publication of local records, especially large collections of them, would allow researchers and historians the opportunity to measure the community's role as instrumental in shaping individual development. Determined to justify the "present tendency" to turn from Turnerian studies about the "outward movement of peoples" to those that established "the effect of the community upon the life of the individual," van Laer published Janse's notarial papers in 1918. They would, he wrote, reveal the "home surroundings, daily occupations, customs and intimate business and family relations of all classes of society."

In many ways, Janse was not the individual whom van Laer expected to emerge from his papers. He was there as background to those in their home surroundings and daily occupations and family relations — to all the others. But van Laer had his concerns and insights about Janse. Biographical notes in his preface to the volume of papers represented him, if I may suggest it, as a figure like Bartelby. For if scholars agree on anything about Melville's intentions in the story of that mysterious scrivener, it is that the tale is about the cessation of writing. Van Laer also understood Janse's life to be one of writing and its cessation. He explained Janse's suicide as follows. In late July 1686, Albany proclaimed a city charter granted by the English governor. At "the very time of the chartering of Albany as a city," Van Laer wrote, "which to him [Janse] may have meant further curtailment of his business as thenceforth all records were kept in English style, he committed suicide by hanging." To van Laer the city charter was not unequivocally a beginning to be remembered and revered. It was a cessation of something old, something Dutch in its precharter ways and in its recording of itself. Janse's ending of his writing career and his life was a suitable, if tragic, metaphor for all of this.

The humiliation of Janse and others as they experienced the loss of language competence and cultural fluency under English rule was real. For him and other townspeople of Albany, the need to abandon the Dutch language and start getting around in English was perhaps a lesser cost of conquest than other deprivations. Yet because the Dutch language was not just a notary's livelihood or a legal system's argot, because it was not just a bureaucracy's life-line but a community's everyday tool for ordering the real world, the wrenching was deep.

Janse's life was inescapably entangled with the English conquest of New Netherland. My purpose in telling his story has been to suggest how subtle and personal that entanglement was. The consequences for the men and women who found themselves subordinated after the 1660s in New York were not unlike those set in train by dozens of armed conquests elsewhere. The conquered had to read their environment, their social and moral space, in a radically different way. They had to change. The first Dutch invaders had forced native Americans to reread their ways of life against the text of an overseas Dutch way of life. Now, in the same places, Dutch colonists were made to read their cultural systems against those of the victorious English.

It became Janse's task to do this kind of reading. He had to read the per-formances of each cultural system in such a way as to find enough meaning to survive, if not to prosper or acquiesce with equanimity. While others could do it, he could not.

Notes and Reflections

1. "New Albanij"

Adriaen Janse's notarial register gives us most of the texts that are his life's story from 1669 to 1676. Almost two hundred years intervened between his death and its first translation. Another fifty years went by before it was retranslated and published by Arnold J. F. van Laer (1918). For most of the other accounts of Janse's life during this time, we are in the debt of local court secretaries who were his contemporaries. Their minutes were also inaccessible to the general public until van Laer's translations and publications began to appear in the 1920s.

If we search for the factors that incited Janse and the court secretaries to write, and to write as they did, we are drawn toward a range of cultural operators in an early modern Dutch way of life. Much about that way of life has been lost to us today, certainly almost everything about the seventeenth-century *notariaat*. We are inheritors of Anglo-American practices and a colonial history which is generally about English settlements and the rise of an Anglo-American world. There is also the irony that New Netherland was conquered by the English. They were a people who deviated from the legal practices of early modern western Europe and elected, among other things, *not* to institutionalize the role of the notary in ways that were common on the Continent. As a result, we have difficulty remembering that the office of notary once existed in colonial North America and that it was essential to one of that multicultured society's legal systems.

The many *notarisboeken*, or manuals for notaries, produced during the early modern period signal the importance of the *notariaat* in Dutch society. Commentaries on the art of the notary written by jurists and experienced notaries and an extensive (and expanding) contemporary Dutch literature on the subject further underlie its significance. They suggest that any understanding of legal practice at the time, especially the functioning of commercial law, is incomplete without a recognition of the place of the notary.

On the engraving:

Redeneerend vertoog
over het
NOTARIS AMPT,
door
ARENT LYBREGHTS

27. Title page of Redenerend Vertoog over 't Notaris Ampt, *Arent Lybreghts, 1736. A gracious female figure, representing the desire for knowledge, is led by Pallas Athena to a learned man of the law. He holds a mirror and points the woman to Lybreghts's book,* A Reasoned Discourse on the Office of the Notary. *Jurisprudence overlooks the scene. Mercury, representing commerce, looks on attentively. (Koninklijke Bibliotheek, The Hague)*

The work of the Dutch historian Adriaan Pitlo provided my entry into this material. As a founder of the Stichting tot Bevordering der Notariele Wetenschap, he initiated the publication of *Ars Notariatus*, a series of studies concerned with all aspects of the profession. Several valuable publications have since appeared in this series: Ankum, van den Bergh, and Schoordijk (1970), Krijgers Janzen (1956), Melis (1982), van den Berg (1979), and Warmelink (1952). Pitlo, however, remains the foremost interpreter of the early modern texts (1948, 1953, 1963, 1981, 1982). He consistently argued that the real professionalization of the *notariaat* came only in the eighteenth century. Before that time, strict rules governing the notary's work were only just being introduced. The notary's training was uneven, and some *notarisboeken* of dubious quality were finding publication. Also, Grotius's comments to the contrary, considerable sections of the Netherlands were still without notaries (Gehlen: 1981; Cacheux: 1960).

Pitlo worked closely with the *notarisboeken* of the early period and identified three types. The majority were *formulierboeken* that offered exact models of acts and some theoretical material. Alongside them were manuals that concentrated on theory. A third sort consisted entirely of models for imitation. Using these and other sources, Pitlo identified the seventeenth-century notary as a "half-intellectual." That is, the notary's training placed him somewhere between the ordinary burgher of limited schooling and (as they all were) university-trained lawyers. At the same time, while he recognized that most notaries were neither scholars nor leading humanists, some of them were. Public perception of them was as practitioners of the *ars dictaminis*. They pursued their profession within the wider body of men learned in the arts of calligraphy, book publication, and various levels of the public *secretariaat* (Pitlo 1948, 1981; Warmelink 1952; Wiarda 1970).

More than most scholars, Pitlo reflected imaginatively on the early *notariaat*. He repeatedly emphasized the creative side of the notary's day-to-day practice, refusing to see a drably conservative man lacking in humor and bored in a world of repetitive work (1948: 2, 25, 40–43; 1963: 6). His ideas have been broadened by studies in the series already mentioned but also by Cacheux (1960), Duinkerken (1988), Gehlen (1981, 1986), and Kok (1971). Kossman (1932) offers a fascinating glimpse of the notaries who sold their services in the precincts of the Binnenhof at The Hague. In 1989 Heersink used the criminal court records of Amsterdam from 1600 to 1800 to measure the degree to which practicing notaries actually met the criteria set out in the prescriptive literature.

The purpose of Pitlo's work, and that of Heersink (1989) and others, was more to explore the evolution of the *notariaat* across the early modern Netherlands than to place it within the broader system of Dutch jurisprudence and international commercial law. Coquillette (1981, 1987), Trakman (1980, 1981), and van Caenegem (1979) are especially useful for such a comparative perspective.

In 1964, Jacob Schiltkamp produced a compendious study of the *notariaat* in the overseas stations of the West India Company, including New Netherland. He concluded that the profession functioned overseas much as it did at home. Although he points out that the notarial registers in the New York archives are more complete than those in other settlements, neither he nor any other scholar has, to my knowledge, used them as a way into the cultural life of early New York. The papers of the notary Salomon Lachaire, for example, await serious consideration (Scott and Stryker-Rodda 1978).

Authors of *notarisboeken* such as Lybreghts (1736), Schoolhouder (1722), Thuys (1590, 1645), van Leeuwen (1678), and van Wassenaar (1746b) suggest the considerable intellectual acumen expected of the notaries who were their readers. Van Leeuwen spoke for many of these commentators, summarizing the central place of the notary and insisting that on him rested the good order of countless Dutch cities (599). Schoolhouder is the best example of a writer determined to offer simplified models for easy imitation by notaries and other clerks. A writer such as Jacob Verwey, in his *Ars Testandi* of 1656, also presented a model will, six pages in length (Pitlo 1948: 39).

Seventeenth- and eighteenth-century commentators on civil and criminal law are also sources for understanding what courts expected of notaries. Van Wassenaar (1746b) followed the usual formula for such treatises. After setting out the simple definition of the notary, he offered rules governing proper practice, advice on the creation of a proper register, commentary on the laws with which the notary needed to be familiar, and finally a dictionary of useful terms. Notaries were also a subject of attention — and particularly of warnings against criminal practices — in Grotius (see Lee 1926; de Damhouder 1618, 1642; Rooseboom 1656: chap. 44; and van Zutphen 1636: 382–84 and passim).

For the office of the notary in England, Brooks, Hemholz, and Stein (1991), Clanchy (1993), Cressy (1980), and Purvis (1957) are helpful. Steven Justice (1994) provides a brief but intriguing interpretation of a bored fifteenth-century English notary. The office of the notary in Scotland is worth studying because Roman law influenced legal codes there as it did in the Netherlands. It is detailed in *Ars Notariatus* (1740) and in Thomson (1790), where, among other things, the examples of acts likely to be executed by a notary point immediately to a society far more concerned about land (and feudal landowners) than, as in the Dutch case, seaborne and inland commerce. Pappafava (1880, 1901) looks at notarial systems across many nations. For those studying early New York, his study on the development of the *notarisambt* in Dutch South Africa is especially intriguing (1901).

JUNE 10, 1669
"Albany"

Court records are the source for Janse's appointment as notary and his first experiences in office (van Laer 1926: 80, 69). They (and earlier court records) also provide data on the magistrates and the court secretary, Ludovicus Cobus, as well as Janse's occupation as schoolmaster.

In 1675 Janse executed a deposition against Robert Livingston. In it he stated his date of birth according to the church calendar (and Julian calendar of the English) and deposited a copy of the act in his own notarial papers (van Laer 1918: 329). In 1668 he granted power of attorney to his wife, naming her as Tryntje Jans (van Laer 1934–35). I have translated a notary's oath of office taken in 1674 from Schiltkamp (1964: 297). Valcooch is quoted in Wouters and Visser (1926: 90). Van Deursen (1979: 5, 28) is one of many scholars who notes that schoolmasters frequently supplemented their income by serving as notaries. Merwick (1980, 1990), van Laer (1927), Weise (1884), and Wilcoxen (1984) have tried to reconstruct the shape of the early Beverwijck community on the basis of the available, but incomplete, data on the natural and built environment. The first maps were constructed under English occupation. They are useful only for the period after about 1690.

Janse could expect to have an active practice as notary because Dirck van Schelluyne had not taken up his commission (Christoph and Christoph 1982: 198, 276; see van Laer 1926: 69 and 1928: 76). Van Schelluyne's papers and the court records show that Becker was distrusted (van Laer 1918: 19, 1926: 107, 115, 143). In any case, he practiced erratically, leaving Cobus, who, despite his heavy drinking, appeared before the court frequently as notary and therefore can also be easily traced in the minutes.

JULY 12, 1669
Albany

Nothing that I have found in Janse's papers suggests that his clientele consisted of anything other than ordinary burghers and farmers. The acts that he executed on this day and then in August (van Laer 1918: 313–14, 308, 309) are part of some 250 documents that came into the hands of the Albany City Council in 1702 and are preserved today in the Albany County Hall of Records. The collection is incomplete. In the early twentieth century, for example, additional documents were found among the papers of Johnson L. Redmond (van Laer 1934–35: 1). At least four additional acts are to be found in papers relating to New York City, and three are in the Gemeentearchief Amsterdam. This is not surprising, but it means that, although van Laer surmised that the register is "almost complete" (and I am in agreement), any attempt at quantification, particularly any attempt to estimate Janse's yearly income, must remain tentative.

Early *notarisboeken* and commentaries by scholars such as Pitlo and Heersink repeatedly point to the care notaries were meant to take in the appearance and preservation of their protocols. Thus we have Pitlo's quote from the notary-commentator Adriaen van Nispen about an act meant to resemble a printed text (Pitlo 1948: xvi). Marginalia were considered to be crucial textual elements in a document because they recorded its ongoing history. They were essential to the management of business (see, for example, Macasar, *Dagregister,* 1790). At the same time, they added to the number of representations of their own *burgerlijke* world which the Dutch so widely craved to see (Hirsch 1991: 104). Spierings (1984: 66) draws attention to the use of *papierstrookjes* as frowned upon in notarial registers. Van der Linde (1983: xxvi) notes an autographed slip of paper pinned to the bottom of a page in a record book, probably by the writer in the 1600s, and I have encountered one or two in my own research.

The writers of manuals for notaries insisted that they observe the obligation of stating the source of their authority and the jurisdiction within which they were authorized to practice. Grotius (Lee 1936) is a fine example of this insistence. Janse's papers carry the account of his wording and rewording of attestations during these days (van Laer 1918: 308, 313, 386, and see act executed before Willem Bogardus of New York City, 312).

Townspeople other than Janse were also confused by the meaning of "Albany" — perhaps today's Albanians are still bewildered. The correspondence of Jeremias van Rensselaer (van Laer 1932b) offers, as it does on many matters, insight into the burghers' misunderstandings immediately after 1664 and is briefly cited in Merwick (1990: 173). If Pretyman and Fernow (1886) are correct in stating that the flag of the New England colonies flew over Beverwijck after 1664, the mistaken notion of townspeople that they were living in New England becomes somewhat more understandable; see La Montagne (1670).

NOVEMBER 26, 1669
Albany

Court minutes and notarial papers, the deacons' account books, and Jeremias van Rensselaer's correspondence all testify to the subsistence living of most burghers and farmers. Hence the prevailing fear of falling at any time into the "poor community." Especially helpful in getting some sense of this fear — and of the episodes explored here — are the minutes published by van Laer and Janse's papers (van Laer 1926: 31, 32, 85, 182, 188, 192, 204, 205, 285; 1918: 36, 365, 366 for *kind van Weelde* and *kind van Armoede*).

The court's hunger for proper books is documented in its own minutes (van Laer 1926: 65, 147, 106, 159, and passim). Janse's call to act as a counselor to the court is in van Laer (1926: 73, 103, 104). Lovelace's failure to recall his commission is in Christoph and Christoph (1982: 309, 310) and reprinted in Munsell (1849–59: 4:10).

THE TRADING SEASON, 1670
Albany

Intermittent violence always marked *handelstijd*, the trading season, and is well documented in the records. Both Shattuck (1993) and Merwick (1990) have reconstructed the affairs of this summer in some detail. In the lead-up to *handelstijd* — and I think the months before May 1 were thought to be that — Janse's papers continued to accumulate. These early 1670 incidents are recorded in them (van Laer 1918: 314, 366–71; for my direct quotes 366, 367, 369, 371). The best extended example of French hostilities around Albany is to be found in the 1665–66 records. Different perspectives on the events are offered in Bell (1862), Eccles (1964), Fernow and O'Callaghan (1853–87: 3), Goldstein (1969), Jennings (1984), O'Callaghan (1849–51: 1:57–84), and Richter (1992). Richter is one of several scholars who enlarge on the distrust with which the Dutch and natives lived, each manipulating the other in a relationship of mutual dependence. He, and Jennings (1984), O'Donnell (vander Donck 1968 [1841]), and Franklin (1979), would read vander Donck, Megapolensis, and other contemporary commentators as I do, that is, as expressing a high regard for Indian ways while at the same time considering them *de wilden*. The term is an ambiguous one. Like *de luiden* (the people), *de naturellen* (those in a state of nature) or *het inwooners* (residents of a given place), *de wilden* should not be taken as unequivocally pejorative. Elsewhere I have explored the use of these terms in the context of the first Dutch-Amerindian contacts, when, I would argue, each side saw the other as (an ambiguous term too) tricksters (1994).

Father de Lamberville's letter to van Rensselaer from Canada is in the director's correspondence, as are van Rensselaer's expressions of his anxiety about the continual intertribal fighting and further French incursions (van Laer 1932b: 447 [as editor, van Laer places the undated letter with other 1671 correspondence], 413, 440).

Janse's confrontations with the disorder of *handelstijd* in June are recorded in his papers (van Laer 1918: 315–17). I have placed them in the context of some of the many descriptions of a flagrant disregard for trading ordinances found in the court minutes (van Laer 1926: 95, 104, 148, and see 96, 111; for choice locations for snagging natives into illicit trading arrangements, see 135 and 306, and Munsell 1849–59: 4:13). The locations of houses like Bruyn's were identified by Pearson in 1859–60 and published by Munsell (1865–72: 4:196). Since he owned several properties, it is impossible to be certain that the house near the south gate was the scene of the incident on June 23.

Stuyvesant's ordinance of 1658 was a harsh attack on notaries. It suggests that any evidence of deceit or avarice on their part quickly aroused a lingering cynicism. Fernow (1897: 2:17) reproduces the ordinance, as does O'Callaghan (1868: 329–33). Krijgers Janzen offers evidence of notaries denounced as vultures and the devil (1956: 19, 20). Suleiman discusses the often widespread fraud found among early modern French notaries (1987: 71, 72). Camporesi cites popular Italian distrust of notaries (1990: 8).

JULY 5, 1670
Albany

Janse's work on Pietersz's behalf is documented in his papers and the court records of Albany and New York City (van Laer 1918: 317–20, 312–13, 1926: 46; Fernow 1897: 6:272). The traditional saying about the devil's punishment of a dishonest or careless merchant is in Yamey, citing the 1547 work of Jan Ympyn (1989: 19).

For the location of Evertsz's house in 1670, I have used Pearson's work in Munsell, since his findings seem consistent with other data on property conveyances (1865–72: 4:193). Early public records offer some evidence on Janse's property transactions during this and an earlier period (Pearson 1869: 28, 64, 65, 78, 99, 100, 278, 298, 319, 355, 395; van Laer 1919: 22n33; Munsell 1849–59: 5:132, 133). They fail, however, to pinpoint his residence with certainty, not least because in 1668 he referred to ownership of "houses and lots," and again in 1682 he declared ownership of two properties but identified neither (van Laer 1934–35: 7, 1918: 495). From later evidence, we can tentatively establish that he lived on Handelaarsstraat near Maiden Lane; see the comments on " 'Nieuw Albanij in America,' " below.

Dutch law expected that wills would be executed before a notary and remain lodged with him even after they were passed before two magistrates and a town secretary. Grotius wrote that witnesses to a will did not give it authenticity (Lee 1936: 141). On the question of the executorial power of notarized acts, see Gehlen, who suggests that the intervention of a judge was not necessary because the notary's acts were public acts, although in the Netherlands the "mere formality" of calling upon a judge was often introduced (1981: 107). For the Duke's Laws concerning the archiving of wills in lower New York during this time, see Christoph (1980: 9 and see 21, 24).

SEPTEMBER 23, 1670
Albany

The uneasy contact between the English soldiers and the inhabitants of Albany is found in court records, the correspondence of van Rensselaer, and especially the correspondence and reports of English officers collected in Fernow and O'Callaghan (1853–87: vols. 3 and 13, and 4:162–64), Christoph (1980), Christoph and Christoph

(1989), Foote (1966), Christoph, Scott, and Stryker-Rodda (1976a, 1976b), Munsell (1849–59: 4:19), and Christoph and Christoph (1982: 69). The minutes of Lovelace's executive council carry his warning about the instability of Dutch-English relations (Palsits 1910: 2:757, or see Christoph and Christoph 1982: 523). The accounts of the Esopus "mutiny" and other disturbances are in Fernow and O'Callaghan (1853–87: 13:406–16).

Baker's appeal to the general is in van Laer (1926: 133–34). The book of general entries kept during the administrations of Nicolls and Lovelace carries the rebuke to Swart (Christoph and Christoph 1982: 305). How and why the burghers "voted" to install Salisbury as *schout* remains unclear (van Laer 1926: 196, 197), as does the choice of Janse as notary by the Lutheran minister Fabricius. References to "those of the Augsburg Confession" and to the property conveyance are in van Laer (1926: 144, 1918: 375, 376). Munsell notes Fabricius's arrival with Lovelace (1849–59: 4:14). I am unable to explain why a disproportionately large number of attestations were taken by Janse from the town's Lutherans.

Janse and Swart were appointed as arbiters during the December 8 court session (van Laer 1926: 206).

LATE DECEMBER 1670
Albany

Janse's first year as notary was not a busy or lucrative one. Although we have some idea of the charges he was allowed to ask for his services, we simply cannot reconstruct the number of occasions when he engaged in other fee-producing work such as offering legal advice, traveling outside the city for clients, or making copies of acts (O'Callaghan 1868: 331, 332; for "client," 330, 332). In Holland, the annual earnings of a master carpenter were close to 468 guilders, or 9 a week, *if* he worked every week of the year. Those of a common laborer were 234, or 4.5 a week. Janse would have had to expect his income to fall somewhere within this range (van der Woude 1991: 300).

Part of the explanation for a disappointing income in 1670 lay in the disastrous trading season. It was a calamity that variously affected every burgher and could not be overcome until the next season (van Laer 1932b: 433, 441–42, 1926: 226). Janse's call upon a by-employment was a widely adopted strategy. Van Deursen emphasizes, correctly I think, that such employments were welcomed by Dutch men and women as much for the expansiveness they provided in one's life as for income (1978a: 29, 30).

The sources are generous in documenting day and night schools in Albany, and some of the evidence is presented in van Laer 1918: 422, 485, 524, 530, 532, 544, 547, 561; and see van Laer 1920: 200, where Janse appears in 1655 to have had only one competitor as schoolmaster. The same sources, however, offer nothing on the average schoolday, nor do they allow an exact estimate of the number of men (and probably women) giving instruction at any one time during this period. It is possible that Albany had its six masters because, if parallels with the Low Countries are valid (and as Valcooch complained), one could pay as little as 13 guilders to be appointed as master in some communities (Durantini 1983: 167).

Becker's appeal and Lovelace's intervention in schooling is in Christoph and Christoph (1982: 345) and van Laer (1926: 170–71). Scholars seem to be in agreement that education came to receive far less attention under English rule; see Vanderbilt (1899: 22), Hamlin (1939: 2), Kilpatrick (1912: 18), Howard (1991). Although Biemer's main interest is in women and criminal law in early New York, her data are also enlightening on female education and the negative effects of the English conquest (1991).

Lovelace's strange identification of Fort Albany is in Fernow and O'Callaghan (1853–87: 13:464).

JULY 6, 1671
Fort James, New York

The distance of Albany from New York City and a recalcitrant populace thwarted the designs of Lovelace (and later English governors) to settle a military frontier that effectively combined the efforts of the Albany garrison and a local "militia." Dutch ignorance of what those designs entailed and their ignorance of English understandings of a local militia were obstacles as well. Fishman is one of many scholars who note the distinction drawn by seventeenth-century Dutch people between an urban burgher guard and "active military men" (1979: 29).

In this episode — in which Janse was unknowingly a pawn — the sources point to disingenuousness on Lovelace's part. They also indicate mutual misunderstanding of deeply embedded cultural practices and assumptions. Munsell can be consulted for the governor's correspondence with Delaval (1849–59: 4:24–26). Janse's role and the roles of local residents such as van Rensselaer are available in the court minutes, Janse's papers, and van Rensselaer's correspondence (van Laer 1918: 321, 322, 324; 1926: 226n, 259, 260, 266; 1932b: 417, 418, 433). Janse's papers documenting his role as clerk in 1672 are in van Laer (1918: 322, 324). The court's apparent indifference to pursuing fines is especially evident in 1657 and is in van Laer (1923: 83–87).

NOVEMBER 1671
Albany

Janse's leave-taking of Gerbertsz is one of the few recorded instances of a leisurely get-together with friends (van Laer 1918: 320, 383, 384). In the 1660s, Gerbertsz dictated a will and in it described their relationship as that of "good friends" (van Laer 1918: 219). Biographical data on him are in van Rensselaer's letters, early public records, and Janse's papers (van Laer 1932b: 182, 216, 339, 406; Pearson 1869: 491; van Laer 1918: 219, 220).

The activity that annually accompanied burghers' business trips to the Low Countries can be found in the notarial papers and court records of New Amsterdam and Beverwijck. Scott and Stryker-Rodda's edition of Lachaire's papers (1978) and van Laer's collection of van Schelluyne's (1918) are especially valuable. Elsewhere I have made some calculations on the number of voyages that Beverwijck's burghers made to the Netherlands, but these are by no means definitive (Merwick 1990: 114, 120). Comparisons of van Schelluyne's and Janse's extant papers on this matter suggest a difference in the number of men and women returning to Holland after the English conquest.

The evidence for a gradual restriction of commerce for Albany's residents is consistent with data on English policies that denied them free trade, including, of course, intercourse with the Netherlands. In their own way, Biemer's findings regarding female traders and proprietors correlate interestingly with this evidence. She finds that the number of traders in Albany fell from 46 in 1654–64 to 10 in 1665–74, 6 in 1685–94, and 0 in 1695–1700. In New York City the number fell from 134 in 1653–63 to 43 in 1664–74. The number of women who were proprietors of businesses in Albany fell from 13 in 1654–64 to 9 in 1675–84 and 3 in 1695–1700. In New York City the number declined from 50 in 1653–63 to 17 in 1664–74 (1991: 76).

Gerbertsz's departure and something about the friends who saw him off is in van Laer (1926: 268, 1928: 374, and 1918: 137, 320, 387, 390). The early appearance in New York City of contracts acceptable in law on the basis of witnesses alone is in Fernow (1897: 6:165).

APRIL 18, 1672
Albany

The magistrates' public recognition of Janse's contribution to the town's well-being is documented in van Laer (1926: 298). Egmond has found that there were more than three hundred largely independent urban or rural first-instance courts in the provinces of Holland, Zeeland, and Brabant alone. Though lacking any particular legal training, magistrates dealt repeatedly, and judiciously, with a range of criminal cases (1993: 12, 23). He also found that magistrates were prone to record "an abundance of concrete and often immensely detailed description of the offenses committed" — even expressing their own "almost personal sense of outrage" at the commission of offenses within their jurisdiction (9).

The Albany court and Janse recorded the minutiae of the community's everyday life in representations that matched the realism of Dutch artists at the time. They took pleasure in representing daily happenings in nothing more than a sort of documentary record (Carroll 1993: 118). For a further discussion of realist representations, see the comments on "Beverwijck," below.

Janse's role as assistant to the court is in van Laer (1926: 158, 285, 291, 298). De Schepper directs us to the term *reilen en zeilen* (1988: 58). For use of the phrase "resting with me," consult Christoph and Christoph (1989: 245). Sullivan et al. (1927: 1867) as well as Yamey (1950) and Edey and Thomson (1963: 9) indicate that "Good Men" or "Tribunal of Well-Born Men" were common terms for counselors (often notaries) who served the courts.

Janse's modest role in the church hierarchy is in van Laer (1926: 298, 304, 305), as are Rooseboom's appointment (62) and his church duties and emoluments (74, 228, 249, and van Laer 1918: 353–54, 1923: 267; Pearson 1869: 92). In appointing Rooseboom and Janse, the town may have been adopting the practice followed in a city such as Utrecht, where two churchwardens were appointed, one specifically as gravedigger and the other as *kerkschout*, that is, someone responsible for order during church services (Leeuwenberg 1988: 93). The Reformed church in Flatbush, Long Island, gave wider scope to its churchmasters than I have been able to establish for Janse (Nooter 1994: 19–21).

A penchant for secrecy — discussed in "*Patria*," below — helps explain the strenuous efforts made by burghers to ensure that the privacy of their incomes was preserved and respected. Van Laer has the figures that Janse sent to Guldewagen in the form of a financial account (1918: 494). Otherwise we have no record of his income or expenses for any single year. Cobus seems to have covered some of his expenses by writing citations for the bench and pursuing people for other sorts of fees; see van Laer (1926: 130, 323). J. G. van Marcken gave up the *notarisambt* (306). Cobus's identification of the courtroom as "the king's house" and the bench's role as actors on a world stage because of England's geopolitical policies are found in Pearson (1869: 489) and Christoph and Christoph (1982: 489). Van Laer carries the account of the quartering of soldiers (1926: 299).

FEBRUARY 14, 1673
Albany

Court minutes give some detail of the execution of Kalcoep and Keketamp from the local officials' point of view (van Laer 1926: 327, 328). A letter of Lovelace to Salisbury as well as the commission for the trial is in Christoph and Christoph (1982: 522, 523). Bridenbaugh's edition of John Pynchon's letters carries his peripheral involvement in this tragic affair (1982: 113, 270). Stuart's name appears several times in the records during these years. See, for example, the account of his shanty in van Laer 1918: 466–68.

Janse never used his patronymic as part of his signature — although court clerks citing him did. We can only guess that he dropped "Janse" out of disdain for his father. The contract here is in van Laer 1918: 408.

AUGUST 9, 1673, TO JUNE 11, 1674
Albany and the Hague

Accounts of the months from August 1673 to November 1674 are few, although for events and changes occurring throughout these months consult Fernow and O'Callaghan (1853–87: 2:540–745) and (presenting some of the same documents) State Historian (1898: 159–264). My reconstruction of the period out of Janse's experiences and from his possible viewpoint is derived from van Laer (1918: 326, 328, 409–11; Fernow and O'Callaghan 1853–87: 2:708, 593, 599, 531, 565–66; van Laer 1928: 12 and see 34; State Historian 1898: app. L, 176).

Both Dutch and English authorities meted out punishments when the province changed hands. My references, including those pertaining to de Dekere, are Naber (1934: 107), Christoph and Christoph (1982: 29, 38, 47, 104, 394, 395), Stokes (1915–28: 4:268), and Weise (1884). Stuyvesant reported de Dekere allegedly oppressing the poor, and elsewhere he is also described as a tough administrator (Stuyvesant 1657; Pearson 1869: 242). The attempt of Dutch merchants such as van Ruyven to convince the States General of the value of the province is in Fernow and O'Callaghan (1853–87: 2:526) and reprinted in Lambrechtsen (1841: 115, 116).

Fernow and O'Callaghan provide the decisions of the States General regarding New Netherland (1853–87: 2:531, 565–66).

MID-OCTOBER 1674
Willemstadt

The list of those invited to van Rensselaer's funeral is held at the Albany Institute of History and Art and reprinted in Schermerhorn (1917). Alterations to the government of Albany (and Esopus and Harlem) can be found in Fernow and O'Callaghan

(1853–87: 2:480, 526, 627; for Esopus, 650; for Harlem, see Pierce 1903: 77). Colve's encouraging words to the natives and his reference to Willemstadt as a city are in Fernow and O'Callaghan (1853–87: 13:480, 2:526). Like the family at home, van Rensselaer expressed concern about control of the province throughout this period (van Laer 1932b: 403, 465, 472, and see Fernow and O'Callaghan 1853–87: 2:541, 542). His words about praying in secret and not expecting the return of the English are in van Laer 1932b: 461.

Maria van Rensselaer's letters are less revealing than those of her husband, Jeremias. It is she, however, who begins to live under the government of Edmund Andros, writing of events and receiving revealing letters from family members such as Stephan van Cortlandt. Schrick (1994: 34) suggests (without documentation) that Andros had mastered the Dutch language while in Holland in the 1650s. Janse assured Guldewagen in 1676 that he had a copy of David Janse's will (van Laer 1918: 334).

JANUARY 28, 1675
Albany

It would be easy to allow the figure of Robert Livingston to overshadow that of Adriaen Janse. The volume of his papers, and not least those he kept himself, is testimony to his important role in early New York history. The meeting with Janse is in van Laer (1918: 329). The Livingston-Redmond Collection contains the account book Livingston kept in Rotterdam from January to December 1670, in which he expressed his hope of recording everything "op de maniere van Italiaens Boeckhouden." Observers' descriptions of Rotterdam during his years there as a youth — and they were prosperous years for the city — are available in Hazewinkel (1943: 26–31), and see Hazelzet (1944). Steven (1832) makes the point that two languages, Dutch and English, were part of Livingston's life in the city.

Livingston's ambition and ruthlessness in Albany as seen by contemporaries is, inter alia, in Fleming (1901: 129). Leder's biography (1961: 13, 14) picks up Livingston's altarcation with Janse and Schaets in this January. Kierner's 1992 study of the Livingston family is useful but, in my judgment, overly sympathetic to Robert Livingston.

Further accounts that provide a context for the meeting of Janse and Livingston are other papers of Janse (van Laer 1918: 441), Weise (1884: 174), court minutes (van Laer 1928: 30, 34, 48, 93, 103, 105), the papers of Edmund Andros (Christoph and Christoph 1989: 421), and Maria van Rensselaer's correspondence (van Laer 1935: 128). The saying about the ruthless man who takes the best for himself is in van Laer (1926: 167).

Carl Carmer offers a version of Nicolaus van Rensselaer's vision in *The Hudson* (1939: 62). For another, see Leder (1961: 21). A contemporary poem also identifies van Rensselaer as a prophet (Murphy 1865: 161). Roodenberg discusses Dutch practices of reconciliation that Janse might have expected Livingston to honor (1991: 172, 173). Pearson (1869) and van Laer (1916, 1919) have published some of Livingston's papers. The court minutes published after 1675 are van Laer's work as well.

Domine Schaets appears regularly in the town records of this period. His name also recurs in the ecclesiastical records, where, for example, he is cited as having been a schoolmaster in Beets in the Netherlands before emigrating to New Netherland (Hast-

28. The Regents of the Lepers' House, *Jan de Bray, 1667. The artist depicts the regents of one of Haarlem's charitable institutions. Had the painting been executed sixteen years earlier, in 1651, Dammas Guldewagen would have been portrayed among the dignified overseers. (Frans Halsmuseum, Haarlem)*

ings 1901–5, Index 1916: 1:308–9). Van der Linde (1983) has sensitively translated Domine Henricus Selijns's papers relating to the congregation in Brooklyn. Nooter (1994) has studied the deaconry and ministry in Flatbush, and Balmer (1989) has published a comprehensive account of religious affairs from the earliest years to the late eighteenth century. We still await a study of what it meant to be a minister in Dutch New York.

SUMMER 1675
Albany

Andros's papers and those of the local court during these months show his intention of subjecting Albany to greater control than had been exerted under either Nicolls or Lovelace (van Laer 1928: 16–23 and passim, and see Pearson 1869: 143; Weise 1884: 175, quoting Dankaerts on the fort; Scott 1983: 30).

The court sessions of August 24 and September 7 are in the minutes (van Laer 1928: 13, and see 11, 12, 16–22). Janse's and Swart's further work on Stuart's estate is in the same volume at 132, 134, 142. Early records in Pearson have Janse's and Swart's sale of Stuart's house (1869: 120). For resentment at the imposition of direct taxes based on personal

Guldewagen.

29. *Guldewagen family coat of arms. The shield of the device is red with the central design of the cornucopia in white. Sheaves and stars are in white as well. (From "Verzameling van Echte Achtbare Heeren Raden in de Vroedschap, sedert den Jare 1618 . . . der Stad Haarlem," Gemeentearchief Haarlem)*

30. Portrait of Dammas Guldewagen, *Cornelis van Noorde, eighteenth-century copy of the original portrait by Jan de Bray. (Gemeentearchief Haarlem)*

wealth, see van Laer (1928: 30–48), and for how extraordinary this public exposusre would be elsewhere among the Dutch, de Schepper (1988: 69).

SEPTEMBER 18, 1675
Albany

Janse would have been doing work for the two merchants about the same time Guldewagen was writing him regarding his inheritance (van Laer 1918: 428–30, and for other attestations taken during these months 432, 433, 435). Albany's merchant community had been calling on Sijbinck's services for many years; see the comments on "Albany," below. Negotiations involving Sijbinck close to this time are in the court minutes and notarized acts held in Amsterdam. See, for example, van Laer 1928: 271, 274; Gemeentearchief Amsterdam (hereafter GA), Sijbinck (1674).

Information on Dammas Guldewagen is surprisingly scarce, given his importance and that of the family in Haarlem. The Haarlem Gemeentearchief holds nothing of significance on him. Fijen, Melching, and Peterse (1977) and Wildeman (1898) offer only sketchy information. Schwartz and Bok (1990) have used inventories to study the career of Pieter Saenredam. They relate the great painter to the Guldewagen family, one of whom — probably in a lateral line — was also a well-known artist of the time.

JUNE 19, 1676, OLD STYLE
"In Albany in America"

Adriaen Janse's first letters to Guldewagen and Sijbinck are in his register (van Laer 1918: 333–36; "In Albany in America" is his identification of his town, 334. For people wanting to dress like burghers, 422). Court minutes refer to Janse's reappointment as schoolmaster (van Laer 1928: 88).

2. *Patria*

1616
Delft, in Holland

Little is known of Jan Janse's life before he sailed to New Netherland. Baptismal, marriage, and burial records are in the Gemeentearchief Leiden (hereafter GL). Archives relating to property ownership are available there as well. In 1992, Kuypers completed a short genealogy of the van Ilpendam family. It offered further biographical detail on Jan Janse as well as his brothers, Joachim and David. The holdings of GL provide further sources pertaining to David, including the will jointly made with his wife; see Oude Notarieële Archieven, archief van de notaris Jacob Fransz. van Merwen, 1635–44, Inv., no. 5438, f. 29ro. Jan's sister Geertruijt Jansdr. van Ilpendam and her family also enter Kuypers's genealogy, and data on her and her family are in the GL. Jan and Adriaen Janse appear in orphanmasters' records also kept there.

Blankert (1978) offers a useful description of Delft when Janse's immediate neighborhood also happened to be that of Jan Vermeer. Dekker (1978) draws attention to the *vrouwenoproer* in Delft in August 1616. Johan Maurits's description of Delftshaven is quoted by Boxer (1957: 71).

Many Leidenaars were eager for overseas adventure with the East India Company (VOC) and West India Company. Bevaart (1989) follows the careers of some of these men. Jan Janse was not alone in casting his fortunes with the West India Company. The risk-taking is an interest of van Deursen (1978a: 104), but Schama (1987: 343 and passim) and other scholars have written of it as well. The engagement of patrician families such as the de Laets and de Foreests in the overseas companies is documented in van Laer (1908). The involvement of Jan Janse's family is in Kuypers (1992); GA, Carel de Beauvois (1685); and "Raad en Vroedschap" (n.d.: 66). Schama (1987: 343) and Duysentdaelers 1659: chap. 1, 22) offer some idea of the fearsome court of bankruptcy in Amsterdam.

1635
Pernambuco

The early years of the West India Company have been described in many studies: Boxer (1957), Hart (1959), Menkman (1947), O'Callaghan (1846, 1848), Rink (1986), and van Winter (1978), to name only a few. The company's papers up to 1700 were sold at public auction in 1821. Of its extant papers, therefore, less than 3 percent concern the first half of the seventeenth century, and those relating to the years between 1626 and 1637 have been lost. Joannes de Laet's multivolume *Jaerlyck Verhael* is in chronicle form but remains the most valuable source for the company's overseas operations in such places as Brazil. De Laet's careful work allows some reconstruction of the voyaging of the *Pernambuco* from 1632 to 1635, as well as the coastal raids and siege of Porto Calvo in 1636 (Naber 1934: 3:84, 108, 136, 197, 209–13, and Naber and Warnsinck 1937: 4:4, 25–31, 46, 72, 152–61, 212–16, plate 6, opp. 212). He registers the names of ships sent out to Brazil annually. The *Pernambuco*, for example, sailed in 1634 and not again before 1636. Either Jan Janse was aboard in 1634 (and therefore saw action as supercargo all through to January 1636, when he was captured) or he sailed in 1635 on another vessel and took up his duties that year. Like the *Windt-hondt* and the *Haringh*, the *Pernambuco* was a larger ship than the 80-to-100-ton vessels the West India Company usually sent out (Hazelzet 1944).

Boxer's elegantly written history is a reliable treatment of the Dutch in Brazil and also tells the story of Porto Calvo (1957). Jan Janse's service on the *Pernambuco* and at Porto Calvo and his return to Amsterdam are documented in Hoffman (1935: 381). Cornelis van Lodesteijn's service and death are also in Hoffman (382) but not corroborated by Kuypers (1992). The field of battle is in de Laet, where it is acknowledged that accounts differ regarding the number of Dutch casualties (Naber and Warnsinck 1937: 4: plate 6, opp. 212, and see 216).

1636
Amsterdam

Overvoorde and de Roo de la Faille offer a careful reconstruction of the buildings of the West India Company and the VOC in the mid-1630s, even though they work with scant evidence (1928). A fully elaborated interpretation of the company's early operations in New Netherland has yet to be written, but Bachman (1969), Hart (1959), Rink (1986), Stokes (1915–28), and van Winter (1978) have convincingly established that its designs were well intentioned but often blundering. Sources that I have used to fill out Jan Janse's (and Adriaen Janse's) years on Manhattan Island are in Fernow and O'Callaghan (1853–87: 1, 12, 13), Innes (1902), Wieder (1925), Scott and Stryker-Rodda (1974a, 1974b, 1974c, 1974d), Stokes (1915–28: 1, 2, 4). Stokes uses "Records of Old West India Co., No. 14, CXV, fol. 177vo." for Janse's capture and return to Holland as well as his plea for lost wages. Following van Laer (1908: 355), he identifies Jan Janse as supercargo (1915–28: 4:84). Kiliaen van Rensselaer's meeting with the directors is in van Laer (1908: 83, 84).

Van Rensselaer's letters and memorandums are by far the most rewarding sources for reconstructing the plans that he and the company had for New Netherland, in which

Jan Janse was briefly caught up (van Laer 1908). In them are van Rensselaer's accounts of his involvement of Leiden partners in the *colonie* (326, 332–41), immediate preparations for the departure of the *Rensselaerswijck* (336, 337), designation of Dirck Corssen (and not Jan Janse) as supercargo (322, 343n19a), claim to it as "my little ship" (351), and later estimate of Jan Janse (417). Jan Janse boards as assistant supercargo under the company's Charter of Freedoms and Exemptions, Article XI (143). Van Rensselaer made strenuous and often laudable efforts to settle the patroonship, and these are given detailed attention by Jussurun (1917), Merwick (1990: 6–67), and Nissenson (1937).

Tiepkesz's log of the *Rensselaerswijck's* Atlantic crossing and its sailing upriver to the *colonie* and back to Manhattan Island are in van Laer (1908: 355–89). We have no information about Tiepkesz's navigational charts. In 1609 Henry Hudson did not have accurate charts, according to Johnson (1993: 132), but later, in the mid-1630s, the production of maps and globes reached its peak, making detailed charts of the coast of northeastern North America readily available. Bagrow's 1964 study of cartography is one of many valuable accounts, and for early New York, nothing excels Stokes for detail and mastery (1915–28: 1, 2). Minuit's maps (as they are called by Stokes) were laid down in 1630. They are usefully studied alongside the Buchalius Map (early or mid-1630s) and the Manatus Map of ca. 1639 (Stokes 1915–28: 2:111–15, 173–79, C plates 38 and 41, plates. 39 and 40). The company's secrecy about its charts was well known and is briefly documented below.

Van Rensselaer's expectation of an uneventful voyage for the *Rensselaerswijck* and evidence that sailors were often left in the dark about their destinations is in van Laer (1908: 339, 419). Beernink's comprehensive, if unduly sympathetic, study of Brant van Slichtenhorst (1916) should be read alongside Kiliaen's letters. He reminds us that the Dutch called the Hudson River *de rivier van d'vorst Mauritius* (151). It was also called *'t noord revier* (complementing *de Suytrivier*, Delaware River). The main settlement of New Netherland was consistently referred to as "the Manhatans." Hendrick de Foreest's journeys are in Stokes (1915–28: 4:84) and van Laer (1908: 31, 75, 197, 345, 382, and passim). Hoffman's genealogy of the van Lodesteijn family links the van Ilpendams to the de Foreests (1935: opp. 376).

1637
At the Manhatans

I have learned most about the early years of Dutch settlement on Manhattan Island by placing the maps and commentaries of Stokes (1915–28: 1, 2), Burke (1956), and Wieder (1925) alongside the reports and memorandums of officials, merchants, and navigators published in Fernow (1897: 1–7), Fernow and O'Callaghan (1853–87: 1, 2, 12, 13), Scott and Stryker-Rodda (1974a, 1974b, 1974c, 1974d), and van Rooijen (1988a).

Early settlement at "the Manhatans" was uneven. Strained by dissension, it was far from being what everyone expected or wanted. But structures familiar in the Low Countries were there or, more precisely, the knowledge was there of how to go about putting them in place by building a powerful trading city if profitable trade allowed. For my interpretation of the trading station that presented itself to Janse in 1637, I have relied on Innes (1902: 1, 2), O'Callaghan (1946: doc. E, 422), van Laer (1924: Special Instructions for the Engineer and Surveyor Cryn Fredericksz and for the Directors and

Council regarding the building of the fort and the houses, April 22, 1624–26, and Special Instructions, 1625 [where the commander's farm is confined to 200 square. feet]), Wassenaar's description of the occupational structure at the Manhatans in Stokes (1915–28: 2:107, 108), and Wieder (1925).

"Earning a beaver" was a colonist's way of declaring his or her right to have some part in the trade (van Laer 1923: 267). Boxer describes Recife and Olinda as "two heaps of sand and stones" (1957: 46). I have found it valuable to compare early Manhattan Island with the Dutch establishment at Table Bay. Dominicus (1919) is a useful authority, and Schrire (1995) has imaginatively reconstructed aspects of early Dutch culture from an archaeologist's viewpoint.

The authority structure which Janse would have encountered on Manhattan Island in the 1630s was a cultural feature of an amphibious people. Early seventeenth-century maps testify to the island nature of the Low Countries. They not only reveal people made islanders or otherwise cut off from one another by waterways and drowned lands but also remind us of the Netherlands' ancient origins in self-contained *terpen* and the development of many of its important communities as dependencies of the Zuider Zee. One is led in this direction also by reading Burke (1956), Schiltkamp (1964), and van Rooijen (1988a) and by encountering the scattered references to copies of *zee-rechten* in New Netherland and the 1643 inventory of Jonas Bronck's estate (Scott and Stryker-Rodda 1974b: 122). Among this Danish man's books were found the *Zeespiegel* of Willem Janse Blaeu (3 vols., Amsterdam, 1623, reprinted in 1626 and 1638), and *'t Gesicht des grooten zeevaerts* by J. H. J. van der Ley (Franeker, 1619).

The authority that early directors established during the founding years of New Netherland is suggested in Schiltkamp: "In the beginning, the authority structure of the trading settlements of the Netherlanders in the West was just an extension of the organization aboard the ships. But also the *materiele* law that was put in place by them as suitable was that to which they were subject on board a ship" (1964: 21). Wieder refers to councils composed of visiting sea captains (1925: doc. C: Instructie voor Willem Verhulst, Januari, 1625, and doc. D: Naerdere Instructie voor Willem Verhulst, April 25, 1625). Schiltkamp, like Wieder, makes reference to the "Orders of Governance" drawn up for the overseas stations (1964: 21–22).

I have used *Boeck der Zee-Rechten* and cited the maritime laws of Wisbuy (in a Dutch edition) to write about such practices as seeking the white hospital ship (Zee-Rechten 1664). Antoniszoon can be consulted for a rudder based on Wisbuy's experience of navigating (1671). The 1664 volume has tables listing prices at major ports of call). Abel Tasman's log cites the customary practice of hoisting a white flag at sea to take counsel with captains of a fleet or convoy. For his explorations, see Eisler (1995). Lachaire's references to *zee-rechten* are in Scott and Stryker-Rodda (1978: 20, 25). Schiltkamp cites the edition to which Lachaire must be referring (1964: 50).

Economic historians emphasize the importance of *lex mercatoria* for trading communities by saying that merchants carried their law with them. The context of this practice was similar to the one I have constructed. Such a context was the essential nexus between merchants and magistrates, law and notaries. A phrase like "Merchants or Shopkeepers who deale in Considerable Estate *by sea and land*" occurs too often to be trivial (Scott 1983: 44).

Van Rensselaer lived with a persistent disquiet about affairs at Rensselaerswijck. He distrusted the colonists, and they, in turn, chafed at his refusal to allow independent trading in furs. All of this is in van Laer (1908; see 375–79 for Tiepkesz's return voyage to the *colonie*; 409, 411, 415, 416 for the colonists' trade with Corssen; 351, 354 for letters of van Rensselaer to Jacob Planck; 327 for prohibitions against trading agricultural produce for furs; 417 for letters condemning Jacobus van Curler and Jan Janse). Elsewhere I have written about van Rensselaer's desperate efforts to get letters with useful information from officials, including Planck and Arent van Curler (1990).

1641
On the South River

Jan Janse's career as commanding officer at Fort Nassau on the Delaware River (Gloucester, New Jersey), and his probable dishonesty, can be pieced together from the council minutes of New Netherland. Much of it, however, remains unknown (Scott and Stryker-Rodda 1974d: office as commissary and deployment of the *Real* and *St. Marten*, 145, 146; investigation for negligence and fraud, 282, 285–86, 289, 297, 299–300). Jan Janse and his wife, Cathalina, are cited for indebtedness in GA (1641). Contemporary commentators would have understood that Jan Janse's appointment to the Delaware River area was to a place of violence; see council minutes (Scott and Stryker-Rodda 1974d: 436) and Fernow and O'Callaghan (1853–87: 13; for the Delaware as a place for hardened criminals, 20). Egmond describes marginal places in the Low Countries where Dutch people assumed that Gypsies, criminals, and roving underworld bands would gather (1993: 52, 60, 91, 101, and passim). The introduction to the 1903 edition of the Aspinwall Papers carries the reference to New Englanders exploring the Delaware River (Aspinwall Papers 1903: v). Kieft's directions to Jan Janse that he "govern himself" are in Scott and Stryker-Rodda (1974d: 145).

The New Netherland archives demonstrate how completely the company depended on the reports and memorandums — and gossip — filed by its overseas employees. Boxer noted this long ago, arguing that such ventures survived only because their men combined "the ledger and the sword" in a "striking fashion" (1957: 10). I would dare to take his insight further, arguing, like Roland Barthes, that for directors at home, only a world of signs brought into reality a world of things — which could then, of course, be exploited (quoted in Gossman 1978). The index to the world of signs of the VOC — and these papers are by no means complete — is itself 634 typed pages, and see Opper (1975) and Colenbrander (1919).

The thirst for documentation is strongly evident in the papers of the Dutch trading station at Curaçao (Gehring, 1987a) as well as in those of New Netherland before 1664. It is the company's and States General's fetish for writing that makes sense of the quantity of the dispatches and their tone. The obsessive concern for correspondence and archiving, for strategies of secrecy and precautions regarding the overseas or intercity transport of papers, all become evident in Fernow and O'Callaghan (1853–87: 1:138–475, and see 2:365–415 for some of the papers that Stuyvesant collected in order to defend his surrender of New Netherland). I have tried to reconstruct some of this in Chapter 3.

The bureaucracy's concern for knowledge resulted in a kind of seventeenth-century information superhighway. By 1612, Rotterdam — which was the headquarters for the post to England — had a daily postal service to Amsterdam (van Houtte 1977: 209). Kiliaen van Rensselaer, working in Amsterdam, readily communicated with a colleague in Leiden "by way of Haerlem" (van Laer 1908: 350). By mid-century mail coaches, *postkoetsen*, were arriving in Amsterdam regularly: on Wednesdays from Italy and parts of Germany; from England "according to how the wind is" (Ten Have 1973b: 14). The correspondence of Jeremias van Rensselaer reveals the place of the New Netherland merchants along the highway, using the transatlantic ships for regular mail. "Write by every ship," he is repeatedly told (van Laer 1932b: 185).

A pervasive secrecy surrounded personal and business papers. Kiliaen van Rensselaer's assurance to Oloff van Cortlandt in 1643 that he would keep his advice "secret" was typical (van Laer 1908: 656). For the sake of secrecy, directors of an exploration venture forbade a printer to reproduce their charts and journals; instructions reached naval captains in cypher — and magistrates corresponded in cypher as well (Fernow and O'Callaghan 1853–87: 1:15, 16, 21; Stokes 1915–28: 2:77, 80, 89; Evertsen Papers 1672; Rowen 1978: 145). As a common procedure, local courts forbade minority decisions to be made public; secretaries and treasurers avoided registering the final credits and debits in their accounts; burghers who "could not keep a secret" were removed from court meetings (Gehring 1987a: 73 and O'Callaghan 1849–51: 1:609; van Laer 1922: 118; Fernow and O'Callaghan 1853–87: 1:305). The secrecy of Dutch merchants about their account books is, of course, legendary (Yamey 1989: 118).

In his history of New Netherland, O'Callaghan records surveying equipment sent to a local official (1846: app. G). In the papers generated by the bitterness of the 1640s and early 1650s, Stuyvesant is found searching for papers in chests and cupboards (Fernow and O'Callaghan 1853–87: 2:27, 33, 64). Van Rensselaer sent Bastiaen Jansz Krol a "wood measure rule" in 1630 (van Laer 1908: 160). Council minutes give the pay meted out to surveyors (Scott and Stryker-Rodda 1974d: 166). For the obligation officials felt to give *de geheele staet* of a settlement or make a "swing around the circle," see Colenbrander (1919: 1:159); Opper (1975: 10); and see Fernow (1897: 1:213). Complainants writing to the company in the 1640s expected Kieft to be out "in this country" examining the environment in an extraordinarily detailed way and reporting on "birds" and "fish" as well as "facts" and "localities" (Fernow and O'Callaghan 1853–87: 1:212, 213).

The expectation that its officials would rise through the ranks from clerk or bookkeeper to commissary contributed greatly to the structure and success of an overseas venture such as the West India Company; see van Winter (1978: 104). An insistence on accurate books corresponded to the "boundless passion for detail" found elsewhere in Dutch literature (Huizinga 1924: 266–68), art (Alpers 1983), piloting (Skelton 1964; Seed 1995), and court testimony (Egmond 1993). Across western Europe and in England, the seventeenth century saw an outpouring of manuals and treatises on bookkeeping. This literature assumed an audience of professional clerks and accountants but also men and women of the merchant classes. The work of Yamey on Dutch bookkeeping is enlightening and entertaining (1950, 1963, 1989) but other valuable commentators are Barbour (1950), Baxter and Davidson (1950), Bywater and Yamey (1982), Green (1930), Littleton (1933), Ong (1971), ten Have (1973a, 1973b), and Vlaemminck (1956).

The format of seventeenth-century Dutch manuals on bookkeeping often overlapped with that of general educational material. Waningen (1672) can be read for the question-and-answer format corresponding to that of many manuals on the *notarisambt* and, of course, popular catechisms. Phoonsen (1677) gave instruction on how to execute bills of exchange. Van Winter offers some idea of the terror felt by company officials and individual merchants when faced with fraudulent or careless bookkeeping (1978: 111).

Jan Janse's final days are documented in council minutes (Scott and Stryker-Rodda 1974d: 214, 215, 282, 286, 289, 297, 299–300, and see the provincial secretary's register, Scott and Stryker-Rodda 1974b: 212). Fernow and O'Callaghan carry the murder of the native sachem (1853–87: 12:54, and see 61). We have evidence of Janse's bankruptcy from GA, Jan Janse van Ilpendam (1651), and Scott and Stryker-Rodda (1974c: 166).

The degree to which Adriaen Janse might have been associated with his father is impossible to establish. The records suggest that he was not on Manhattan Island much before 1647. His father was, of course, still living in that year, and both he and Adriaen Janse stood as witnesses at baptisms within a month of one another. His mother was perhaps the "Catalina Straet" who appeared as a witness at the same baptism as Adriaen (Baptisms, Collections 1901: 2:21, 22). The smallness of the settlement would also suggest some contact, although there is nothing to link him with his father's years along the Delaware River or his final days. Regarding later years, links can be made between traders whom Jan Janse would have known and who were trading with Fort Orange and then Beverwijck. For example, Adriaen Janse received goods in 1678 from Pieter Jacobsz Marius, who earlier traded regularly with Claes Bordingh, who was hired by the company in Amsterdam just four days after Jan. After his arrival at the Manhatans, Bordingh was imprisoned for running guns to Fort Orange and dealing with Egbert van Borsum, whose illegal trading along the Delaware was part of the indictment against Jan Janse (Scott and Stryker-Rodda 1974d: 286, 531, 537; van Laer 1918: 225). There must have been several men like Bordingh known to both father and son — Oloff van Cortlandt is another (Scott and Stryker-Rodda 1974b: 174; and see Chapter 6. Exactly what this might have meant in Adriaen Janse's life we cannot say.

FEBRUARY 1646
At the Manhatans

We know something of Jan Janse's trial and the year of his death from Scott and Stryker-Rodda (1974d: 289, 297, 299) and GA, Jan Janse van Ilpendam (1651). The deposition of 1651 also refers to Adriaen Janse as a schoolmaster already residing at Rensselaerswijck.

SUMMER 1649
At the Manhatans and Leiden

Seventeenth-century Leiden has been the object of many studies. Stone-Ferrier (1985) describes the textile industry in close detail and gives a good sense of a confident and hardworking city. Eekhof is one of many scholars pointing to the university's prominence among other European educational institutions (1921, 1926). Van Houtte (1977: 237) refers to "professors' bread"; van Laer presents Kiliaen van Rensselaer's intimidation by the university-educated lawyers (1908: 534).

David Janse van Ilpendam was, like his brother Joachim, a notable Leidenaar, yet we know little of his life when Adriaen Janse was in the city and somehow obtained his copy of the will made in 1640. Kuypers (1992) is a reliable source for biographical detail, and municipal records provide information on the family, their properties, and their bequests.

Nowell-Smith and Wooten alert readers to the special bond between universities and booksellers in European cities (1984: 143). Contemporary descriptions of Leiden are many, but Marselije (1989) has been especially useful to me. Orlers offered a particularly sensitive point of view (1641: 180–95). Van Selm is an authority on book fairs such as those held in The Hague and Leiden (1987: 31–42, 373–81). Much of his research is based on catalogs of public and private book sales. Gruys and de Wolf supply David Janse's name and, after 1640, that of his widow among the book publishers in Leiden (1989: 257). De Vrankrijker writes of the popular use of almanacs, throwaway *wegwijzers* (travel guides), and cheap pictures or pages of script pinned to the walls of rooms in Dutch houses (1981: 171, 172).

New Amsterdam, of course, had no book market to compare with that of Leiden. The large collection of books possessed by Gysbert van Imbroch in Wiltwijck may have been exceptional but gives some sense of comparative prices at a moment in the 1660s (Christoph, Scott, and Stryker-Rodda 1976b: 568, 569, 574). For the price of a Borstius in Holland (1 stiver), see Nooter (1994: 132). It seems unlikely that the number of children's schoolbooks on Manhattan Island available to a young teacher in the 1640s would have been anything other than minimal. A suggestion that estate auctions were always a possible source is in van Laer (1932: 13). In this book I have tried to address the question of literacy in New Netherland (see Chapter 5) but have made no effort to discuss or tabulate the range of books available there.

Although Salomon de Bray's illustration of a typical Netherlands bookstore and van Selm's work (1987: 377) are helpful in reconstructing David Janse's bookshop, we have almost no detailed information about it other than its ownership and location. Kuypers, who offers that information, also notes that in 1637 Janse helped produce a *Statenbijbel* in Leiden, that is, a version of the Bible adapted to the prescriptions of the 1619 Synod of Dordrecht and one of many brought to publication (1992).

The GL holds van Merwen's protocols (1635–44) in Oude Notarieële Archief, nos. 533–42. The introduction to the inventory of the collection, dated January 18, 1916, is a brief but useful explanation of the role of the notary — who sometimes served as municipal secretary — and of the advantaged position that Leiden's notaries had because of the city's leading role as a clothmaking and university town. As in the case of Janse's papers, numbering and indexing individual notarial acts did not become common practice until the end of the seventeenth century. See Oude Notarieële Archieven, Archief Alewijn Claasse de Man (1635–37) for van Merwen's colleague. David Janse's will, Testament de eersamen David Jansz. van Ilpendam ende de eerbare Aefjen Dammasdr. vander Horn echteluijden, 1640 juni 20, is inv. no. 538, f. 29ro. (There is also an earlier will, inv. no. 536, no. 54). Pitlo gives detailed consideration to Verwey in his 1948 study, 37–41.

Adriaen Janse's early education — for example, how and where he qualified to be a schoolmaster — remains unknown. *Dutch Schoolsystem* (1960: 15) points to a compulsory education act of 1957 intended to ensure the education of children of bargemen, and Durantini cites a 1634 directive of the Synod of South Holland ordering those in state employment (including bargemen) to send their children to school (1983: 36). Adriaen Janse sailed for New Netherland sometime before February 10, 1647, when he acted as witness at a baptism on Manhattan Island (Baptisms, Collections 1901: 2:22).

Sullivan et al. (1927: 2028) asserted that learned men were more evident in New Netherland than we have credited. Whether or not that statement is tenable, there is evidence of some men who were studying at the University of Leiden in the 1630s and 1640s (Sullivan et al. 1927: 1858n10 quoting Walsh, *History of Medicine in New York* [1917: 1:19–20], and see Hamlin [1939: 73, 84n3]).

Pitlo (1948: 7) describes the notary as a half-intellectual and elsewhere comments extensively on his social status. Among others, Heersink (1989: 51) and Sprenger van Eyck (1928: 16) point out that the *notariaat* was a family business in many Dutch towns.

3. The Manhatans

AUGUST 19, 1649
At the Manhatans

The settlement on Manhattan Island in the late 1640s was one of dissension that raged between the West India Company's highest officials and an emerging merchant elite who would eventually succeed in getting municipal privileges for New Amsterdam, but only in 1653. The exchanges are copiously documented, especially in Fernow and O'Callaghan (1853–87: 1:126–553). The same documentation and the vicious tenor of the conflict, however, can easily draw attention toward dissent about law and government — and individual personalities — and away from the structures within which the altercations were taking place. Misapplication of law there certainly was, and especially on the governing body's side, but not the absence of legal structures. They were in place and on them rose the foundation of New Netherland in the two cities, thirteen villages, two forts, and three colonies that Nicasius de Sille listed in 1660 (Stokes, 1915–28: 2:349–51, C pls. 83 and 84).

As a notary, Janse was part of the Dutch legal system in New Netherland. James Sullivan offered a description of it in 1927. New Netherland, he asserted, was meant to be a "provincial establishment . . . in line with the legal and civil systems of the homeland." By its charter, "the will of the West India Company was supreme and all power was vested in the Director-General and Council, who were to be governed by the Dutch Roman Law, the imperial statutes of Charles V, and the edicts, customs and resolutions of the United Netherlands." The "superstructure of it all was a vision of the Roman, German and Dutch municipal systems." That is, the Dutch "were governed by a league of commercial guilds, represented in the States-General in order that they might protect the organized interests of each class of people. . . . This principle of conserving the ancient rights of all the people as against any portion thereof, even a majority, and as against government itself, was the foundation principle of the province as of the mother country." Legitimate government and popular rights, he concluded, resided in the courts and not in legislatures, where we are accustomed to look for them in our colonial and later history (Sullivan et al. 1927:1848). Tilly's 1989 article usefully illuminates this interpretation.

Sullivan's insight seems crucial for understanding that the development of Dutch jurisprudence, universally regarded as remarkable in the seventeenth century, did not somehow bypass New Netherland, as so many of early New York's historians have contended. Rather, it confirms patterns of government in places such as New Amsterdam and Beverwijck that are latent in the sources.

Officials such as Stuyvesant, together with notaries and court secretaries, were (and had to be) familiar with the major legal commentaries of the day. De Damhouder (1618, 1642, 1660) went through several editions throughout the seventeenth century. It was present in Rensselaerswijck after 1634 and cited in the Albany court records in the last quarter of the seventeenth century (van Laer 1908: 281, 283, 294, 1928: 147). Stuyvesant cited it in 1647 in order to pronounce on criminally dishonorable gestures (Scott and Stryker-Rodda (1974d: 410). He cited de Damhouder later in the same case, this time quoting closely from the volume and advising listeners and readers to consult a particular page and adding references to Johannes Bernardinus Muscatellus (*Praxis criminalibus*), Macrobius, and Albricus (410). Shortly afterward and still in council, he cited "the Imperial statutes of Charles the Fifth which are in force in our country" (409, and see 415, 447). Other treatises on criminal and civil law were in New Netherland as well. Stuyvesant (1657) wrote of "books" expected sometime before 1657. Schiltkamp records that twelve copies of Duysentdaelers (1659) and an unknown number of copies of Rooseboom (1656) were in the province and that van Zutphen's *Nederlandtsche Practycque* was sent to Stuyvesant in 1662 (1964: 47, 48). Although van Zutphen's is a demanding text, 551 pages in length, it is set out in the helpful question-and-answer format adopted by many commentators (1636; see, for example, 382–84).

Once New Amsterdam came into existence, Amsterdam's ancient privileges became rights on which local burghers and city officials felt they had a call. So, in the court records a farmer of the burgher excise, the burgomasters, and *schepenen* all refer to the compilation of Amsterdam's laws and ordinances published in *Handvesten* (1613), citing an ordinance passed on July 10, 1586, at page 293 (Fernow 1897: 2:234). Rooseboom's *Recueil* was called upon repeatedly as well (229 and passim*).* When the English arrived in 1664, they found attached to the burgomasters' courtroom a small library of legal works. One item was the "Wisbuste [Wisbuy] Admiralty Laws" (Fernow 1897: 7:139). We may never know exactly what law books were available to officials in New Netherland. It seems illogical, however, that notaries took pains to provide themselves with such books while officials, who needed to know the rules governing such men and the citations they were likely to present in court, did not. In Chapter 5 I introduce notary Lachaire and the books he consulted (Scott and Stryker-Rodda 1978). Christoph, Scott, and Stryker-Rodda carry the inventory of Gerrit van Imbroch's books made in 1665, among which van Zutphen and Rooseboom were listed (1976b: 568).

The sorcery practiced by company officials and their opponents is evident in Fernow and O'Callaghan (1853–87: 1; for allegations of Kieft as homosexual, see 204, and see Scott and Stryker-Rodda 1974d: 399; learned papers written against Kieft, 205–9; "little blue book," 206, and for Kieft's embellishment of it, 212; complaints with citations in Latin and laced with footnotes, 262–70, 457; the Remonstrance, 271–318 [the transcription indicates 49 pages, but an 83-page copy is cited in the Royal Archives of The Hague, 272]; Stuyvesant's destruction of a man's personal papers [Roberts n.d: 231], but see Vreeland, in which a colonist insists that Stuyvesant was "always very careful of . . . [their] lives" [1956: 13]). For Stuyvesant's "highly embellished writings" and people frightened to "associate" with others, see Fernow and O'Callaghan (1853–87: 1:455). Scott and Stryker-Rodda document the ransacking of houses (1974d: 537). For the general hatred of van Tienhoven, see below. Kiliaen van Rensselaer's rebuke to his secretary is in his correspondence (van Laer 1908: 485, 486). Corbin's 1992 study of violence in a nineteenth-century rural French village is an unforgettable portrayal of the social power of rumor. Interestingly Roth, in his study of Washington Irving's writings, sees Kieft creating a "logocracy" by inciting "democrats" all around him (1976: 144, 158, 159).

For the burghers' awareness of New Amsterdam as a place for merchants and their expanding enterprises, see, inter alia, the Remonstrance or the Petition of October 13, 1649, in Fernow and O'Callaghan (1853–87: 1:260, 271–318). Ten Have gives us contemporary notions of European trade patterns (1973b: 15). References to "nations" resident in Dutch trading cities are in Carroll (1993), Fernow (1897: 1:122), and see Hazelzet for English and Scots merchants in Rotterdam (1944: 114). Bewes (1923) writes about merchants carrying their law with them, but Coquillette (1981, 1987) and Trakman (1980, 1981) discuss international business law far more critically.

The portrayal of Stuyvesant as playing the patron rather than introducing free trade is in van Laer (1918: 10). New Netherland is identified as a "republic" in Scott and Stryker-Rodda (1974d: 131, 132, and see Fernow and O'Callaghan 1853–87: 1:214); the call for "suitable" government is in Fernow and O'Callaghan (1853–87: 1:260; New Amsterdam as the "capital" of New Netherland is on 265n111).

Janse's first years on Manhattan Island cannot be reconstructed in any detail. For the favorable career he might have left behind in Leiden, I have used GL 1635–44, Introduction to the *Oude Notarieële Archieven* (1916: 2), and Fijen, Melching, and Peterse (1977: n.p).

The papers of the company's secretary show that by 1649, Janse was assisting Laurensz (Scott and Stryker-Rodda (1974c: 10, 11, and see 1974d: 356, 359; consult too Fernow and O'Callaghan 1853–87: 12:53, 54). Van Deursen attests to the place of fate in Dutch lives, stating that even riches were taken to be a matter not of diligence but of luck or belief (1978a: 104). The appearance of Leidenaars in Janse's life will be recurrent — and among them is Adriaen Janse Appel (or van Leyden) who is in New Amsterdam and Beverwijck at the same time as Janse and easily confused with him. Janse's presence at baptisms in 1650 is documented in Baptisms, Collections 1901: 27. Janse's marriage has not been recorded. Nevertheless, he refers to a marriage of thirty-one years in 1682 (van Laer 1918: 495). Later court records show that his wife was ill in the early 1650s (van Laer 1920: 75).

Janse lived with people who had a craving to get things in writing. New Netherlanders placed considerable significance on institutionalizing educational practices adopted at home. The literature on schooling in the seventeenth-century Low Countries is vast. Dirck Adriaensz Valcooch's 1591 book of rules for primary school teachers is the best place to begin (De Planque 1926). His prescriptions to schoolmasters were highly influential and offer excellent insight into curricula, tuition, qualifications for schoolmasters, and parents' expectations of schools. Most commentators on seventeenth-century schooling return to Valcooch, generally measuring his observations against the practices of one or another local Dutch community. The studies of De Booy (1977), Fortgens (1958), Frederiks (1960), ter Schegget (1976), and Van Eck (1927) are particularly useful. Wouters and Visser (1926) present a careful examination of lower school education based on data collected by provincial synods acting in response to directives of the Synod of Dordrecht.

In 1912 Kilpatrick worked with the fragmented data about education on Manhattan Island. His study is not strongly interpretive but is still the most comprehensive account available. I have also used Sullivan et al. (1927:2127, 2130), Fernow and O'Callaghan (1853–87: 1:155), and van Vechten (1897: 321–44). Council minutes allow us to follow the sad career of Roelandsz (Scott and Stryker-Rodda 1974d: 93, 330, 348, 351, 376). Together with church records such as those published by Hastings (1901–5, Index 1916), they allow some reconstruction of the lives of other schoolmasters. For Janse as master of a private school, see below. For comparison of Stevensz's salary with those in the Low Countries, see Downer, who cites the salary of a master in circumstances equivalent to Janse's as 107:10 guilders (1989: 25). In 1660 the Flatbush congregation was paying 200 guilders (Nooter 1994: 137). Stuyvesant's and van Tienhoven's positive appreciation of private schools is in Sullivan et al. (1927: 2129).

One can only suspect that over the years Janse maintained some contact with his family in Leiden. But only once is contact recorded before his letters to Guldewagen beginning in the 1670s. Van Tienhoven's clerk records Janse's appearance at the secretary's house in August 1649. The minute is among the secretary's papers (Scott and Stryker-Rodda 1974c: 165, 166, and see Stokes 1915–28: 4:119). To contextualize the episode, I have reconstructed something of the career and character of van Tienhoven and used Stokes 1915–28: 2:266–68 for the location of his house and those of near neighbors who figure in this narrative; Kilpatrick 1912: 61 for his boast about the many schools on Manhattan Island; Scott and Stryker-Rodda 1974b: 170, 126–27, 386; Fernow and O'Callaghan 1853–87: 1:308, 309, 454–56, and see 316 for Stuyvesant's directive of 1649 invalidating documents not written by his secretary; 517 and 335 for van Tienhoven's physical description. Regarding van Tienhoven's probable suicide, see Stokes (1915–28: 2:238) and Kessler and Rachlis (1959: 211). The New Netherland Papers (Bontemantel Collection), New York Public Library, contain a letter in which Stuyvesant admitted that his secretary was widely despised (Stuyvesant 1655a).

The arrival of van Schelluyne signaled the waning of van Tienhoven's power. His career is discussed in Chapter 5, but valuable for his education and first years in New Netherland are references in Fernow and O'Callaghan (1853–87: 1:454 and passim), van Laer (1918: 10, 11), Schiltkamp (1964: 130–34 [de Deckere as notary in 1655, 133]), and Hamlin (1939: 73). Van Schelluyne is referred to briefly at The Hague examining a copy of the Remonstrance (Fernow and O'Callaghan 1853–87: 1:318). Kossman does not comment on van Schelluyne's presence there but presents a careful mapping of the notaries' stalls and offices — and the "swarm" of personnel — at the Binnenhof during his time (1932: xi). Melis also cites the presence of the notaries but uses it as evidence that Dutch notaries were less professional in the seventeenth century than their French counterparts (1982: 25).

Hardenberch's dealings with Janse and his role as fur trader and leading merchant are in the secretary's papers collected in Scott and Stryker-Rodda (1974c: 10, 165, 166).

Council minutes edited by the same scholars (1974d: 342–43, 439, 537) as well as Hoffman (1939: 254, 255) and Fernow and O'Callaghan (1853–87: 12:53, 54) cite Laurensz's trafficking on his behalf at the south river, where he might have encountered Jan Janse. We know from council minutes that Stuyvesant searched his house (Scott and Stryker-Rodda 1974d: 537 and O'Callaghan 1846: 394–95). Documents in Fernow and O'Callaghan tell us that he sailed on the *Valckenier* with the petition (1853–87: 1:259–61, 318, 324).

The secretary's clerk registered Claesz's acceptance of Janse's power of attorney (Scott and Stryker-Rodda 1974c: 165). Elsewhere are records of Claesz's property holdings, including a house next to that of Cornelis Melijn, one of Stuyvesant's fiercest critics (Pierce 1903: 9). Claesz's petition is in Fernow and O'Callaghan (1853–87: 1:327–30, and see 191 for a document he signed condemning Kieft in 1644). Teunisse's petition and the captain's connivance at bringing him aboard as well as van Tienhoven's voyaging on the *Valckenier* are in the same volume at 326, 327, and 324. See 330 for the resolution of the States General on the petitions and 448 for the burghers' fears at not knowing with whom they could associate in safety.

Van Tienhoven's papers record Cathalina's dealings with him in 1647 and her house rental arrangements (Scott and Stryker-Rodda 1974b: 483–84, 486–88). She rented from Dirck Cornelissen of Wensveen. Although he was a lifetime carpenter of the city, Stokes has no record of his house. Laurensz seems to have been a small time trader in merchandise. Fernow and O'Callaghan's documents and those of Scott and Stryker-Rodda offer only some of the fragmentary data available on him (1853–87: 12:53, 54; 1974d: 205, 350). Nothing about Janse as a trader can be found.

No one — a member of council, a minister, or a solicitous parent — wrote of Janse as schoolmaster. In 1897 van Vechten asserted that "one Adriaen Janse van Ilpendam" had opened a school in 1646 and charged as tuition "two dried beaver skins per annum." Mistakenly, she also claimed that his school was so successful that it continued for over a decade (328). In fact, Janse's precise activities remain a mystery, although much about his daily routine is informed by studies completed on men in similar circumstances, that is, those making their way in rural districts and small towns in the Netherlands. I have already cited most of these, but for specific details about the day's routine and a master's desk and schoolroom I have also consulted De Booy (1977: 45), Frederiks (1960: 191, 209 [relying on Valcooch]), Nooter (1994: 138), and van Vechten (1897: 341).

The desire of the mercantile community at the Manhatans that its children be proficient in elementary reading, writing, and numeracy must be arrived at indirectly. Walter J. Ong's essay "Ramist Method and the Commercial Mind" (1971) helped me understand those expectations more clearly. There, and without parodying a bourgeois mentality, he explored the link between a consumer culture, a quasi-intellecutual commercialism, and the Ramean method, which so appealed to the merchants and artisans who could see knowledge in terms of intake, output, and consumption (173). It is possible to look, with Ong, at the extraordinary diffusion of Ramus's works in the sixteenth and seventeenth centuries and find assumptions about education being put into practice (however primitively) in New Amsterdam. Ramus's concern for mathematics and his desire to found it on the practices of "bankers, merchants, architects, painters, and mechanics" (171) is a theoretical expression of New Amsterdammers' well-documented con-

31. Detail of Temperancia, *engraving from the series* The Seven Virtues, *Pieter Bruegel the Elder, late 1550s. In the larger picture, a female figure of Temperance is shown surrounded by scenes illustrating the Seven Liberal Arts. The figures in "Arithmetic" are a merchant or banker (or perhaps a money changer) and two clerks doing mathematical calculations. The hooded figure appears to be a woman. Women often acted as bookkeepers for their husbands and needed, as one visitor to the Low Countries noted, neither servants nor friends for guidance. (British Museum, London; drawing in Boijmans–van Beuningen Museum, Rotterdam)*

cern to establish schools and apprenticeships for their children. See Howard (1991) on apprenticeships and Biemer's evidence that even women were expected to have some command of "ciphering and the arithmetic of commerce" (1991: 73). Sullivan et al. found that ciphering was taught in New Amsterdam in 1658 (1927: 2130). Although it can be pointed out that copies of Ramus's treatises were among the books of Domine Megapolensis in 1643, my point is not to attempt to show the direct influence of Ramus but to suggest a wider relationship between culture and education (O'Callaghan 1846: 454).

Stuyvesant's order of 1647 that all traders keep accounts and, similarly, that those clearing the port have proper papers are in Scott and Stryker-Rodda (1974d: 384, and see 368, 382, 386, 390). Minutes of the New Amsterdam court of burgomasters and *schepenen* carry repeated directives that burghers keep accounts and pay attention to public placards (Fernow 1897: 3:108 and passim).

Van Tienhoven's script can be seen in Kieft (1645). Eekhof quotes a seventeenth-century minister on the sonority of the Dutch language (1910: 47, quoting Bastiaen Jansz Krol). Stokes refers to a prominent New Amsterdammer who employed a private tutor

32. Portrait of a Merchant, *Jan Gossaert, c. 1530. The artist depicts a man of commerce writing in a ledger. He is surrounded by the tools of his trade, many of which were also those of Adriaen Janse's trade as notary: batches of papers, twine, a shaker for sand, an inkpot, a metal receptacle for sealing wax, and pens. The portrait suggests the arithmetic of commerce just as a portrait of Janse with his papers would suggest the literature of commerce. (Ailsa Mellon Bruce Fund, © 1996 Board of Trustees, National Gallery of Art, Washington)*

(1915–28: 2:212). Stuyvesant's employment of a secretary to write letters in English is in the council minutes (Scott and Stryker-Rodda 1974d: 378).

The confidence of Wouters and Visser in stating that in the Netherlands "naturally there were, in a *koopmansland* like ours, arithmetic teachers and little arithmetic books" cannot be ours regarding New Netherland (1926: 113). But we can observe the pressures for education that fell on parents, churchmen, and officials alike — and that gave Janse his chance. Parents expected the company (in conjunction with the church) to take a lead in providing the practical kind of elementary education that Ramus systematized. When it failed to do so, their outcry reached into the records and cannot have surprised officials because similar expectations (and clamor) were expressed in such places as Zwolle in the Netherlands (Frederiks 1960: 201). At the same time, parents expected much of schoolmasters, anticipating that they would be "public persons," men who (like the minister) could be turned to for advice and be counted on to comport themselves with dignity (Kilpatrick 1912: 19). They were watchful. On one occasion, they openly condemned excessive disciplining of their children (Fernow 1907: 76). Stuyvesant seems to have taken control in school matters, dismissing van Curler and remaining alert to the demand for schools prompted by the continual increase of population (Fernow 1897: 2:348; Sullivan et al. 1927: 2130; Fernow 1897: 1:6; 2:404, 220).

Across the Low Countries and in New Netherland, the salaries of teachers rested either on the determination of the local court or (infrequently) the capacity of an individual to demand a given salary (Wouters and Visser 1926: 98 and passim). Janse's income during these years cannot be calculated with any accuracy. I have estimated house rent and the general cost of living using Stokes, Fernow (1897: 1–7), and Kilpatrick. On Manhattan Island, a teacher's income may have been adversely affected by the number of other masters who seem to have served for short periods of time. At least seventeen schoolmasters gave lessons at one time or another in the years immediately before and after 1650. This number has led one scholar to conclude that the system in place for "popular education" was a solid one. It is worth noting that the same scholar finds that education suffered a "decided setback" under English rule, when "royal governors were not generally in favor of the education of the people, and the sentiment of the ruling classes in England was directly opposed to it" (Sullivan et al. 1927: 2127, 2138, 2139). Kilpatrick agrees with these findings (1912: 18, 21). Wouters and Visser, whose 1926 study included a brief comparison of the educational practices of the Low Countries with those of England, were led to conclude that the system in the Low Countries was far superior (1926: 79, and see Brugmans 1973: 249). Elliott's brief comments on early New England education would seem to support the findings as well (1975: 48, 50, 59).

Schoolmasters considered the *notariaat*, or the position of town secretary, as a useful by-employment or possible step up the social ladder. It was one of a cluster of jobs open to men who had become skilled in writing. Several authorities cite Valcooch's explicit suggestion that schoolmasters supplement their income in this way (Kilpatrick 1912: 27; Wouters and Visser 1926: 92; see De Planque 1926: 126n1 and 15). Commentators on the *notariaat* are less inclined to draw similarities between teaching and the work of the notary, but they write extensively on the congruence that seventeenth-century Dutch people saw between notaries, masters of calligraphy, secretaries, printers, and publishers

(Warmelink 1952). Wiarda's study of Dirck Volkertszoon Coornhert points to a man who acted as notary, secretary, bookseller, and printer (1970).

Heersink describes apprenticeships for notaries in Holland and the fees that a young family member (like Adriaen van Tienhoven) might earn acting as witness in his father's or uncle's rooms (1989: 51). Fernow and O'Callaghan tell of van Schelluyne's harsh treatment when he first arrived at Manhattan Island (1853–87: 1:454). Schiltkamp provides an accurate list of New York's notaries (1964: 322, 323).

Janse put his name forward as secretary for Beverwijck in 1652 (van Laer 1920: 29). From 1640 to his death in 1686, eighty-two men served as secretaries in the company or as town clerks in the New Netherland/New York settlements. Another eight are mentioned in passing in the records (Schiltkamp 1964: 309–12). I have compiled a description of the position from council and court records of New Netherland and Curaçao (Gehring 1987a). Specific references are Scott and Stryker-Rodda (1974d: 378), O'Callaghan (1849–51: 1:651, 649; for de Sille's "Description . . . of New Utrecht," 651–52), van Laer (1920: 39, 40, 57–60,182), Gehring (1987a: 71–73, an excellent description of a secretary's ordinary routine).

Even in the course of New Netherland's short history, secretaries' salaries varied according to circumstances. As examples, 720 guilders as company secretary in 1644; 360 guilders at Rensselaerswijck in the mid-1650s; 1,200 guilders yearly from 1654 to 1664 as New Amsterdam's secretary, but 400 guilders there in 1666 (Fernow and O'Callaghan 1853–87: 1:155; van Laer 1908: 825; Fernow 1897: 6:228, 17). Serving under the English administration, Johannes Nevius complained in 1665 that he could not live on his salary (Fernow 1897: 5:265, 4:1).

SEPTEMBER 9, 1650
Rensselaerswijck

My reconstruction of affairs at Fort Orange and Rensselaerswijck is largely from van Laer (1922, 1908), Fernow and O'Callaghan (1853–87: 13), Pearson (1869), Nissenson (1937), Weise (1884), and Folkerts (1991). Beernink (1916) writes about these years as a historian of Gelderland. He is as interested in the accomplishments of Brant van Slichtenhorst's scholarly son Arent, who was one of Gelderland's earliest historians, as in the director himself, but his perspective is different and valuable. Meij et al.'s 1975 study is useful as well. Slichtenhorst's disputes with Labatie, Dyckman, and Stuyvesant are readily available in the court records of Rensselaerswijck (van Laer 1922).

Beernink identifies *de Geldersche Vallie* (1916: 183). The colloquial forms of Dutch speech and the quaint phrases that he mentions there can be found in the court minutes, and Egmond too notes the localism in judicial terminology used across the Dutch provinces, especially "verbosity" and the adoption of more ornate styles outside Holland (Beernink 1916: 14; van Laer 1922: 150 and passim; Egmond 1993: 9). Janse's installation as schoolmaster and van Curler's willingness to act as an administrator are in Beernink (1916: 294) and Weise (1884: 91).

Van Laer used Kiliaen van Rensselaer's papers to compile a list of those who arrived in Rensselaerswijck yearly from 1630 to 1658 (1908: 805–46). He also provided generous biographical footnotes when he edited the court minutes of later years. They frequently refer back to this period. Van Rensselaer's opinion on colonists is in van Laer (1908: 647). For bridges and railings over kills, see van Laer (1922: 141; the settler who could not survive in the *colonie*, 130; natives squatting in vacated houses, 214).

NOVEMBER 28, 1650
Rensselaerswijck

The incident surrounding "the Owl" is in the court records (van Laer 1922: 131, 132), as is Labatie's bargaining with van Slichtenhorst and refusal to meet with the Mohawk (129, and see 128).

The sources allow a confident reconstruction of the men Janse would have come to know during this time. When not quarreling in public, van Slichtenhorst — the "gray thief" (van Laer 1908: 819) — was there worrying over his books, stabbed while writing, using van Wenckum to make up his accounts and final inventory, urging tenants to present vouchers (van Laer 1922: 148, 201–18 [and here van Wenckum's wages are entered], 146). Something of de Hooges's family background, personality, and contribution to the *colonie* can be pieced together from van Laer (1922) and Beernink (1916: 159n3). Among van Rensselaer's papers are the young man's log, instructions he received from the patroon, and accounts of his friendship with van Curler (van Laer 1908: 580–603, 663, 704, 649).

Van Curler's incapacity to concentrate on accounts, inventories, and correspondence was picked up by Kiliaen and raged against in his letters (van Laer 1908: 438 and passim). I have written an interpretative account of this episode (1990: 45–59). Van Curler's account book with Latin phrases and Greek lettering is van Curler (1634–38).

The books that we know to have been in Rensselaerswijck during these years are those sent by Kiliaen and others in the possession of Megapolensis and van Slichtenhorst. Van Rensselaer sent a box of pious books, including *The Practice of Godliness*, and specifically mentions sending de Damhouder's works on civil and criminal law and Thuys's *Ars Notariatus* in correspondence of 1634 (van Laer 1908: 418, 281, 283, 294). Megapolensis's library (including the work of Ramus) is listed in O'Callaghan (1846: 454, 455). Van Slichtenhorst's possession of Grotius's work on jurisprudence is in van Laer (1922: 202). My references to de Damhouder are from the 1618, 1642, and 1660 editions; those from Thuys are the 1590 edition (1–54) — excepting the model of an inventory, which is from the 1645 edition (190, 191). Strubbe takes notice of de Damhouder's desire to be "clear and accurate" but also of his plagiarism (1970: 53, 25). Gehlen points to Thuys's plagiarism as well and notes that the first edition was 1587 and the last 1675 (1981: 97). De Smidt argues that Grotius's *Introduction* was "short, clearly formulated . . . [and] easily discernable" (1984: 181).

NOVEMBER 23, 1651
Rensselaerswijck

Janse's petition regarding house rent and the court's reply are in the minutes (van Laer 1922: 173). For rental costs and designations of properties that were central to the settlement as compared to those located at the margins, I used the minutes and relied on my own work on early settlement (van Laer 1922: 74; Merwick 1990: 6–67). Kiliaen van Rensselaer maneuvered constantly for "friends in the game" and the phrase is his (van Laer: 1908: 268). We can know nothing of Janse's "friends" in the fur trade at this time, nor can we estimate how deeply, if at all, he was involved. Gehring has a brief but solid account of Stuyvesant's founding of Beverwijck (1990: xxi–xxx).

4. Beverwijck

1652
Beverwijck

It is easy to overlook the importance of Stuyvesant's first act in establishing Beverwijck. Before anything else, he set up a local court. It was the guarantor of the residents' freedoms and liberties. New Netherlanders were obsessive about protecting their rights — we have already seen no dearth of evidence for that. They directed that energy into a close scrutiny of the bench. They were not ambitious for local assemblies or centralized legislative bodies. In this respect, they set themselves off from the political culture of mid-seventeenth-century England and Anglo-America. Consequently, some measure of the deep-seated dislocation that occurred as English rule got under way can be taken from observing the burghers' and farmers' interaction with the local court of Beverwijck.

James Sullivan wrote for fellow New Yorkers in 1927. He tried to explain to them the state's earliest legal system. He took as his starting point later confusions about it during the Dutch period. A failure to understand the fundamental difference between Dutch and English institutions, he insisted, meant an inability to appreciate the evolution of their own legal structures. By the late seventeenth century, England was a sovereign state. It vested (or tried to vest) supreme power in a balanced constitution of executive and legislature. The United Provinces, Sullivan went on, were a federated republic. They made the judiciary supreme against the encroachments of arbitrary power. But this intention was institutionalized by devolving authority to provincial and local or first-instance courts. The localism that supported the empowerment of popular rights through the courts, Sullivan concluded, made the whole structure elusive to his twentieth-century New York readers. It resembled an "irregular mosaic, in which might be found all the principles as well as the details of a most enlightened system of jurisprudence, but in a form so confused as to make it exceedingly difficult to master it" (1927: 1849n1, 1876n27, and see Egmond quoting a relevant Amersfoort document of 1694 [1993: 34]).

In places like Beverwijck, the court provided such a structure to daily life. It also acted as a kind of bi- or triweekly listening post for the stories of its townspeople. For these reasons, historians have leaned heavily on its records to interpret the town's history. In 1920 and 1923, van Laer edited the minutes for the years 1652 to 1660. They stand alongside his editions of secretaries' and notaries' legal papers (1916, 1918, 1919) and Pearson's publication of other early records in 1869. They make possible an ethnographic account of the town — and an ethnography of Janse's life.

The geography of early Beverwijck, even the distribution of house lots, is not easily gleaned from the records. See, however, the efforts of Beernink (1916), Merwick (1980,

1981, 1990) and Wilcoxen (1984). Van Laer (1927) tried to locate early properties on the south side of Jonckerstraat (State Street). Pearson constructed diagrams and a key to early lots, but they are not wholly reliable (1871). Janse mentions Beverwijck as "inland" from New York City in 1676 (van Laer 1918: 334). For an estimate of pelts leaving Fort Orange and New Netherland for Holland, see Merwick (1990: 71), Rink (1986), and van Laer (1932b: 29 for the figure of 36,000 pelts).

Janse's public appearances during these years are few. He is already the obscure figure that he will be over the coming seventeen years, that is, until his appointment as notary in 1669. Like the burghers, however, he was caught up in the conflict between the *colonie* and the company's officials and, like the others, he came under the scrutiny of Johannes Dyckman, who wrote his name into the records. For one man's worries about divided allegiances and de Hooges's sense of time in 1650, see van Laer (1922: 196, 117n2). Dyckman's many activities in settling the town are in van Laer (1920: 16, 17, 20, 23, 28; signs of his madness are referred to at 12; see also Pearson 1869: 188n1, and below).

Janse's petition for the position of secretary interested me because of the degree of self-confidence it seemed to suggest (van Laer 1920: 29). I tried to fill in the social role of this office by using, among other sources, those that pertained to the court messenger (van Laer 1920: 68, 87), earlier court minutes (van Laer 1922: 55, 159), council minutes from New Amsterdam (Scott and Stryker-Rodda 1974d: 93, 376, and passim); Sullivan et al. (1927: 1852n5) and Stokes (1915–28: 2:227). The hours of work and possible income from acting as secretary are based on Beverwijck's extant minutes, for example, 221 pages from January 8, 1658, to December 31, 1659, and 332 from 1668 to 1673 (van Laer 1923, 1926; for the secretary's role in reading documents for others, see van Laer 1922: 56). For the most part, Dyckman carried on as his own clerk, and in 1656 de Deckere was forced to do so as well (van Laer 1920: 13, 249). When Johannes La Montagne assumed office, Provoost became secretary, and he held the post until 1664. Data on his brother are generally available, but consult van der Zee and van der Zee (1978: 148, 238, 371).

1653
Beverwijck

Not surprisingly, the burghers' aesthetic appreciation of the Hudson River has gone unrecorded. Their use of it as a trade route, however — north to the Mohawk Valley and Canada, south to the Esopus and New Amsterdam, downriver and along Long Island to Boston, across the seas to Holland — fills the public records. Dyckman's memorandums of 1657 give some idea of traffic during one season of *handelstijd* (Pearson 1869: 244–47). Van Slichtenhorst's letter to seven skippers is documented in Beernink (1916: 172), and van Laer (1922: 88) provides a further sense of the ready flow of goods and passengers. Court minutes, published early records, and Jeremias van Rensselaer's correspondence, however, provide the amplest evidence (van Laer 1920, 1923; Pearson 1869; van Laer 1918, 1932b). I have tried to estimate the volume of traffic and the turn-around time between Beverwijck and New Amsterdam elsewhere (Merwick 1990: 111–14), but my work is by no means exhaustive. Van Houtte comments on merchant adventurers' practice of regularly accompanying their cargoes of goods overseas (1977: 209).

Janse continued to be reappointed as a schoolmaster in Beverwijck (van Laer 1920: 57, 65; 1923: 295; 1928: 88). He also seems to have been engaged in the fur trade, although the extent of his involvement — and with wholesale merchants such as Keyser — remains uncertain (van Laer 1920: 75, and for further data on Keyser in 1649, refer to Chapter 2 and Fernow and O'Callaghan 1853–87: 1:308). Debts to Sybout Claesz cited in the *Year-Book of the Holland Society* and Janse's part in the *rederij* of 1668 suggest that he kept more of a hand in the trade than appears in the records (Banta 1900: 170). He also seems to have had dealings with Sijbinck before his letter of 1676. Finally, his meager income as schoolmaster would not seem to have offered him the funds for properties bought during this time. Janse's role as adjudicator is in van Laer (1920: 57), and Jan Janse's debts are in a letter cited in Fernow and O'Callaghan (1853–87: 14:137).

During these years, the fur trade was a determinant of every burgher's economic well-being. Being a participant in the activities of the trade — being in the game, even along the margins — was a way of reinforcing a worldview of interconnected values (see Geertz 1975b). Van Rensselaer's correspondence and the court minutes offer just some of the data on the significance of seemingly trifling sums in an economy like Beverwijck's (van Laer 1932b: 355, 1928: 426). Janse's indebtedness for his wife's care on Manhattan Island is in the minutes (van Laer 1920: 75).

The arable land immediately around the old fort has a history of its own, often bitter and full of contest. It is enough to say here that the land, sometimes referred to as the *plein,* appears repeatedly in early grants and conveyances but rarely are boundaries of lots within it accurately given. The earliest land grants refer to house lots and gardens drawn by lot (Pearson 1869: 202–4; van Laer 1920: 48, 64; for Janse's property see below but note here Pearson 1869: 195, 226). Abraham Staats's property sold for 2,325 guilders (195). The ordinance to fence house lots and its enforcement by Stuyvesant and Dyckman are in the minutes (van Laer 1920: 65, 76, 77, 82, 83).

Janse's failure to summon Stoll to court is, I think, evidence that he was a mild, somewhat withdrawn man — perhaps even what the Dutch called *onderborig,* dependent (van Laer 1920: 104, 105, 111). This interpretation is consistent with everything I have discovered about him from other records. The court records and correspondence of Jeremias van Rensselaer give us something of the rhythm of the town's activities during winter, including the festivities of Shrove Tuesday and gatherings at which nicknames were concocted (van Laer 1920: 199, 248, 251). Stoll was frequently charged with extreme acts of violence (van Laer 1922: 135, 136; 1920: 26, 27, 59, 96, 119, 238–39, 248).

NOVEMBER 7, 1657
Beverwijck

The only way of tracing Janse as a property owner during these years is by tediously searching the early papers collected by Pearson. The results, however, are far from satisfactory. No survey of the early town was conducted, nor were boundaries of lots recorded. Unidentified parcels of a property were sold off by owners; notarized contracts of sale were drawn but the deeds were not consistently recorded. In all, men and women looked upon properties as they did other commodities: as much to be exchanged, divided, and alienated as consolidated and passed on to children.

In some sense, however, Janse's experiences as one of the earliest property owners are typical of those of others of his generation. That is, he received his lot and garden directly from Stuyvesant and by means of a lottery; he sold off part of it in a short time; he purchased another property (the brickyard), which he sold off in about ten years' time; at a later date, he saw his original lot enlarged by a piece of land granted by the magistrates to him and a neighbor; along the way, he acquired a property which he rented — and in 1668 he was able to write of owning "houses and lots" (which are impossible to identify). There is nothing here that marks his place in the property market (if we may use that term) as anything out of the ordinary. What is perhaps remarkable is the meagerness of his portfolio of other investments. As far as we can know, and unless his activities in the fur trade were such that they eluded the records that caught up most others, his sources of income were his school tuitions and, after 1657, whatever profits he earned on the brickyard. He may also have been receiving payments for rentals of a house or house lot.

Pearson's collection records most of this (property) activity to 1660 (1869: 56, 57 for Janse's purchase of the brickyard, and see 7, 228, 229, 440; van Laer 1919: 22; 1934–35: 7). A patent in the Van Vechten Papers dated April 25, 1667, refers (without accurate detail) to lands of Abraham Staats and Adriaen Gerritsz van Papendorp in the vicinity of Janse's (Van Vechten Papers 1667). Janse's original allotment is also mentioned in court records (van Laer 1920: 65, 83). The Huntington Library holds the original of Stuyvesant's land grant to Janse, dated simply October 1653. (A transcript is in the Manuscripts and Special Collections, State Library of New York, Albany.) Dyckman's purchase is in Pearson (1869: 226).

Jeremias van Rensselaer arrived in the *colonie* in 1656. His correspondence from that date until his death in 1674 provides the only reflective account of life in Beverwijck during this time. It is an arresting chronicle of an engaging young man (van Laer 1932b). Jeremias's letters give us information on pelts sent to Holland and the sale of a yacht for a cargo of merchandise. He comments that 1657 was a reasonably profitable trading year when the burghers might have had surplus capital to invest (van Laer 1932b: 29, 34). When Janse bought his brickyard, Ryer Eldertsz already owned one (Pearson 1869: 32, 109, 132, 268, 413), and elsewhere reference is made to a "former brickyard" owned by the company but providing residence for Hendrick Janse Westerkamp (van Laer 1922: 194). In their accounts, the deacons of the church costed the building of the poorhouse (van Laer 1931–32: 253); the magistrates kept records on the erection of the church building (van Laer 1923: 14).

The Leidenaars' business transactions are in Pearson, as is the apparent contempt of de Hulter and Appel for Beverwijck's ordinances (1869: 56, 58, 242, 243). Among the Leidenaars who came with de Hulter to Rensselaerswijck in 1654 were Pieter Bont Quackenbosch, Pieter Jacobsz Borsboom, and Pieter Meese Vrooman, each of whom was involved in a *steenbakkerij* or otherwise associated with de Hulter during this time; consult Hoffman (1938: 345; Pearson 1869: 56–59 *and* passim).

I have simply presented a series of canvases or scenes in Janse's life from 1655 to 1658 because they allow me to be true to the record: these *are* his only appearances in the town's public records. A detailed reconstruction of them is possible because of the abundant concrete detail that Dutch men and women of Beverwijck enjoyed bringing before the court and that officers such as Dyckman customarily recorded. For the auctions, see Pearson (1869: 16, 17, 206, 207, and for confirmation of Halenbeeck's house sale and Janse's bid for the brickyard, 31, 32, 56, 57). The incident in the courtroom together with Janse's meeting with three other men and then the scene in the fort are in the minutes and other early papers (van Laer 1920: 200, and see 10; Pearson 1869: 7, 228; in 1657 Janse was summoned to court but defaulted, 77).

I think it is not coincidental that the abundance of concrete detail in the records suggests canvases that are in the manner of the realist paintings of the Golden Age. Among others, Freedberg and de Vries (1991) have made us aware of the vigorous debate over the matter of realism among today's art historians. My own researches in the Dutch local records and notarial papers, as well as in the notarial manuals and treatises on accounting, navigation, and education, have led me to accept the validity of Svetlana Alpers's position in this debate, namely, that the aim of Dutch painters was to "increase the visual knowledge of reality" by striving for *schijn zonder zijn,* semblance without being (Sluijter 1991: 175). Alpers's 1983 study is a comprehensive presentation of her position. Her work in relating "pictorial phenomena to notions of knowledge" has guided me in what I have tried to do here and elsewhere, that is, relate scribal phenomena in New Netherland — the products of notaries and bureaucrats, of navigators and merchants — to notions of knowledge as well (Schwartz and Bok 1990: 1). Alpers believes that the Dutch placed a high value on pictorial phenomena — paintings but also maps and well-crafted legal documents — but not because they called forth abstract principles or ideal models. Rather, they strove to resemble "the thing itself" (Sluijter 1991: 182). And so it was with notarial papers. In a notary's act, for example, a distancing and universalizing word like the article "a" (*een*) seldom appears. Rather, "the" (*het* or *de*) is there to establish the concrete.

Lyckle de Vries recalls something further about the realist style in Dutch seventeenth-century painting and indirectly comments on the way New Netherlanders enjoyed living their lives. Everything, he writes, "is orchestrated to give the impression that what is represented is not the dramatic highpoint of an exceptional event but a fairly arbitrary moment taken from an incident in daily life. The painted figures perform without drama or emphasis. The rendering of space, the composition, and the placement of figures underscore the impression of coincidence" (1991: 225).

Dyckman's illness is recorded in letters of de Deckere in Pearson (1869: 232, 234, 242; and see 246 for his "sayings") and a letter of Stuyvesant, de Sille, and La Montagne to the company directors at home (Stuyvesant 1655b). The community's care of him is documented in Munsell (1865–72: 1:28, 32, 35).

The new courthouse is described in a 1660 memorandum of La Montagne to Stuyvesant and his council and quoted in van Laer (1920: 10, 11). The deacons' accounts show that Johanna de Hulter was getting 1 guilder for 50 bricks in 1656 (van Laer 1931–32: 3).

Details of the auction held in July 1658 are in early records edited by van Laer (1919: 53–55, 78–80).

5. Beverwijck: The Final Years

SEPTEMBER 1, 1660
Beverwijck

I interpret the events of this summer as the burghers' efforts to confront the company with their determination to take control of the fur trade and move the market town toward the status of a city. At the same time, the arrival of the notary Dirck van Schelluyne further empowered residents to consider themselves as *poorters,* or citizens of a city. His professional skills dramatized how transactional the character of the townspeople's relationships were, how contractual and urban, indeed interurban, their enterprises. In this sense it is not surprising that in 1937 the major scholar on the early *colonie* pointed out that the office of notary developed in the Mohawk Valley only after the establishment of Beverwijck, that is, "primarily in connection with the affairs of the townsmen" (Nissenson 1937: 145).

The violence of 1660 can be traced in the court minutes and in van Rensselaer's correspondence (van Laer 1923: 249–302; 1922: see 71 for sending notes to the natives; 1932b). Shattuck (1993) and Merwick (1990: 88–99) have studied these months closely. If van Laer is correct, 1660 was one of many years when Janse was instructing youth rather than younger children (1918: 21). His demands for tuition were heard in court on September 1. I have cited the court cases and consulted other sources for suitable context: his suit against van Valkenbergh (van Laer 1923: 295 and see 40, 80, 277, 339; for data on Jochem van Valkenbergh, see Pearson 1869: 228, 339); against Lookermans (van Laer 1923: 295 and see Pearson 1869: 7, 57, 228–29, 335); against Brouwer (van Laer 1923: 295 and see 80, 264, 279, 280); against Teunisse (van Laer 1923: 189, 193, 201, 221, 260, 267, 298, 300, and passim, and see Pearson 1869: 43, 56, 283). The surgeon's fees are in the court minutes (van Laer 1923: 21).

It is impossible to arrive at an exact estimate of Janse's income as schoolmaster during these years. The numbers of youth and schoolmasters (and possibly schoolmistresses) offering classes at any one time as well as the tuitions they charged remain uncertain. Still, there is no evidence that during these years Janse was earning anything more than a subsistence living. De Planque (1926), Kilpatrick (1912), Van Eck (1927), and Wouters and Visser (1926) found that, with some variation, notoriously low wages were fairly standard across the Low Countries and New Netherland. Wouters and Visser discovered evidence of many complaints about salaries set at less than 100 guilders a year (1926: 98). I have used Kilpatrick's figures (1912: 68) and find they accord with Flatbush salaries cited in Nooter (1994: 137). Curaçao papers include the cost of quills and other writing materials in 1655 (Gehring 1987a: 68).

De Ridder-Symoens notes that whenever family income fell in the Low Countries, cutting corners on school tuition was an immediate way of economizing. This practice contributed significantly to keeping schoolmasters at the level of "an intellectual proletariat" (1988: 204). Wouters and Visser point to the trivial amount a rich merchant might budget for schooling as opposed to wearing apparel (1926: 92). Frederiks found people of Overijssel inclined to compare the schoolmaster with a housewife, and Luykas Gerritsz hoped in 1676 that the magistrates of Albany would appoint him as schoolmaster because he had the use of only one hand (1960: 207; van Laer 1928: 98).

Records of these years point to Janse as a man pursuing his affairs very much on his own. While Kiliaen van Rensselaer spoke for most people in saying that he was always looking for "friends in the game," Janse seems to have gone his own way, unsupported by merchants, family, or patrons (van Laer 1908: 268). Data about the van Lodesteijns are from van der Linde's edition of Selijns's papers (1983: 79, 97), and see Fernow and O'Callaghan for reference to the family member Joost van Lodesteijn, who was chosen to represent the Delft chamber of the West India Company to the States General regarding New Netherland in 1652 (1853–87: 1:467).

Prominent among the happenings of *handelstijd* in 1660 was the recording of them by the leading merchants who made up the local court and were intent upon presenting their worrying story to Stuyvesant in early autumn. The assiduous record-keeping of the *colonie* was going ahead as well, making a good beginning to manor papers that would, by 1780, include 200 volumes of ledger and journal accounts, 1,000 letters, 3,000 leases, 500 maps and surveys, and 25,000 miscellaneous manuscripts.

Examples of the *colonie*'s involvement with record-keeping during these years are in Jeremias van Rensselaer's correspondence. His work checking van Slichenhorst's accounts is in van Laer (1932b: 141, 144–46, 171, 173, 174, 182, 191, 202). Something of his own interest in books may be found at 231, 273, 467. It is possible that newspapers arrived regularly for him since Rychart writes in 1659 that he would "again [be] sending" them except that Jan Baptiste was doing so, and Stephan van Cortlandt forwarded three newspapers to him from Jan Baptiste in early 1664 (149, 347).

JANUARY 1661
Beverwijck

Van Schelluyne's papers seem to have been preserved by being given into the custody of Adriaen Janse. They then became the property of the city council of Albany and were translated and published by van Laer in 1918. Today they are held at the Albany County Hall of Records and bound with Janse's papers. They are certainly not complete, but they served as a basis for my analysis. Van Schelluyne seemed to work carefully. He cut his pen to a less fine point than Janse so his script is less attractive but consistently readable. His penmanship suggests a self-assured individual. Although his signature is outdone in grace by those of Jeremias van Rensselaer, Anthonij de Hooges, and Arent van Curler, it is nonetheless forceful. Schiltkamp considers van Schelluyne to have been a skillful notary and traces his career back to 1644, when he was admitted to practice in Gorinchem and probably had his first contact with New Netherland (1964: 130n2). Hamlin asserts that he kept his library near him, but Hamlin is not always reliable (1939: 73).

It is difficult not to think that van Schelluyne taught Janse the skills of his office — his own son, for example, was, at least at times, engaged in other kinds of work — but we cannot be certain (van Laer 1918: 201). Schiltkamp has, of course, an interest in van Schelluyne and documents his call to Rensselaerswijck (1964: 133). Adriaen Janse's self-conscious identification of himself as "testis" is in van Schelluyne's papers, December 7, 1661 (van Laer 1918: 137).

I first became aware of the confidentiality that rested with a notary by examining the papers of Kiliaen van Rensselaer. He expected his notary to be the "secret professional," a term used in the title of a nineteenth-century French treatise on notaries (Pappafava

1880, referring to Muteau, *Du Secret Professionel... Traite théoretique et practicque a l'usagé des Advocats... Notaires* [Paris, 1870], n.p.). Lachaire's greeting to van Schelluyne as a "confrater" appears in his papers (Scott and Stryker-Rodda 1978: 170). Rooms were set aside for notaries not only in the Amsterdam town hall but in the Binnenhof at The Hague (Brugmans 1973: 103; Kossman 1932: xx–xxiv, 26, 64–66, 71, and passim).

It is not surprising that van Schelluyne's papers give evidence of a high degree of literacy in Beverwijck from 1660 to 1664: 78 percent of men and 40 percent of women could sign their names. (Shattuck, using a larger sample — that is, early records published by Pearson and those published by van Laer in 1916, 1918, and 1919 — presents tentative figures of 66 percent and 49 percent [1993: 59–61]). The quantitative evidence, although limited, supports other accounts that Beverwijck's residents chose to leave behind. Together, these accounts point to a culture grounded in the handwritten word, the culture of a people who considered it proper to entrust a great many social relationships to the circulation of texts. Baumann (1985: 18) deals usefully with definitions and descriptions of scribal cultures, as do Chartier (1987), Certeau (1984), Goody (1986: 72), Love (1987: 133), Ong (1977), and Sweeney (1987).

A brief comparison of Dutch- and English-speaking communities in the seventeenth century suggests that literacy in a place like Beverwijck was not likely to be promoted under English rule. Research on literacy across the Low Countries points to variation from province to province but to "extremely high" levels prevailing in the western provinces, where the majority of the population lived (Parker 1980: 214). Jan de Vries, using the data of Simon Hart from Amsterdam marriage registers, quotes the proportion of grooms who were literate in 1680 as 70 percent and brides as 44 percent (1974: 212). The data are substantiated by the comments of contemporary foreign observers such as Guicciardini — "even the peasants at least know how to read and write" (quoted in Kilpatrick 1912: 37) — and, more substantially, scholars of early modern Dutch education. De Hulla cites the example of 3,450 letters handed over to Governor-General Hendrick Brouwer in 1632 by sailors aboard two ships sailing for the VOC to the Indies (1914: 350).

The levels of literacy appear to have been lower in England. See Spufford, who cites the well-known 1642 data stating that literacy in the countryside ranged from 17 to 38 percent but with considerable variation (1974: 181, 182). Cressy, using his own research and quoting that of Kenneth A. Lockridge, states that in mid-seventeenth-century England two-thirds of men and three-fourths of women "could not sign their own name." In New England two-fifths of males and two-thirds of females were similarly illiterate (1987: 217, and see Kett and McCluny, whose figures for Virginia are comparable (1984: 100, 136). There is general agreement that "signature literacy" is not a wholly satisfactory indicator of reading and writing skills. Functional literacy — which suggests more satisfactory results — needs further examination. Gilmore (1992) and Reay (1991) are worth consulting here.

SATURDAY, MAY 26, 1663
Beverwijck

Van Schelluyne's papers give the setting for this episode (van Laer 1918: 217, 218). Other sources that allow a context are early property records and court minutes (Pearson 1869: 278, 279, and passim; van Laer 1920: 64, 276–77). Bensingh's indebtedness is documented frequently in the late 1650s, but see van Laer 1923: 152.

Thomassen's encounter with Lachaire is recorded in the notary's register, edited by Scott and Stryker-Rodda (1978: 189, and see 71, 73, 88, and 194). The register makes it possible to reconstruct Lachaire's practice in considerable detail. Direct references are made to the commentators cited at 20, 54, 80, 105, 118, 119, 148, 195, 160, 178, 200, and 201. *Zee-rechten* are noted at 20 and 25. In addition, Lachaire referred in passing to a range of other books, but they are those he encountered as he made up inventories of others' estates. The reference to the sea, land, city, and church as giving a notary his employment is Lybreghts (1736, quoting [in quatrains] Abraham van Limburg de Jonge n.p.) Lachaire's papers are held in the New York municipal archives. They suggest a man who often wrote in haste, often inscribing (as was customary) "Amsterdam" rather than "New Amsterdam," trying his hand at English, sometimes embroidering the date of an attestation into the flourishes of his signature.

FEBRUARY 2, 1664
New Amsterdam

Van der Zee and van der Zee offer a detailed account of the seizure of New Amsterdam by the English (1978). Archdeacon (1976), Balmer (1989), Goodfriend (1992), Maika (1995), Merwick (1990), Rink (1986), and Ritchie (1977) are only some of the scholars who have sought to interpret it. For the most part, there is agreement that the seizure was an unlawful act. Carried on outside a declaration of war, it was known to be an illicit act of aggression both at the court of Charles II and at The Hague. Differences center on the cost of the subsequent cultural dislocation to the Dutch. Many have argued that Dutch residents gladly embraced the blessings of conquest and "benign English governors" (Balmer 1989: 9, and see Roeber 1991: 221). The view seen through the conqueror's eyes has been particularly challenged by recent scholarship, which instead looks to recover a Dutch way of life that was different from that of the English — indeed, that needed no comparison with things English to establish its own validity (see, among others, Narrett 1992, Nooter and Bonomi 1988, van der Linde 1983, van Zwieten 1996, Voorhees 1994, and the work of the New Netherland Project located at the State Library of New York, Albany).

My reconstruction of the surrender of New Amsterdam is from Stokes (1915–28: 4:232–42). Fernow (1897: 5:15–116) and Fernow and O'Callaghan (1853–87: 2:230–72) can be read along with this daily chronology. The saying regarding conscience and political loyalties is in Struik (1981: 60, quoting Simon Stevin, *Het Burgerlijke Leven*). Documents among the Curaçao papers and those of New Amsterdam give some sense of the public confidence that New Netherland would one day be restored to the Dutch (Gehring 1987a: 205; see Merwick 1990: 134–47).

WEDNESDAY, JULY 16, 1664
New Amsterdam

The suicide of Hendrick Janse Smitt is documented in Stokes (1915–28: 4:238; for another source, see Fernow 1897: 5:93). Stokes allows us to locate Janse's house and the Kalckhoek near the Fresh Pond, where he hanged himself. For his house, see Stokes

1915–28: 2:267–68, Block F, no. II. Schiltkamp (1964: 48) writes of a copy of Duysent-daelers in New Netherland in 1659, and for cases of suicide handled by Leiden's magistrates, see comments on " 'Nieuw Albanij in America,' " below.

6. Albany

1665, 1666
Albany

This chapter concerns Adriaen Janse's first four years under the English occupation. For most of the time, he was silent. It would be convenient to interpret this silence as emblematic of the town's mute acquiescence in a military regime and the first imposition of new cultural ways. More properly, however, it was coincidence. Janse's unimportance as a townsman and his seemingly reticent personality — why *would* his voice be heard? — coincided with a public silence that had more complex origins.

The unexplained disappearance of the court records from 1661 to 1668 suggests only one of many reasons why a silence about the military occupation hangs over these years. Yet the void left in public records that were otherwise remarkably full from 1648 to the 1690s is also a telltale sign of disruption, perhaps one as powerful as any of the few recorded events we have. There are fugitive references to resistance, most of them in official English reports and van Rensselaer's correspondence (Fernow and O'Callaghan 1853–87: 3:117, 13:387; van Laer 1932b: 356, 465; and see Weise 1884: 141, 147). Yet those who recorded the passing events generally describe a period of sullen accommodation (Christoph 1980; Fernow and O'Callaghan 1853–87: 3, 13; van Laer 1932b; Pretyman and Fernow state that the flag of the New England colonies flew over Albany (1886: n.p.). This policy of accommodation is in sharp contrast to tactics of resistance adopted in Kingston (see immediately below). Governor Lovelace's reminder to the local commanding officer that the residents could not be expected to "love us" is in his papers (Christoph 1980: 32).

Janse's role in the town auctions can be gleaned from memorandums and records kept by the town's secretary (Pearson 1869: 343–44, 65, 68, 69, 78–82, 88–90; for the price of a cow, 63; for "dangling a line," van Laer 1908: 322). The auction of valuable items is carried in Pearson (1869: 83–86; for Janse's willingness to act as guarantor, 396, 397).

The *Hollandtze Mercurius* (*Hollandtze* is variously spelled) was published in Haarlem and ranks among the earliest Dutch *couranten*. Its Amsterdam counterpart appeared only in 1672; the *Weeckelijke Courante van Europa* began to appear in Haarlem after 1656 (van Rooijen 1988b: 241). Like the *Hollandtze Mercurius*, such publications were purely informative. The later *Europische Mercurius* (1691+) set itself to be interpretive, looking in a new way for causation and consequences. Hazewinkel describes the life of Gerard van Spann and his *Amerikaansche Wegwijzer* (1943: iv, v).

References to the disturbing events that a *Mercurius* might have reported in the Albany vicinity for 1665 and 1666 are in van Laer (1932b: 375, 376); Christoph, Scott, and Stryker-Rodda (1976a: 232, 233); Weise (1884: 148); and Fernow and O'Callaghan (1853–87: 3:118, 119; 13:406–16, "Papers Relating to the Esopus Mutiny"). Data on the

French expeditionary force that threatened Albany in 1666 are in Fernow and O'Callaghan (1853–87: 3:118, 119, 132 [and see 128–30], 157). Interpretations are offered by Bell (1862: 1:219), Eccles (1964: 95), Goldstein (1969: 95), and Jennings (1984: 131). Schoonmaker offers a detailed and sympathetic history of Kingston during these years (1888).

APRIL 20, 1667
Albany

Janse's role in the renewal of Gerritsz's land patent is in Pearson (1869: 418–19). English orders for such reconfirmations are in Christoph, Scott, and Stryker-Rodda (1976a: 315, and see van Laer 1916: 8). The fees collected by the English authorities are referred to in Ritchie (1977: 55); surveyors' fees are mentioned in Pearson (1869: 407). Fernow and O'Callaghan have published some of the records of the court-martial proceedings related to the Kingston rising (1853–87: 3:149, 150), and Gerritsz's presence at the Lyndraer auction is given in Christoph, Scott, and Stryker-Rodda (1976b: 640). Other meetings regarding land confirmations are detailed in Pearson (1869: 410–23). For the burgher's admission of neglect in 1679, see van Laer (1928: 422); for Janse's renewal of his own grant, van Laer (1919: 18n26). The land granted to Staats is recorded in the Van Vechten Papers (April 25, 1667)

JULY, AUGUST 1668
Albany

The only sources for Janse's voyage to Holland are Pearson (1869: 446 [where the translator identifies him as "Arent"]), Fernow and O'Callaghan (1853–87: 2:178, 179, "Petition"), van Laer (1934–35: 8, 9). Van Rensselaer's preparations and concerns are in his correspondence (van Laer 1932b: 405, 406, 411, 413; for the "generals," 408). For an interpretation of van Rensselaer's relationship with Nicolls, see Merwick (1990: 148–65). Jeremias refers to his quartering of soldiers on 411. Hartgers's confiscated property is referred to in van Laer (1932b: 315, 357, 358, 405).

Van Schelluyne, acting as the town's secretary, assisted the six Albany burghers with their preparations for reaching Holland (Pearson: 1869: 406, 407, 439–49, 499). Schermerhoorn's affairs in Dordrecht are recorded in van Laer (1920: 177, 178, 216). His agency for Maria Dyckman is in van Laer (1934–35: 4–6). Van Eps's order of trading goods appears in the court minutes (van Laer 1926: 92). Some of the dense evidence for the portfolios of the Albany travelers and their mutual associations is in Pearson (1869: 275, 400). Bancker's and Vedder's overseas dealings with the major Amsterdam merchant houses are taken up by Rink (1986: 187, 189, 190). Janse's preparations can be pieced together from Pearson (1869: 446) and van Laer (1934–35: 8). In a town as small as Albany, Janse would have known each of the other travelers. Only some of his business with them can be reconstructed, but it appears to have been incidental (Pearson 1869: 60, 365, 407). Schermerhoorn's conflict with Stuyvesant is in Fernow and O'Callaghan (1853–87: 1:428). Laurensz's partnership with van Aecken is in the council of New Netherland minutes (Scott and Stryker-Rodda 1974d: 205).

Fragmentary data on the *King Charles*'s early history is in Stokes (1915–28: 4:156) and van Laer (1932b: 404–8). Hardenbroeck's assignment of power of attorney to Sijbinck establishes that the ship was still in New York Harbor on August 21, 1668 (GA, Sybinck 1669, January 5). Bestevaer is identified as captain in van Rensselaer's correspondence (van Laer 1932b: 412); van Rensselaer's spellings of the ship's name are at 408, 412, 413; Nicolls's departure is at 411 and referred to by him in Fernow and O'Callaghan 1853–87: 3:172).

A *rederij* or *charterpartij* was a common way among the Dutch of underwriting a ship and freighting it with cargo for a single voyage. The practice is discussed by Bruijn, who examined the seventeenth-century Dutch merchant's understanding of a "profitable" voyage and found it entailed a return of not less than 10 percent (1990: 179, 184). Also worth consulting are ten Have (1973b: 15), Barbour (1950), and Gehlen (1986: Document 19 for a notarized agreement to a *charterpartij*, June 1675). Van Laer presents the inventory of the expenses of a *rederij* entered into by Jan Baptiste van Rensselaer, Abel de Wolff, and others — including drinks and meals in Amsterdam at the Golden Lion and other eateries (1908: 795–803).

Ritchie (1977: 59 and *passim*) and Matson (1991, 1994) have reconstructed the impact of England's navigation acts on New York's trade. The complaint of English merchants to the Board of Trade about allowances made to Dutch New York traders during November 1668 is worth consulting (Fernow and O'Callaghan 1853–87: 3:175, 176). Rink (1986) remains the best authority on the ties between the merchant communities of Holland and New Netherland, although I think he ascribes too little inventiveness to the New World merchants. He describes some of the activities of de Wolff and Vedder on 189 and 190; see also the work of Maika (1995). Jan Martensz van Wolphen was an Amsterdam merchant and partner of Jan Baptiste van Rensselaer in July 1668 (van Laer 1932b: 315, 357, 358a, 363, 376, 390, 405). He would seem to be the partner whom the translator of the petition identifies as "John Martens." (For words mangled in translation, note the translator's identification of Oloff van Cortlandt as "Olive Stuyvesant van Cortlandt.") In transcription, the petition records the names of seventeen partners. They may have been sixteen, however, with "John Jansen, Koster van Aken" actually identifying only van Aecken.

Janse's days in Holland are a mystery. I have used Cosimo de' Medici's journal notes because he was in Holland about the same time as Janse (Hoogewerff 1919). His observations also offer some sense of a visitor's way of traveling in the Low Countries. Hoogewerff writes a splendid introduction to the account, and my citations are at xxvii, xv, and, in the diary, at entries for February 1–3, 1668 (130) and December 20, 1667 (42).

Brugmans's lively description of seventeenth-century Amsterdam includes references to the Schouwberg and its critics, street and tavern music, the waterfront, Catholic worship, rooms for notaries in the great town hall, the administrative practices of Valckenier, and the impressive status of the *schout* (1973: 128, 124, 207, and see 11, 145, 103, 184, 185, 74). This work, which attends so usefully to popular culture, can be filled out by van Deursen (1978b), Schama (1987), and Zumthor (1962). Kermis as a time of violence with knives is in van Deursen, and see *De Wandelende Beschouwer* and *De Twee Beschouwende Vrienden* (1978b: 52; 1820).

My references to Amsterdam's booksellers are in Gehring (1987a: 137 for the sale of manifests in the 1650s by Françoys Lieshout) and Vanderbilt (1899: 54). Ships laden with exotic cargoes from Batavia are cited in *Hollandtz Mercurius* (1667: [October] 162). Den Oosterling's papers are archived in GL Den Oosterlingh 1668.

I have raised the question of Janse's feeling himself to be a stranger in Holland during these weeks although I have no answer to it. How seriously he took the self-identification of the petitioners as "sworn subjects" of the king of England cannot be known. Neither can we know the degree to which he considered himself to be counted among the "strange" Americans, the *barbaren* or the exotic Americans (te Lintum 1909: 25; ten Have 1973b: 15; Fernow and O'Callaghan 1853–87: 1:262 [Adriaen vander Donck et al.], "Additional Observations . . . October 13, 1649"). Although New Netherland had fallen to the English four years before, several of the partners continued to identify themselves as residing in New Netherland or on Manhattan Island (GA, Sijbinck 1668, December 22 and 28; and 1669, January 5, February 14, July 17).

Jan Hendricksz Sijbinck's name occurs repeatedly in the early records of New Netherland. His role in various merchants' affairs is documented, inter alia, in Pearson (1869: 78 and passim), van Laer (1935: 170), and GA, Sijbinck 1651, where I have collected references to relevant notarized acts (March 17, 1651; May 20, 1654; March 15, 1657; April 1, 1657; March 16, 1660; November 1, 1662; March 24, 1663; March 27, 1663; July 27, 1663; April 12, 1666). He, of course, continued to do business with customers in New York and Albany after 1669. GA, Sijbinck 1670, April 30, documents such arrangements and refers to the examination of pelts in his house. Rink's account of Sijbinck in his 1986 study is brief but valuable.

Very little about the voyagers' activities in Holland can be pieced together. The data I have cited are from Sijbinck's papers and those of nine notaries consulted by one or another of them during this time (GA, Sijbinck 1668, December 27 and 28; 1669, January 5, February 14, March 29, June 19, July 17; and 1670, May 28). Albany court records document van Eps's return home with cloth sometime before August 4, 1669 (van Laer 1926: 92). I have based the probability that Janse met with Sijbinck during this time on his 1676 reference to a relationship arising "from old acquaintance" and the fact that both men did business with Pieter Jacobsz Marius (van Laer 1918: 335; GA, Sijbinck 1663, March 27, and 1668, December 22; van Laer 1918: 337). The delay of the *King Charles* and the *reders*'s awareness of the serious weather hazard it created is in Fernow and O'Callaghan (1853–87: 3:178, and for the Order in Council agreeing to the petitioners' request, 179). Several of the notarized acts cited immediately above document the delay. See particularly GA, Sijbinck 1668, December 27.

1669
Holland

The conflict of Cousseau, Philipse, and Steenwyck over *'t Fort Albanie* [*Hopewell*] is in GA, Sijbinck 1668, December 27; 1669, March 8, May 29, June 19; and 1670, May 28. The ship's earlier voyaging as the *Hopewell* is mentioned in van Laer (1932b: 371) and in Sijbinck's papers, dated April 12, 1666. The date of the *King Charles*'s departure from Texel in unknown. The disappointingly sketchy diary of young Kiliaen van Rensselaer gives the cost of transport from Amsterdam to Texel (Kiliaen van Rensselaer 1685: entry of July 25). De Ruyter's defenses for the sound between North Holland and Texel are mentioned in Keyes (1990: 167).

MAY 12, 1669
Rensselaerswijck

Jeremias van Rensselaer's letters convey a poignant sense of the cost of the English presence in Albany and the pervasive uncertainty of living on the edge of the wilderness (van Laer 1932b: 403, 413, 416; see 413 for Reyersz's imminent departure for Holland). Janse returned to these conditions by May 13, 1669 (van Laer 1926: 69). Vedder seems to have been present in the New York City court by early April, but his case may have been put by an attorney (Fernow 1897: 6:176).

The Dutch Labadist visitor Jasper Dankaerts filled a journal in 1680 with negative comments about Dutch New Yorkers. Here his remarks about Albany's residents are taken from Weise (1884: 171).

7. "Nieuw Albanij in America"

These last years of Janse's life leave us with the question that began this book. How did England's imperial designs in the last decades of the seventeenth century catch up the life of so insignificant a man as Janse? Largely our narrative must be surmised. We can know only that the particularities of Janse's life were being enfolded by the generalities that were taking England toward being a more centralized state and territorial aggressor. Circumstance and structure, as they always are, were being merged, and contradictions were being found. As a notary, Janse symbolized business practices that contradicted the centralizing of state powers. He also represented a system that sustained itself without the powers and privileges of landownership. Janse came to personify something obsolescent. The king's representative in New York imposed a unified and London-based economic policy on a province that had been remarkably free of state interference. The scramble for land and for manorial grants showed how much the landscape of this new order needed to be changed. We see these contradictions and this obsolescence in Janse's papers. In them we can see, or think we see, what drove Janse's life and the visions held by Englishmen miles away toward their tragic meeting.

SEPTEMBER 19, 1678
Albany

Janse's experiences during these years can be reconstructed from the court records and his register. Many of these experiences were his efforts to maneuver between the Dutch and English languages. Others were between the demands of a receding Dutch legal system and those of an English system being steadily but erratically put into place. The latter changes in all their torturous twists and turns are documented by Goebel (1970).

Goebel's research shows that before the mid-1680s, when Governor Thomas Dongan arrived with instructions for revising the government of New York, Janse was, to a certain degree, in the same position as the non-Dutch justices of the peace appointed after 1664. Both were in the dark in respect to knowing precisely what the laws of New York were. It was a time when judicial commissions were "intentionally" vague, so that even "from the [English] subjects' point of view," the laws and precedents that justices of the peace were meant to administer were "nowhere to be known." Only beginning in 1684 were models of the laws of England put in place that could clarify law for justices and (if it were asked for) present a notary like Janse with an unambiguous body of law to consult. Only then could county justices, most of them English New Yorkers, get help from legal textbooks printed in England. Those they selected — Lambarde's *Eirenarcha*, Dalton's *Countrey Justice* — were either amateurish or outdated. Yet they at least provided rules of English practice (Goebel 1970: 43, 45–47). Lambarde (1635) sets out the duties of constables but offers no role for notaries (Read 1962). Meriton, a London jurist writing for constables, concluded in 1668 that Lambarde's rules were "unsafe" to follow (1685: n.p). Seavey's work demonstrates that the powers allowed to an English or Anglo-American justice of the peace would cancel out those of a Dutch notary (1894).

I have set Janse's inability to comply with the street paving ordinance within other events noted in the court minutes (van Laer 1928: 16, 23, 38, 53–55, 64, 71, 76, 91, 105, 107, 124, 243, 245, 262; see 246n1 and 404 for proclamations in Dutch and English; see 107 for fencing thrown in the river. Court minutes also carry the episodes surrounding Janse's work for van Curler and her criticism of Becker, 233, 314, 410; see also van Laer 1926: 44, 216, and 1932a: 107, 108).

Janse's letters to Guldewagen and Sijbinck are in his papers (van Laer 1918: 334–38; for his later account with Sijbinck, 494). Sijbinck's association with Marius is in the comments on "Albany," above. Janse had every reason to worry about Algerian pirates (van Laer 1928: 349, 360). "Turk rates" were imposed for the release of captives, including Jacob Leisler, and are cited in Fernow and O'Callaghan (1853–87: 13:533). Evidence for Janse's increasing difficulties in earning an income can be gathered from the court minutes (van Laer 1928: for taxes laid, 17, 23, 105, 267, 273, 376; for poor agricultural returns, 71; for difficulties supporting the minister, 69).

The burghers' confusion about the status of legalized documents is evidenced in Governor Andros's papers (Christoph and Christoph 1990: 64–65). The uncertain status of depositions is in the court minutes (van Laer 1928: 223, 224, and see 240). Andros's directive against taking depositions was possibly aimed at people like Lewin who were collecting them against *him* (Ritchie 1977: 124). For the distinction between formal and infomal land transactions, see van Laer (1919: 4:18n24 and de Smidt 1984: 189 quoting Grotius). Lovelace's misunderstanding is in the book of general entries, 1664–73 (Christoph and Christoph 1982: 309).

Changes in court procedures — and men such as Domine van Rensselaer and Cobus as points of entry to the courts — are of the subtlest sort, but see van Laer (1928: 19, 21, 254, 255, 258, 422). Van Laer (1916: 8, 9) refers to the assembly's law regarding mortgages drawn before June 13, 1684. Alterations in words and presentation of proof are in van Laer (1928: 89, 146, 147, 204, 206, 321). The separate cases involving the English soldier, Schuyler, and Livingston are also in van Laer (1928: 315–18; 1932a: 338; 1928:

266). Documentation about the English townsman who carried his case to New York City is in Andros's papers (Christoph and Christoph 1990: 317, 329). Janse served on a jury in 1676, and its garbled verdict is in van Laer (1928: 104).

Evidence of Janse's and the town's attempt to cope with translations and Livingston's calculations about the advantages are in van Laer (1918: 400, 403, 345, 468, 573, 577, and see Christoph and Christoph 1990: 248 for the merchant's signature as "Willson"); van Cortlandt (1681); Leder (1961: 19); van Laer (1928: 226; 1926: 36 for payment of the *spin-huyssedeel*). Pitlo points out that notaries were expected to be at home in the language they were using (1948: 23).

Janse's notarial papers and the court records hold the wills he executed at this time as well as Willson's request for a patent in English (van Laer 1918: 345, 450–56, 466–67). Rooseboom's commentary on the legality of a will first authenticated in private and then passed before two local *schepenen* and a secretary is in *Recueil* (1656: 218).

Janse (1918: 464) records his meeting with van Loon in December 1678. His name on the list of those commandeered to provide palings is in van Laer (1928: 396, 397, and see 384).

FRIDAY, MAY 2, 1679
Extraordinary Session Held in Albany

Court minutes carry the account of the burghers' petition to retain the city's right to trade overseas and the governor's dismissive rejection of it. Their acquiescence hides an intense and long-standing concern. At stake were not just the fortunes of the city's twenty or thirty principal peltry merchants. Rejection of the petition was emblematic of a shift in which state power was beginning to count more than market power. Albany was changing from a Dutch city to an agricultural county seat. For the petition, its rejection, and the burghers' response, see van Laer (1928: 406, 407, 409, 412, 413, 480, 481). Goebel's account of the slow attrition of the power of city magistrates in the face of county judges sitting in quarter sessions is excellent (1970: 20, 39–42).

Court minutes and Janse's papers give details of his collating a disputed act written by Cobus and recording bids at an auction (van Laer 1928: 422; 1918: 510, 511). Janse's letter to Guldewagen dated November 4, 1681, is in his register (van Laer 1918: 493, 494).

MARCH 7, 1682
Albany

Janse's professional lapse regarding the Ouderkerk contract was made a subject of the court minutes, as was his role in an earlier episode of "drunken man's business" (van Laer 1932a: 213, 214; 1928: 301, 302). The secretary also recorded the community's difficulties with and care for old and senile people (van Laer 1932a: 261, 278, 303). Duysentdaelers (1659: 5) comments on the treatment of senile persons and Brugmans (1973: 289) presents the rules of the old men's house in Amsterdam.

The deacons' account books record (inconsistently) the days of prayer for the king, and church attendance. There is no way of knowing why Janse chose to draw up a contract on

May 29, 1682, but we have to think that he knew of the prohibition against working on that day (van Laer 1918: 538). Weise cites the ordinance (1884: 169).

SOMETIME IN NOVEMBER 1682
Albany

Once again stories in the court records and in Janse's papers testify to the burghers' loss of language competence — and their efforts to cope — as part of the cost of conquest. Janse's awareness of all of this cannot be directly established, but we have to recognize that the transformation was taking place in the very small community around him and that coming to terms with English was a demand placed on everyone, to one degree or another.

In his letter to Guldewagen, written sometime in November, Janse seems withdrawn, enclosed in worries and fears for the future (van Laer 1918: 495). The original letter, now in the Albany County Hall of Records, is torn, folded, and interleaved between blank pages pencil-marked 287 and 291. Fijen, Melching, and Peterse document Guldewagen's death in 1684 (1977: n.p).

Documents used for people stumbling around in English and Dutch are Weise (1884: 175 for the non-Dutch-speaking commander at the fort); van Laer (1932a: 97, 98; see 113, 114, for Lewin's investigations and, for his report, see also Fernow and O'Callaghan [1853–87: 3:303]; van Laer [1932a: 15 for the English soldier translating a document for a Dutch trader]). Van Laer's translation of Maria van Rensselaer's correspondence carries her strategies (and those of the family) for accommodating to English demands (1935: 56–58).

Nicolaus van Rensselaer, perhaps more than any other figure, focused the burghers' attention on the high cost of the English occupation because he made ambiguous the previously undisturbed place of the Dutch language and protocols in church practice. By all accounts, he was either unbalanced or deliberately provocative, but see Schrick for a sympathetic portrayal (1994). The inventory of his estate is in the court minutes (van Laer 1932a: 48–51). His prophecy to Charles II is in Murphy (1865: 160, "Op 't Conterfeijt van D. Nicolaus Renselaer [*sic*]"). For other Dutch self-appointed prophets who felt called to write to princes and magistrates, see Hylkema's study of the Amsterdam mystic Jan Rothe (1900: 37–43).

Livingston's attempt to make himself knowledgeable in English law at this time is in Maria van Rensselaer's correspondence, as is her friend's offer to consult a London jurist (van Laer 1935: 86, 118). An invoice for law books dated May 10, 1683, may be consulted among the Livingston-Redmond Papers. His provocation of de Laval is in van Laer (1932a: 153–55, and see Leder 1961: 42).

The knowledge of prevailing laws that Dutch notaries were expected to have is evident in the seventeenth- and especially eighteenth-century *notarisboeken*; see Lybreghts (1736: Dedication of Albaham van Limburg, de Jonge, n.p.; see also 1); van Wassenaar (1746b: 2); van Zutphen (1636: 382–84). Spierenburg cites the laws covering sluices and bridges (1984: 135). Uncertainty about the laws of England (as distinct from the Duke's Laws) is caught in the words of the New York Assembly (van Laer 1916: 9). The shift toward oath-taking in court merits more extensive consideration, but something of its disturbing impact is in the court minutes (van Laer 1932a: 300) and Fernow (1897: 5: 226). The wisdom of relying on the written word is offered by Kiliaen van Rensselaer and the learned notary Arent Lybreghts (van Laer 1908: 648; 1736: Dedication of Abraham van Limburg, de Jonge, n.p).

JULY 23, 1683
Albany

Although the deacons' records from 1677 to 1681 are missing, those of other years provide reasonably complete accounts of the Reformed congregation's finances. These transactions and the occasion of Janse's rental of the pall are published in Munsell (1865–72: 1:43, and see 51 for costs of a coffin and *aanspreker*). Maria van Rensselaer's correspondence carries the account of Philip Pietersz Schuyler's death (van Laer 1935: 108). Court minutes offer evidence about the fear of dying alone and the interrogation of the French couple. They also record the sudden death of the commander, claims on estates on the day of death, and the role of de Hooges in comforting a depressed man (van Laer 1928: 285; 1932a: 306–7, 249–51, 410, 411; 1922: 192, 193, 195–96).

DECEMBER 3, 1684
Albany

Available sources allow only an incomplete reconstruction of the city's topography in 1684. Tracing land titles is a highly unsatisfactory task. Even those that are available — such as the papers establishing Livingston's ownership of land just north of the palisades — are indistinct; see van Laer (1916: 251). By this date, Governor Thomas Dongan had established Albany as a county. Yet the evidence convinces me that the townspeople did not know exactly where the boundaries of the county were or, for that matter, the meaning of "county" in this vast upriver area (Merwick 1990: 204, 205). For the episode in which Janse takes his oath as assessor and its context, see court minutes (van Laer 1932a: 489, 490, and see 450, 451, 484).

Almost everything about Janse's house must remain conjectural. Identification of the house lot on which it stood is made even more problematic because he owned two houses (van Laer 1918: 495). Fragmentary evidence, however, points to a lot near the corner of (today's) Maiden Lane and Broadway (van Laer 1916: 397; Pearson 1869: 452n1). Pearson's plotting of house lots and owners is not accepted as entirely accurate (1871: see 203 for Janse's property). Van Laer criticizes his work in a collection of early records (1916: 46, 47n1).

The Dutch house itself can be reconstructed from a variety of sources such as Gehring (1987b), Kenney (1975: 79), Munsell (1849–59: 8:169–73), Piwonka (1987), van Laer (1928: 403; 1918: 565–66), and Zantkuijl (1987). Talk of old streets and substantial houses is in the minutes (van Laer 1928: 136). De Vrankrijker (1981) and Sluyterman (1918) are excellent references on house interiors and alert us to the wide assortment of storage spaces with which Dutch people provided themselves. Pitlo cites the notaries' unspoken rule about guarding their notes (1948: 1). Janse's reference to papers in his custody is in van Laer (1916: 388; see 15 for his probable oversight of van Schelluyne's papers).

I have used Bachelard's *Poetics of Space* (1964: 11, 40, 41) to reconstruct a late winter's afternoon in Janse's house. Kalma and de Vries (1978) describe the hours of Domine Schotanus's writing in Friesland. Brugmans (1973: 119) wrote of Rembrandt's old age and withdrawal from society. Watermarks have been carefully studied by Churchill (1935), Gravell (1979), and Labarre (1950). One can still see watermarks on Janse's papers.

Janse's work during this time can be pieced together only from the extant notarial papers. For examples cited, see van Laer (1918: 566–67, 571, 575, 574, 566). Van Laer presents a mortgage of 1686 which refers to an "old Dutch" mortgage of 1671 (1916: 296). My calculations about the kinds of acts Janse and van Schelluyne were executing — and therefore the different bases of their incomes — are (despite their incompleteness) based on their notarial papers in van Laer's edition of 1918. Biemer has calculated the drop in the number of female traders in Albany from 1654 to 1700 (1991: 76).

For some of the acts legalized by Livingston from 1675 to 1684, see van Laer (1916). Those drawn up to ensure the sale of Indian lands in the mid-1680s appear in the same volume at 141, 84, 229–30, and passim. The title to Livingston's manor lands is at 191, 192. Seventeenth-century *notarisboeken* were clear about the nonexecutorial role of the notary in papers affecting immovable property (Gehlen 1981: 73). For Lovelace's understanding that they were so empowered, see General Entries, 1664–73 (Christoph and Christoph 1982: 309). The inebriated townsman's awareness that land was slipping out of locals' hands is in the court minutes (van Laer 1932a: 416). See Wilstach for Livingston's clear perception of this development (1933: 273).

The magistrates' efforts to use English to identify themselves as justices of the peace is in van Laer (1916: 246, 247, 253). These errors — like "Note Republic" (van Ilpendam 1685) — point to an ignorance that colonialized people have exhibited elsewhere in using the colonizers' language, that is, an ignorance of contexts. Roman Jakobson (1956) was not alone in asserting that to know a word is to know its significative universe, only part of which is also knowing the words for which it can substitute or with which it can combine; Stubbs (1980) offers the same considerations. A hold on this universe, it seems to me, was what burghers such as Schuyler and Janse lacked again and again — and what they were made to know they lacked.

The assessors' misunderstanding of the assets that were taxable under the English is in the minutes (van Laer 1932a: 459, 461). The same volume cites Janse's duties as clerk of the burgher guard on December 11 (499).

JANUARY 20, 1685
Albany

Janse's effort to write "notary public" in English is recorded in a contract of sale presently held by the New-York Historical Society (van Ilpendam 1685). While he was writing up his very few acts, winter made the heightened incidence of fires a worry (van Laer 1932a: 506–8 and, for the old man Albert Bradt, see also van Laer 1908: 676n78). 'T Hart and Fisher offer an example of "notary" and "public" separated in a Dutch text of 1560 (1963: 84–85).

Janse's last letter to Madame Sijbinck together with acts notarized at this time are in van Laer (1918: 583–86). In the letter he identifies himself as in "Nieuw Albanij in Amer-

33. "Self-murderers," woodcut in Practycke in Criminele Saecken, *by Joost de Damhouder, 1618. The suicides pictured here must be made to feel the full punishment of the state because they have, as de Damhouder prepares to argue, killed their bodies and their souls. (Koninklijke Bibliotheek, The Hague)*

ica" (584). Teller signs himself as notary in one of van Rensselaer's account books (Jeremias van Rensselaer 1658–74). The community's care for Wesselsz's wife is in the court records (van Laer 1932a: 528, 533, 534, and see Pearson 1869: 229).

MARCH 12, 1686
Albany

The date of Janse's suicide is attested to in a deposition given by Willem Bancker in Amsterdam (GA, Sijbinck 1693). Van Laer, Schiltkamp, and I were wrong in assuming his death was closer to July 29 when the disposition of his property was made (van Laer 1918: 17; Schiltkamp 1964: 206; Merwick 1990: 197). Van Leeuwen was one of many doctors of law who commented on the evil of self-murder (1678: bk. 4, chap. 34, p. 458, point 12, "Van Misdaad tegen het leven . . ."). The catechism of Johannes Naeranus (1640: 36) asks readers about the raising of the dead. De Damhouder presents the example of Judas Iscariot (1660: 136), and see Camporesi (1990: 131). Camporesi uses literary evidence to argue that at no time did hell exert such a general attraction and repulsion as it did in the seventeenth century (28).

The Van Ness family Bible holds the entry about the passing of winter in 1772 (Van Ness 1772: entry of March 25). Munsell records weather on March 12, 1848 (1849–59: 1:220).

Court minutes documenting the possible suicide by drowning in 1677 are in van Laer (1928: 285). The municipal archives of Leiden hold an annotated inventory of criminal cases handled by the court there from 1533 to 1811 (GL 1533–1811). Only thirty cases of suspected suicide were investigated between 1600 and 1669, after which no cases were recorded for the remainder of the seventeenth century. Enough detail is offered about each case — the autopsy, the visit of officials to the family home or, infrequently, to the prison, the court's findings — to make this a valuable resource. The material is especially useful in confirming the findings of Noordam on suicide in nearby Delft (1989: 215, 220, 223, 230).

For Adriaen Janse's estate, see comments on "The Costs of Conquest," below, but note here van Laer (1934–35: 8) and GA, Adriaen van Ilpendam 1693.

8. The Costs of Conquest

Representations of Adriaen Janse have always been vulnerable to the present's need to reconfigure the past. They have thus been subject to changing patterns of archiving and to shifting choices about making or not making English translations of Dutch records. They have been vulnerable to the ebb and flow of xenophobia. They have felt the hand of a community's nostalgia.

Jan van Loon's were only the first of these choices. Like most, they were made without explanation. Townspeople's decisions to tell or to suppress the story of Janse's suicide went unexplained as well. So did those of Jacobus de Beauvois in selling Janse's property. What we know is that Janse's name came to be misspelled, that the last of the Dutch notaries died, that there was apparently no need to remember him in folklore or in the other representational repertoires that a city uses to recall its past. (For van Loon, see Munsell 1849–59: 2:101; 4:136, 138, 151; 9:88; van Laer 1918: 17, 358–59; Christoph 1987b: 9–12; Pearson 1871: 194. For de Beauvois, see Fernow 1902b: 49; van Laer 1918: 17; van Laer 1919: 154–57; Pearson 1869: 452n1, 183n1, and consult 452–53, 457–58, 488.) The contract of 1701 referring to earlier work of Janse (and misspelling his name) is in van Laer (1916: 389). The tale about the van Rensselaer manor house and ghosts is in Read (1807). For Grotius's comment on the immortality of notaries' registers, see Lee (1936: 235).

The literature on suicide is far more comprehensive than I am suggesting here. I found it especially valuable to discover correlations between the cases of suicide in early modern Leiden and Delft (see the comments on " 'Nieuw Albanij in America,' " above) and those in the English material discussed by Barrington (1980), MacDonald (1986, 1988), MacDonald and Murphy (1990), and Zell (1986). The explanations for self-murder that I cite are in Ferngren (1980: 172), Kushner (1981: 481), Oates (1980: 162), and Zell (1986: 307, 308). Ferngren discovered a widespread assumption in early modern Europe that melancholy was a physiological disturbance (1980: 172). For the reluctance of Dutch courts to search for motivation in crimes of self-murder (or of any kind), see Egmond (1993: 24).

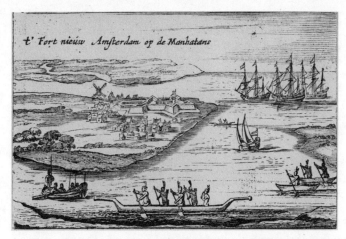

34. 't Fort nieuw Amsterdam op de Manhatans *(The Hartgers View), 1651. This view de-picts New Amsterdam in about 1628. It accompanied two articles on the front page of the* Christian Science Monitor, *November 7, 1942. A story headed "Memo about the Dutch: You Just Can't Nazify Some People" occupied left-hand columns. Arthur Seyss-Inquart,* Reichskommissar *for the Netherlands, had just written in Joseph Goebbels's weekly* Das Reich *that the chances of establishing "the National Socialist way" in the Netherlands were not looking favorable.*

Another story under the headline "The Dutch Contribution to America" told how "the British took New Amsterdam." This "seizure of a peaceful colony by invading Britishers was surely an altogether lawless act. But I suppose the Roosevelts and other Americans of Dutch descent are happier now, speaking English in New York, than they would be speaking Dutch in a little New Amsterdam threatened on all sides by a New England, New France and New Spain." (I. N. Phelps Stokes Collection, Miriam and Ira D. Wallach Division of Art, Prints, and Photographs, The New York Public Library, Astor, Lenox, and Tilden Foundations)

Fragmentary data about the final years of Albany's last Dutch notaries, Jan Juriaensz Becker and Ludovicus Cobus, are in published notarial papers and records of Schenec-tady (van Laer 1918: 18–22, 28; Becker's inventory, 589–92; his will, 593–94; his papers, 595–608; an earlier will is in van Laer 1919: 135–37). Cobus is last recorded as active in Schenectady in 1686 (Burke 1991: 48); the loss of his papers is in Pearson (1880: 56). The attestation regarding the disappearance of Dutch notaries in New York City is in GA Adriaen van Ilpendam 1693. For comparative purposes, see the place of notaries in early seventeenth-century Massachusetts Bay (Aspinwall 1644–51; Trumbull 1867).

Janse's image as a Dutch notary was affected by the English conquest and particu-larly the replacement of the Dutch-Roman legal system by one driven by English com-mon law. Goebel's 1970 study is a remarkable attempt to chart the changes that oc-curred after 1664, and something of his findings are cited in the comments on "Nieuw Albanij in America," above. The transformation may also be approached by considering

van Ilpendam

*35. Van Ilpendam family coat of arms. By the 1930s, genealogists were discovering Dutch New Yorkers whose ancestry linked them to the royal families of Europe. This coat of arms exists because one of the van Lodesteijns ("of distinguished Dutch ancestry") married into the family. It could claim a direct line to the house of Holland-Hainaut — well, an illegitimate branch of it (Hoffman 1935: 376, 381). (*The New York Genealogical and Biographical Record *66 [October 1935]: 381)*

the wider changes that occurred in English jurisprudence from the late sixteenth century to the third quarter of the eighteenth. I found Clark (1991), Coquillette (1981, 1987), Trakman (1980, 1981), and van Caenegem (1979) most helpful here. Blackstone is quoted damning the changeable practices of merchants, and Prynne is cited in Coquillette (1981: 354, 359n242; and for common law advocates' derision of "foreign law," 1987: 296). Cheney concludes that the notary in England "remained exotic" (1972: 139). Kenney documents the controlling power of English-speaking lawyers in early eighteenth-century Albany (1969: 28).

Scholars of many disciplines have commented on ridicule as a weapon of negation used by European and North American imperialists against conquered peoples (Dening 1992, Greenblatt 1992, Hulme 1992, Price 1989, Said 1978). Stallybrass and White have analyzed the invention of the grotesque (1986). Slanders against the Dutch as interlopers along the Hudson — careless of international rights and of their own governing institutions — accompanied the English landing at New Amsterdam in 1664 (Stokes 1915–23: 4:240). Later versions of the Dutch as ignorant, indeed comic, figures were expressed by Governor Richard Coote, Lord Bellomont (Hastings 1901–5, Index 1916: 2:1299), opponents of Livingston (Leder 1961: 119), Edwards (1867: 112), and Battershall (1899: 9, 10). Janvier offered his estimate of Dutch civic virtue in a 1903 study (195). In 1993 the Institute for Early American History and Culture sponsored a forum on law in early America. Nothing was mentioned of the early Dutch legal system (Forum 1993).

The recovery of Janse's life within the wider revival of interest in New York's seventeenth-century Dutch past is as exciting a story as his disappearance. It was, of course, his papers that were recovered — and by nineteenth-century rummagers like Munsell who were humble enough to admit that they couldn't fully explain what their value was

(Campbell 1879: 6, 15; Munsell 1865–72: 1: "Preface," n.p.; Munsell 1849–59: 5: "Preface," iv, and see 8:v). Munsell's dismissal of the city council's synopses is in his *Annals* (1849–59: 2:88, and see van Laer 1932a: 9, 10).

For van Laer's apologia for publishing Janse's register, see 1918: 8. His hypothesis regarding Janse's suicide is on 17. For Melville's introduction to Bartelby's bewildered employer, see Melville (1995: 1).

References

Accounts. 1651–60, 1673. "Anno 1660, this 12th February, Amsterdam. Memorandum of what New Netherland has cost the [West India] Company . . . during the past year, 1659." Bontemantel Collection, New Netherland Papers, box 2, folder "1651–1660: Accounts of the Dutch West India Co., slave trade, etc., 1651–1660, 1673 (Transcripts and Translations)." Rare Books and Manuscripts Division, New York Public Library.

Agnew, Jean-Christophe. 1986. *Worlds Apart: The Market and the Theater in Anglo-American Thought, 1550–1750.* Cambridge: Cambridge University Press.

Alpers, Svetlana. 1983. *The Art of Describing: Dutch Art in the Seventeenth Century.* Chicago: University of Chicago Press.

Andrew, Donna T. 1988. "Debate: The Secularization of Suicide in England, 1660–1800 [Reply to Michael MacDonald]." *Past & Present* 119: 158–70.

Ankum, J. A., G. C. J. J. van den Bergh, and H. C. F. Schoordijk, eds. 1970. *Plus Est en Vous: Opstellen over Recht en Cultuur Aangeboden aan Prof. Mr. A. Pitlo ter Gelegenheid van Zijn 25-Jarig Hoogleraarschap.* Haarlem: H. D. Tjeenk Willink & Zoon.

Anon. 1866. *The Beauties of Washington Irving,* illustrated by George Cruikshank. London: William Tegg.

Antoniszoon, Cornelis. 1671. *The Safeguard of Sailors, or, Great Rutter containing the courses, distances, soundings, floods, and ebbs, with the marks for the entring of sundry harbours of England. Scotland, France, Spain, Ireland, Flanders, Holland, and the sounds of Denmark, also the coasts of Jutland and Norway . . . published for the use and benefit of all honest mariners.* [Translation by Robert Norman of *Het Leeskaartboek van Wisbuy,* 1671.] London: Fisher & Hurlock.

Archdeacon, Thomas J. 1976. *New York City, 1664–1710: Conquest and Change.* Ithaca: Cornell University Press.

Ars Notariatus. 1740. *Ars Notariatus: or, The Art and Office of a Notary-Publick, As the Same is Practised in Scotland. In Two Parts, I. Giving an Account of the Rise and Institution of the Office, and Ancient and Present State thereof, II. Containing Notarial Instruments of all kinds. To which is added, by way of Conclusion, An Avice to Notaries, touching the right discharging of their Office.* Edinburgh: Sands, Brymer, Murray and Cochran.

Aspinwall, William. 1644–51. "William Aspinwall, notary public. Mss 42 [Notarial records, Boston, 1644–51]." Boston Athenaeum, Boston. [Published in 1903 as *A Volume Relating to the Early History of Boston Containing the Aspinwall Notarial Records from 1644 to 1651, Boston, Municipal Printing Office, 1903: Volume 32 of the Records of the Boston Commissioners,* ed. W. H. Whitmore and W. K. Watkins.]

————. 1655. *An Abstract of Laws and Government. Wherein as in a Mirrour may be seen the wisdom & perfection of the Government of Christ's Kingdom. Accomodably to any State or form of Government in the world, that is not Antichristian or Tyrannicall. Collected and digested into the ensuing Method, by that Godly, Grave and Judicious Divine, Mr. John Cotton, of Boston in New-England, in his Life-time, and presented to the generall Court of the Massachusetts. And now published after his death, by William Aspinwall.* London: M. S. for Livewel Chapman.

————. 1656. *The Legislative Power Is Christ's Peculiar Prerogative, Proved from the 9th of Isaiah, vers. 6. 7. by W. A.* London: Livewel Chapman.

Bachelard, Gaston. 1964. *The Poetics of Space.* Translated by Maria Jolas. New York: Orion Press.

Bachman, Van Cleaf. 1969. *Peltries or Plantations: The Economic Policies of the Dutch West India Company in New Netherland, 1623–1639.* Baltimore: Johns Hopkins University Press.

Bagrow, Leo. 1964. *History of Cartography,* rev. and enl. by R. A. Skelton. Cambridge: Harvard University Press.

Bailyn, Bernard, and Philip D. Morgan, eds. 1991. *Strangers within the Realm: Cultural Margins of the First British Empire.* Chapel Hill: University of North Carolina Press.

Balmer, Randall. 1989. *A Perfect Babel of Confusion: Dutch Religion and English Culture in the Middle Colonies.* New York: Oxford University Press.

Banta, M., ed. 1900. *Year Book of the Holland Society of New York, 1900.* New York: By the Society, Knickerbocker Press.

Baptisms, Collections. 1901. *Records of the Reformed Dutch Church in New Amsterdam and New York: Baptisms from 1639 to 1730 in the Reformed Dutch Church, New York,* ed. Thomas Grier Evans. Collections of the New York Genealogical and Biographical Society, vol. 2. New York: Printed for the Society.

Barbour, Violet. 1950. *Capitalism in Amsterdam in the Seventeenth Century.* Baltimore: Johns Hopkins University Press.

Barrington, Mary Rose. 1980. "Apologia for Suicide." In *Suicide: The Philosophical Issues,* ed. M. P. Batlin and David J. Mayo, 90–103. New York: St. Martin's Press.

Barthes, Roland. 1970. "Historical Discourse." In *Structuralism: A Reader,* ed. Michael Lane, 145–55. New York: Jonathan Cape.

Bates, E. S. 1911. *Touring in 1600: A Study in the Development of Travel as a Means of Education.* Boston: Houghton Mifflin.

Battershall, Walton W. 1899. "Albany." In *Historic Towns of the Middle States,* ed. Lyman P. Powell, 1–38. New York: Putnam.

Baumann, Gerd, ed. 1985. *The Written Word: Literacy in Transition. Wolfson College Lectures.* Oxford: Clarendon.

Baxter, William T. 1962. "Credit, Bills, and Bookkeeping in a Simple Economy." In *Studies in Accounting Theory,* ed. Baxter and Sidney Davidson, 31–48. London: Sweet & Maxwell.

Baxter, William T., and Sidney Davidson, eds. 1950. *Studies in Accountancy,* 3d ed.. London: Institute for Chartered Accountants in England and Wales. [In 1962, published as *Studies in Accounting Theory*].

Beernink, G. 1916. *De Geschiedschrijver en Rechtsgeleerde Dr. Arend van Slichtenhorst en zijn vader Brant van Slichtenhorst, Stichter van Albany, Hoofdstad van der Staat Neu-York.* Arnhem: S. Gouda-Quint.

Bell, Andrew. 1862. *History of Canada from the Year of Its Discovery till the Union Year, 1840–1841.* Trans. of *L'Histoire du Canada of F. Y. Garneau, Esq. and Accompanied with Illustrative Notes.* 2d ed. Montreal: J. Lovell.

Benson, Egbert. 1848. "Memoir, Read before The Historical Society of the State of New York, December 31, 1816." In *Collections of the New-York Historical Society,* 77–148. New York: Bartlett & Welford.

Bevaart, D. C. J. 1989. "Leidenaars op het wereldzeeïn in de 17de eeuw." In *Uit Leidse Bron Geleverd,* ed. J. W. Marsilje, 220–28. Leiden: Gemeentearchief Leiden.

Bewes, Wyndham A. 1923. *The Romance of the Law Merchant, being an Introduction to the Study of International and Commercial Law with Some Account of the Commerce and Fairs of the Middle Ages.* London: Sweet & Maxwell; rpt. Littleton, Colo.: F. B. Rothman, 1986.

Biemer, Linda. 1991. "Criminal Law and Women in New Amsterdam and Early New York." In *A Beautiful and Fruitful Place: Selected Rensselaerswijck Seminar Papers,* ed. Nancy Anne McClure Zeller, 73–82. New Netherland Project. Albany: New Netherland Publishing.

Blankert, Albert. 1978. *Vermeer of Delft: Complete Edition of the Paintings.* Oxford: Phaidon.

Bogardus, Willem. 1680. "Obligation of Adolph Meier to Paulus Richard for 1908:90 guilders before W. Bogardus, May 5, 1680, Protocol en Register der Notulen van Constable en Officiers ten Durpe Nieuw Haerlem, Gehouden door Hendrick J. Vander Vin, Jan Tibout en Guiliaem Berthof, 1679–1691, Deel 6." Riker Collection, vol. 12. Rare Books and Manuscripts Division, New York Public Library.

Bond, J. 1685. *A Complete Guide for Justices of Peace, According to the Best Approved Authors, in Two Parts. The First Containing the Common and State Laws of England, relating to the Office of a Justice of Peace. The Second consisting of the Most Authentick and Useful Precedents, which do properly Concern the Same.* London: T. B. for Hannah Sawbridge.

Booth, Mary L. 1880. *History of the City of New York.* New York: Dutton.

Boxer, Charles R. 1957. *The Dutch in Brazil, 1624–1654.* Oxford: Clarendon.

Bridenbaugh, Carl, ed. 1982. *The Pynchon Papers,* vol. 1, *Letters of John Pynchon, 1654–1700.* Charlottesville: University Press of Virginia.

Broadsides. 1643. "Printed Broadsides, Insinuatie, Protestatie, en de Presentatie. September 8, 1643 [Badly Burned]." VRMP, SC7079, box 3, folder 4, Manuscripts and Special Collections, State Library of New York, Albany.

Brooks, C. W., R. H. Hemholz, and P. G. Stein. 1991. *Notaries Public in England since the Reformation.* London: Erskine Press for the Society of Public Notaries of London.

Brown, James C. 1935. "The Origin and Early History of the Office of Notary." *Juridical Review* 47: 201–40, 355–417.

Brugmans, H. 1973. *Geschiedenis van Amsterdam*, vol. 3, *Bloeitijd, 1621–1697*. Utrecht: Spectrum.

Bruijn, Jaap R. 1990. "Productivity, Profitability, and Costs of Private and Corporate Dutch Ship Owning in the Seventeenth and Eighteenth Centuries." In *The Rise of Merchant Empires: Long-Distance Trade in the Early Modern World, 1350–1750,* ed. James D. Tracy, 174–94. New York: Cambridge University Press.

Burke, Gerald L. 1956. *The Making of Dutch Towns: A Study in Urban Development from the Tenth to the Seventeenth Centuries.* London: Cleaver-Hume.

Burke, Thomas, Jr. 1991. *Mohawk Frontier: The Dutch Community of Schenectady, New York, 1661–1710.* Ithaca: Cornell University Press.

Bywater, M. F., and Basil S. Yamey, eds. 1982. *Historic Accounting Literature: A Companion Guide.* London: Scholar Press.

Cacheux, Albert 1960. "Les Notaires dans de ressort de la coutume de Mons en Hainaût Français aux XVIIe et XVIIIe siècles." *Tijdschrift voor Rechtsgeschiedenis* 28: 42–58.

Campbell, Douglas. 1879. *Historic Fallacies Regarding Colonial New York, an Address delivered before the Oneida Historical Society, Utica, N.Y. . . . January 14, 1879.* New York: F. J. Ficker.

Camporesi, Piero. 1990. *The Fear of Hell: Images of Damnation and Salvation in Early Modern Europe.* Trans. Lucinda Byatt. Cambridge: Polity.

Carmer, Carl. 1939. *The Hudson.* New York: Farrar & Rinehart.

Carroll, Margaret D. 1993. " 'In the Name of God and Profit': Jan van Eyck's Arnolfini Portrait." *Representations* 44: 96–132.

Certeau, Michel de. 1984. *The Practice of Everyday Life.* Trans. Stephen Rendell. Berkeley: University of California Press.

Chartier, Roger. 1987. *The Cultural Uses of Print in Early Modern France.* Princeton: Princeton University Press.

Cheney, Christopher R. 1972. *Notaries Public in England in the Thirteenth and Fourteenth Centuries.* Oxford: Clarendon.

Christoph, Peter R., ed. 1980. *New York Historical Manuscripts: English,* vol. 22, *Administrative Papers of Governors Richard Nicolls and Francis Lovelace, 1664–1673.* Baltimore: Genealogical Publishing Co.

———, ed. 1987a. *New York (Colony) Council: Calendar of Council Minutes, 1668–1783,* ed. Berthold Fernow. *[New York State Library Bulletin* no. 58, 1902.] Harrison, N.Y.: Harbor Hill Books.

———. 1987b. "The Time and Place of Jan van Loon: A Roman Catholic in Colonial Albany." Pt. 2. *Halve Maen* 60: 9–12.

———, ed. 1993. *The Dongan Papers, 1683–1688,* pt. 1, *Admiralty Court and Other Records of the Administration of New York Governor Thomas Dongan.* Syracuse: Syracuse University Press.

Christoph, Peter R., and Florence A. Christoph, eds. 1982. *New York Historical Manuscripts: English. Books of General Entries of the Colony of New York, 1664–1673.* Baltimore: Genealogical Publishing Company.

———, eds. 1989. *The Andros Papers, 1674–1676: Files of the Provincial Secretary of New York during the Administration of Governor Sir Edmund Andros, 1674–1680.* Syracuse: Syracuse University Press.

————, eds. 1990. *The Andros Papers, 1677–1678: Files of the Provincial Secretary of New York during the Administration of Governor Sir Edmund Andros, 1674–1680.* Syracuse: Syracuse University Press.

————, eds. 1991. *The Andros Papers, 1679–1680: Files of the Provincial Secretary of New York during the Administration of Governor Sir Edmund Andros, 1674–1680.* Syracuse: Syracuse University Press.

Christoph, Peter R., Kenneth Scott, and Kenn Stryker-Rodda, eds. 1976a. *New York Historical Manuscripts: Dutch, Kingston Papers,* trans. Dingman Versteeg (with Revision of Pages 1–171 by Samuel Oppenheim), vol. 1, *Kingston Court Records, 1661–1667.* Baltimore: Genealogical Publishing Co.

————, eds. 1976b. *New York Historical Manuscripts: Dutch, Kingston Papers,* trans. Dingman Versteeg (with Revision of Pages 1–171 by Samuel Oppenheim), vol. 2, *Kingston Court Records, 1668–1675 and Secretary's Papers, 1664–1675.* Baltimore: Genealogical Publishing Co.

Churchill, W. A. 1935. *Watermarks in Paper, in Holland, England, France, Etc., in the XVII and XVIII Centuries and Their Interconnection.* Amsterdam: Menno Hertzberger.

Clanchy, M. T. 1993. *From Memory to Written Record: England, 1066–1307.* Oxford: Blackwell.

Clark, Jonathan. 1991. "Sovereignty: The British Experience: Blackstone, Bentham and the Origins of Parliamentary Absolutism." *Times Literary Supplement,* Nov. 29, 1991, 15–16.

Colenbrander, Herman T., ed. 1919. *Jan Pietersz Coen: Bescheiden Omtrent Zijn Bedrijf in Indie.* The Hague: Martinus Nijhoff.

Colquhoun, Patrick M. 1849. *A Summary of the Roman Civil Law, Illustrated by Commentaries on and Parallels from the Mosaic, Canon, Mohammedan, English and Foreign Law.* London: V. & R. Stevens and Sons.

Coquillette, Daniel R. 1981. "Legal Ideology and Incorporation II: Sir Thomas Ridley, Charles Molloy and the Literary Battle for the Law Merchant, 1607–1676." *Boston University Law Review* 61: 315–71.

————. 1987. "Legal Ideology and Incorporation III: Reason Regulated — The Post-Restoration Civilians, 1653–1735." *Boston University Law Review* 67: 289–361.

Corbin, Alain 1992. *The Village of Cannibals: Rage and Murder in France, 1870.* Trans. Arthur Goldhammer. Cambridge: Harvard University Press.

Cressy, David. 1980. *Literacy and the Social Order: Reading and Writing in Tudor and Stuart England.* New York: Cambridge University Press.

————. 1987. *Coming Over: Migration and Communication between England and New England in the Seventeenth Century.* New York: Cambridge University Press.

Davis, Natalie Zemon. 1987. *Fiction in the Archives: Pardon Tales and Their Tellers in Sixteenth-Century France.* Stanford: Stanford University Press.

De Booy, E. P. 1977. "Het 'Basisonderwijs' in de Zeventiende en Achttiende Eeuw — De Slechtse Dorpsscholen." *Bijdragen en Mededelingen betreffende de geschiedenis der Nederlanden* 92: 208–22.

De Damhouder, Joost. 1618. *Practycke In Criminele Saecken ghemaecht door Joost De Damhouder van Brugge. Nut en Proffytelyck vooral le Souvereins, Baillius, Borgem ende Schepenen, etc. Alles met schoone Figuren daer toe dienende vercist. Item hier is noch by ghevoecht d'Ordinantie op t'stuck van de Criminele Justitie in dese Nederlanden.* Rotterdam: Jan van Waesberghe de Jonge.

———. 1642. *Practycke In Criminele Saecken ghemaecht door Joost De Damhouder van Brugge. Nut en Proffytelyck vooral le Souvereins, Baillius, Borgemrs ende Schepenen, etc. Alles met schoone Figuren daer toe dienende vercist. Item hier is noch by ghevoecht d'Ordinantie op t'stuck van de Criminele Justitie in dese Nederlanden.* Utrecht: Johan van Waesberge.

———. 1660. *Practycke in Civile Saken, Zeer nut proffijtelijck ende noodigh allen Schouten, Burgermeesteren, Schepenen, ende andere Rechteren. Beschrevan door den vermaerden Heere Joost de Damhouder Van Brugge, Ridder, Doctor in beyde de Rechten ende Raedt-ordinaris van de Keyserlycke Majesteyt Karel de Vijfde.* Rotterdam: Pieter van Waesberge.

De Hooges, Anthonie. 1643–48. "Memorandum Book Kept by A. de Hooges [Title Page: Copie van eenige Acten en andere aenmerckelyke Notitien, 1646]." VRMP 7079, box 31. Manuscripts and Special Collections, State Library of New York, Albany.

De Hulla, J. 1914. "De Matrozen en Soldaten op de Schepen der Oost-Indische Compagnie." *Bijdragen tot de Taal-, Land- en Volkenkunde van Nederlandsch-Indie* 69: 318–65.

Dekker, R. M. 1978. "De Rol van Vrouwen In Oproeren in de Republiek in de 17de en 18de Eeuw." *Tijdschrift voor Sociale Geschiedenis* 12: 305–16.

———. 1979. *Oproeren in Holland Gezien door Tijdgenoten: Ooggetuigeverslagen van Oproeren in de Provincie Holland ten Tijde van de Republiek (1690–1750).* Assen: Van Gorcum.

Dening, Greg. 1992. *Mr. Bligh's Bad Language: Passion, Power and Theatre on the Bounty.* New York: Cambridge University Press.

Den Oosterlingh, Adriaen. 1668. "Notariële Instrumenten d'Anno 1668, A. den Oosterling [Adriaen den Oosterlingh]." Notarieël Archief: 1067, GL, Leiden.

De Planque, Pieter Antonie. 1926. *Valcooch's Regel Der Duytsche Schoolmeesters, Bijdrage tot de Kennis van het Schoolwezen in de Zestiende Eeuw.* Groningen: P. Noordhoff.

De Ridder-Symoens, H. 1988. "Steden en Hun Onderwijs." In *Steden en Hun Verleden: De Ontwikkeling van de Stedelijke Samenleving in de Nederlanden tot de Negentiende Eeuw,* ed. Maurits Van Rooijen, 201–24. Utrecht: Teleac.

De Schepper, H. 1988. "Steden en Hun Bestuur." In *Steden en Hun Verleden: De Ontwikkeling van de Stedelijke Samenleving in de Nederlanden tot de Negentiende Eeuw,* ed. Maurits Van Rooijen, 57–80. Utrecht: Teleac.

De Smidt, J. Th. 1984. "The Expansion of Dutch Private Law outside Europe in the Seventeenth and Eighteenth Centuries." In *The World of Hugo Grotius, 1583–1645: Proceedings of the International Colloquium Organized by the Grotius Committee of the Royal Netherlands Academy of Arts and Sciences, Rotterdam, 6–9 April 1983,* 179–93. Amsterdam: APA–Holland University Press.

De Vrankrijker, A. C. J. 1981. *Mensen, Leven en Werken in de Gouden Eeuw.* The Hague: Martinus Nijhoff.

De Vries, B. M. A. 1988. "Steden en Hun Nijverheid." In *Steden en Hun Verleden: De Ontwikkeling van de Stedelijke Samenleving in de Nederlanden tot de Negentiende Eeuw,* ed. Maurits van Rooijen, 153–76. Utrecht: Teleac.

De Vries, Jan 1974. *The Dutch Rural Economy in the Golden Age, 1500–1700.* New Haven: Yale University Press.

———. 1978. *Barges and Capitalism: Passenger Transportation in the Dutch Economy, 1632–1839.* Published by Afdeling Agrarische Geschiedenis Landbouwhogeschool, Wageningen, as *A. A. G. Bijdragen* 21: 33–398.

———. 1991a. "Introduction." In *Art in History / History in Art: Studies in Seventeenth-Century Dutch Culture,* ed. David Freedberg and Jan de Vries, 1–6. Santa Monica: Getty Center for the History of Art and the Humanities.

———. 1991b. "Art History." In *Art in History / History in Art: Studies in Seventeenth-Century Dutch Culture,* ed. David Freedberg and Jan de Vries, 249–82. Santa Monica: Getty Center for the History of Art and the Humanities.

De Vries, Lyckle. 1991. "The Changing Face of Realism." In *Art in History / History in Art: Studies in Seventeenth-Century Dutch Culture,* ed. David Freedberg and Jan de Vries, 209–44. Santa Monica: Getty Center for the History of Art and the Humanities.

Dominicus, F. C. 1919. *Het Huiselik en Maatschappelik Leven van de Zuid-Afrikaner in de eerste helft der 18de Eeuw.* The Hague: Martinus Nijhoff.

Downer, W. 1989. "De Schoolmeester van Wilsveen in de 17de en 18de Eeuw." In *Uit Leidse Bron Geleverd,* ed. J. W. Marsilje, 256–59. Leiden: Gemeentearchief Leiden.

Ducruet, M. 1884. *Notice Historique sur le Notariat.* Paris: Oudin Frères.

Duinkerken, B. 1988. *Notariaat in Overgangstijd, 1796–1842.* Deventer: Kluwer.

Durantini, Mary Frances. 1983. *The Child in Seventeenth-Century Dutch Painting.* Ann Arbor: UMI Research Press.

Dutch Schoolsystem. 1960. Netherlands Government Information Center, for Ministry of Education, Arts, and Sciences.

Duysentdaelers, Nicolai. 1659. *Notae Nicolai Duysentdaelers I. C. Op en Ordonnantie Ende Maniere, Van Procederen, voor den Gerechte der Stadt, Amsterdam, Gecorrigeert ende Geamplieert.* Amsterdam: Isaac de la Tombe.

Eccles, W. J. 1964. *Canada under Louis XIV, 1663–1701.* Toronto: McClelland & Stewart.

Edelstein, David S. 1950. *Joel Munsell: Printer and Antiquarian.* New York: Columbia University Press.

Edwards, Charles. 1867. *Pleasantries about Courts and Lawyers of the State of New York.* New York: Richardson.

Edwards, Philip, ed. 1988. *Last Voyages: Cavendish, Hudson, Ralegh: The Original Narratives.* Oxford: Clarendon.

Eekhof, A. 1910. *Bastiaen Jansz. Krol, Krakenbezoeker, Kommies en Kommandeur van Nieuw-Nederland (1595–1645). Nieuw Gegevens voor de Kennis der Vestiging van ons Kerkelijk en Koloniaal Gezag in Noord-Amerika.* The Hague: Martinus Nijhoff.

———. 1921, *De Theologische Facultiet te Leiden in de 17de Eeuw.* Utrecht: G. J. A. Ruys.

————. 1926. *Jonas Michaëlius, Founder of the Church in New Netherland.* Leiden: A. W. Sijthoff.

Egmond, Florike. 1993. *Underworlds: Organized Crime in the Netherlands, 1650–1800.* Cambridge: Polity.

Eisler, William. 1995. *The Farthest Shore: Images of Terra Australis from the Middle Ages to Captain Cook.* Cambridge: Cambridge University Press.

Elliott, Emory. 1975. *Power and the Pulpit in Puritan New England.* Princeton: Princeton University Press.

Evertsen Papers. 1672. "Cypher for the Squadron . . . 12 October, 1672." New Netherland Papers. Bontemantel Collection: Evertsen Papers — List of the papers in J. C. Brevoort's hand. Rare Books and Manuscripts Division, New York Public Library.

Faber, Sjoerd, ed. 1989. *Nieuw Licht op Oude Justitie: Misdaad en Straf ten Tijde van de Republiek.* Muiderberg: Dirk Coutinho.

Ferngren, Gary B. 1980. "The Ethics of Suicide in the Renaissance and Reformation." In *Suicide and Euthanasia: Historical and Contemporary Themes,* ed. Baruch A. Brody, 155–81. Dordrecht: Kluwer.

Fernow, Berthold, ed. 1897. *The Records of New Amsterdam from 1653 to 1674.* 7 vols. Rpt. Baltimore: Genealogical Publishing Co., 1976.

————, ed. 1902a. *The Minutes of the Orphanmasters of New Amsterdam, 1655 to 1663.* New York: Francis P. Harper.

————, ed. 1902b. *New York (Colony) Council: Calendar of Council Minutes, 1668–1783. New York State Library Bulletin* no. 58: *History 6.* Albany: University of the State of New York.

————, ed. 1907. *Minutes of the Orphanmasters Court of New Amsterdam, 1655–1663: Minutes of the Executive Boards of the Burgomasters of New Amsterdam and the Records of Walewyn Van der Veen.* Vol. 2. New York: Francis P. Harper.

Fernow, Berthold, and E. B. O'Callaghan, eds. 1853–87. *Documents Relative to the Colonial History of the State of New-York.* 15 vols. Albany: Weed, Parsons.

Fijen, L. A. M., W. F. B. Melching, and L. S. Peterse, eds. 1977. "Secretarissen en Pensionarissen van Haarlem (1573–1795)." Gemeentearchief Haarlem. Typed inventory.

Fishman, Jane Susannah. 1979. *Boerenverdriet: Violence between Peasants and Soldiers in Early Modern Netherlands Art.* Ann Arbor: UMI Research Press.

Fleming, Walter L. 1901. "The Public Career of Robert Livingston." *New York Genealogical and Biographical Record* 32: 129–33.

Fock, Willemijn. 1987. "Culture of Living on the Canals in the Seventeenth and Eighteenth Centuries: The Rapenburg in Leiden." In *New World Dutch Studies: Dutch Arts and Culture in Colonial America, 1609–1776,* ed. Roderic H. Blackburn and Nancy A. Kelley, 131–42. Albany: Albany Institute of History and Art.

Folkerts, Jan 1991. "Van Rensselaer and Agricultural Productivity in His Domain." In *A Beautiful and Fruitful Place: Selected Rensselaerswijck Seminar Papers,* ed. Nancy Anne McClure Zeller, 295–308. New Netherland Project. Albany: New Netherland Publishing.

Fortgens, H. W. 1958. *Schola Latina, uit het Verleden van Ons Voorbereidend Hoger Onderwijs.* Zwolle: Tjeenk Willink.

Forum. 1993. "Forum: Explaining the Law in Early American History — A Symposium." *William and Mary Quarterly* 50: 3–50.

Franke, Herman. 1985. *De Dood in het Leven van Alledag: Twee Eeuwen Rouwadvertenties en Openbare Strafvoltrekkingen in Nederland.* The Hague: Nijgh & Van Ditmar.

Franklin, Wayne. 1979. *Discoverers, Explorers, Settlers: The Diligent Writers of Early America.* Chicago: University of Chicago Press

Frederiks, Jan. 1960. *Ontstaan en Ontwikkeling van het Zwolse Schoolwezen tot Omstreeks 1700: Een Historische Studie.* Zwolle: J. J. Tijl.

Freedberg, David, and Jan de Vries, eds. 1991. *Art in History / History in Art: Studies in Seventeenth-Century Dutch Culture.* Santa Monica: Getty Center for the History of Art and the Humanities.

GA, Carel de Beauvois. 1685. "Power of attorney Gellis Hoornbeeck to Tobias van Hoornbeeck, April 27, 1685." Not Arch 2325, fol. 325. Nots Jac. de Winter.

GA, Jan Hendricksz Sybinck. 1651. "Agreement of Partnership Gerrit Janse Cuijper and Jan Hendricks Sybinck, Mar. 17, 1651." Not Arch 1300/40v. Nots H. Schaef. See also acts of May 20, 1654; Mar. 15, 1657; April 1, 1657; Mar. 16, 1660; Mar. 24, 1663; April 12, 1666; April 30, 1670; Nov. 20, 1670; Aug. 5, 1672; Mar. 13, 1674. For Pieter Jacobsz Marius, Mar. 27, 1663.

———. 1668. "Power of Attorney Lizbeth Dirckx van Eps to Abel de Wolff, Dec. 28, 1668." Not Arch 2297 III, fol. 28, 29. Nots Jac. de Winter; "Power of attorney Sybout Claesz and Sybinck to Pieter Jacobsz Marius at Hoorn, Dec. 22, 1668." Not Arch 2788, fol. 713, 714. Nots P. van Buytene; "Deposition of Gellis van Hoornbeeck against Margareta Hardenbroeck and J. Cousseau, Dec. 27, 1668." Not Arch 2228, fol. 1150 Nots Adr. Lock.

———. 1669. "Power of Attorney J. Cousseau to J. H. Sybinck." Not Arch 2788, fol. 337. Nots P. van Buytene; "Contract of Partnership J. Cousseau and Frederick Rihel, May 29, 1669." Not Arch 3198/fol. 294, Nots H. Outgers; "Deposition J. Cousseau, June 19, 1669." Not Arch. 3503V acte 28, Nots G. van Breugel. "Power of attorney Gerrit van Slichtenhorst to J. H. Sybinck, Feb. 14, 1669" (and see Oct. 2, 1670). Not Arch 3620/No. 6, Nots Jacob de Vlieger. For van Cortlandt, "Power of Attorney to J. B. van Rensselaer, July 17, 1669," see Not Arch 2230, fol. 832–34, Nots Adr. Lock; for Hardenbroeck, "Power of attorney to Sybinck, Jan. 5, 1669," see Not Arch 2788, fol. 43, 44, Nots P. van Buytene.

———. 1670. "Deposition of Gerrit J. Kuijper and Albert Bartels, April 30, 1670." Not Arch 3891/137 Nots Leendert Fruijt; "Deposition of F. Philipse against J. Cousseau, May 28, 1670." Not Arch 3619/Nr 52, Nots Jacob de Vlieger; "Power of Attorney, Gerrit van Slichtenhorst to Sybinck, Oct. 2, 1670." Not Arch 3620/Nr. 6, Nots Jacob de Vlieger; "Deposition J. H. Sybinck, Nov. 20, 1670." Not Arch 3205 fol. 311–13, Nots H. Outgers.

———. 1671. "Deposition of Sybinck, Andries Hardenbroeck, Nic. Governeur and others as part owners of 't Fort Albania, Jan. 2, 1671." Not Arch 3206/fol. 9. Nots H. Outgers.

———. 1672. "Power of Attorney, Sybinck to Goose Gerritsz van Schaick, Aug. 5, 1672," Not Arch 3893/153. Nots Leendert Fruijt.

———. 1674. "Power of Attorney J. J. Schermerhoorn to Sybinck, Nov. 22, 1674." Not Arch 2304, 3e reg, fol. 14. Nots Jac. de Winter.

———. 1680. "Deposition of Adriaen Janse Croon as guardian of the children of Dirck Adriaensz, Jan. 27, 1680." Not Arch 3940/129. Nots. Nic. Brouwer.

GA, Adriaen van Ilpendam. 1680. "Power of attorney Adriaen Janse Croon, et al to Jac. van Ulenbroeck, May 27, 1680." Not Arch 5120/198. Nots Jac. van Ulenbroeck.

———. 1682. "Obligation Rychart van Rensselaer to Hendrick Wijbrants, April 20, 1682." Not Arch 4703, akte 47. Nots Jacob Lansman.

———. 1693. "Deposition Willem Bancker, May 19, 1693." Not Arch 2342, acte 51–69. Nots Jacob de Winter.

GA, Jan Janse van Ilpendam. 1641. "Power of Attorney Anna Jansdr. to Jan Jochumss Cappel, April 11, 1641." Not. Arch. 1283/66. Nots. H. Schaeff.

———. 1651. "Deposition Willem Thomas and Jan Hendrickss, Dec. 8, 1651." Not Arch 2279 III, fol. 18. Nots Jac. de Winter.

Geertz, Clifford. 1975a. "Thick Description: Toward an Interpretive Theory of Culture." In *The Interpretation of Cultures: Selected Essays*, 3–30. London: Hutchinson.

———. 1975b. "Deep Play: Notes on the Balinese Cockfight." In *The Interpretation of Cultures: Selected Essays*, 412–53. London: Hutchinson.

Gehlen, A. Fl. 1981. *Het Notariaat in het Tweeherig Maastricht: Een Rechtshistorische Schets van de Inrichting en Practijk van het Maastrichtse Notariaat vanaf Zijn Opkomst tot aan het Einde van de Tweeherigheid over de Stad (1292–1794)*. Assen: Van Gorcum.

———. 1986. *Notariële Acten uit de 17E en 18E Eeuw*. Zutphen: De Walburg Pers.

Gehring, Charles T., ed. 1983. *New York Historical Manuscripts: Dutch*, vol. 5, *Council Minutes, 1652–1654*. Baltimore: Genealogical Publishing Co.

———, ed. 1987a. *New Netherland Documents*, vol. 17, *Curaçao Papers, 1640–1665*. Transcr. J. A. Schiltkamp. Trans. Charles T. Gehring. Interlaken, N.Y.: Heart of the Lakes.

———. 1987b. "Material Culture in Seventeenth-Century Dutch Colonial Manuscripts." In *New World Dutch Studies: Dutch Arts and Culture in Colonial America, 1609–1776*, ed. Roderic H. Blackburn and Nancy A. Kelley, 43–49. Albany: Albany Institute of History and Art.

———, ed. 1990. *Fort Orange Court Minutes, 1652–1660*. Syracuse: Syracuse University Press.

Gilmore, William G. 1992. "Elementary Literacy on the Eve of the Industrial Revolution: Trends in Rural New England, 1760–1830." *Proceedings of the American Antiquarian Society* 92: 87–178.

GL 1533–1811. "De Criminele Vonnisboecken van Leiden, 1533–1811." Inventory and Introduction by H. M van den Heuvel.

GL 1635–1644. De Oude Notariële Archieven, Inventaris 43: "Archief van de notaris Jacob Fransz van Merwen, 1635–1644: 533–542, Minuten van notariële acten, 10 deelen. [Will of David Janse van Ilpendam, 20–6–40, Deel 538]." "Archief van de notaris Alewijn Claesz de Man, 1635–1644: 544–549."

Goebel, Julius, Jr. 1970. *Law Enforcement in Colonial New York: A Study in Criminal Procedure (1664–1776)*. Montclair, N.J.: Patterson Smith.

Goldstein, Robert A. 1969. *French-Indian Diplomatic and Military Relations, 1609–1701.* The Hague: Mouton.

Goodfriend, Joyce D. 1992. *Before the Melting Pot: Society and Culture in Colonial New York City, 1664–1730.* Princeton: Princeton University Press.

Goody, Jack. 1986. *The Logic of Writing and the Organization of Society.* London: Cambridge University Press.

Gossman, Lionel. 1978. "History and Literature: Reproduction and Signification." In *The Writing of History: Literary Form and Historical Understanding,* ed. Robert Canary and Henry Kozicke, 3–40. Madison: University of Wisconsin Press.

Grant. 1653. "Land Grant, October, 1653, signed by P. Stuyvesant [in Dutch] Original in Huntington Lib. Collections, HM9724." Box SC 16676–8, Manuscripts and Special Collections, State Library of New York, Albany.

Gravell, Thomas A., and George Miller. 1979. *A Catalogue of American Watermarks, 1690–1835.* New York: Garland.

Green, Wilmer L. 1930. *History and Survey of Accountancy.* Brooklyn: Standard Text Press.

Greenblatt, Stephen. 1992. *Marvelous Possessions: The Wonder of the New World.* Chicago: University of Chicago Press.

Gruys, J. A., and C. de Wolf. 1989. *Thesaurus, 1473–1800: Nederlandse Boekdrukkers en Boekverkopers, Met plaatsen en jaren van werkzaamheid* [Dutch printers and booksellers, with places and years of activity]. The Hague: De Graff.

Hamilton, Alexander. 1971. *Hamilton's Itinerarium, Being a Narrative of a Journey from Annapolis, Maryland, through Delaware, Pennsylvania, New York, New Jersey . . . from May to September, 1744 by Doctor Alexander Hamilton.* Ed. Albert B. Hart. New York: Arno Press and New York Times Reprint.

Hamlin, Paul M. 1939. *Legal Education in Colonial New York.* New York: New York University Law Quarterly Review.

Handteekeningen. n.d. "Verzameling van Echte Handteekeningen van de Edele Achtbare Heeren Raden in de Vroedschap, sedert den Jare 1618 benevens der Secretarissen sedert 1690 en Pensionarissen van 1678 der Stad Haarlem, met Alphabetisch Register, biographische aanteekeningen en Wapend." Gemeentearchief Haarlem.

Harrison, Francis. 1730. *The English and Low-Dutch School-Master.* New York: W. Bradford.

Hart, Simon. 1951. "De Stadskolonie Nieuwer-Amstel aan de Delaware Rivier in Noord-Amerika." *Amstelodamum Maandblad voor de Kennis van Amsterdam* 38: 89–94.

———. 1959. *The Prehistory of the New Netherland Company. Amsterdam Notarial Records of the First Dutch Voyages to the Hudson.* Amsterdam: City of Amsterdam Press.

———. 1966. "Fiscal History of the West India Co." *Halve Maen* 41 (April): 10.

Hastings, Hugh, ed. 1901–5 [Index, 1916]. *Ecclesiastical Records, State of New York.* Albany: James B. Lyon.

Hazelzet, Kees. 1944. *Rotterdam: Van Visschersdorp tot Wereldhaven.* Rotterdam: Nijdh & Van Ditmar.

Hazewinkel, H. C., ed. 1943. *Beschrijvinge der Stad Rotterdam en Eenige Omleggende Dorpen Behelst Rotterdam's beginopkomst en uitlegging, alsmede de voornaamste gebouwen en Kerken, Kloosters, Kapellen en andere Gestichten. Van authentyke stukken, handvesten en privilegien voorzein door Gerard van Spaan voor onzen tijd bewerkt door H. C. Hazelwinkel.* Antwerpen: A. D. Donker.

Hazewinkel, H. C., and J. E. Van der Pot, eds. 1942. *Vier Eeuwen Rotterdam, Citaten uit Reisbeschrijvingen, Rapporten, Redevoeringen, Gedichten en Romans.* Rotterdam: W. L. & J. Brusse.

Heersink, Wim. 1989. " 'Van oude tijden bij alle volkeren geacht': Amsterdamse notarissen van schrijftafel tot schepenbank, 1600–1800." In *Nieuwe Licht op Oude Justitie: Misdaad en Straf ten Tijde van de Republiek,* ed. Sjoerd Faber, 48–64. Muiderberg: D. Coutinho.

Hirsch, Edward. 1991. "The Fidelity of Things." Review of Zbigniew Herbert, *Still Life with a Bridle,* trans. John and Bogdana Carpenter. *New Yorker,* December 23, 100–107.

Hoffman, William J. 1935. "An Armory of American Families of Dutch Descent: Van Lodensteyne." *New York Genealogical and Biographical Record* 66: 376–82.

———. 1939. "An Armory of American Families of Dutch Descent: Van Hardenberg." *New York Genealogical and Biographical Record* 70: 253–55.

Hoogewerff, G. J., ed. 1919. *De Twee Reizen van Cosimo de' Medici Prins van Toscane door de Nederlanden (1667–1669): Journalen en Documenten.* Werken Uitgegeven door het Historisch Genootschap, derde serie, no. 41. Amsterdam: Johannes Muller.

Howard, Ronald W. 1991. "Apprenticeship and Economic Education in New Netherland and Seventeenth-Century New York." In *A Beautiful and Fruitful Place: Selected Rensselaerswijck Seminar Papers,* ed. Nancy Anne McClure Zeller, 205–18. New Netherland Project. Albany: New Netherland Publishing.

Howell, George R., and Jonathan Tenney, eds. 1886. *Bicentennial History of Albany: History of the County of Albany, New York, from 1609 to 1886. With Portraits, Biographies & Illustrations.* Vol. 2. New York: W. W. Munsell.

Huizinga, Johan. 1924. *The Waning of the Middle Ages: A Study of the Forms of Life, Thought, and Art in France and the Netherlands in the Fourteenth and Fifteenth Centuries.* Rpt. New York: Penguin, 1971.

Hulme, Peter. 1992. *Colonial Encounters: Europe and the Native Caribbean, 1492–1797.* London: Routledge.

Hylkema, Cornelis Bonnes. 1900. *Reformateurs, Geschiedkundige Studiën over de Godsdienstige Bewegingen uit de Nadagen onzer Gouden Eeuw, Eerste Stuk.* Haarlem: H. D. Tjeenk Willink & Zoon.

Innes, J[ohn] H. 1902. *New Amsterdam and Its People: Studies, Social and Topographical, of the Town under Dutch and Early English Rule.* 2 vols. New York: Scribner.

Jakobson, Roman. 1956. "Two Aspects of Language and Two Types of Aphasic Disturbances." In *Fundamentals of Language,* ed. Roman Jakobson and Morris Halle. The Hague: Mouton.

Janvier, Thomas A. 1903. *The Dutch Founding of New York.* New York: Harper.

Japenga, C. J., and M. E. M. Sommer. 1988. "Steden en Hun Ommelanden." In *Steden en Hun Verleden: De Ontwikkeling van de Stedelijke Sameleving in de*

Nederlanden tot de Negentiende Eeuw, ed. Maurits Van Rooijen, 273–94. Utrecht: Teleac.

Jennings, Francis. 1984. *The Ambiguous Iroquois Empire: The Covenant Chain Confederation of Indian Tribes with English Colonies from Its Beginning to the Lancaster Treaty of 1744.* New York: Norton.

Johnson, Donald S. 1993. *Charting the Sea of Darkness: The Four Voyages of Henry Hudson.* Camden, Me.: International Marine.

Johnson, Herbert Alan. 1963. *The Law Merchant and Negotiable Instruments in Colonial New York, 1664 to 1720.* Chicago: Loyola University Press.

———, ed. 1981. *Essays on New York Colonial Legal History.* Westport, Conn.: Greenwood.

Jussurun, Jacob S. C. 1917. *Kiliaen van Rensselaer van 1623 tot 1636.* The Hague: Martinus Nijhoff.

Justice, Steven. 1994. "Inquisition, Speech, and Writing: A Case from Late-Medieval Norwich." *Representations* 48: 1–29.

Kalma, J. J., and D. de Vries, eds. 1978. *Beschrijvinge van de Heerlyckheydt van Frieslandt door Christianus Schotanus (1664 [Franeker]).* Amsterdam: Theatrum Orbis Terrarum.

Katz, Stanley N. 1984. "The Problem of a Colonial Legal History." In *Colonial British America: Essays in the New History of the Early Modern Era,* ed. Jack P. Greene and J. R. Pole, 457–80. Baltimore: Johns Hopkins University Press.

Keller, Arthur S., Oliver J. Lissitzyn, and Frederick J. Mann. 1938. *Creation of Rights of Sovereignty through Symbolic Acts, 1400–1800.* New York: Columbia University Press.

Kenney, Alice P. 1975. *Stubborn for Liberty: The Dutch in New York.* Syracuse: Syracuse University Press.

Kessler, Henry H., and Eugene Rachlis. 1959. *Peter Stuyvesant and His New York.* New York: Random House.

Kett, Joseph F., and Patricia A. McCluny. 1984. "Book Culture in Post-Revolutionary Virginia." *Proceedings of the American Antiquarian Society* 94: 97–154.

Keyes, George S., ed. 1990. *Mirror of Empire: Dutch Marine Art of the Seventeenth Century.* Cambridge: Minneapolis Institute of Arts with Cambridge University Press.

Kieft, Willem. 1645. "Grant from Willem Kieft . . . of a piece of land named the Bouwerie No. 5, December 13, 1645 [signed: Tienhoven]." Bontemantel Collection. New Netherland Papers, box I, folder "Lands, 1645, Doc. 13." Rare Books and Manuscripts Division, New York Public Library.

Kierner, Cynthia A. 1992. *Traders and Gentlefolk: The Livingstons of New York, 1675–1790.* Ithaca: Cornell University Press.

Kilpatrick, William Heard. 1912. *The Dutch Schools of New Netherland and Colonial New York.* Washington: Government Printing Office.

Knuttel, G. 1951. *De Letter als Knutwerk: Beschouwingen en confrontaties met andere gelijktijdige knustuitingen van de romeinse tijd tot op heden.* Amsterdam: N. V. Lettergieterij-Amsterdam, voorheen N. Tetterode.

Kok, G. Chr. 1971. *Het Nederlandse Notariaat.* Deventer: Kluwer.

Kossmann, E[rnst] F. 1932. *De Boekverkoopers, Notarissen en Cramers op het Binnenhof.* The Hague: Martinus Nijhoff.

Krijgers Janzen, W. C. 1956. *De Notaris in de Literatuur.* Haarlem: H. D. Tjeenk Wellink & Zoon.

Kushner, Howard I. 1981. "The Suicide of Meriwether Lewis: A Psychoanalytic Inquiry." *William and Mary Quarterly* 38: 464–81.

Kuypers, H. M. 1992. "Jan Joachimsz. van Ilpendam, een Leidse Bezitter van de Barbara-prebende in de 16de Eeuw." *Genealogische Bijdragen Leiden en Omgeving* 7: 476–79.

Labarre, E. J. 1950. *Monumenta Chartae Papyraceae Historiam Illustrantia, or Collection of Works and Documents Illustrating the History of Paper,* vol. 1, *Watermarks, Mainly of the 17th and 18th Centuries by Edward Heawood.* Hilversum: Paper Publications Society.

Lambrechtsen, Nicolaas Cornelis. 1841. "A Short Description of the Discovery and Subsequent History of the New Netherlands, a Colony in America (at an Early Period) of the Republic of the United Netherlands, ed. and tr. Francis Adrian van der Kemp. Middelburg, S. van Benthem, 1818." In *Collections of the New-York Historical Society* 1, 2d ser.: 79–122.

La Montagne, Jan. 1670. "Act executed before Jan la Montagne [*sic*], October 23, 1670, Register and Protocol Gehoûden ten Durpe Nieuw Haerlem door Jan la Montagne en Hendrick J. Van der Vin, 1670–1674, Book 3." James Riker Collection, 11:5, Rare Books and Manuscripts Division, New York Public Library.

Laws. 1896. *The Colonial Laws of New York from the Year 1664 to the Revolution, Including the Charters to the Duke of York, the Commissions and Instructions to Colonial Governors, Duke's Laws, the Laws of the Dongan and Leisler Assemblies, the Charters of Albany and New York and the Acts of the Colonial Legislatures from 1691 to 1775 Inclusive.* Vol. 1. Albany: James B. Lyon.

Lechford, Thomas. 1971. *Note-Book Kept by Thomas Lechford, Esq., Lawyer, in Boston, Massachusetts Bay, from June 27, 1638, to July 29, 1641.* New York: Johnson Reprint.

Leder, Lawrence H. 1961. *Robert Livingston, 1654–1728, and the Politics of Colonial New York.* Chapel Hill: University of North Carolina Press.

Lee, R. W., ed. 1926. *The Jurisprudence of Holland by Hugo Grotius, the Text Translated with Brief Notes and a Commentary by R. W. Lee,* vol. 1, *Text Translation and Notes.* Oxford: Clarendon.

———. 1936. *The Jurisprudence of Holland by Hugo Grotius, the Text Translated with Brief Notes and a Commentary by R. W. Lee,* vol. 2, *Commentary.* Oxford: Clarendon.

Leeuwenberg, H. L. Ph. 1988. "Steden en hun kerken." In *Steden en Hun Verleden: De Ontwikkeling van de Stedelijke Samenleving in de Nederlanden tot de Negentiende Eeuw,* ed. Maurits Van Rooijen, 81–104. Utrecht: Teleac.

Littleton, Ananias C. 1933. *Accounting Evolution to 1900.* New York: American Institute.

Littleton, Ananias C., and Basil S. Yamey, eds. 1956. *Studies in the History of Accounting.* Homewood, Ill.: R. D. Irwin.

Love, Harold 1987. "Scribal Publication in Seventeenth-Century England." *Transactions of the Cambridge Bibliographical Society* 9: 130–46.

Lucas, E. V. 1929. *Vermeer the Magical.* London: Methuen.

Lybreghts, Arent. 1736. *Redenerend Vertoog over 't Notaris Ampt; Behelzende eene duidelyke en nette Verklaring van deszelfs Gronden, omtrent veelerleye gevallen in de Practyk; Alles volgens Placaten en Costumen dezer Landen; Als mede door Gewysdens van de hoge Gerechtsboven, en Advyzen van voorname Rechtsgeleerden, bevestigt. Zynde Dus Eene bequame handleiding tot eene algemene kennisse der Rechten, voor zo verre zulks tot 't Notaris Ampt betrekkelyk is; Niet alleen voor min geoeffenden, maar ook voor meêr gevorderen. Eerste Deel Opgesteld, vermeerderd, en gecorrigeert, door Arent Lybreghts, Notaris in 's-Gravenhage. Tweden Druk.* Amsterdam: J. Ratelband.

Macasar, Dagregister. n.d. "Geheim Dagregister Macasar." Reel no. 02 [Photographed 7/6/1977 ARSIP National Republik Indonesia. Bundel 95: 1769–1791.] [See here "Register der Marginaalen op het Vervolg van het Secreet Dag-verhaal van anno 1790."]

MacDonald, Michael. 1986. "The Secularization of Suicide in England, 1660–1800." *Past & Present* III: 50–97.

———. 1988. "Debate: The Secularlrization of Suicide in England, 1660–1800." *Past & Present* 119: 158–70.

MacDonald, Michael, and Terence R. Murphy. 1990. *Sleepless Souls: Suicide in Early Modern England.* Oxford: Clarendon.

MacMurray, J. W., ed. 1883. *A History of the Schenectady Patent in the Dutch and English Times; Being Contributions toward a History of the Lower Mohawk Valley by Prof. Jonathan Pearson, A.M., and Others.* Albany: J. Munsell's Sons.

Maika, Dennis J. 1995. "Commerce and Comunity: Manhattan Merchants in the Seventeenth Century." Ph.D. diss., New York University.

Marechal, G. M. O. 1988. "Steden en Hun Sociale Zorg." In *Steden en Hun Verleden: De Ontwikkeling van de Stedelijke Samenleving in de Nederlanden tot de Negentiende Eeuw,* ed. Maurits Van Rooijen, 249–72. Utrecht: Teleac.

Margry, P. J. 1988. "Steden en Hun Verkeer." In *Steden en Hun Verleden: De Ontwikkeling van de Stedelijke Samenleving in de Nederlanden tot de Negentiende Eeuw,* ed. Maurits Van Rooijen, 105–52. Utrecht: Teleac.

Marsilje, J. W., ed. 1989. *Uit Leidse Bron Geleverd.* Leiden: Gemeentearchief Leiden.

Matson, Cathy. 1991. "The 'Hollander Interest' and Ideas about Free Trade in Colonial New York: Persistent Influences of the Dutch, 1664–1764." In *A Beautiful and Fruitful Place: Selected Rensselaerswijck Seminar Papers,* ed. Nancy Anne McClure Zeller, 251–68. New Netherland Project. Albany: New Netherland Publishing.

———. 1994. "'Damned Scoundrels' and 'Libertisme of Trade': Freedom and Regulation in Colonial New York's Fur and Grain Trades." *William and Mary Quarterly* 51: 389–418.

McIlwain, Charles H., and Paul L. Ward, eds. 1957. *Archeion, or A Discourse upon the High Courts of Justice in England.* [Originally *Archeion or, A Discourse Upon the High Courts of Justice in England. Composed by William Lambard, [sic] of Lincolnes Inne, Gent. Newly Corrected, and enlarged according to the Authors Copie. London, E. P. for Henry Seile, 1635.*] Cambridge: Harvard University Press.

Megapolensis, Johannes. 1644. "A Short Sketch of the Mohawk Indians in New Netherland, Their Land, Stature, Dress, Manners and Magistrates, Written in the Year, 1644, by Johannes Megapolensis Jr., Minister There. Revised from the

Translation in Hazard's Historical Collections, with an Introduction and notes by John Romeyn Brodhead." *Collections of the New-York Historical Society* 3, ser. 2: 137–60.

Meij, P. J., et al. 1975. *Geschiedenis van Gelderland, 1492–1795.* Bk. 2. Zutphen: Walburg Pers.

Melis, J. C. H. 1982. *Dr Notariswet.* Zwolle: W. E. J. Tjeenk Willink.

Melville, Herman. 1995. *Bartleby and the Lighning-Rod Man.* Ringwood, Victoria: Penguin.

Menkman, W. R. 1947. *De West-Indische Compagnie.* Amsterdam: P. N. Van Kampen & Zoon.

Mercurius, Hollandtze. 1667. *Hollandtze Mercurius Vervarende de Voornaemste Geschiedenissen Voor-gevallen in 't Gantze Jaer 1667, in Christenryck: Het Achttiende Deel.* Haarlem: Pieter Casteleyn.

Meriton, George. 1685. *A Guide for Constables, Churchwardens, Overseers of the Poor, Surveyors of the High-ways, Treasurers of the County-Stock, Masters of the House of Correction, Bayliffs of Mannors, Toll-takers in Fairs, etc. . . . The English Edition Enlarged, collected by Geo. Meriton, Gent.* London: Richard and Edward Atkins.

Merwick, Donna. 1980. "Dutch Townsmen and Land Use: A Spatial Perspective on Seventeenth-Century Albany, New York." *William and Mary Quarterly* 37: 53–78.

———. 1981. "Becoming English: Anglo Dutch Conflict in the 1670s in Albany, New York." *New York History* 62: 389–414.

———. 1989. "Being Dutch: An Interpretation of Why Jacob Leisler Died." *New York History* 70: 373–404.

———. 1990. *Possessing Albany, 1630–1710: The Dutch and English Experiences.* New York: Cambridge University Press.

———. 1994. "The Work of the Trickster in the Dutch Possession of New Netherland." In *Dangerous Liaisons: Essays in Honour of Greg Dening,* ed. Donna Merwick, 115–34. Melbourne: University of Melbourne, Department of History.

Montias, John Michael. 1991. "Works of Art in Seventeenth-Century Amsterdam: An Analysis of Subjects and Attributions." In *Art in History / History in Art: Studies in Seventeenth-Century Dutch Culture,* ed. David Freedberg and Jan de Vries, 331–72. Santa Monica: Getty Center for the History of Art and the Humanities.

Moore, Charles B. 1887. "Laws of 1683 — Old Records and Old Politics." *New York Genealogical and Biographical Record* 18: 49–63.

Morris, Richard B. 1978. "The New York City Mayor's Court." In *Courts and Law in Early New York: Selected Essays,* ed. Leo Hershkowitz and Milton M. Klein, 19–29. Port Washington, N.Y.: Kennikat Press.

Muller, Sheila D. 1985. *Charity in the Dutch Republic: Pictures of Rich and Poor for Charitable Institutions.* Ann Arbor: UMI Research Press.

Munsell, Joel, ed. 1849–59. *The Annals of Abany.* 10 vols. Albany: J. Munsell.

———, ed. 1865–72. *Collections on the History of Albany, from Its Discovery to the Present Time.* 4 vols. Albany: J. Munsell.

Murphy, Henry C., ed. 1865. *Anthology of New Netherland, or Translations from the Early Poets of New York.* New York: Bradford Club; rpt. Port Washington, N.Y.: Friedman, 1969.

Naber, S. P. L'Honore, ed. 1932. *Joannes de Laet: Jaerlyck Verhael van de Verrichtinghen der Geoctroyeerde West-Indische Compagnie in derthien Boecken: Tweede Deel.* Bks. 4–7 (1627–30). The Hague: Martinus Nijhoff.

———, ed. 1934. *Joannes de Laet: Jaerlyck Verhael van de Verrichtingen der Geoctroyeerde West-Indische Compagnie in derthien Boecken, Derde Deel.* Bks. 8–10 (1631–33). The Hague: Martinus Nijhoff.

Naber, S. P. L'Honore, and J. C. M. Warnsinck, eds. 1937. *Joannes de Laet: Jaerlyck Verhael van de Verrichtingen der Geoctroyeerde West-Indische Compagnie in derthien Boecken, Vierde Deel.* Bks. 11–13 (1634–36). The Hague: Martinus Nijhoff.

Naeranus, Johannes, ed. 1640. *Onderwijsinge Inde Christelijcke Religie, Ghestelt bij Vraghen ende Antwoorden nae de Belijdenisse der Romanstrants-Ghereformeerde Christenen, Mitsgaders Der Selfder Formulieren ende Ghebeden, des Heijlighen Doops, ende des H. Avontmaels. De Tweede Druck, Verbetert en vermeerdert met een aensprake tot de Siecken en eenige Ghebeden.* Rotterdam: Voor Johannes Naeranus Boeck-verkooper.

Narrett, David E. 1992. *Inheritance and Family Life in Colonial New York City.* Ithaca: Cornell University Press.

Nissenson, S[amuel] G[eorge]. 1937. *The Patroon's Domain.* New York: Columbia University Press.

Noordam, Dirk Jaap. 1989. "Strafrechtspleging en Criminaliteit in Delft in de Vroeg-Moderne Tijd." *Tijdschrift voor Sociale Geschiedenis* 15: 209–44.

Nooter, Eric, and Patricia Bonomi, eds. 1988. *Colonial Dutch Studies: An Interdisciplinary Approach.* New York: New York University Press.

Nooter, Willem Frederik (Eric). 1994. "Between Heaven and Earth: Church and Society in Pre-Revolutionary Flatbush, Long Island." Diss., Vrije Universitiet te Amsterdam.

Nowell-Smith, Geoffrey, and David Wootton, eds. 1984. Lucien Febvre and Henri-Jean Martin, *The Coming of the Book: The Impact of Printing, 1450–1800.* Trans. David Gerard. London: New Left Books.

Nussbaum, Martha C. 1991. "The Literary Imagination in Public Life." *New Literary History* 22: 877–910.

Oates, Joyce Carol. 1980. "The Art of Suicide." In *Suicide: The Philosophical Issues,* ed. M. P. Batlin and David J. Mayo, 161–68. New York: St. Martin's Press.

O'Callaghan, E. B. 1846, 1848. *History of New Netherland: or, New York under the Dutch.* 2 vols. New York: D. Appleton.

———, ed. 1849–51. *The Documentary History of the State of New-York.* 4 vols. Albany: Weed, Parsons; Charles van Benthuysen.

———, ed. 1868. *Laws and Ordinances of New Netherland, 1638–1674.* Albany: Weed, Parsons.

Ong, Walter J. 1971. "Ramist Method and the Commercial Mind." In *Rhetoric, Romance, and Technology: Studies in the Interaction of Expression and Culture,* ed. Walter J. Ong, 165–89. Ithaca: Cornell University Press.

———. 1977. *Interfaces of the Word: Studies in the Evolution of Consciousness and Culture.* Ithaca: Cornell University Press.

Opper, Edward. 1975. "Dutch East India Company Artisans in the Early Eighteenth Century." Ph.D. diss., Indiana University.

Orlers, J. J. 1641. *Beschrijvinge der Stadt Leyden, Inhoudende 't Begin den Voortgang ende den Wasdom der Selver: De Stichtinge van de Kerken, Cloosteren, Gasthuysen, ende Andere Publycque Gestichten, etc. Desgelijcx de Oprechtinge van de Academie, ende de Collegien Theologie. Mitsgaders Verhael van Alle de Belegeringen, ende Aenslagen, die de Selve Stade zedert den Jare 1203, Geleden Heeft, tot te Laeste Strenge Belegeringe ende Verlostinghe Ghevallen inden Jaere 1574, J. J. Orlers.* Leyden: Andries Jansz Cloeting tot Delft ende Abraham Commelijn tot Leyden.

Overvoorde, J. C., and P. de Roo de la Faille. 1928. *De Gebouwen van de Oost-Indische Compagnie en van de West-Indische Compagnie in Nederland.* Utrecht: A. Oosthoek.

Paltsits, Victor Hugo, ed. 1910. *Minutes of the Executive Council of the Province of New York: Administration of Francis Lovelace, 1668–1673.* 2 vols. Albany: J. B. Lyon.

Pappafava, Vladimiro. 1880. *Della Opera che Illustrano il Notariato.* Zara: Nicolò Solic.

———. 1901. *Etude sur le notariat dans la République Sud-Africaine.* Rpt. from *Bulletin de la Societé de Législation comparée.* Paris: Générale Lahure. Pamphlet.

Parker, Geoffrey. 1980. "An Educational Revolution? The Growth of Literacy and Schooling in Early Modern Europe." *Tijdschrift voor Geschiedenis* 93: 210–20.

Pearson, Jonathan, ed. 1869. *Early Records of the City and County of Albany and Colony of Rensselaerswyck (1656–1675), translated from the Original Dutch, with Notes.* Albany: J. Munsell.

———. 1871. "Diagrams of the Home Lots of the Village of Beverwyck." In *Collections on the History of Albany, from Its Discovery to the Present Time, with Notices of Its Public Institutions, and Biographical Sketches of Citizens Deceased,"* vol. 4, ed. Joel Munsell, 184–224. Albany: J. Munsell.

———. 1880. *Nisi Dominus Frustra. Two Hundreth Anniversary of the First Reformed Protestant Dutch Church of Schenectady, N.Y. June 20th & 21st . . . 1880 . . . ,* pt. 3, *History of the Church, by Professor Jonathan Pearson,* 54–263. Schenectady: Steam Printing House.

Phoonsen, J. 1677. *Wissel-Styl tot Amsterdam, Vervattende Niet Alleen het geene dat men gewoon, maar ooch wat een voorsichtigh Koopman, tot sijn securiteyt, in de Wissel-handel dienstigh en noodigh is te observeren. Mitsgaders De Ordonantiën, Willekeuren, en Reglementen van Wisselen tot Amsterdam, Rotterdam, Antwerpen . . . en Lions. Als ooch de Ordonnances de Louis XIV. . . Beschreven, en by een vergadert door J. Ph[oonsen].* Rotterdam: Barent van Santbergen.

Pierce, Carl Horton. 1903. *New Harlem, Past and Present.* New York: New Harlem.

Pitlo, A. 1948. *De Zeventiende en Achttiende Eeuwsche Notarisboeken, en Wat Zij Ons Omtrent Ons Oude Notariaat Leeren.* Haarlem: H. D. Tjeenk Willink & Zoon.

———. 1953. *Taal en Stijl der Notariële Akten.* Wageningen: Zomer & Keunings.

———. 1963. *De Lach in het Recht.* Haarlem: H. D. Tjeenk Willink & Zoon.

———. 1981. "Figuratief–Non-Figuratief Legisme — Vrije Rechtsvinding." In *Pitlo en de Muzen, Bundel Opstellen van de Hand van Prof. Mr. A. Pitlo, Jurist en Kunstminnaar, Hem Aangeboden ter Gelegenheid van Zijn Tachtigste Verjaardag,* ed. A. Pitlo, 11–38. Arnhem: S. Gouda Quint–D. Brouwer & Son.

———. 1982. *Niet Alleen Artikel Eén: Een vleug notariële Cultuurgeschiedenis.* Deventer: Kluwer.

Piwonka, Ruth. 1987. "New York Colonial Inventories: Dutch Interiors as a Measure of Cultural Change." In *New World Dutch Studies: Dutch Arts and Culture in Colonial America, 1609–1776*, ed. Roderic H. Blackburn and Nancy Kelley, 63–81. Albany: Albany Institute of History and Art.

Poole, Robert. 1995. " 'Give Us Our Eleven Days!': Calendar Reform in Eighteenth-Century England." *Past & Present* 149: 95–139.

Potter, Jonathan, and Margaret Wetherell. 1987. *Discourse and Social Psychology: Beyond Attitudes and Behavior*. London: Sage.

Preston, Colonel Rupert. 1974. *Seventeenth Century Marine Painters of the Netherlands*. Leigh-on-Sea: F. Lewis.

Pretyman, William, and B. Fernow. 1886. *The Flags Which Floated over Albany and the Present State of New York when under Dutch, English and American Government, with a Few Historical Data*. Pamphlet.

Price, Sally. 1989. *Primitive Art in Civilized Places*. Chicago: University of Chicago Press.

Purvis, J. S. 1957. *Notarial Signs from the York Archiepiscopal Records*. London: St. Anthony's Press.

Quinn, David, ed. 1982. *Colonies in the Beginning: Early Maryland in a Wider World*. 2d ed. Detroit: Wayne State University Press.

"Raad en Vroedschap der Stad Haarlem van 1583–1813." n.d. Gemeentearchief Haarlem.

Raesly, Ellis Lawrence. 1945. *Portrait of New Netherland*. Rpt. Port Washington, N.Y.: Friedman, 1965.

Read, Conyers. 1962. *William Lambarde and Local Government: His "Ephemeris" and Twenty-nine Charges to Juries and Commissions*. Ithaca: Cornell University Press for Folger Shakespeare Library.

Read, John Meredeth. 1807. Letter of John Meredeth Read to Mrs. John Cruger, March 14, 1807. MS11346 (8). Manuscripts and Special Collections, New York State Library, Albany.

Reay, Barry. 1991. "The Context and Meaning of Popular Literacy: Some Evidence from Nineteenth-Century Rural England." *Past & Present* 131: 89–129.

Regin, Deric. 1976. *Traders, Artists, Burghers: A Cultural History of Amsterdam in the 17th Century*. Assen / Amsterdam: Van Gorcum.

Reps, John. 1965. *The Making of Urban America: A History of City Planning in the United States*. Princeton: Princeton University Press.

Richter, Daniel K. 1992. *The Ordeal of the Longhouse: The Peoples of the Iroquois League in the Era of European Colonization*. Chapel Hill: University of North Carolina Press.

Rink, Oliver A. 1986. *Holland on the Hudson: An Economic and Social History of Dutch New York*. Ithaca: Cornell University Press.

Ritchie, Robert C. 1977. *The Duke's Province: A Study of New York Politics and Society, 1664–1691*. Chapel Hill: University of North Carolina Press.

Roberts, George S. n.d. *Old Schenectady*. Schenectady: Robson & Adel.

Robinson, O. F., T. D. Fergus, and W. M. Gordon. 1985. *An Introduction to European Legal History*. London: Professional Books.

Roeber, A. G. 1991. " 'The Origin of Whatever Is Not English among Us': The Dutch-Speaking and the German-Speaking Peoples of Colonial British America." In *Strangers within the Realm: Cultural Margins of the First British Empire,* ed. Bernard Bailyn and Philip D. Morgan, 220–283. Chapel Hill: University of North Carolina Press.

Roodenburg, Herman. 1991. " 'The Hand of Friendship': Shaking Hands and Other Gestures in the Dutch Republic." In *A Cultural History of Gestures: From Antiquity to the Present Day,* ed. Jan Bremmer and Herman Roodenburg, 152–89. Cambridge: Polity.

Rooseboom, Gerard. 1656. *Recueil van Verscheyde Keuren, en Costumen. Midtsgaders Maniere van Procederen binnen de Stadt Amsterdam. Eerst gecollecteert en beschreven, door Gerard Rooseboom in zijn leven Secretaris de voorsz. Stadt. Den tweeden Druck, nu merkelijck vermeerdert en verbetert.* Amsterdam: Jan Hendricks.

Roth, Martin. 1976. *Comedy and America: The Lost World of Washington Irving.* Port Washington, N.Y.: Kennikat Press.

Rowen, Herbert H. 1978. *John de Witt: Grand Pensionary of Holland, 1625-1672.* Princeton: Princeton University Press.

Said, Edward. 1978. *Orientalism.* New York: Random House.

Schama, Simon. 1987. *The Embarrassment of Riches: An Interpretation of Dutch Culture in the Golden Age.* New York: Knopf.

Schatborn, Peter, and István Szénássy. 1971. *Iconographie du notariat: Documentation de la Fondation pour le progrès de la science notariale.* Groningen: H. D. Tjeenk Willink.

Schermerhorn, Richard, Jr. 1917. "An Early Colonial Manuscript and Biographical Notes Thereon." *New York Genealogical and Biographical Record* 48: 236–43.

Schiltkamp, Jacob Adriaan. 1964. *De Geschiedenis van het Notariaat in het Octrooigebied van de West-Indische Compagnie.* The Hague: L. Smits.

Schoolhouder, Jacob. 1722. *Offenschoole Der Beamptschryvers, Geopent voor alle Leerlingen, die begeerig zyn, hen in dezelve Konst te oeffenen . . . door Jacob Schoolhouder.* Amsterdam: Jacobus Wolffers.

Schoonmaker, Marius. 1888. *The History of Kingston, New York, from Its Early Settlement to the Year 1820.* New York: Burr.

Schrage, E. J. H. 1986. "Sale Breaks Hire — or Does it? Medieval Foundations of the Roman-Dutch Concept." *Tijdschrift voor Rechtsgeschiedenis* 54: 287–96.

Schrick, C. R. 1994. "The Philipse Jewel: A Legend Is Born." *Halve Maen* 67: 30–36.

Schrire, Carmel 1995. *Digging through Darkness: Chronicles of an Archeologist.* Charlottesville: University Press of Virginia.

Schwartz, Gary, and Marten Jan Bok. 1990. *Pieter Saenredam: The Painter and His Time.* London: Thames & Hudson.

Scott, Kenneth, ed. 1983. *New York Historical Manuscripts: Minutes of the Mayor's Court of New York, 1674–1675.* Baltimore: Genealogical Publishing Co.

Scott, Kenneth, and Kenn Stryker-Rodda, eds. 1974a. *New York Historical Manuscripts: Dutch,* trans. and annotated by Arnold J. F. van Laer, vol. 1, *Register of the Provincial Secretary, 1638–1642.* Baltimore: Genealogical Publishing Co.

———. 1974b. *New York Historical Manuscripts: Dutch,* trans. and annotated by Arnold J. F. van Laer, vol. 2, *Register of the Provincial Secretary, 1642–1647.* Baltimore: Genealogical Publishing Co.

———. 1974c. *New York Historical Manuscripts: Dutch*, trans. and annotated by Arnold J. F. van Laer, vol. 3, *Register of the Provincial Secretary, 1648–1660*. Baltimore: Genealogical Publishing Co.

———. 1974d. *New York Historical Manuscripts: Dutch*, trans. and annotated by Arnold J. F. van Laer, vol. 4, *Council Minutes, 1638–1649*. Baltimore: Genealogical Publishing Co.

———. 1978. *New York Historical Manuscripts: Dutch: The Register of Salomon Lachaire, Notary Public of New Amsterdam, 1661–1662*, trans. E. B. O'Callaghan. Baltimore: Genealogical Publishing Co.

Seavey, W. M. 1894. *The Powers and Duties of Notaries Public and Justices of the Peace in Massachusetts*. Boston: Little, Brown.

Seed, Patricia. 1995. *Ceremonies of Possession in Europe's Conquest of the New World, 1492–1640*. New York: Cambridge University Press.

Shattuck, Martha Dickinson. 1993. "A Civil Society: Court and Community in Beverwijck, New Netherland, 1652–1664." Ph.D. diss., Boston University.

Shomette, Donald G., and Robert D. Haslach. 1988. *Raid on America: The Dutch Naval Campaign of 1672–1674*. Columbia: University of South Carolina Press.

Skelton, R[alph] A[shlin], ed. 1964. Willem Janse Blaeu (William Johnson), *The Light of Navigation, Amsterdam, 1612*. Theatrum Orbis Terrarum, Series of Atlases in Facsimile, 1st ser., vol. 6. Amsterdam: N. Israel.

Slothouwer, D. F., Jr. 1928. *Amsterdamsche Huizen, 1600–1800*. Amsterdam: P. N. Van Kampen & Zoon.

Sluijter, Eric J. 1991. "Didactic and Disguised Meanings? Several Seventeenth-Century Texts on Painting and the Iconological Approach to Northern Dutch Painting of This Period." In *Art in History / History in Art: Studies in Seventeenth-Century Dutch Culture*, ed. David Freedberg and Jan de Vries, 175–207. Santa Monica: Getty Center for the History of Art and the Humanities.

Sluyterman, Karel. 1918. *Huisraad en Binnenhuis in Nederland in Vroegere Eeuwen*. The Hague: Martinus Nijhoff.

Spierenburg, Pieter. 1984. *The Spectacle of Suffering: Executions and the Evolution of Repression from a Preindustrial Metropolis to the European Experience*. Cambridge: Harvard University Press.

Spierings, M. H. M. 1984. *Het Schepenprotocol van 's-Hertogenbosch, 1367–1400*. Tilburg: Stichting Zuidelijk Historisch Contact.

Sprenger van Eyk, J. P. 1928. *De Wetgeving op het Notaris-Ambt*. Haarlem: F. Bohn.

Spufford, Margaret. 1974. *Contrasting Communities: English Villagers in the Sixteenth and Seventeenth Centuries*. New York: Cambridge University Press.

Stallybrass, Peter, and Allon White. 1986. *The Politics and Poetics of Transgression*. Ithaca: Cornell University Press.

State Historian. 1897. *Second Annual Report of the State Historian of the State of New York*. Albany: Wynkoop Hallenbeck Crawford.

———. 1898. *Third Annual Report of the State Historian of the State of New York, 1897, transmitted to the Legislature, March 4, 1898 . . .*, Appendix L, *New York Colonial Archives, Transcriptions of the Records between the Years 1673 and 1675*. New York: Wynkoop Hallenbeck Crawford.

Steven, William. 1832. *The History of the Scottish Church, Rotterdam.* Edinburgh: Waugh & Innes.

Stokes, I[saac] N[ewton] Phelps. 1915–28. *The Iconography of Manhattan Island: 1498–1909.* 6 vols. New York: Robert H. Dodd.

Stone-Ferrier, Linda A. 1985. *Images of Textiles: The Weave of Seventeenth-Century Dutch Art and Society.* Ann Arbor: UMI Research Press.

Strubbe, Eg. I. 1970. "Joos de Damhouder Als Criminalist." *Tijdschrift voor Rechtsgeschiedenis* 38:1–65.

Struik, Dirk J. 1981. *The Land of Stevin and Huygens: A Sketch of Science and Technology in the Dutch Republic during the Golden Century.* Dordrecht: D. Reidel.

Stubbs, Michael 1980. *Language and Literacy: The Sociolinguistics of Reading and Writing.* London: Routledge & Kegan Paul.

Stuyvesant, Petrus. 1655a. "Suyvesant to Directors in Amsterdam, October 28, 1655 [Extract]." New Netherland Papers. Bontemantel Collection, box 2, folder "1655 — Extracts of Letters from Director-General Stuyvesant to the Directors in Amsterdam, dated 28 October, 30 October and 7 November, 1655." Rare Books and Manuscripts Division, New York Public Library.

———. 1655b. "Stuyvesant, de Sille, La Montagne to Directors in Amsterdam, October 30, 1655 [Extract]." New Netherland Papers. Bontemantel Collection, box 2, folder "1655 — Extracts of Letters from Director-General Stuyvesant to the Directors at Amsterdam, dated 28 October, 30 October and 7 November, 1655." Rare Books and Manuscripts Division, New York Public Library.

———. 1657. "Stuyvesant to Directors at Amsterdam, May 31,1657." New Netherland Papers. Bontemantel Collection, box 2, folder "1657 — Extracts of papers from New Netherland that arrived on the ship 'Bever,' July 1657 (Transcripts and Translations)." Rare Books and Manuscripts Division, New York Public Library.

Suleiman, Ezra N. 1987. *Private Power and Centralization in France: The Notaries and the State.* Princeton: Princeton University Press.

Sullivan, James, E. Melvin Williams, Edwin P. Conklin, and Benedict Fitzpatrick, eds. 1927. *History of New York State: 1523–1927.* 6 vols. New York: Lewis Historical Publishing Co.

Sweeney, Amin. 1987. *A Full Hearing: Orality and Literacy in the Malay World.* Berkeley: University of California Press.

Te Lintum, C. 1905. *De Merchant Adventurers in de Nederlanden: Een Bijdrage Tot de Geschiedenis van den Engelschen Handel met Nederland.* The Hague: Martinus Nijhoff.

———. 1909. "De Rotterdamsche Handel in Vroeger Dagen." In *Rotterdam in den Loop der Eeuwen,* ed. Kees Hazelzet, 3:25–40. Rotterdam: W. Nevens.

Temple, Sir William. 1673. *Observations upon the United Provinces of the Netherlands.* London: A. Maxwell.

Ten Have, Onko. 1973a. *De geschiedenis van het Boekhouden.* Wassenaar: Delwel.

———. 1973b. *De Leer van het Boekhouden in de Nederlanden Tijdens de Zeventiende en Achttiende Eeuw.* Delft: J. J. Waltman.

Ter Schegget, H. 1976. *Het Kind van de Rekening: Schetsen uit de Voorgeschiedenis van de Kinderbescherming*. Alphen aan den Rijn: Samson.

'T Hart, G., and H. F. W. D. Fischer. 1963. *Costumen van 's-Gravenhage, 1451–1609*. Utrecht: Kemink en Zoon.

Thomson, Robert. 1790. *The Duty and Office of a Messenger at Arms, with a Copious Introduction, Containing Plain and Necessary Directions for Practice, to Which is Added an Appendix, Relative to the Office of a Notary-Public, and Some Useful and Necessary Tables*. Edinburgh: Grant & Moir for Silvester Doig.

Thomson, Rodney M. 1983. "England and the Twelfth-Century Renaissance." *Past & Present* 101: 3–21.

Thuys, Jacques. 1590. *Ars Notariatus, Dat is: Conste en Stijl van Notarischap: begreven in Theorijcke ende Practijcke. Allen Practisienen, Rentieren, Cooplieden, ende andere, seer nut, oirboor ende dienstelijck. Dese derden druck grootelijcken vermeerdert ende verbeteert sou de Tafel dat uitwijsen sal*. Antwerp: Arnout s'Coniner.

———. 1645. *Ars Notariatus, Dat is: Konste en Stijl van Notarischap: Begrepen in Theorijcke en Practijcke. Met Verklaringhe van vele duystere Latijnsche als Francoysche Woorden ende Termen, die men gemeynelijck in de Practycke is ghebruyckende. Allen Practisenen, Rentenieren, Kooplieden en andere zeer nut oozvooz en dienstigh*. Utrecht: David van Hoogenhuysen.

Tilly, Charles. 1989. "History, Sociology, and Dutch Collective Action." *Tijdschrift voor Sociale Geschiedenis* 15: 142–57.

Trakman, Leon E. 1980. "The Evolution of the Law Merchant: Our Commercial Heritage." *Journal of Maritime Law and Commerce* 12: 1–24.

———. 1981. "The Evolution of the Law Merchant: Our Commercial Heritage." Pt. 2. *Journal of Maritime Law and Commerce* 12: 153–82.

Trumbull, J. Hammond, ed. 1867. [Thomas Lechford], *Plain Dealing or News from New England*. Boston: J. K. Wiggen and Wm. Parsons Lunt.

Twee Beschouwende Vrienden. 1820. *De Twee Beschouwende Vrienden, als Wandelaars op de Amsterdamsche Kermis, 1820*. Amsterdam: M. van Kolm.

Vachon, Andre. 1962. *Histoire du notariat*. Quebec: Presses de l'Université, Laval.

Valentine, David T., ed. 1862. *A Compilation of the Laws of the State of New York Relating Particularly to the City of New York*. New York: Edmund Jones.

van Caenegem, R. C. 1979. "The English Common Law: A Divergence from the European Pattern." *Tijdschrift voor Rechtsgeschiedenis* 47: 1–7.

van Cortlandt, Hephanus (Stephen). 1681. "Sale of land from van Cortlandt to Dirck Teunis van Vechten, October 20, 1681." Van Vechten Papers, LZ15213, folder 25. Manuscripts and Special Collections, State Library of New York, Albany.

van Curler, Arent. 1634–38. "Ledger, debit–credit account, 1634–1638, for Colonists at Rensselaerswyck," VRMP, SC7079, box 14, ledger no. 1. Manuscripts and Special Collections, State Library of New York, Albany.

van den Berg, J. 1979. "Ervaringen als Streekkandidaat-Notaris in Zeeuws-Vlaanderen." *Ars Notariatus* 17: 17–21.

Vanderbilt, Gertrude Lefferts. 1899. *The Social History of Flatbush, and Manners and Customs of the Dutch Settlers in Kings County*. New York: D. Appleton.

vander Donck, Adriaen. 1968 [1841.] *A Description of the New Netherlands*. Ed. Thomas F. O'Donnell. Trans. Jeremiah Johnson. Syracuse: Syracuse University Press.

van der Linde, A. P. G. Jos, ed. 1983. *New York Historical Manuscripts: Dutch. Old First Dutch Reformed Church of Brooklyn, New York: First Book of Records, 1660–1752*. Trans. van der Linde. Baltimore: Genealogical Publishing Co.

van der Veen, Walewyn. 1900. "Walewyn van der Veen's Record: Dutch Records in the City Clerk's Office, New York." In *Year Book of the Holland Society of New York, 1900*, ed. M. Banta, 152–58. New York: Knickerbocker Press.

van der Woude, Ad. 1991. "The Volume and Value of Paintings in Holland at the Time of the Dutch Republic." In *Art in History / History in Art: Studies in Seventeenth-Century Dutch Culture*, ed. David Freedberg and Jan de Vries, 285–329. Santa Monica: Getty Center for the History of Art and the Humanities.

van der Zee, Henri, and Barbara van der Zee. 1978. *A Sweet and Alien Land: The Story of Dutch New York*. New York: Viking.

van Duersen, A. Th. 1978a. *Het Kopergeld van de Gouden Eeuw*, vol. 1, *Het Dagelijks Brood*. Assen: Van Gorcum.

———. 1978b. *Het Kopergeld van de Gouden Eeuw*, vol. 2, *Volkskultuur*. Assen: Van Gorcum.

———. 1979. *Het Kopergeld van de Gouden Eeuw*, vol. 3, *Volk en Overheid*. Assen: Van Gorcum.

van Eck, P. L., Jr. 1927. *Hoe 't Vroeger Was: Schetsen ter Inleiding tot de Geschiedenis van Onderwijs en Opvoeding*. Groningen: J. B. Wolters.

van Harderwijk, K. J. R., and G. D. J. Schotel, eds. 1862. *Biographisch Woordenboek der Nederlanden, bevattende Levensbeschrijvingen van Zoodanige Personen, Die Zich op Eenigeslei wijze in ons Vaderland Hebben Vermaard Gemaakt*. Vol. 5. Haarlem: J. J. van Brederode.

van Herwaarden, J. 1988. "Steden en Hun Verleden." In *Steden en Hun Verleden: De Ontwikkeling van de Stedelijke Samenleving in de Nederlanden tot de Negentiende Eeuw*, ed. Maurits Van Rooijen, 9–33. Utrecht: Teleac.

van Houtte, J. A. 1977. *An Economic History of the Low Countries, 800–1800*. London: Weidenfeld & Nicolson.

van Ilpendam, Adriaen Janse. 1669–86. Notarial Papers 1, 1660–76, and 2, 1677–95. [Papers numbered in pencil. Vol. 1, papers 1–477 are those of Dirck van Schelluyne; 484–616 are van Ilpendam's. Vol. 2, papers 1–532 are van Ilpendam's; the remainder are those of or pertaining to Jan Juriaensz Becker.] Albany County Hall of Records, Albany.

———. 1684. "Statement of Sale of Land of Moordenaar's Kill by Cornelis Michelis to Jurien Teunis Tappan. 1684." MS 955, Albany Institute of History and Art, Albany.

———. 1685. "Agreement between Sybrant van Schaick and Tierck van Visscher, before Adriaen van Ilpendam, January 20, 1684/5." Albany Papers, folder "1680–1689." Collections of the New-York Historical Society, New York.

van Keulen, Jan. 1682. *Le Grand Nouvel Atlas de la Mer. On Monde Aquatique, Estant augmenté, E nous represente toutes les Costes, Maritimes de la terre, consistant en tres belles Cartes, si bien plattes, que celles qui ont des degrés croissantes, dont il y en a aucunes corrigées de la variation de buxolle. Ce qui se foit au titre des Cartes. Fort utile a des Mariniers, Pilottes en Amateurs de la grand navigation.* Amsterdam: Jean van Keulen.

van Laer, A. J. F., ed. 1908. *Van Rensselaer-Bowier Manuscripts, Being the Letters of Kiliaen van Rensselaer, 1630–1643, and Other Documents Relating to the Colony of Rensselaerswyck.* Albany: University of the State of New York.

——, ed. 1916. *Early Records of the City and County of Albany and Colony of Rensselaerswyck.* Vol. 2, *Deeds 3 and 4, 1678–1704. Translated from the Original Dutch by Jonathan Pearson.* Albany: University of the State of New York.

——, ed. 1918. *Early Records of the City and County of Albany and Colony of Rensselaerswyck.* Vol. 3, *Notarial Papers 1 and 2, 1660–1696. Translated from the Original Dutch by Jonathan Pearson.* Albany: University of the State of New York.

——, ed. 1919. *Early Records of the City and County of Albany and Colony of Rensselaerswyck.* Vol. 4, *Mortgages 1, 1658–1660, and Wills 1–2, 1681–1765. Translated from the Original Dutch by Jonathan Pearson.* Albany: University of the State of New York.

——, ed. 1920. *Minutes of the Court of Fort Orange and Beverwyck, 1652–1656.* Albany: University of the State of New York.

——, ed. 1922. *Minutes of the Court of Rensselaerswyck, 1648–1652.* Albany: University of the State of New York.

——, ed. 1923. *Minutes of the Court of Fort Orange and Beverwyck, 1657–1660.* Albany: University of the State of New York.

——, ed. 1924. *Documents Relating to New Netherland, 1624–1626, in The Henry Huntington Library.* San Marino: Henry Huntington Library.

——, ed. 1926. *Minutes of the Court of Albany, Rensselaerswyck, and Schenectady, 1668–1673.* Albany: University of the State of New York.

——. 1927. "The Dutch Grants along the South Side of State Street: A Contribution Toward the Early Topography of the City of Albany." In *The Dutch Settlers Society of Albany,* 2 (Year-Book 1926–27):11–27.

——, ed. 1928. *Minutes of the Court of Albany, Rensselaerswyck, and Schenectady, 1675–1680.* Albany: University of the State of New York.

——. 1931–32. "Deacon's Account Book, 1652–1664." In *The Dutch Settlers Society of Albany Year-Book,* 7:1–11.

——, ed. 1932a. *Minutes of the Court of Albany, Rensselaerswyck and Schenectady, 1680–1685.* Albany: University of the State of New York.

——, ed. 1932b. *Correspondence of Jeremias van Rensselaer, 1651–1674.* Albany: University of the State of New York.

——. 1934–35. "Albany Wills and Other Documents, 1668–1687." In *The Dutch Settlers Society of Albany Year-Book,* 10:1–14.

——, ed. 1935. *Correspondence of Maria van Rensselaer, 1669–1689.* Albany: University of the State of New York.

van Leeuwen, Simon. 1678. *Het Rooms-Hollands-Regt, Waar in de Roomse Wetten, Met het huydendaagse Nederlands Regt, In alles dat tot de dagelijkse onderhouding kan dienen, met een byzondre kortheit, so wel in de vaste Regts-stoffen, als in de manier van*

Regts-vordering over een gebragt werden. Met allerhande Ordonnantien, Placaten, Hand-vesten, Keuren, Gewoonten, en Gewijsden deser en omleggende Landen bevestige. Ten vijfemaal hersteld, en vermeerderd door Mr. Simon van Leeuwen, R. G. Amsterdam: Hendrick en Dirk Boom.

van Lennep, Jacob, and Johannes ter Gouw. 1868. *De Uithangteekens in verband met Geschiedenis en Volksleven beschouwd.* 2 vols. Amsterdam: Gebroeders Kraay.

———. 1869. *Het Boek der Opschriften.* Amsterdam: Gebroeders Kraay.

van Ness. 1772. "Van Ness Family Bible Records, 1696–1740, 3 p. Trans. Charles T. Gehring, March, 1985. [Bible in possession of Robert Weibezahl.]" Entry of March 25, 1772. MS 18445. Manuscripts and Special Collections, State Library of New York, Albany.

van Rensselaer, Hendrick. 1735–40. "Account Book." MS SC16673, Manuscripts and Special Collections, State University of New York, Albany.

van Rensselaer, Jeremias. 1658–74. "Rekeningen aengaande De Colonie Renselaerswyck onder de Directie van Jeremias van Renselaer sedert anno 1658 tot anno 1674" [Faithfulness of these accounts, signed Andries Teller as notary public, 1685]. VRMP SC7079, box 19A. Manuscripts and Special Collections, State Library of New York, Albany.

van Rensselaer, Kiliaen. 1685. "Extracts from a Diary of Kiliaen van Rensselaer, Written in Dutch, 1685." Original now in collection of Morton Pennypacker, Easthampton, N.Y. FG80/, box 2, folder 1, "Genealogy." Albany Institute of History and Art, Albany.

van Rensselaer, Mrs. Schuyler. 1909. *History of the City of New York in the Seventeenth Century,* vol. 1, *New Amsterdam.* New York: Macmillan.

van Rooijen, Maurits. 1988a. "Steden en Hun Verdediging." In *Steden en Hun Verleden: De Ontwikkeling van de Stedelijke Samenleving in de Nederlanden tot de Negentiende Eeuw,* ed. Maurits Van Rooijen, 33–56. Utrecht: Teleac.

———. 1988b."Steden en Hun Culturele Leven." In *Steden en Hun Verleden: De Ontwikkeling van de Stedelijke Samenleving in de Nederlanden tot de Negentiende Eeuw,* ed. Maurits Van Rooijen, 225–48. Utrecht: Teleac.

van Selm, B. 1987. *Een Menighte Treffelijcke Boeken: Nederlandse Boekhandelscatalogi in het Begin van de Zeventiende Eeuw.* Utrecht: HES.

van Twiller, Wouter. 1636. "Letter of Wouter van Twiller to Directors of the Amsterdam Chamber of the West India Company, August 14, 1636. [Tr. *New-York Historical Society Quarterly,* October 1919]." SC16675, Manuscripts and Special Collections, State Library of New York, Albany.

van Vechten Papers. 1667. "Reconfirmation of land near fort to A. Staets . . . [Recorded] 25 April, 1667." AQ 7006. Patents no. 1, folder 27. Manuscripts and Special Collections, State Library of New York, Albany.

van Vechten, Emma. 1897. "Early Schools and Schoolmasters." In *Historic New York,* ser. 2, vol. 2, ed. Maud Wilder Goodwin, A. Royce, R. Putnam, and E. Brownell, 319–44. Rpt. Port Washington, N.Y.: Friedman, 1969.

van Wassenaar, Gerard. 1746a. *Practyck Judicieel ofte Instructie Op de forme en manier van Procederen Voor Hoven en Recht-Banken, Soo in 't generaal, als in verscheide particuliere, meest voorvallende materien . . . Gestelt door Mr Gerard van Wassenaar,*

Naeuwkeurig naergezien, en van zeer veele grove fouten gezuïvert door Mr. Egbertus Cotius. Eerste Deel. Utrecht: Jacob van Poolsum.

————. 1746b. *Practyck Notariael ofte Instructie Tot het maken ende instelling van de voornaamste Instrumenten en allerley Contracten, Acten, Handelingen en Dispositien Die voor Notaris en Getuigen, Of in 't particulier by Partyen opgerecht en gedaan worden, Bekleedt met Redenen, Rechten en Rechtsgeleerden, van alles dat in de Practyck kan voorvallen . . . Gestelt door Mr Gerard van Wassenaar. Tweede Deel.* Utrecht: Jacob van Poolsum.

van Winter, P. J. 1978. *De Westindische Compagnie ter kamer Stad en Lande.* The Hague: Martinus Nijhoff.

van Zutphen, Bernhard. 1636. *Nederlandtsche Practycque van verscheyden daghelijcksche soo civile als criminele questiene Gecolligeert bij Bernhard van Zutphen, Advocaet voor den Ed. Hove Provinciael van Utrecht.* Utrecht: Jan van Doorn.

van Zwieten, Adriana. 1996. "The Orphan Chamber of New Amsterdam." *William and Mary Quarterly* 53: 319–40.

Venema, Jenny. 1991. "Property in Seventeenth-Century Albany." *Halve Maen* 64: 1–8.

Vlaemminck, Joseph H. 1956. *Histoire et doctrines de la comptabilité.* Bruxelles: Treurenberg.

Voorhees, David William. 1994. " 'The 'Fervent Zeale' of Jacob Leisler." *William and Mary Quarterly* 51: 447–72.

Vreeland, Louis Beach. 1956. *Annals of the Vreeland Family.* Charlotte, N.C. : Privately printed.

Wandelende. 1820. *De Wandelende Beschouwer: Gedurende de Amsterdamsche Kermis, Behelzende het meest merkwaardige daar op te zien geweest, zoo in de Speel-en Nacht-Huizen; als op openbare plaatzen — en de afloop derzelve. [1820].* Amsterdam: M. van Kolm Jr.

Waningen, Hendrick. 1672. *'t Recht Gebruyck van 't Italiaens Boeck-Houden, Waer in begrepen staet, Een Memoriael, Journael, ende Schult-boeck: Inhoudende Hondert schoone Partyen, noch 530 Vragen ende Antwoorden, verciert met schoone Verklaringen. Alles zeer nut ende bequaem voor Kooplieden, Factoors, Boeck-houders, etc. door Hendrick Waningen, Boeck-houder tot Amstelredam, Vermeerdert met het Italiaens Boeck-Houden van Johannes Buingha.* Amsterdam: Marcus Doornick.

Wardhaugh, Ronald. 1976. *The Contexts of Language.* Rowley, Mass.: Newbury House.

Warmelink, H. A. 1952. *De Notarissen, de Calligraphie en de Drukkunst: De Bibliographie van het Notariaat.* Wageningen: Zomer & Keunings.

Washburn, Emory. 1840. *Sketches of the Judicial History of Massachusetts, from 1630 to the Revolution in 1775.* Boston: Charles C. Little & James Brown.

Weise, Arthur James. 1884. *The History of the City of Albany, New York, from the Discovery of the Great River in 1524, by Verrazzano, to the Present Time.* Albany: E. H. Bender.

Weslager, C. A. 1961. *Dutch Explorers, Traders, and Settlers in the Delaware Valley, 1609–1664.* Philadelphia: University of Pennsylvania Press.

White, Richard. 1991. *The Middle Ground: Indians, Empires, and Republics in the Great Lakes Region, 1650–1815.* New York: Cambridge University Press.

Wiarda, J. 1970. "Dirck Volkertzoon Coornhert." In *Plus Est en Vous: Opstellen over Recht en Cultuur Aangeboden aan Prof. Mr. A. Pitlo ter Gelegenheid van Zijn 25-Jarig*

Hoogleraarschap, ed. J. A. Ankum, G. C. J. J. van den Bergh, and H. C. F. Schoordijk, 381–402. Haarlem: H. D. Tjeenk Willink & Zoon.

Wieder, F. C. 1925. *De Stichting van New York in Juli, 1625: Reconstructies en nieuwe gegevens outleend aan de Van Rappard Documenten [met 28 kaarten en platen].* The Hague: Martinus Nijhoff.

Wilcoxen, Charlotte. 1984. *Seventeenth-Century Albany: A Dutch Profile.* Albany: Albany Institute of History and Art.

Wildeman, M. J. 1898. "Genealogische Aantekeningen Suyderhoef, Gerlings, Guldewagen, Duyvesteijn, etc." Gemeentearchief Haarlem.

Wilstach, Paul. 1933. *Hudson River Landings.* Rpt. New York: Friedman, 1969.

Wouters, D., and W. J. Visser. 1926. *Geschiedenis van de Opvoeding en het Onderwijs Vooral in Nederland.* Groningen: P. Noordhoff.

Yamey, Basil S. 1950. "Scientific Bookkeeping and the Rise of Capitalism." In *Studies in Accountancy,* ed. W. T. Baxter, 13–30. London.

———. 1989. *Art and Accounting.* New Haven: Yale University Press.

Yamey, Basil S., H. C. Edey, and Hugh Thomson, eds. 1963. *Accounting in England and Scotland, 1543–1800: Double Entry in Exposition and Practice.* London: Sweet & Maxwell.

Zantkuijl, Henk J. 1987. "The Netherlands Town House: How and Why It Works." In *New World Dutch Studies: Dutch Arts and Culture in Colonial America, 1609–1776,* ed. Roderic H. Blackburn and Nancy A. Kelley, 143–60. Albany: Albany Institute of History and Art.

———. 1988. "Steden en Hun Huizen." In *Steden en Hun Verleden: De Ontwikkeling van de Stedelijke Samenleving in de Nederlanden tot de Negentiende Eeuw,* ed. Maurits Van Rooijen, 177–200. Utrecht: Teleac.

Zee-Rechten, 't Boeck der. 1664. *'t Boeck der Zee-Rechten. Inhoudende Dat Hoogste ende Dudtste Gotlantsche Waterrecht dat de gemeene Koop-lieden ende Schippers geordineert ende gemaeckt hebben tot Wisbuy. De Zee-Rechten gemaeckt by Keyser Karel als mede die gemaeckt zijn ten tijde van Koningh Philippus de derde mede inhoudende sekere Ordonnantie op 't stuck van de Assurantien, Bodemerije ende Toerustinge van Schepen. Mitsgaders de Schips rechten ghemaeckt by de Oude Hanze-Steden . . . Op nieuws vermeerdert ende verbetert.* Middelburgh: François Kroock.

Zell, Michael 1986. "Suicide in Pre-industrial England." *Social History* 11: 303–17.

Zumthor, Paul. 1962. *Het dagelijks leven in de Gouden Eeuw.* 2 vols. Utrecht: Prisma-Boeken.

Index

Janse, Adriaen, van Ilpendam (*cont.*)
as figure in local scenes, 1655–57, 105, 106
in fur trade, 99, 110
in historical memory, 178–85, 240, 241, 242
honored by court, 27, 28
income: in Albany, 11, 21, 24, 26, 30, 35, 119,
146, 147, 149, 153; annuity from inheritance, 41–42, 148–49, 157, 160, 174, 176; in
Beverwijck, 99; in *colonie*, 87; inheritance,
35, 43, 81; on Manhattan Island, 82, 84; uncertainty of, 32, 149, 155, 157, 158, 160, 169,
194, 223
and David Janse, 64
jury duty, 152
in Leiden, 43
letters to Guldewagen, 41–43, 148–49, 157–58,
159–60
and Robert Livingston, 35–37, 167, 171
with natives, 14, 15, 89, 90
as notary: clientele of, 20, 21, 170, 191; with
clients, 4, 5, 10, 11, 14–20, 25, 26, 30, 31, 35,
39, 40, 120, 155, 158, 159, 169, 172, 173, 174;
commissioned and sources of authority, 2,
6, 7, 9, 33, 40
as orphan, 46
papers of, 6, 35, 187, 191; compared to Livingston's, 170, 171; compared to van Schelluyne's, 170, 195; custody of, 5, 29, 167; custody of will and letters, 35, 42–43, 149, 158,
160, 173; executed (1673–74), 31–35; formalities and style of, 6, 16, 32, 33, 69, *116*, 153,
154, 173; history of, 176–78, 187, 243; orthographic blunders, 153, 173; watermarked,
42, 160, *168*, 174
and patronymic, 31, 82
petitions to be town secretary, 93, 97, 98
professionalism of, 20, 26, 40, 42, 43
as property owner, 99, 101, 103, 104, 135, 223
as provost, 22–25
as *reder* on *King Charles*, 135–45
residence of: in 1670, 3; in 1684, 166–69, 179,
180, 193
as schoolmaster: in Albany, 3, 5, 21, 41; in
Beverwijck, 97, 101, 105, 109–12; in *colonie*,
87, 90, 91, 93; on Manhattan Island, 63, 67,
78, 82–86
as servant, 77, 78
and Sijbinck, 14, 142; correspondence with,
41–43, 148–49
suicide of, xv, 174–76, 185
and Swart, 17, 18, 20, 39
and van Schelluyne, 113–15; retains papers of,
168
and wife, Tryntje Jans, 2, 3, 163–65

as witness, 89, 90, 117, 118
Janse, David, van Ilpendam, 47, 63–69, 73
as bookseller, 65, 67, 68
will of, 42, 43, 64, 68
Janse, Hendrick, Westerkamp, 223
Janse, Huybert, 10, 15
Janse, Jan, van Aecken, 131
Janse, Jan, van Ilpendam, 44, 45, 46, 47, 81
accused of defrauding West India Company,
61–63
arrival at the Manhatas, 55, 56
death and estate of, 63, 99
at Delaware River, 58–63
in employ of West India Company, 48, 49,
50, 52–54, 204
livelihood of, 45, 48, 62
marriages and occupations of, 45–47
relations with Kiliaen van Rensselaer, 53, 58
residence and family in Leiden, 46–48
Janse, Joachim, van Ilpendam, 46
Janse, Rem, 99, 106
Janse, Stoffel, Abeel, 134, 142
Jans, Tryntje, 2, 3, 78, 100, 135, 158, 160, 163, 179
Janvier, Thomas, 183
Jonckerstraat, 3, 104, 166, 167

Keyser, Adriaen, 81, 100
Kieft, Willem, 59, 78, 82
enemies of, 74, 75
"Little Blue Book" of, 75
relations with Jan Janse, 59, 61, 62, 63
Kinderhoek, 171
King Charles (*Cingh Carels, Konigh Carel*), voyagers on, 137–44
dealings with Sijbinck, 142, 143
disputes among, 143
petition to Charles II, 135, 136, 143
residences cited as New Netherland, 141
Kuyper, Jan Andriesz, 16

Labatie, Jan, 89, 90
Lachaire, Salomon, 118–20
acquainted with van Schelluyne, 116, 137
learned books of, 118
papers of, 120, 228
La Montagne, Jan, 100
La Montagne, Johannes, 71, 100, 106, 125
La Montagne family, 48, 78
landownership
in Albany, 132, 170, 171
in Beverwijck, 99, 100, 101, 103, 104
in the Manhatas, 55, 56, 60, 205
valued differently, Dutch and English, 233
language, Dutch, in Albany, 185, 186